The Management of Nonprofit and Charitable Organizations in Canada

Vic Murray, Ph.D.
General Editor

LexisNexis®
Butterworths

The Management of Nonprofit and Charitable Organizations in Canada

© LexisNexis Canada Inc. 2006

July 2006

Members of the LexisNexis Group worldwide

Canada	LexisNexis Canada Inc, 123 Commerce Valley Dr. E., MARKHAM, Ontario
Argentina	Abeledo Perrot, Jurisprudencia Argentina and Depalma, BUENOS AIRES
Australia	Butterworths, a Division of Reed International Books Australia Pty Ltd, CHATSWOOD, New South Wales
Austria	ARD Betriebsdienst and Verlag Orac, VIENNA
Chile	Publitecsa and Conosur Ltda, SANTIAGO DE CHILE
Czech Republic	Orac sro, PRAGUE
France	Éditions du Juris-Classeur SA, PARIS
Hong Kong	Butterworths Asia (Hong Kong), HONG KONG
Hungary	Hvg Orac, BUDAPEST
India	Butterworths India, NEW DELHI
Ireland	Butterworths (Ireland) Ltd, DUBLIN
Italy	Giuffré, MILAN
Malaysia	Malayan Law Journal Sdn Bhd, KUALA LUMPUR
New Zealand	Butterworths of New Zealand, WELLINGTON
Poland	Wydawnictwa Prawnicze PWN, WARSAW
Singapore	Butterworths Asia, SINGAPORE
South Africa	Butterworth Publishers (Pty) Ltd, DURBAN
Switzerland	Stämpfli Verlag AG, BERNE
United Kingdom	Butterworths Tolley, a Division of Reed Elsevier (UK), LONDON, WC2A
USA	LexisNexis, DAYTON, Ohio

Library and Archives Canada Cataloguing in Publication

The management of nonprofit and charitable organizations in Canada / Vic Murray, general editor.

Includes bibliographical references and index.
ISBN 0-433-45047-9

1. Nonprofit organizations—Canada—Management. 2. Charitable uses, trusts, and foundations—Canada. I. Murray, Victor V.

HD62.6.M358 2006   658'.0480971   C2006-903551-2

Printed and bound in Canada.

To Professor Mel Moyer

**Pioneer scholar, researcher and counsellor
in the field of nonprofit management in Canada**

PREFACE

I first began to take a serious interest in the subject of the management of nonprofit and voluntary sector organizations in 1982 when my colleague at York University, Professor Mel Moyer, persuaded me that this was an important and neglected field of study. At that time, few scholars in Canada or elsewhere had recognized the sector as a sector, let alone one that deserved to be researched. Similarly, most managers did not think of themselves as part of anything beyond the group of organizations in their own sub-sector. Nor was there much in the way of pressure from funders, clients, government regulators or the public to change the status quo. Nonprofit organizations were typically viewed as groups of well-meaning people trying to help others and their good intentions were sufficient to justify their activities.

By the early 1990s, however, this situation had begun to change. Umbrella organizations such as the Canadian Centre for Philanthropy (now Imagine Canada) began publishing the first systematic surveys of the size, scope and impact of the sector as a whole in Canadian society. Most importantly, mounting government deficits were creating great pressures to cut spending and this included their support for nonprofit organizations in big sub-sectors such as social services, health, education and the arts. More and more nonprofits had to learn to manage themselves more efficiently *and* seek alternative sources of funding. The overall environment was becoming much more fast-paced, complex and demanding. Stress, burnout and turnover among nonprofit managers began to increase.

All this gave rise to a growing interest in acquiring management skills in a way somewhat comparable to the growth of interest in business management as a profession in the 1950s after the Second World War. In the latter case, however, this demand led to the creation of many schools of business in universities and colleges throughout North America and Europe. Along with this came a wave of research that tried to systematically test the validity of various theories in all areas of management.

Paradoxically, however, the growth of interest in the management of nonprofit organizations in the 1990s did *not* lead to the rapid emergence of programs of study and research at universities and colleges in Canada (though it did to a greater extent in the U.S. and Britain). This may be in large part because many of those managing in the sector, though interested, have had so little time and resources available to devote to education at that level.

Thanks in large part to the Voluntary Sector Initiative and other factors, this situation is now beginning to change. Though research is still sparse, the number of courses in nonprofit management has been increasing steadily since 2000. Unfortunately, however, the availability of Canadian oriented educational materials has not kept pace with this trend. This book is the first attempt to provide a comprehensive overview of all the main subject areas in nonprofit management with a Canadian focus. The main features of the book are the following:

- Each chapter provides an introduction to its subject that is written for general managers and students of nonprofit management who are *not* specialists in that area. For those who seek more depth, a variety of references and resources are provided for further study.

- Every effort is made to recognize the great diversity of the nonprofit world ranging, as it does, from small all-volunteer groups to large professionally managed institutions. Many management tools and methods do not necessarily fit every situation and this is highlighted throughout.

- The chapters also attempt to note the differences between so-called "best practices" and systematically researched hypotheses. At this stage in the development of the field of nonprofit management studies, much that is recommended as the best way to do things has not been carefully tested as to its validity in a wide range of situations.

- Finally, though there is no question that it pays for leaders in the sector to become more skilled and knowledgeable about management, it is not the intention of this book to suggest that nonprofit organizations must become more "businesslike" — coldly efficient, impersonal, driven only by the financial bottom line. None of the contributors to this book forget that the critical feature of this sector is that it exists because those who lead in it believe in the cause their organizations represent. We recognize that they can never survive if they lose sight of what is known as "the expressive dimension" — the opportunity for volunteers and staff to work with others who share their values and commitment. No improvement in management skills should be made at the cost of losing this defining dimension of work in the sector.

Whatever value this book may provide to new and aspiring managers in the Canadian nonprofit and voluntary sector comes entirely from the excellent people who contributed the chapters that make it up. Each of them is a recognized authority in his or her field providing original work summarizing years of practice and research. My thanks go out to them and to our editor at LexisNexis Butterworths, Gian-Luca DiRocco, for his support and encouragement of the project from the beginning.

Vic Murray, Editor
Victoria, B.C., 2006

CONTRIBUTORS

Carolyn Bodnar-Evans, C.A.

Carolyn Bodnar-Evans most recently served as the Chief Financial Officer for the Canadian Cancer Society and the National Cancer Institute of Canada from 1996 to 2005. Previously, she held senior financial positions in the nonprofit sector in the areas of international development and the performing arts. For over 17 years, she has actively contributed to the nonprofit sector, as both a board member and an academic lecturer. She currently serves on the Not-for-Profit-Advisory Committee, Accounting Standards Board of the Canadian Institute of Chartered Accountants. She has served on the Advisory Committee for the Program in Interdisciplinary Studies in Nonprofit and Voluntary Sector Management at Ryerson University, the Board of Directors for the Canadian Association of Professional Dance Organizations, and as Treasurer of the Danny Grossman Dance Company in Toronto. She also held part-time lecturer positions with the University of Toronto accounting program, and Ryerson University's nonprofit and voluntary sector management program.

Kathy Brock, Ph.D.

Kathy Brock is an associate professor at the School of Policy Studies and Department of Political Studies, Queen's University, and past director, Public Policy and Third Sector, School of Policy Studies. She has published numerous books, academic articles and reports on voluntary organizations, citizen engagement, politics and Aboriginal issues. Active in public affairs, she has served on the National Survey of Nonprofit and Voluntary Organizations, acted as an advisor to the Canadian Government/Voluntary Sector Initiative, was Co-Chair of the Agnes Etherington Art Centre Membership Drive, a member of the National Voluntary Sector Forum Selection Committee, policy advisor to the Minister of Aboriginal Affairs, Manitoba Government, political advisor to the Grand Chief, Assembly of Manitoba Chiefs, and research director of the Meech Lake Constitutional Task Force. She currently serves as an associate editor (*Canadian Public Policy*) and is a member of three nonprofit boards.

Terrance Carter, LL.B.

Terrance Carter practises at Carters Professional Corporation in the area of charity and nonprofit law and is counsel to and affiliated with Fasken Martineau DuMoulin LLP. He is a member of the Canada Revenue Agency's Charity Advisory Committee, and the Technical Issues Committee advising the Canada Revenue Agency, past Chair of the National Charity and Not-for-Profit Section of the Canadian Bar Association, a past member of the Uniform Law Conference of Canada Task Force on Uniform Fundraising Legislation, and has been recognized as one of the leading experts in the area of charity and nonprofit law in Canada by Lexpert. Mr. Carter is also a frequent writer and speaker in the area of charity and nonprofit law across Canada and internationally, as well as co-editor of *Charities Legislation & Commentary*, 2006 Edition, contributing author to Industry Canada's *Primer for Directors of Not-for-Profit Corporations*, co-author of the soon-to-be-published *Branding & Trade-Marks Handbook for Charitable and Not-For-Profit Organizations*, and editor of <www.charitylaw.ca>, <www.churchlaw.ca> and <www.antiterrorism.ca>.

Karen Cooper, LL.L.

Karen Cooper is a member of Carters Professional Corporation's charity and not-for-profit law group in the Ottawa office, and was formerly Senior Rulings Officer with the Income Tax Rulings Directorate of the Canada Revenue Agency. Her practice focuses on tax issues and she has considerable experience before the Tax Court. Called to the Ontario Bar in 1995, she became counsel for the Department of Justice in tax litigation before moving to Lang Michener and finally to the Canada Revenue Agency. In addition to her considerable legal experience, Ms. Cooper has extensive teaching experience, including the Estates (Tax) section of the Ontario Bar Admission Course, sessional lecturer at Carleton University School of Business teaching Business Law, and part-time professor at the University of Ottawa, Faculty of Common Law.

Michael Hall, Ph.D.

Michael Hall is Vice-President, Research at Imagine Canada, where his work focuses on building the body of knowledge about Canada's nonprofit and voluntary sector and the ways in which Canadians support one another and their communities. His publications on nonprofit organizations, philanthropy and volunteering include: *The*

Canadian Nonprofit and Voluntary Sector in Comparative Perspective; *Cornerstones of Community: Highlights of the National Survey of Nonprofit and Voluntary Organizations*; *Charitable Fundraising in Canada*; and *Assessing Performance: Evaluation Practices and Perspectives in Canada's Voluntary Sector*. He was the founding President of Parks and Recreation Ontario, is a former member of the board of the Association for Research on Nonprofit Organizations and Voluntary Action and currently serves as an Associate Editor of *Nonprofit Management and Leadership*. Dr. Hall holds a Ph.D. in social psychology from York University.

Yvonne Harrison, Ph.D.

Yvonne Harrison is Assistant Professor in the Center for Nonprofit and Social Enterprise Management at Seattle University. In 2005, she received her Ph.D. from the School of Public Administration at the University of Victoria, British Columbia, Canada. Since 2001, she has specialized in the adoption of information and communications technology (ICT) in volunteerism and has conducted two national research studies in Canada exploring the impact of ICT on the management of volunteer resources. Other research interests include the new governance environment, volunteerism, innovation, organizational effectiveness, leadership, change, and the management of public-private partnerships. At Seattle University, she teaches courses at the graduate and undergraduate levels in nonprofit and public sector managaement. She is an active consultant and the author of several research reports, book chapters, and journal articles on ICT adoption and effectiveness and e-government partnership management challenges.

Andrea McManus, CFRE

Andrea McManus is principal of The Development Group, a strategic philanthropic consulting firm based in Calgary, Alberta and is a Certified Fundraising Executive. Her extensive experience with a wide variety of nonprofit organizations has led to a conviction that philanthropy, and its technical catalyst of fund development, generally plays an undervalued and misunderstood role in Canadian nonprofit organizations. The focus of her work is on integrating fundraising throughout the organization and nurturing a philanthropic culture. Andrea has been a key force in establishing the Association of Fundraising Professionals in Canada and has held a variety of leadership roles that include terms on the AFP International Board Executive Committee,

Chair of the AFP Canadian Council and Chair of the AFP Foundation for Philanthropy, Canada. She currently chairs the Calgary Chamber of Voluntary Organizations and is a member of the Advisory Council for the Institute of Non-Profit Studies at Mount Royal College in Calgary.

Agnes Meinhard, Ph.D.

Agnes Meinhard is Associate Professor of Organizational Behaviour and Theory in the Faculty of Business at Ryerson University. She is the founding director of the Centre for Voluntary Sector Studies at Ryerson. Her research has focused on the formation, growth and demise of voluntary organizations; strategic responses of voluntary organizations to changing policy; women's voluntary organizations; volunteer behaviour and development; and leadership and organizational change. Recent research projects include a study of the responses of 645 Canadian nonprofit organizations to the changing political, social and economic environment; an investigation of volunteering in community service programs in Ontario high schools; the evolving partnership among government, nonprofit and for-profit organizations; a comparative study of partnerships between nonprofit and for-profit organizations in Israel and Canada; and ethnic diversity, multiculturalism and the role of voluntary organizations in the integration of immigrants. Her work has been published in several peer-reviewed, academic journals.

Vic Murray, Ph.D.

Vic Murray is currently Adjunct Professor in the School of Public Administration at the University of Victoria. From 1983 to 1995, he was Director of the Voluntary Sector Management Program and professor in the Schulich School of Business at York University, Toronto. He specializes in the study of leadership and management of voluntary sector organizations of all types, with particular emphasis on the areas of board governance, strategic planning, inter-organizational collaboration and the assessment of organizational effectiveness. He is also an active consultant and volunteer in these areas. As Director of the Nonprofit Leadership and Management Program at York University he developed several of the first certificate and master's level courses in that field. He is the author of numerous books, articles and papers in the fields of organizational behaviour and nonprofit management.

Susan Phillips, Ph.D.

Dr. Susan Phillips is Professor and Director of the School of Public Policy and Administration, Carleton University and Senior Scholar with the Centre for Voluntary Sector Research and Development, also located at Carleton. She has published extensively in the areas of citizen engagement, shared governance, the voluntary sector and urban public policy. Her current research focuses on a comparative analysis of responsive regulation of the third sector, which has been funded by the Social Sciences and Humanities Research Council of Canada. She has served as an Associate Editor of *Canadian Public Policy*, an editor of *How Ottawa Spends*, and is a member of the editorial board of the *Philanthropist*. She is also a Senior Academic Fellow with the Canadian School of Public Service and was Research Director of the Broadbent Panel on Accountability and Governance in the Voluntary Sector, as well as policy advisor to the Voluntary Sector Initiative, national voluntary organizations, urban governments and a variety of federal departments.

Keith Seel, M.A.

Keith Seel, Ph.D. (Candidate) is the Director of the Institute for Nonprofit Studies at Mount Royal College. He designed and wrote curriculum for Canada's only baccalaureate degree focused on the nonprofit sector. As well, he has been actively researching issues of concern to the nonprofit sector including legal issues, executive director job quality, governance and social policy. He has published numerous articles and has been a contributor to several nonprofit management textbooks. As a long-time contributor to the nonprofit sector, he has served on numerous boards including, most recently, the inaugural board of the Human Resources Council for the Voluntary/Non-profit Sector, which is addressing employment issues across the country.

Tatyana Teplova

Tatyana Teplova is currently working at the Public Service Human Resource Management Agency of Canada as a policy analyst. Previously, she has worked with the Canadian Policy Research Networks and the Centre for Voluntary Sector Research and Development, a joint program of Carleton University and University of Ottawa, on a number of projects, including the Voluntary Sector Evaluation Research Project. Her areas of interest and expertise include measurement and evaluation in the voluntary sector, social and childcare policies, welfare state transformation, ethics and accountability in government. Tatyana is completing her Ph.D. in public policy at the School of Public Policy and Administration, Carleton University.

Thea Vakil, M.A.

Thea Vakil is a former senior executive and educator with extensive experience in a number of large portfolios in the British Columbia government. She has special expertise in finance, human resource management, public policy and organizational change. She has taught widely in the areas of management, public policy and strategic planning in the School of Public Administration and in the Faculty of Business. She is also a Senior Fellow at the Centre for Public Sector Studies at the University of Victoria. She is a recipient of the 2002 Award for Teaching Excellence in the Faculty of Human and Social Development and of the 2004 Faculty Award of Excellence in the Faculty of Business. She holds a Master's degree from the University of British Columbia and is working on a Ph.D. in public administration.

TABLE OF CONTENTS

Preface... v
Contributors.. ix

**Chapter 1: Introduction: What's So Special About
Managing Nonprofit Organizations? — Vic Murray**
How Do Nonprofit Sector Organizations Differ from Those in the
    Business and Government Sectors?.. 3
    Organizational Mission and Values 3
    Organizational Goals and Strategic Priorities 5
    Use of Volunteers... 6
    Governance by a Nonprofit Board of Directors 7
How Do Nonprofit Organizations Differ from One Another and
    What Do These Differences Mean for Their Leaders? 8
    Types of Nonprofit Organization 8
    Degree of Voluntarism... 11
    Sources of Funds.. 12
    Degree of Resource Scarcity and Competition for Resources 13
    Age and Stage of Development.. 14
    Summary 16
A Framework for Understanding Nonprofit Management 16
    External Concerns 17
        Politics 18
        Economics 18
        Social Values 19
        Technology 19
        Demographics... 19
    Internal Concerns 20
        People 21
        Money... 21
        Information 21
        Organization and Planning 21
Outline of this Book.. 22
References... 23

**Chapter 2: The Canadian Nonprofit and Voluntary Sector
in Perspective — Michael H. Hall**
Introduction... 25
Defining and Classifying Nonprofit Organizations 26
    Defining Nonprofit Organizations 27
    Legal Distinctions 28

Area of Activity.. 28
Type of Function 29
The Size and Scope of Canada's Nonprofit Sector...................... 30
Geographic Area of Focus... 32
Public vs. Mutual Benefit.. 32
Economic Contributions 32
A Substantial Workforce... 34
International Comparisons.. 35
Financial and Human Resources.. 37
Financial Resources 37
Concentration of Revenues 39
Human Resources.. 40
The Challenges Nonprofit Organizations Face............................. 43
Problems with External Funding.. 46
Conclusion 48
References... 50

Chapter 3: Managing the Governance Function:
Developing Effective Boards of Directors — Vic Murray
Introduction.. 53
The Four Controllable Dimensions of Board Functioning 55
The First Dimension: Board Roles and Responsibilities.............. 56
Roles of Board Members 58
Decision-maker/Evaluator.. 58
Advisor... 59
Implementer 59
Patterns of Board Responsibility and When They Are
Appropriate 59
The Working Board... 60
The Governance-only Board 61
"Mixed Model Boards"... 61
Confusion over What Is "Strategic" 63
Problems in the Fiscal/Legal Oversight Function of Boards
and the Responsibility for Risk Assessment 67
The Responsibility for Selection and Evaluation of the
Executive Director 67
The Board's Responsibilities for Community Relations 68
The Board's Role in Fundraising... 70
The Board's Role in the Development and Assessment of
Management Systems.. 71
The Balanced Scorecard... 72
The CCAF-FCVI Framework for Performance
Reporting 72

The Second Dimension: Board Structure and Formal Operating
    Procedures 73
    Structuring the Board.. 73
    Board Size... 74
    Formal Offices.. 75
    Board Committees 76
    A Word about Informal Groups in Boards 79
    Terms of Appointment and Reappointment....................... 79
    Attendance 80
    Meeting Frequency and Times 80
    Meeting Agenda Formats and Meeting Rules 82
    Board Orientation, Development and Evaluation
        Procedures 83
The Third Dimension: Board Composition............................... 84
    Should Boards be Composed Primarily of Prestigious
        People? 85
    The Diversity Dilemma 85
    How Well Should Candidates Know the Organization?........ 86
    How Much Should "Business Skills" Be Emphasized? 87
    What Individual Personal Qualities Should Be Sought? 87
    The Special Problems of Low-profile and Non-popular
        Organizations 88
    A Final Word on Board Composition................................. 89
The Fourth Dimension: Board Culture and Leadership 89
    Elements of the How-to-Run-a-Meeting Culture 90
    Openness to Change 90
    Acceptance of Diversity and Equity 91
    Commitment to Action 91
    Deep-Seated Convictions about Board Roles and
        Responsibilities 91
    What Can Be Done to Change Board Cultures? The
        Importance of Leadership 92
        The Chair.. 92
        The Executive Director 94
Conclusion 95
References... 96

**Chapter 4: Executive Leadership in Nonprofit Organizations
— Keith Seel**
Introduction.. 99
Terminology 100
The Role of the Executive Director 101
Leadership and the Executive Director....................................... 103

Personal Beliefs and Values 109
Executive Director Effectiveness.. 110
The Board and ED Effectiveness... 111
The ED-Staff Relationship 114
The ED and Financial Oversight 117
The ED and the Community 119
Challenges... 120
Conclusion 122
References.. 123

**Chapter 5: The Legal Context of Nonprofit Management —
Terrance S. Carter and Karen J. Cooper**
Introduction — Definitions and Legal Environment........................ 127
  Defining Charitable and Nonprofit Organizations 128
Legal Environment 130
  Applicable Federal and Provincial Legislation 131
    Income Tax Act 132
    Canada Corporations Act.. 132
    Other Federal Legislation 132
    Provincial Legislation.. 133
    Provincial Legislation Aimed at Regulating Charities 133
Legal Structures for Nonprofit Organizations 134
  Overview of Types of Legal Structure.. 134
    Trusts 135
    Unincorporated Association 136
    Corporation without Share Capital 138
    Co-operative without Share Capital....................................... 139
  Advantages and Disadvantages of Different Legal Structures... 139
    Set-up Costs.. 140
    Legal Capacity 140
    Liability (Organization, Directors, Officers, Members)...... 141
    Perpetual Existence.. 142
  National Nonprofit Corporate Structures 142
    National Association Model 142
    Centralized Chapter Model.. 143
    Association Agreements 144
Registered Charities under the *Income Tax Act*.............................. 145
  Types of Registered Charities 145
    Charitable Organization... 145
    Charitable Foundation 146
  Specific Rules Affecting Registered Charities........................... 146
    Relationship between Directors/Trustees and Control 146
    Disbursement Quota Rules 149
    Related Business... 151

Charitable Activities 151
Borrowing.. 152
Control of Other Corporations.. 152
New Regulatory Regime 155
Interim Sanctions.. 155
Appeals Process.. 157
Risk Management and Liability.. 157
Level of the Organization/Corporation 158
Choice of Nonprofit or Charitable Structure 158
Standard of Care 159
Vicarious Liability (Directors, Officers, Staff,
Volunteers)... 159
Anti-terrorism Legislation Compliance 162
Level of Directors and Officers... 163
Role and Duties of Directors and Officers........................... 163
Liability of Directors and Officers...................................... 164
Rights and Powers 165
Statutory Protection 166
Other Means of Reducing Risks.. 166
Indemnification and Insurance 166
Due Diligence in Operations (Maintaining the
Corporation).. 167
Legal Risk Management Committees.................................... 168
Independent Legal Advice.. 168
Size of the Board 168
Transfer of Assets 169
Checklists... 169
References... 169

**Chapter 6: Government and Community Relations —
Kathy Brock**
Introduction: Managing Up and Outwards 173
Government to Governance: Trends in Government–Nonprofit
Relations... 176
Accountability, the Westminster Model of Government and
Nonprofit Services 177
Understanding the Nature of the Relationship with
Government 180
Challenges in Developing and Maintaining Relationships with
Governments... 187
Sector Wide Relations: The Significance of the Voluntary
Sector Initiative.. 191
Partnering with the Corporate Sector: From Antagonists to Allies .. 195
The Shift Towards Partnerships 195

The Types of Relationships.. 197
Finding the Right Partner.. 199
Building with Other Nonprofits: The Challenges of Forming
    Alliances... 201
Public and Media Relations: With Influence Comes Scrutiny 204
Conclusion 206
References.. 207
Further Resources 211

Chapter 7: Resource Development Basics — Andrea McManus
What is "Resource Development"? 215
Clarifying Terminology.. 215
Understanding the Differences Between Non-profits and
    Registered Charities 217
Typical Sources of Income 219
Recent Trends in Fund Development 224
Six Key Fundraising Principles 227
Overview of a Development Program 230
Categories within an Integrated Development Program.................. 231
Annual Giving... 232
Major and Special Giving 239
Identifying Donors... 243
Individual Donors.. 245
Corporate Donors 246
Foundations 251
Groups and Associations.. 252
Fundraising for Core Operating Needs....................................... 252
Identifying What Works for Your Nonprofit................................. 252
Resourcing the Development Function... 257
Organizational Structure 257
Staffing.. 258
Non-staff Resources 258
Fundraising Costs.. 259
Planning and Evaluating Development Activities 261
Philanthropic Culture 261
Planning and Implementation.. 261
Strategic and Annual Planning.. 262
Evaluation and Measurement.. 263
Roles and Responsibilities... 263
Development Committees.. 266
Accountability, Stewardship and Ethics 267
Accountability and Stewardship... 267
Ethical Fundraising 268
Percentage-based Fundraising.. 269
Privacy Legislation.. 269
Future Trends... 270

References... 271
Additional Resources... 272
   Web-based Resources 272
   Print Resources.. 272
      Social Enterprise.. 272
      Cause Marketing.. 272
      Fundraising 273
      Planned Giving 273

Chapter 8: Planning and Organizing for Results — Thea Vakil
Introduction... 275
Strategic Management 276
   Strategic Planning 279
      Get Agreement on the Strategic Planning Process 281
      Confirm Mandate and Conduct Stakeholder Analysis........ 281
      Review Mission, Vision and Values.................................. 282
         Mission.. 282
         Vision.. 283
         Values... 284
      External and Internal Environmental Analysis................... 284
         External Scan 284
         Internal Scan.. 285
         Strength, Weaknesses, Opportunities and Threats
         (SWOT)... 286
      Definition of Strategic Issues 287
      Strategy Formulation and Plan Implementation.................. 289
      Project Management.. 291
         Project Life Cycle 292
Organizational Form... 294
Organizational Design 296
   Mechanistic and Organic Design 297
   Vertical and Horizontal Structures... 299
      Vertical Structures 299
         Hierarchy... 299
         Formalization 301
         Horizontal Structure.. 301
         Information Systems 302
         Task Forces and Cross-functional Teams 303
Conclusion 303
References... 304

Chapter 9: From Control to Learning: Accountability and Performance Assessment in the Voluntary Sector — Susan Phillips and Tatyana Teplova

Introduction... 307
A Tide of Rising Expectations: Evaluation Practices in Canada's
   Voluntary Sector 309
   A Changing Environment... 310
   A Survey of Current Practices.. 314
   Performance Assessment as a Management Tool 318
      From Evaluation to Performance Assessment..................... 318
      Using Performance Assessment as a Management Tool 319
Evaluation Issues: The Meta-Questions 320
   Why: Evaluation Purpose and Audience................................. 320
   When: Program Readiness 322
   What: Focus of Evaluation... 323
      Needs Assessment or Context Evaluation 323
      Process Evaluation... 323
      Outcome Evaluation 324
      The Limits of Outcome Measurement............................... 325
      Logic Models as a Means of Linking Contexts,
         Processes and Outcomes 326
   Who: Choice of Evaluator and Participant Involvement........... 328
      Insiders or Outsiders? 328
      Participatory Performance Assessment 329
   How: Data Collection Methods and Sources of
      Information 330
Toward Performance Assessment and Management 334
   Using Assessment Results.. 334
   The Political Dimensions of Performance Assessment.............. 336
   Building the Capacity for Performance Assessment.................. 338
Conclusion 339
References... 341

Chapter 10: Financial Management in Nonprofit Organizations — Carolyn Bodnar-Evans

Introduction... 345
Responsibility for Financial Management....................................... 346
How This Chapter Is Organized 347
Budgeting — The Financial Component of the Planning
   Process... 348
   Characteristics of a Well-prepared Budget 351
   Types of Budgets.. 351
      Capital Budget 352
      Cash Budget... 353

Operating Budget 353
Board and Staff Roles and Responsibilities in Budgeting 354
Board of Directors 354
CEO 355
CFO or Senior Financial Manager 356
Program, Unit, Activity or Department Managers 357
Others 357
Steps in the Budget Preparation Process 358
Budget Review and Adoption 359
Budget Implementation 360
Evaluation 360
Other Budget-setting Methods 360
Zero Based Budgeting 360
Rolling Budgets 361
Activity-based Budgets 361
Internal Control 362
Elements of an Internal Control System 364
What an Internal Control System Cannot Do 365
Responsibility for Internal Control Systems 365
The Role of Board Committees 366
Finance Committee 366
Audit Committee 367
What to Expect from an External Audit 369
Fraud 369
What Happens When Fraud Is Discovered? 371
Financial Reporting 372
Generally Accepted Accounting Principles 373
Financial Statements 374
Statement of Financial Position or Balance Sheet 374
Statement of Operations 375
Statement of Changes in Net Assets or Fund Balances 376
Statement of Changes in Cash Flow 376
Unique Aspects of Nonprofit Accounting and
Financial Reporting 376
Contributions 377
Financial Statement Analysis 380
Comparative Financial Statements 380
The Bottom Line 380
Expense or Cost Ratios 381
References 383
Additional Resources 384

Chapter 11: Managing the Human Dimension in Nonprofit Organizations: Paid Staff and Volunteers — Agnes Meinhard
Introduction 387
Labour and Volunteer Participation in the Nonprofit Sector 388
Human Resource Management in Canadian Nonprofit
    Organizations 389
    A Brief History of Human Resource Management 390
    Human Resource Management as Practised in
        Canadian Nonprofit Organizations 391
    The Benefits of Human Resource Planning 392
    The Challenge of Human Resource Management for
        Nonprofit Organizations 393
        Dearth of Relevant Guidelines 393
        Lack of HR Management Training 394
        Insufficient Financial Resources 394
        Employment Uncertainty under Project Funding 395
        Tension between Volunteers and Paid Staff 395
    The Role of the Board in Human Resource Management 397
The Special Case of Volunteers 398
    Who Volunteers and Why? 401
    Attracting Volunteers 403
        Membership Orientation 404
        Task/program Orientation 404
    New Trends 405
        Education 405
        Employer-supported Volunteering 407
        Entrepreneurial Initiatives 408
    Volunteer Diversity 409
    Managing Volunteers 411
        Incentive Structure 411
        Workplace Climate and Job Design 412
Board, Staff and Volunteers Working Together for Organizational
    Success 415
    Basic Human Resource Functions 415
        Recruitment 415
        Selection 416
        Orientation 416
        Supervision 417
        Performance Appraisals 417
        Termination 418
Conclusion 418
References 419

Chapter 12: Optimizing the Potential of Information and Communications Technology in Nonprofit Organizations — Yvonne Harrison

Introduction 429
What Is Information and Communications Technology (ICT)? 431
What Are the Common Types of ICT Applications? 434
    People 434
    Direct ICT Applications 435
        Email 435
            Collect 436
            Respond 436
            Humanize 437
            Responsible 437
            Trusting 437
            Relationship 438
        Instant Messaging (IM) 438
        Web Conferencing 439
        Online Learning 439
    Indirect ICT Applications 440
        Blogs 440
        Podcasting 441
    Operations 442
        Web Sites 442
        Virtual Volunteering 444
    Financial Resources 445
        Online Fundraising 445
    Performance 447
How Much Success Have Nonprofits Had With the Use of
    ICT Tools? 450
What Factors Influence the Adoption and Use of ICT
    Applications? 452
    Factors Associated with ICT Availability for
        Volunteer Programs 452
    Factors Associated with How Much ICT Is Actually Used 453
How Should the Management of ICT Change Be Approached by
    Nonprofits? 455
Conclusion 457
References 457

Index 465

Chapter 1

INTRODUCTION: WHAT'S SO SPECIAL ABOUT MANAGING NONPROFIT ORGANIZATIONS?

Vic Murray
University of Victoria

"Running an organization like this can be really frustrating at times. Trying to provide the services our clients need, find funders who will support us and get enough good volunteers to help us out is not an easy job."

"We're here to serve our members but they never seem satisfied. They want more and more but don't want to pay for it."

"When volunteers and staff are working together on the same program it can get a bit tricky. Sometimes the staff wants to treat them as 'gofers' and sometimes the volunteers think the staff work for them."

"The competition for funds out there is getting intense. People are getting 'donor fatigue' and the granting organizations say the demands for their funds have doubled in the past five years."

"We used to be a small friendly organization where everybody helped everybody else and everyone had a say in deciding what we were going to do. But now we've tripled in size in the last three years and things are getting a bit chaotic. I've also noticed more 'washroom grumbling'. I think we have to get better organized but I don't want to lose our old way of doing things."

The above are just a few of the kinds of remarks made by those who run Canada's nonprofit and voluntary organizations in the early part of the 21st century. They reflect some of the special challenges that face leaders in this unique sector comprising those organizations that are neither government-run nor private businesses. In it are an estimated 161,000 organizations (Hall *et. al.* (2004) hereinafter "NSNVO") that provide a vast array of services that affect the quality of life of almost all Canadians.[1]

With the growing awareness of the importance of this sector in society has come the realization that we know very little about how these organizations differ from those in business and government. Also, given that they provide paid jobs for over two million people, employ the services of some 19 million volunteers and receive over $110 billion in revenues a year (NSNVO), we need to pay more attention to the special problems they encounter as they seek to achieve their missions.

This book is an attempt to pull together what we know (and identify what we do not know) about managing nonprofit and voluntary organizations (henceforth referred to at times as "NPOs") in Canada. It is aimed specifically at those who are (or who aspire to be) in positions of leadership in these organizations: executive directors, members of boards of directors, program managers, volunteer leaders, and students in the many new university and college programs that have been created to prepare future leaders in this important sector.

We begin with a brief overview of just what the nonprofit and voluntary sector is (henceforth to be referred to simply as "the nonprofit sector"). How does it differ from the business and government sectors? How does it differ within itself? Next we will look at the special management challenges created by the unique characteristics of the sector for those in leadership positions within it. This will lead to the presentation of a simple framework for understanding these management challenges. It will be seen that this framework provides the basis for the organization of the remainder of the chapters in the book.

---

[1]   This number excludes an unknown, but probably very large, number of small, informal, "grass roots" groups that do not qualify as "organizations" but that help themselves and others in myriad ways.

HOW DO NONPROFIT SECTOR ORGANIZATIONS DIFFER FROM THOSE IN THE BUSINESS AND GOVERNMENT SECTORS?

There are many kinds of organizations in the nonprofit sector. They range from large and institutional bodies such as the International Red Cross to small and non-formal associations such as a self-help group of former alcoholics or a line dancing club. Some are entirely voluntary such as a children's hockey league while others are made up of all paid staff and no volunteers other than the board of directors, such as a children's mental health agency.

In spite of this diversity, and on the understanding that one cannot generalize about all nonprofits, it *is* possible to describe how they resemble government-run services on the one hand and for-profit businesses on the other while being distinctly different from both in yet other ways. These unique differences create special kinds of leadership issues even though many other issues might be shared with the other two sectors. The main areas of difference lie in:

(a)   Organizational Mission and Values;

(b)   Organizational Goals and Strategic Priorities;

(c)   The Use of Volunteers; and

(d)   The Governance Practices of the Board of Directors.

Organizational Mission and Values

The ultimate purpose of government-run organizations is to serve the political process. They exist because legislators determine the services they are to provide and they survive only as long as political leaders want them to. Hence they must always be conscious of the political agenda of elected officials. Business organizations, on the other hand, have the ultimate goal of making profits for their owners or shareholders. The growth or continued existence of a business depends on its rate of return on investment.

More than organizations in either of the other two sectors, those in the nonprofit sector are driven by a sense of mission — a strong commitment to "the cause" for which the organization was created, be it finding food for the hungry, "saving souls", showing great art or finding a cure for cancer.

There is also a strong belief in certain values that must be upheld as the organization seeks to achieve its mission. One of the most important of these values for many is the "expressive" side of how the organization should work. In addition to achieve its goals in an efficient way, many NPOs want to provide an atmosphere in which staff and volunteers can develop a sense of community and mutual support. It is a major mistake for leaders of NPOs to act as though their only responsibility is to make their organizations "more businesslike". Ignoring the expressive dimension is to invite eventual ruin.

In sum, then, the NPO's mission and values lie at the heart of its existence. They do not change at the whim of political leaders and do not depend on making surplus money.

This unique "mission and values driven" characteristic of most nonprofit organizations has both positive and negative implications for those who must lead them. For example, it is easier to attract and motivate staff and volunteers who believe in "the cause". Commitment can be harder to achieve in the other sectors where more people are likely to view their work as "just a job". But the same strong values can also make nonprofits more difficult to change because, without political masters or profit-seeking owners to drive them, they may find it easier to ignore signals from their environment that their missions may no longer be relevant to the needs of those they serve or that their programs are ineffective.

As well, like government organizations, the lack of a profit motive means that nonprofits can slip into operating inefficiently as long as there is a ready supply of money from their funders. For most businesses, competition and the market mechanism means that their income depends *directly* on their customers buying the products or services they offer. Declining sales sends the unavoidable signal that the business has problems. If the customer cannot be satisfied, the organization will eventually go bankrupt. In both the public and much of the nonprofit sector, however, there is *no* direct connection between income and output. Except for nonprofits created solely to serve fee-paying members, the clients of most nonprofits are *not* the main providers of the organization's funds. Their money comes from funders who are not the organization's "customers". This has several implications for leadership:

• Nonprofit organization leaders must often be "Janus-faced" — having to look in two directions at once. In order to get future funding they have to be able to keep funders satisfied that they are using their money the way they want it used; while in the other direction they must provide clients the services they need and want. Sometimes these two groups, funders and clients, do not have the same agenda for the organization.

• Funders do not always demand efficient operations the way a competitive market place can "demand" efficiency from a business whose customers will desert it if they can find a better quality or lower priced product elsewhere. For many clients of nonprofits, there may not even be any "elsewhere" to turn to for the services they need. When this happens, special challenges arise in developing efficient operations.

• Because of the "power of the purse", much time can be taken up keeping funders happy, resulting in a comparative neglect of the voice of the client or user of a nonprofit's services.

Organizational Goals and Strategic Priorities

How an organization achieves its mission depends on it having a set of more specific goals or objectives. In the public sector and many nonprofit organizations, these goals are often multiple, vague, difficult to measure and even, at times, mutually contradictory. Businesses, on the other hand, have the iron rule of "the bottom line" to hew to. For example, take the goal of a modern dance company which might be: "to bring the best and the latest developments in modern dance to the community". What does this mean exactly? Who should define "the best"?

Or how about a charity created to help those with certain health problems (*e.g.*, cancer, heart, kidney, diabetes) which has the goals of raising money to find a cure for the disease, educating the public about the disease and helping victims of the disease deal with their affliction. Each of these goals is very general and it can be difficult to clearly measure progress toward them. It is also the case that, if more money is poured into one area there may be less available for the others (so they can be mutually conflicting).

As another example, consider an international aid organization which may wish to be able to provide emergency help to developing countries where there is famine or disaster but also seek to provide longer term aid that will allow people to help themselves in the future. Similarly, a community service centre may have the mission of improving the quality of life of the citizens of a given area but it has to decide what groups to serve (seniors? youth? immigrants? the poor?) and what services to provide. Too much for one group or one problem area may mean less for others.

Being very clear about what goals the organization should pursue and what priority each should have at any given time is one of the most challenging tasks for nonprofit leaders. They must constantly ask themselves and their followers these questions:

• What services do we want to provide to whom at what cost?

• How will we raise the resources we need to provide these services?

• How will we measure our effectiveness and efficiency in carrying out these activities?

In this respect nonprofits are similar to government-run organizations except usually they are smaller and they do not have to bow to the changing winds of politics; hence they are potentially easier to manage. Incidentally, it should not be inferred from the above that all nonprofits are inherently less efficient than businesses. If pressed by funders or concerned leaders, they have been shown to be as efficient as many businesses and more than some, such as those which do not face a lot of competition (see Weisbrod (1998)).

Use of Volunteers

Eighty per cent of Canadian nonprofit organizations depend on volunteers to help them operate with the remaining 20 per cent utilizing volunteers as members of their boards of directors. In this respect they are, of course, uniquely different from business and government organizations. Obviously, they do not have the expense of having to pay this part of their workforce but it is a major error to think that the use of volunteers is cost free. Successfully managing volunteers requires a considerable investment of both time and money if they are to be used effectively.

The biggest single difference between volunteer and paid staff is that the former do not *have* to be there. This means that, whenever they become dissatisfied (or other activities become more appealing), they may leave. As a result, more time and effort must be put into attracting the right kind of people to volunteer, training them and motivating them well enough to keep them coming back.

Governance by a Nonprofit Board of Directors

All registered charitable organizations are required by law to have a board of directors or trustees, as are NPOs registered as corporations under provincial legislation. As well, the vast majority of nonprofit organization board members cannot be paid (unlike members of business boards) so form a critical group of volunteers.[2] The nonprofit board, like its business counterpart, is legally responsible for the "governance" of the organization. This means it must ensure that the organization is achieving its mission and is being run in a fiscally and legally responsible way. Should the organization get into financial or legal difficulties, board members may be personally liable for any liabilities or damages that ensue if it can be shown that they failed to govern with "due diligence".

The problem often is, however, that board members are volunteers who may not have extensive experience in organizational governance or as specialists in the mission of the organization. As a result, many boards experience difficulties in carrying out their duties. Too often there is confusion and conflict between some board members and the paid executives as to who is responsible for what. The latter may feel the board is meddling in matters it knows too little about while the former may feel the managers should be more willing to bow to the board's ultimate authority. Managing the board by helping it to be clear about what its role is and ensuring that its members are able to carry out their responsibilities becomes, therefore, a critical task for the organization's leaders.

---

[2] Board members of *registered charities* are prohibited by law from being paid. In addition many other NPOs do not pay their board members. However, aside from registered charities, NPOs are not *legally prohibited* from paying their board members. For example, legislation governing nonprofit *corporations* permits payment to directors. (See Chapter 5 for a full description of the various legal forms that nonprofits can take.)

HOW DO NONPROFIT ORGANIZATIONS DIFFER FROM ONE ANOTHER AND WHAT DO THESE DIFFERENCES MEAN FOR THEIR LEADERS?

Let us now consider the ways that nonprofit organizations differ from one another. Each of these differences can create special problems or issues of leadership for those responsible for managing them.

Types of Nonprofit Organization

There are several different ways of categorizing the differences between organizations in the nonprofit and voluntary sector. Perhaps the most meaningful difference from the point of view of leadership issues is that between membership benefit organizations and public benefit organizations.

Membership benefit nonprofits exist primarily to serve the needs of their members. They are usually created by and for members who make the conscious decision to join and often pay fees to do so. In many cases the members also do the work of the organization and manage it, all as volunteers (though larger and better off organizations, such as recreational or social clubs may hire both staff and managers).

In all membership benefit organizations the key leadership issue is member service — getting members and keeping them satisfied. Such organizations come the closest to resembling businesses of all nonprofits because their income in the form of membership fees depends directly on keeping the "customers" (*i.e.*, members) happy. If competition lures members away, the organization suffers (unlike the case of non-member based nonprofits where external funders may keep on providing money even when "clients" are unhappy).

Within the broad category of membership benefit organizations there are two sub-categories: those that are organized as "self help" groups and those that are related to work and professional activities. Among the self help groups are those that are organized for "expressive" purposes, to further personal interests such as spiritual needs or recreational interests. Examples are some churches,[3] sports clubs,

---

[3]   This would not include large, hierarchically organized religious organizations such as the Catholic or Anglican churches. These are closer to the service-providing organizations discussed below.

outdoors groups, bridge clubs, *etc.* In these kinds of membership organizations, organized primarily for self-interest, the critical management task above all is keeping the members satisfied and watching out for competitive threats that might lure them elsewhere.

Another kind of self help group is organized as an instrument for solving problems. Members join, not to have a good time, but to help themselves deal with difficulties that they have a hard time dealing with alone, such as loneliness, substance abuse (alcohol or drugs), abusive relationships (support groups for women), or neighbourhood security (such as Neighbourhood Watch groups). In many of these types of self help organizations the members do not have much money. Thus they cannot afford to pay high membership fees. The special skill in running this type of organization is how to provide services on little or no income and how to get work done by volunteers, many of whom have had little opportunity to learn the skills necessary to do the work required.

The work-related type of membership organization refers to trade and professional associations created to further the interests of members who are in the same business or occupation. Running a trade or professional association presents the leader with a number of special kinds of problems. Since members are interested primarily in what the organization can do for them professionally, they can be quite critical and very conscious of what they are getting for their fees (which can often be substantial). This easily leads to members protesting that they are not getting enough services for their dues. Trade and occupational associations are also prone to factionalism. Different groups of members have differing ideas about what the organization should be doing, so keeping all the interest groups from attacking one another or trying to overthrow the current leaders can be a major problem.

Public Benefit Organizations are the other major category of nonprofit. These are the typical "charities" created to provide services which, for the most part, are for persons other than those who run them or volunteer for them. This would include most social service organizations, cultural organizations such as museums, galleries or performing arts companies, health-related organizations such as the Cancer Society, civic benefit organizations such as the Red Cross, and many others. Their unique characteristic from a leadership point of view is that discussed earlier — the split between those who fund the organization (government grants, foundations, United Ways, public donors, *etc.*) and those who use its services. Leaders have to learn how to find, appeal to, and retain funders while not losing sight of the needs of clients. To dwell too much on one side of the equation to the exclusion of the other usually creates problems eventually.

Within the public benefit category, it is possible to distinguish between those organizations created primarily to provide services (*e.g.*, to immigrants, children at risk, the poor, seniors, *etc.*) and those created primarily to advocate a cause. Advocacy organizations exist to persuade governments or others to change their policies and/or "educate" the public to better understand and support their cause (*e.g.*, environmental protection groups such as Greenpeace, anti-poverty organizations, *etc.*). Of course, many organizations of both member and public benefit types may have some element of advocacy in their agendas, however, this is not their primary reason for existence. In fact, they have to be careful about how much and what kind of advocacy they engage in because nonprofits that exist primarily to lobby governments are not allowed to become legally registered charities and give tax deductible receipts for donations. And those that are registered, but become too active as advocates, will eventually lose their charitable status.

Service-providing nonprofits are often organized around professional staffs that run the programs. Volunteers, if used, usually provide only assistance to the staff. One of the major dangers for leaders in these kinds of organizations is that the professional staff can lose touch with the clients. They end up providing these people only what they, the professionals, think ought to be provided (in accordance with what they learn through their professional training), even when the clients may not want or need what they are getting.

The American scholar John McKnight has taken this critique even further. He maintains that many social service, health and educational organizations have helped to create a "culture of dependency" in which the organization's clients are encouraged to believe that they are weak, that they are "victims", and that only by depending on the professional counsellors, social workers, care providers and the like, can they survive. If McKnight could have his way, most government and nonprofit social service providers would be dismantled and replaced by community-run organizations headed by members of the community who would lead in helping community members by emphasizing their strengths and assets, rather than their weaknesses.

Any help provided by "professionals" would be strictly on terms regulated by the persons with the problems rather than the other way round (see McKnight (1995)).

Advocacy-oriented public benefit organizations, because they are so strongly driven by people committed to "the issues", are more likely than others to suffer from factionalism. For example, in environmental organizations, it is common to find a split between "radicals", who want mainly to organize adversarial confrontations with those they see as "the enemy", and "reformers" or "gradualists", who would prefer to work "within the system", negotiating improvements without trying to overturn the established order. Trying to find workable compromises among divergent factions is one of the most difficult challenges facing leaders in these types of organizations. A failure to do so frequently results in breakaway groups being formed or nasty internal squabbles being created that lead to large-scale resignations or dismissals.

Degree of Voluntarism

It has already been indicated above that a key distinctive feature of many nonprofits is their use of volunteers. Clearly when the ratio of volunteers to paid staff is high, such as in the Girl Guides or churches, the critical factor for success is managing them. This requires learning special skills and knowledge about:

- where to locate a reliable supply of good people;
- how to attract them to join;
- how to keep them once they have joined;
- how to make the best use of them (job design, training); and
- how to minimize volunteer-staff conflict in those cases where volunteers and paid staff must work together.

In those organizations where the use of volunteers is low, there is greater dependence on a well-trained, highly motivated paid staff. Since many nonprofits often find it difficult to pay top wages, they depend on their employees being committed to the mission of the organization and therefore willing to do more than the bare minimum in their jobs. Thus, a key leadership success factor is being able to inspire staff to become committed to their work and the mission without many of the typical incentives of steady pay increases and opportunities for promotion (the expressive dimension of management identified earlier).

In the case where there is a high proportion of professionally trained staff members (*e.g.*, teachers, nurses, social workers, doctors, psychologists, *etc.*) the "McKnight problem" discussed above is an ever-present danger. It is all too easy for people who have received credentials to slip into the mindset that says they know it all and the client knows nothing. It is also, sadly, often the case that professionals in the course of their training unconsciously absorb a status ranking in which other professional groups are considered inferior to their own. Then, when these groups are required to work with one another, they clash. This is most common in the health field among doctors and the members of other health care professions, but it can affect relationships between many occupational groups as well as those who come from other kinds of backgrounds, *e.g.*, people from nonprofit sector backgrounds working with those from business or government. What all this means for the nonprofit leader is that team building and conflict management skills become highly important in staff management and in building collaborative relationships with external stakeholders.

Sources of Funds

Another way that nonprofit organizations differ is in terms of the sources from which they receive their money. We have already discussed the important distinction between those that are dependent mainly on fees paid by members and those funded by "outside" sources. Now we will consider the impact of having differing degrees of concentration in funding sources.

Many social service and health-related nonprofits are almost totally dependent for their existence on government grants or purchases of service. For example, they may run group homes for former patients with mental illness or provide children's services or family counselling on behalf of provincial departments. Organizations facing this type of funding environment have two kinds of special leadership problems. The first is the problem of overdependence. As the old saying goes: "He who pays the piper calls the tune", so when programs are supported mainly by a single funder, that funder's agenda can have a significant influence on how they operate. If the funder's approach happens not to agree with that of the delivery organization, the leader is faced with a major dilemma — conform or terminate the contract. The former destroys the organization's independence; the latter may push it into bankruptcy. To navigate between these two extremes requires the leader to develop excellent skills in relating to these key outside funders so as to keep them "on board" in terms of what the organization is doing and trying to prevent major rifts from developing.

What about the other extreme, where the sources of funds are many and varied with no one funder predominating. This is the case in those organizations that raise their money through appeals to the public (mail or phone campaigns, special events, *etc.*) plus seeking grants from United Ways (and similar "federated funders"), private foundations, corporations, the sale of services or products and the like. In this situation the secret to success lies in being highly skilled at fund development. As governments cut back their funding of nonprofits, many are being forced for the first time to become serious fund raisers yet have chief executive officers who have never had to do this before. As a result, a whole new career path has arisen in the past ten years for fund development specialists and consultants.

Degree of Resource Scarcity and Competition for Resources

One of the most common problems in many of today's public service nonprofits is having to cope with budget cuts due to reductions in government grants. When this occurs, most attempt to combat the situation by seeking alternative forms of income. This creates increased competition for the remaining resources. The number of mail, telephone and Internet appeals for donations has increased many times in the past five years along with every other known fund development method — appeals to foundations, sales, 'thons (run-a-thons, *etc.*), gaming (bingo, lotteries, *etc.*), corporate sponsorships, online auctions, *etc.*

Several leadership problems commonly arise when an organization is hit by hard times. Management often becomes obsessed with short-term, money-saving schemes to the exclusion of almost everything else, including concerns over client needs and quality service. The phenomenon of the "bunker mentality" sets in during which top management stops communicating downward or listening to messages from below. This in turn creates major morale problems with staff and volunteers, especially when one of the actions taken is the laying off of staff.

It is a challenge for nonprofit organization leaders to handle hard times with creativity and to get through them with minimal pain. Conversely, the provision of adequate funds is no guarantee of a problem-free life. At the other extreme, when there is little or no scarcity and minimal competition from others for funds, equally serious problems can arise, namely, those of slackness, inefficiency and empire building. No one *intends* to be inefficient or "fat", but it is all too easy to think up reasons to expand employee numbers and other expenditures when there is little incentive to do otherwise. This in fact happened to some of the larger mainstream nonprofits just as it did to government and business organizations during prosperous periods in the past.

Age and Stage of Development

Organizations, like people, go through stages of growth, from birth, through adolescence, to maturity, old age and even death. The movement through these stages for organizations is nothing like as inevitable nor as uniform in duration as it is for people. Nevertheless, each stage in an organization's life creates a probability that certain kinds of leadership problems will arise. In the case of nonprofits, a simple three-stage model will suffice to illustrate the point. When a nonprofit is new it is also usually quite small and must concern itself with basic survival. It usually does this by focusing strongly on "the cause" for which it was founded and a strong "missionary" flavour pervades its every action. While this commitment on the part of the founders provides much of the energy needed to get going, it can also mean that there is a tendency to ignore key stakeholders (volunteers, users of the service) unless they are supportive. Neglecting messages that are critical of what is going on can sometimes be fatal. This phenomenon is so common it has even acquired a name: "founder's syndrome" to refer to the unwillingness of some of those who start organizations to recognize the need for change and make room for new people with differing ideas.

Another tendency at the early stage of a nonprofit's life is for little attention to be paid to organization. The lack of formal job descriptions, structures, systems and policies can cause terrible problems once the organization gets even slightly successful and grows past the stage when a small handful of volunteers or staff can cover everything informally. Miscommunication, confusion and conflict abound because of gaps, overlaps and poor memories.

Once the organization gets past its initial founding stage and begins to grow, it enters a transitional or "adolescent" stage. It is at this stage that the greatest risk of not surviving occurs. Several things have to happen before maturity can be reached. Often, initial funding dries up. In fact, many foundations and government grants are given only as "seed money" to help in the early stages with the expectation that other sources will be secured after, say, five or seven years.

The transition stage is also the point at which it is not uncommon for the founding head of the organization to retire, or sometimes even be forced to retire by the board, because of being unable to change with the times. It is a time when the founders may need to "let go" — to find their successors and delegate responsibilities to others. They will even *say* they are going to do this but, in the final analysis, cannot do it so keep second-guessing and contradicting the suggestions of the new leaders.

In the case of organizations started and run by volunteers, this is the stage at which many attempt to bring in a professional manager as paid head. These first paid staff often have a very frustrating time of it because some of the former volunteer managers cannot delegate their authority.

It is at this stage, too, when boards of directors can run into problems and become quite a headache for the paid CEO. In the early stage, the board often must be a "working board" whose members not only meet to discuss major policy issues but also manage important functions such as fundraising or some of the programs. But as the organization grows and acquires more staff to do the actual work, the board could and should give up some of its involvement in everyday operations, keeping only those few things that staff cannot do and focusing more and more on purely "governance" issues. Often it has trouble doing this so it ends up dabbling in matters that belong to the CEO, second-guessing his or her decisions and generally being more of a nuisance than a help.

By the time an organization passes through the transition stage (and this can take quite a long time — or never occur — for some) it usually has grown quite large in terms of both budget and people. There are often multiple programs and quite a complicated formal organization structure with several levels of hierarchy, numerous departments or program groups, manuals of policies and procedures, *etc*. In other words, it has become a "mature bureaucracy" with all the dangers that entails — dangers such as tendencies toward empire building, loss of commitment to the cause, interdepartmental rivalries, *etc*. Some large, professionally staffed nonprofits also find it too easy to neglect what is happening to their environments until powerful external stakeholders create a crisis. For example, in the past many hospitals, social service agencies, universities and colleges refused to believe that large-scale government cutbacks would occur so they did no planning in advance and were caught in a desperate crisis when budgets were finally slashed.

Summary

This section has outlined some of the major ways in which nonprofit organizations can differ from one another and some of the managerial and leadership issues that can come to the fore under these different conditions. Understand that they will not always do so and that problems that are most common in one set of conditions can also occur, albeit less frequently, in other conditions.

A FRAMEWORK FOR UNDERSTANDING NONPROFIT MANAGEMENT

The chapters that make up the remainder of this book focus on all of the unique aspects of the management of nonprofit organizations that were identified above. To get a better idea of how the chapters fit together, consider the following simple framework of the elements of nonprofit management — the things that leaders must pay attention to if the organization is going to survive and thrive (see Figure 1).

Figure 1: The Elements of Nonprofit Organization Management

External Elements   *Internal Elements*

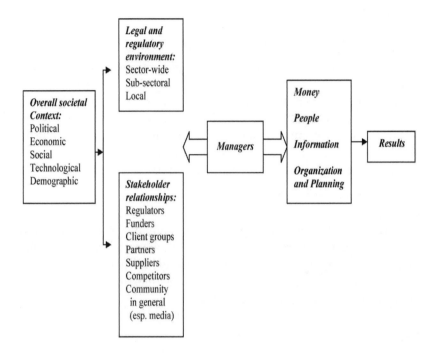

External Concerns

All nonprofit organizations exist in an external environment. It is made up of forces that will determine whether the organization survives or dies. The first responsibility of those who lead is to manage that external world. But few can do it alone. Leaders (and they may be one or several) need resources; therefore, their second responsibility is to manage the "inside" so as to secure, and get the most out of, those resources.

Figure 1 shows most of the elements of the external and internal worlds that must be managed. Looking first at the external world, there are, in the most general sense, a wide range of forces at work that strongly influence how we live as both individuals and organizations. Consider the following:

Politics

Political processes and ideologies matter greatly for many in the nonprofit world. For example, until the collapse of the Soviet empire, there was little in the way of a nonprofit and voluntary sector at all in most of the countries that made it up. This sector has been slowly emerging as these countries develop various forms of democratic political systems. Similarly, until the 1950s in Quebec, the provincial government formed a close partnership with the Roman Catholic Church which, in effect, dominated the charitable sector for Quebeckers.

In recent years, political ideology in Canada has shifted away from favouring the direct provision of many health and social services by government-run organizations. Instead many of these services have been devolved to nonprofit organizations but with government funding supporting them. Clearly, any nonprofit organization that receives money from, or is regulated by, governments must pay close attention to trends in political beliefs and attitudes.

Economics

The state of the economy in whatever regions nonprofits operate for fundraising or program delivery is another critical area to attend to. When times are tough economically (unemployment, rampant inflation, *etc.*), money is short, which makes it much more difficult to raise funds yet, paradoxically, creates a greater demand for services among whole sub-sectors of the nonprofit world. Conversely, "good times" (with high levels of employment, rising wages, *etc.*) can create the opposite problem of making it difficult to find and retain the best employees and volunteers.

Social Values

These are another set of influences that are perhaps more subtle but no less real. They are the underlying beliefs, attitudes and values that are held in common by members of society in general and by various sub-groups within society. They make up what is generally known as the "culture" of society. Many of these are vital to the survival and growth of nonprofit organizations. For example:

- Beliefs about giving and volunteering — to whom and how much should one donate? Why volunteer and for what?

- Degrees of trust and respect that members of communities have for one another and for the social institutions they deal with such as governments, businesses, schools, hospitals. For example, according to Putnam, growing cynicism and feelings of distrust in the United States have led many to give up on all forms of participation in community life, from voting to volunteering (see Putnam (2000)). Without this kind of involvement (or investment of "social capital" as Putnam calls it), the very basis of democracy is threatened. Since research comparable to Putnam's has not been done in Canada, it is unclear the extent to which his conclusions apply to this country, however, fragmentary evidence suggests that at least some areas of society such as large urban centres face the same declines.

Technology

The revolution in electronic information and communications systems (computers, the Internet, the World Wide Web, cell phones, *etc.*) has been a striking feature of modern society for the past 15 years and continues apace. Even the smallest NPOs can benefit from learning to use this technology in communicating with volunteers, staff, funders and other key stakeholders.

Demographics

A final broad contextual condition that NPO leaders must be aware of is population demographics. Ever since the popular success of Foot and Stoffman's 1997 book *Boom, Bust and Echo* (Foot and Stoffman (2001)), there has been a growing consciousness of the effect of changing population demographics on society. In the case of the voluntary sector, the two salient demographic segments are the aging baby boom generation, now mostly in their mid-to-late 50s and rapidly approaching retirement, and the comparative dearth of young people available to fill their shoes when they go. Though retirees are not the most frequent volunteers compared to other groups, their sheer numbers over the next decade will mean that many boomers will look to volunteering but with their usual attitude that nothing that has gone before could be of any value. Just as they had to "discover" relationships, birth, aging, menopause, *etc.* for themselves, so they will insist on discovering late life volunteering and put their own imprint on it. Probably they will be more demanding, want more say in what they do, be more impatient with poorly organized volunteer programs and, just maybe, prove to be more effective than those who have gone before.

The point about this review of broad environmental conditions in which NPOs exist is not to say that their leaders ought to try to change them (though as individuals they may well wish to join groups that do), but that it is often necessary to adapt to the pressures they bring to bear and that it is better to do this before they become major crises; hence the need to carry out regular "environmental scans" to spot critical threats and opportunities in the external world.

For most practical purposes, however, the external world impacts NPOs directly through the actions of its major stakeholders — those outside the organization who have an interest in it or whose support the NPO needs in order to survive. These stakeholders include: regulators; funders; client groups; partners; suppliers; competitors; and the community in general (especially the media and influential individuals who shape community opinion). It is a major part of the leader's job to learn what these stakeholders are doing, what their "agendas" are in areas that can impact the organization's functioning, what kind of influence they have and how they use it. This knowledge is necessary to enable the leader to effectively generate the support the organization needs.

Internal Concerns

To successfully manage the environment, NPO leaders need four critical internal resources: People; Money; Information; and Organization and Planning.

People

It is a cliché to say that without an adequate number of the right kind of volunteers and staff little can be accomplished. It is critical that the NPO manager understand how to attract, develop and motivate staff and volunteers as well as help them to communicate effectively, work co-operatively together and constantly be on the lookout for better ways to do things.

Money

Even though many small, all-volunteer organizations operate with very little money, most need some and, of course, those who employ staff and provide extensive services need a great deal. As mentioned, the unique feature of most NPOs is that their funds do not come from the users of their services, which creates the special challenge of fund development. The second key aspect of managing funds is the need to keep track of it through proper systems of money management — from budgeting to keeping records that can pass an external audit. The death knell of many NPOs is the charge that they mismanage or waste their funds.

Information

The key function of those who manage NPOs is making decisions: what programs to offer or terminate, whom to serve, *etc*. And the basis for effective decision-making is information. Leaders who do not obtain sufficient and accurate information about how their organizations are performing and what threats and opportunities they will face in the immediate future will not last long. This means that the design of proper information systems and a knowledge of the information and communications technology that they use is important.

Organization and Planning

Once an NPO grows beyond a very small handful of volunteers working together informally, it needs agreed-upon structures and processes regarding who will do what and who has the authority to make which decisions. It also needs to think about how to move forward in achieving its mission and to put these thoughts in terms that all those involved can understand and subscribe to. This means developing plans, and the policies and guidelines that will lead to their fruition.

OUTLINE OF THIS BOOK

Identifying the external and internal elements that leaders of nonprofit organizations must attend to in order to succeed is useful but says nothing about *how* they should handle them. It is the purpose of this book to provide an introduction to what it takes to manage each of these areas.

Chapter 2, "The Canadian Nonprofit and Voluntary Sector in Perspective", looks at the broad environment by summarizing the latest information available on the size, scope and importance of the sector as a whole. It also presents the challenges faced by many NPOs in seeking to achieve their missions in order that leaders can see how much they share with others who might seem to be in quite different lines of work.

Chapters 3 and 4, "Managing the Governance Function" and "Executive Leadership", look at the central figures in the management of NPOs — the board of directors and the executive director. They focus on what each does and what makes the difference between those who create first-class organizations and the rest.

Chapter 5, "The Legal Context of Nonprofit Management", continues the examination of the larger context of the NPO world by focusing on their legal and regulatory environments — laws and regulations at federal, provincial and even municipal levels with which NPOs must comply in order to exist. It includes a review of the risks and potential liabilities that need to be considered when making crucial decisions.

Chapters 6 and 7, "Government and Community Relations" and "Resource Development Basics", look at how NPO leaders should relate to their critical external stakeholder groups: government regulators and contractors, potential partners, key community influentials and the all-important people who do provide, or have the potential to provide, needed financial resources to the organization.

The remaining chapters turn the focus inward to the four critical components of effective management within the organization.

Chapter 8, "Planning and Organizing for Results", addresses the constant challenge of deciding how best to achieve the organization's mission and designing a system of organization that will guide it toward the successful implementation of its plans.

Chapter 9, "From Control to Learning: Accountability and Performance Assessment in the Voluntary Sector", reviews of one of the areas that many NPOs find the most difficult — tracking their performance and using this information both for internal decision-making purposes and for reporting to the external and internal bodies to whom their leaders are accountable.

Chapter 10, "Financial Management", provides an introduction to what NPO leaders need to know about budgeting, controlling and accounting for the use of the ever-scarce funds they need to fulfil their missions.

Chapter 11, "Management of the Human Dimension: Paid Staff and Volunteers", looks at the many factors involved in how to attract, retain, motivate and make the best use of paid staff and volunteers.

Chapter 12, "Optimizing the Potential for Information and Communications Technology", focuses on how managers can make the best use of the new technology that has been revolutionizing the way organizations work over the past 10 years, with special emphasis on what is possible in the cash-short world of nonprofits.

REFERENCES

Foot, D.K., & D. Stoffman (2001), *Boom, Bust and Echo* (Toronto: Stoddart, 2001).

Hall, M.H. *et al.* (2004), *Cornerstones of Community: Highlights of the National Survey of Nonprofit and Voluntary Organizations* (Ottawa: Ministry of Industry for Statistics Canada, 2004).

McKnight, J. (1995), *The Careless Society* (New York: Basic Books, 1995).

Putnam, R. (2000), *Bowling Alone: The Collapse and Renewal of American Community* (New York: Simon and Shuster, 2000).

Weisbrod, B.A., ed. (1998), *To Profit or Not to Profit: The Commercial Transformation of the Nonprofit Sector* (Cambridge, Mass.: Harvard University Press, 1998).

Chapter 2

THE CANADIAN NONPROFIT AND VOLUNTARY SECTOR IN PERSPECTIVE

Michael H. Hall
Imagine Canada

INTRODUCTION

Nonprofit organizations make vital social and economic contributions to Canada. They provide important vehicles for collective action enabling Canadians to come together to address the issues and interests that matter most to them. Canadians and their governments also rely upon nonprofit organizations to deliver a wide array of services that underpin the quality of life of our communities.

Canada has one of the largest nonprofit sectors in the world with a unique composition and focus that in many ways reflects the values that its citizens embrace. It is remarkable that, until recently, there has been little information to help nonprofit managers and others understand the size and scope of the Canadian nonprofit sector, the resources they rely on and the challenges these organizations face.

This chapter provides an overview of the latest research about the size and scope of Canada's nonprofit sector and the role it plays in Canadian society. It outlines the various areas in which nonprofit organizations work and shows how organizations vary in terms of the financial and human resources they rely upon to fulfil their missions. Lastly, it provides some insights into the types of challenges that nonprofit organizations report that they face as they work to fulfil their missions.

The chapter draws on the results of four main Canadian research initiatives.[1] The main data source is the National Survey of Nonprofit and Voluntary Organizations (NSNVO) conducted by a consortium of nonprofit research organizations and Statistics Canada in 2003 (Hall *et al.* (2004)). The NSNVO collected data from approximately 13,000 nonprofit organizations that were formally incorporated or registered with provincial, territorial or federal governments. Estimates of volunteer hours come from the 2000 National Survey of Giving, Volunteering and Participating (Hall *et al.* (2001)), while estimates of the nonprofit and voluntary sector's contribution to the nation's gross domestic product are drawn from the Satellite Account of Nonprofit Institutions and Volunteering (Hamdad & Joyal (2005)). To provide comparative perspectives about the Canadian nonprofit sector the data from these studies were integrated with that collected on the nonprofit sectors of 37 countries around the world through the Johns Hopkins Comparative Nonprofit Sector Project conducted under the leadership of Lester Salamon, much of which has been reported elsewhere (Hall *et al.* (2005)).

The chapter begins by providing a definition for "nonprofit organizations" and outlining some of the common ways nonprofit organizations can be classified. Next, it reviews evidence about the economic impact that nonprofit organizations make and compares the size and scope of Canada's nonprofit sector with that of other countries. It then presents information about the key financial and volunteer resources that nonprofit organizations rely upon. The chapter concludes with a discussion of the challenges that organizations face in their efforts to fulfil their missions.

DEFINING AND CLASSIFYING NONPROFIT ORGANIZATIONS

Before providing a statistical portrait of the Canadian nonprofit sector, it may be helpful to explain how nonprofit organizations are being defined in the discussion that follows. As will be seen, the concept of a nonprofit organization is very broad and includes a very diverse set of

---

[1]   In most of these studies organizations are referred to as "nonprofit and voluntary organizations". There are many terms used to describe the various organizations that are the subject of this chapter — voluntary, nonprofit, charities, third sector, civil society and community-based. We have chosen the term "nonprofit and voluntary". For a discussion of these terms and a rationale for using them, see Febbraro *et al.* (1999).

actors in Canadian society. It is also useful to consider the types of useful distinctions that can be drawn among nonprofit organizations.

Defining Nonprofit Organizations

Most of the research that is presented in this chapter employs the structural-operational definition of nonprofit organizations developed by Salamon and Anheier or some variant thereof (Salamon & Anheier (1997)). This definition considers organizations to be nonprofits if they are:

- organized (*i.e.*, having some structure and regularity to their operations)[2]

- non-governmental (*i.e.*, institutionally separate from governments)

- non-profit distributing (*i.e.*, do not return any profits generated to their owners or directors)[3]

- self-governing (*i.e.*, are independent and able to regulate their own activities)

- voluntary (*i.e.*, benefit to some degree from voluntary contributions of time or money)

In applying this definition, hospitals, universities and colleges are included as part of the nonprofit sector. Despite the fact that these organizations receive substantial amounts of public funding and are extensively regulated by government, they are generally governed by volunteer boards, registered as charities and receive substantial contributions of volunteer time.

Although small in number, hospitals, universities and colleges are typically very large in terms of the size of their revenues and the number of people they employ. Although they are non-governmental

---

[2]   The NSNVO excluded "grass-roots" organizations or citizens' groups that are not formally incorporated or registered with provincial, territorial or federal governments. It also excluded some organizations that may be registered charities but are normally considered to be public sector agencies (*e.g.*, school boards, public libraries and public schools). These types of organizations are also not included in the Satellite Account of Nonprofit Institutions and Volunteering.

[3]   A small number of co-operatives were included in the NSNVO. Jack Quarter (1993) notes that some co-operatives — including credit unions and groups that deal with farm marketing and food retailing — do allow members to hold shares in the organization. The mission of these organizations is typically not to maximize profits and, unlike the shares of a business, the shares of such co-operatives do not entitle holders to dividends of any year-end surplus.

in terms of being institutionally separate from government, they are nevertheless tightly controlled by government, particularly in the case of hospitals and community colleges. It is helpful therefore to distinguish these organizations from other nonprofit organizations when presenting economic statistics because of their disproportionate impact. Economic statistics are presented in this chapter both for the entire nonprofit sector (with hospitals, universities and colleges included) and for what has been termed the "core nonprofit sector" (*i.e.*, all organizations except hospitals, universities and colleges).[4]

Legal Distinctions

Turning to the matter of how to distinguish among this broad set of organizations, let us focus first on an important legal distinction. About half of all nonprofit organizations are formally registered as charitable organizations with the Canada Revenue Agency. In order to be eligible for registered charity status an organization's major purpose must fall into one of four areas: the relief of poverty, the advancement of education, the advancement of religion, or other purposes of a charitable nature beneficial to the community as a whole, including health. Charitable status provides two main advantages for organizations. It gives their donors access to tax incentives for the donations they make and enables organizations to access funding from charitable foundations which are restricted by law to registered charities and a small number of other "qualified donees".

Area of Activity

People commonly identify organizations according to their area of activity and are quite familiar with terms such as arts organizations, sports clubs or social service organizations. Along these lines, this chapter employs a version of the International Classification of Nonprofit Organizations (ICNPO), a system developed by Salamon & Anheier (1997) and modified by Hall *et al.* (2004) for the Canadian context. Table 1 outlines the 15 categories into which organizations have been classified based on their primary area of economic activity. While organizations may operate in more than one area (*e.g.*, providing

---

[4]   This follows the practice adopted by the *Satellite Account of Nonprofit Institutions and Volunteering*.

recreation opportunities and day care), they are classified into the single ICNPO category that describes where most of their time and resources are allocated.

Type of Function

Finally, it is important to recognize that nonprofit organizations perform a variety of functions in Canadian life ranging from the provision of human and social services to offering vehicles for citizens to express their interests and address community needs through collective action and advocacy. Salamon has proposed two broad categories of functions (Salamon (1999), at pp. 15-17):

- **Service functions** involve the delivery of direct services such as education, health, housing, community and economic development promotion, animal welfare and social services.

- **Expressive functions** involve activities that enable the expression of cultural, spiritual, professional, and other, interests and beliefs. Organizations serving expressive functions include sports and recreation groups, religious organizations, arts and cultural organizations, labour and professional associations, advocacy groups and those working on environmental issues.

Table 1: Nonprofit Organization Activity Types

Arts and culture	organizations operating in general or specialized fields of arts and culture
Sports and recreation	organizations operating in general or specialized fields of sports and recreation
Education and research	organizations administering, providing, promoting, conducting, supporting and servicing education and research, excluding public school boards, universities, colleges and postsecondary institutions
Universities and colleges	universities and colleges, postsecondary institutions
Health	organizations engaging in health-related activities, providing and administering both general and specialized health care services, as well as health support services, excluding hospitals
Hospitals	hospital facilities that provide inpatient or outpatient medical care organizations and institutions providing social services to a community or target population
Social services	organizations and institutions providing social services to a community or target population

Environment	organizations promoting and providing services in environmental conservation, pollution control and prevention, environmental education and health, and animal protection
Development and housing	organizations promoting programs and providing services to help improve communities and promote the economic and social well-being of society
Law, advocacy and politics	organizations working to protect and promote civil and other rights, advocating the social and political interests of general or special constituencies, offering legal services and promoting public safety
Grant-making, fundraising and voluntarism promotion	philanthropic organizations and organizations promoting charity and charitable activities, including grant-making foundations, voluntarism promotion and support, and fundraising organizations
International	organizations promoting cultural understanding between peoples of various countries and historical backgrounds, as well as those providing relief during emergencies and those promoting development and welfare abroad
Religion	organizations promoting religious beliefs and administering religious services and rituals (such as churches, mosques, synagogues, temples, shrines, seminaries, monasteries and similar religious institutions); and related organizations and auxiliaries of such organizations
Business and professional associations and unions	organizations promoting, regulating and safeguarding business, professional and labour interests
Organizations not elsewhere classified	a small number of organizations that were unable to locate their primary activity within any of the specified activity categories

Source: National Survey of Nonprofit and Voluntary Organizations.

In the sections that follow these various ways of classifying nonprofit organizations are employed to provide a portrait of their size and scope and the resources that they rely upon.

THE SIZE AND SCOPE OF CANADA'S NONPROFIT SECTOR

An estimated 161,000 nonprofit organizations operated in Canada in 2003. As Figure 1 shows, the sector is very diverse in terms of its activities, with most organizations serving expressive functions. The two largest areas of activity involve expressive functions: Sports & Recreation (21 per cent of all organizations) and Religion (19 per cent). Social service organizations are the next largest group, comprising 12 per cent of all organizations.

Figure 1: Types of Nonprofit Organizations

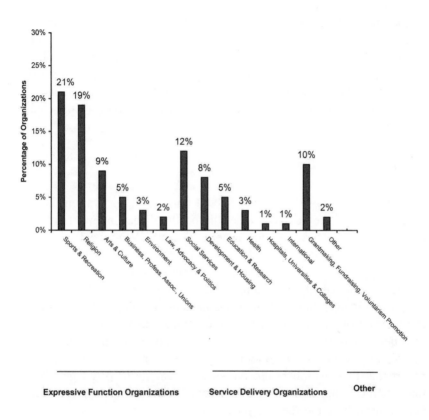

Source: National Survey of Nonprofit and Voluntary Organizations.

About half of all nonprofit organizations are registered charities. Their areas of activity reflect the requirement that they engage in specific types of activities to obtain charitable status. Registered charities make up over 70 per cent of all organizations operating in the areas of Religion, Social Services, Health, Hospitals, Universities & Colleges, Education & Research, International Development, and Grantmaking, Fundraising & Voluntarism Promotion. Over half of the Arts & Culture and Education & Research Organizations are also registered charities.

Geographic Area of Focus

The ability of nonprofit organizations to understand the needs of the communities in which they are based is often cited as one of their key strengths. Most nonprofit organizations (64 per cent) operate at the local level serving a neighbourhood, town or regional municipality. About one-fifth (19 per cent) serve a region, while about one in ten (9 per cent) serve a province or territory. A small minority operate in more than one province (2 per cent) or at a national level (3 per cent) or international level (3 per cent).

Public vs. Mutual Benefit

One of the questions that is raised about nonprofit organizations is the extent to which they exist to meet the needs of their members rather than to provide a larger public benefit. The NSNVO reveals a Canadian nonprofit sector that serves, and is extensively supported by, the Canadian public. Most organizations (76 per cent) have individuals as members, collectively reporting a total membership of 139 million people (an indication that many Canadians hold multiple memberships in nonprofit organizations). Of those organizations with individuals as members, more than half (57 per cent) place no restrictions on membership and allow anyone to join. Only 27 per cent of all organizations report that their members receive special benefits or privileges from their membership, and only 39 per cent indicate that their members benefit most from the services provided.

ECONOMIC CONTRIBUTIONS

Nonprofit organizations are significant players in the Canadian economy. In 2000, they accounted for 6.4 per cent of the nation's gross domestic product (GDP). When the value of volunteer activity is included, the contribution to GDP increases to 7.8 per cent of GDP (see Table 2).

Table 2: Economic Contribution of Nonprofit Organizations to the Canadian Economy

---

Total Nonprofit Sector

$79 billion added to national economy (including value of volunteers)

7.8% of Gross Domestic Product

$65 billion added (excluding value of volunteers)

2,073,032 full-time equivalent workforce

1,524,032 full-time equivalent paid employees

549,000 full-time equivalent volunteers

12.1% of the economically active population

Core Nonprofit Sector (excluding hospitals, colleges and universities)

$35 billion added to national economy (including value of volunteers)

3.5% of the economy

$23 billion added (excluding the value of volunteers

1,541,345 full-time equivalent workforce

1,016,856 full-time equivalent paid employees

524,489 full-time equivalent volunteers

9% of the economically active population

Source: Johns Hopkins Comparative Nonprofit Sector Project, Statistics Canada Satellite Account of Nonprofit Institutions and Volunteering, 2000 National Survey of Giving, Volunteering and Participating, and National Survey of Nonprofit and Voluntary Organizations.

If one sets aside the one per cent of Canadian organizations that are hospitals, universities and colleges, the remaining organizations (the core nonprofit sector) contribute 3.5 per cent of the nation's GDP. The contribution of the core nonprofit sector is larger than many other well-recognized industrial sectors including Accommodation and Food Services, Agriculture and Motor Vehicle Manufacturing (see Figure 2).

Figure 2: Comparative Contribution to GDP

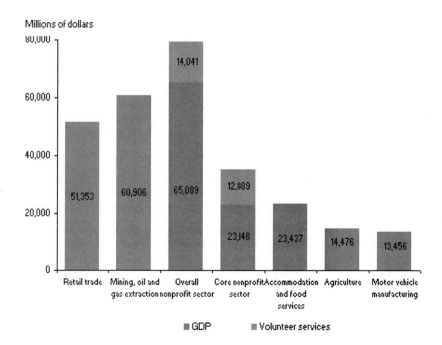

Source: Satellite Account of Nonprofit Institutions and Volunteering: 1997-2000, Catalogue No. 13-015-XIE (Ottawa: Statistics Canada).

A Substantial Workforce

The nonprofit sector is also a major employer. With a workforce of 1.5 million full-time equivalent (FTE) paid staff and 549,000 FTE equivalent volunteers, it engages 12 per cent of the economically active population. To put this in perspective, the workforce is almost the size of the entire manufacturing industry in the country (see Figure 3).

Figure 3: The Relative Size of the Nonprofit Workforce
(Paid Employees and Volunteers)

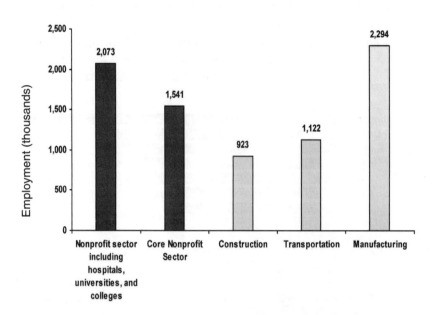

Source: 2000 National Survey of Giving, Volunteering and Participating; and National Survey of Nonprofit and Voluntary Organizations.

The core nonprofit sector alone engages one million FTE paid staff and 524,489 FTE volunteers or 9 per cent of the economically active population. It has a workforce that is one-third larger than the transportation industry and more than one-and-one-half times larger than the construction industry.

INTERNATIONAL COMPARISONS

How does Canada's nonprofit sector compare to that of other countries? Is it bigger or smaller? Does it engage in the same types of activities? Answers to these questions are available from research conducted as part of the Johns Hopkins University, Comparative Nonprofit Sector Project (CNP) (Hall *et al.* (2005)).

Many will be surprised to learn that Canada has the second largest nonprofit sector in the world when expressed as a share of the economically active population.[5] Moreover, on this basis, it is far larger than the nonprofit sectors in the United States, the United Kingdom, France or many other developed countries (see Figure 4).

Figure 4: Nonprofit Sector Workforce (Paid Employees and Volunteers) as a Share of the Economically Active Population, by Country

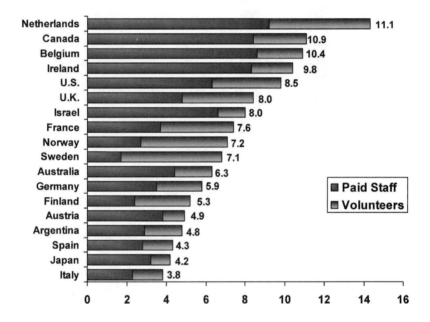

Source: Johns Hopkins Comparative Nonprofit Sector Project; 2000 National Survey of Giving, Volunteering and Participating; National Survey of Nonprofit and Voluntary Organizations.

The Canadian nonprofit sector is not only relatively large compared to many other countries, it also is more professionalized, drawing more on the efforts of paid employees. Paid employees comprise three-quarters of the full-time equivalent workforce of Canadian nonprofit organizations compared to 62 per cent in the 37 countries that participated in the CNP.

Nevertheless, Canadian nonprofit organizations also engage more volunteers in their activities than do nonprofit organizations in many other countries. Three per cent of the economically active population

---

5   International comparisons performed by the CNP exclude religious organizations.

in Canada contributes volunteer time to nonprofit organizations, an amount that is almost double the average for developed countries in the CNP (1.6 per cent) and larger than the overall CNP international average (2.7 per cent), but less than the amount of volunteer effort contributed in Sweden, Norway, the United Kingdom, France and the United States.

FINANCIAL AND HUMAN RESOURCES

Securing adequate financial and human resources is a key aspect of nonprofit management. With that in mind, it is useful to understand how nonprofit organizations are typically resourced and the particular types of resources that different types of organizations depend upon.

Financial Resources

Most nonprofit organizations rely on two main sources of revenue, earned income and government funding (often in the form of payment for services delivered). Looking at the nonprofit sector as a whole, 49 per cent of all revenues comes from government compared to 35 per cent from earned income[6] and 13 per cent from private giving (*i.e.*, individual donations, foundation grants and corporate contributions) (Hall *et al.* (2004)). With respect to government funding it is important to note that 83 per cent of all government funding comes directly from provincial or territorial governments.

For the core nonprofit sector, 43 per cent of revenues come from earned income, followed by 36 per cent from government and 17 per cent from gifts and donation. The most important sources of earned income are fees for goods or services (21 per cent of all revenues) and membership fees (16 per cent). With respect to government funding, almost one-quarter of all revenues for this group come from provincial governments and 9 per cent from the federal government. The leading sources of revenue from gifts and donations are contributions from individuals (11 per cent of all revenues) and from corporations (3 per cent).

---

[6] The earned income category does not include payments from government for goods or services, such revenues are classified as government funding.

Nonprofit managers may find it informative to examine how the revenue profiles for their own organizations compare to those for their sub-sector overall. Government funding is dominant among social services, health, hospitals, and universities and colleges (see Figure 5). On the other hand, earned income sources of revenue predominate among sports and recreation, arts and culture and business, professional associations and unions, development and housing and environmental organizations. Religious organizations are unique in their reliance on private giving as the primary source of their revenue.

Generally speaking, service delivery organizations rely more on government funding than do expressive function organizations, which rely more upon earned income and donations (see Figure 5). This undoubtedly reflects the role that these organizations play in delivering human and social services on behalf of government departments.

Figure 5: Sources of Revenue by Area of Activity

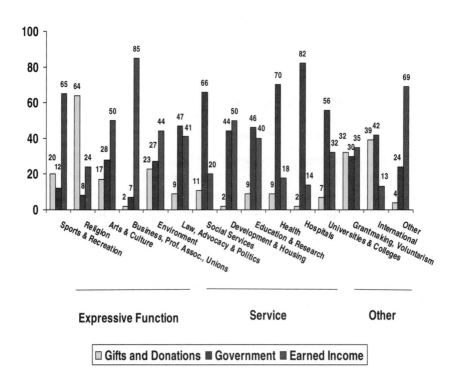

Source: National Survey of Nonprofit and Voluntary Organizations.

There are also substantial variations among sub-sectors in terms of the amount of revenues that organizations receive. Hospitals, universities and colleges have average annual revenues that far outstrip those of other organizations ($31.4 million and $24.7 million, respectively). Figure 6 displays the average annual revenues of core nonprofit organizations. Health organizations ($1.7 million average annual revenues), international development organizations ($1.2 million) and business, professional associations and unions ($1.3 million) have substantially larger revenues than other types of organizations. In contrast, sports and recreation, religious and arts and culture organizations have the smallest revenues. As will be seen, these organizations rely much more on volunteers to operate and much less on paid staff.

Figure 6: Average Annual Revenues by Type of Organization

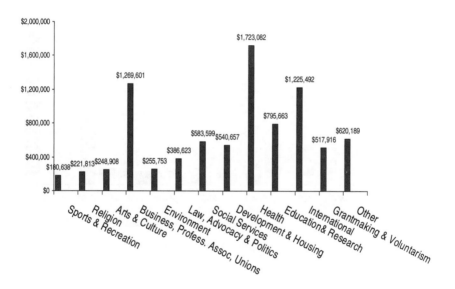

Source: National Survey of Nonprofit and Voluntary Organizations.

Concentration of Revenues

While the nonprofit sector as a whole commands substantial revenues, it is apparent that some types of organizations receive more in annual revenues than others. In fact, large revenue organizations command the bulk of resources in the nonprofit sector. As Figure 7 shows, the 1 per cent of organizations that have annual revenues of $10 million or more receives 58 per cent of all revenues in the nonprofit sector and the 7 per cent that have annual revenues over $1 million receive 84 per cent of all revenues. This concentration of economic activity is a pattern that is also found in the for-profit sector where small businesses predominate in terms of numbers, but a small number of large companies dominate economically. With 63 per cent of nonprofit organizations operating on revenues of under $100,000, it is clear that many nonprofit managers have to know how to operate their organizations without an abundance of resources.

Figure 7: Distribution of Revenues by Size of Organization

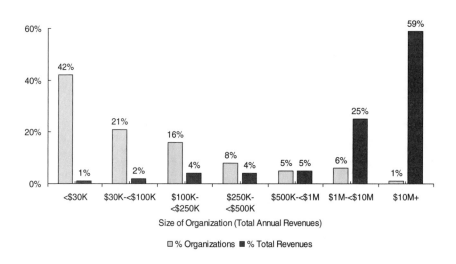

Source: National Survey of Nonprofit and Voluntary Organizations.

Human Resources

One of the unique aspects of Canadian nonprofit organizations is the extent to which they engage volunteers in their activities. In many nonprofit organizations, managers need to attend to two distinct types of human resources: volunteers and paid staff.

The majority of nonprofit organizations (54 per cent) rely solely on volunteers for their operations (see Figure 8) and only 12 per cent have paid staff complements of 10 or more. All-volunteer organizations are most common in a number of sub-sectors, particularly those in Grantmaking, Fundraising & Voluntarism (82 per cent have no paid staff), Sports & Recreation (73.5 per cent), Environmental and Arts & Culture (see Figure 9). Organizations with relatively large staff complements, on the other hand, are more likely to be operating in the areas of Health, Hospitals, Universities & Colleges and Social Services. Generally, Service Delivery organizations tend to have larger staff complements than expressive function organizations, with the exception of the Development & Housing sub-sector (56 per cent have no paid staff).

Figure 8: Distribution of Nonprofit Organizations by Staff Size

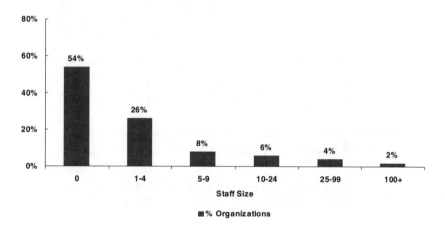

Source: National Survey of Nonprofit and Voluntary Organizations.

Volunteers perform a variety of functions. Most (93 per cent) are engaged in the delivery of programs and services or in fundraising and campaigning activities. Less than one in 10 (7 per cent) participate in the governance of the organization by serving on boards of directors. The extent to which nonprofit organizations rely on volunteers varies according to area of activity in which the organization is engaged and its size.[7]

---

[7] NSNVO data.

Figure 9: Size of Paid Staff by Area of Activity

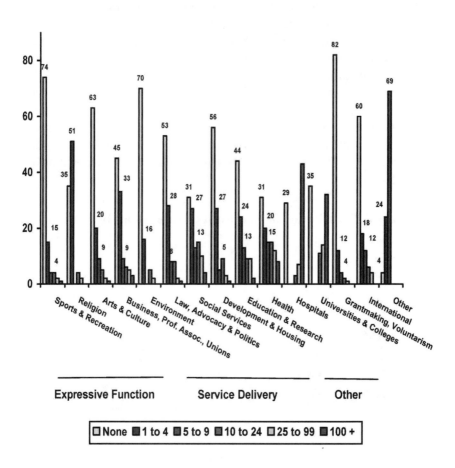

Expressive Function   Service Delivery   Other

☐ None ■ 1 to 4 ■ 5 to 9 ■ 10 to 24 ☐ 25 to 99 ■ 100 +

Source: National Survey of Nonprofit and Voluntary Organizations.

Not surprisingly, the extent to which organizations have paid staff is directly related to the size of their revenues (see Figure 10). Most organizations with annual revenues of $100,000 or less do not have any paid staff while over half of the organizations with revenues between $100,000 and $250,000 have between one and four paid staff. In contrast, at least half of organizations with annual revenues of $1 million or more have staff complements of 25 or more.

Figure 10: Paid Staff Employment by Size of Revenues

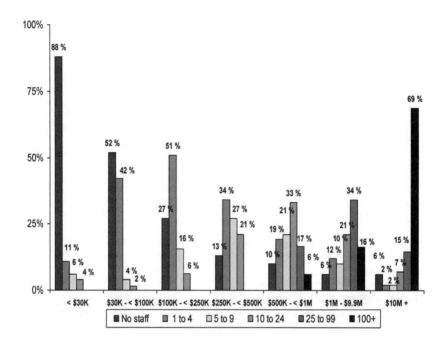

Source: National Survey of Nonprofit and Voluntary Organizations.

THE CHALLENGES NONPROFIT ORGANIZATIONS FACE

Despite the significant role that Canadian nonprofit organizations play in the Canadian economy, there are signs that many are under strain. The challenges of running nonprofit organizations can be considerable. As the foregoing has demonstrated, Canadian nonprofit organizations, in the main, operate on the energy that their volunteers provide, along with the modest revenues that they can generate from earned income and donations. The areas that appear to pose the greatest problems are those that involve recruiting and retaining volunteers, planning for the future and obtaining funding.

The National Survey of Nonprofit and Voluntary Organizations explored the challenges organizations were experiencing in fulfilling their missions. Survey respondents were asked to indicate the extent to which their organizations were experiencing problems in five general areas:[8]

•   human resources — the capacity to recruit and utilize volunteers and paid staff

•   finances — the capacity to obtain and deploy revenues

•   planning and development — the capacity to develop and draw on organizational strategic plans, program plans, policies and procedures

•   relationships and networks — the capacity to draw on relationships with clients, members, funders, partners, government and other stakeholders

•   infrastructure and processes — the capacity to deploy or rely on internal administrative systems, information technology, software or databases

•   external factors that affect the organization overall — such as the level of demand for services or products.

Respondents were presented with a list of potential challenges pertaining to these five areas and asked to indicate whether each potential challenge posed "no problem", "a small problem," "a moderate problem" or "a serious problem".

The majority of organizations (56 per cent to 58 per cent) report problems planning for the future, recruiting the types of volunteers the organization needs, and obtaining board members (see Figure 11). Close to half (48 per cent to 49 per cent) report problems retaining volunteers, difficulty obtaining funding from other organizations such as government, foundations or corporations, and difficulty obtaining funding from individual donors. A substantial number report that they are experiencing *serious* problems, particularly with respect to difficulties obtaining funding from individual donors (20 per cent report serious problems), planning for the future (15 per cent), and recruiting the type of volunteer the organization needs (15 per cent).

Close to 40 per cent of respondents reported problems with: increasing demands for services or products, competition with other organizations for funding or revenues, difficulty earning revenues, difficulty adapting to change, lack of internal capacity, difficulty

---

[8]   For a discussion of the conceptual model of organizational capacity that guided this research and the results of qualitative research that informed the development of the survey items used by the NSNVO, see Hall *et al.* (2003).

participating in the development of public policy and difficulty providing training for volunteers (see Figure 12). Problems with respect to paid staff such as staff retention, obtaining the type of staff the organization needs, providing staff training and development appeared to pose relatively less of a problem for most organizations (less than 30 per cent identified these as problem areas). In addition, relatively fewer organizations reported that problems collaborating with other organizations kept them from fulfilling their mission (24 per cent reported problems in this area).

Figure 11: Top Six Problems that Keep Organizations from Fulfilling their Missions

Source: National Survey of Nonprofit and Voluntary Organizations.

Figure 12: Other Problems that Keep Organizations from Fulfilling their Missions

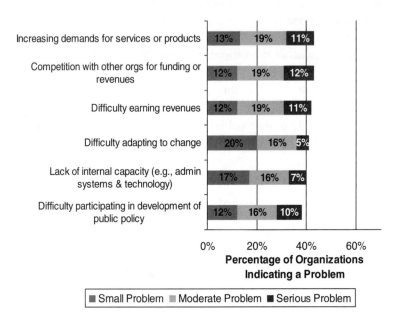

Source: National Survey of Nonprofit and Voluntary Organizations.

Problems with External Funding

The most serious problems appear to be among those organizations that rely on external funding from governments, corporations and foundations. According to the NSNVO, these organizations are much more likely than others to report that they are facing serious problems in fulfilling their missions (see Figure 13). Almost two-thirds reported that reductions in government funding were a problem, with over one-third indicating that it was a serious problem. Six in 10 reported problems arising from the unwillingness of funders to fund core operations and almost 3 in 10 reported that it was a serious problem. Similar numbers reported difficulties because of an over-reliance on project funding. Close to half indicated problems arising from the need to modify programs in order to receive funding and just over 4 in 10 reported problems with the reporting requirements of funders.

Figure 13: Problems Related to External Funding

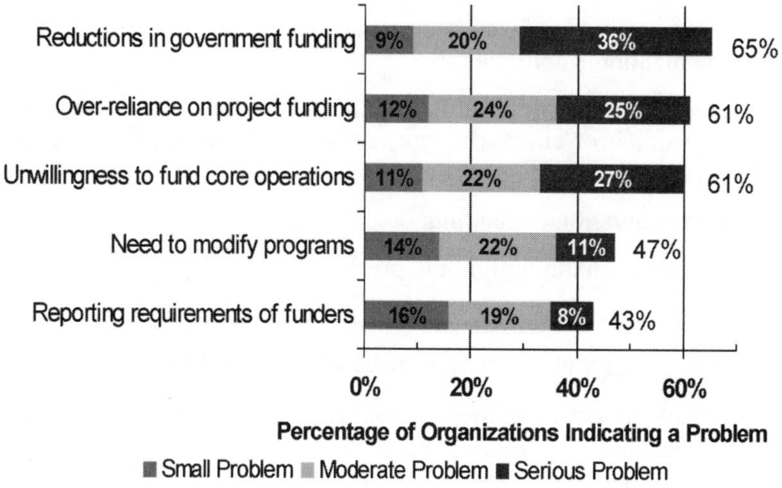

Percentage of Organizations Indicating a Problem

■ Small Problem ■ Moderate Problem ■ Serious Problem

Source: National Survey of Nonprofit and Voluntary Organizations.

Note: Based on responses of 39 per cent of organizations that had been active for at least three years and that had received funding from governments, foundations or corporations over that period. Government funding accounted for the bulk of their funding.

Many of the difficulties that organizations are experiencing as a result of their reliance on external funding revolve around their relationships with government funders. Many organizations appear to be still struggling to adapt to reverberations emanating from the radical cuts in government program spending that occurred during the 1990s. Between 1992 and 1999, total government program spending was reduced by approximately 20 per cent.[9] The funding regime for many nonprofits changed significantly and, as Hall *et al.* (2003) and Scott (2003) have noted, many are still attempting to cope with changes such as:

• reductions in funding;

• the introduction of competitive bid processes for government funding (particularly among health and social service organizations)

---

[9]   Measured as a percentage of GDP, government program spending fell from an all-time high of 43 per cent in 1993 to 34 per cent in 1999 (Stanford (2001)).

that in some instances have included competition with private business;

- a move to fund projects rather than provide general support for an organization's activities;

- the restriction of funding to direct program costs, with little provision for infrastructure or the administrative overhead associated with program delivery;

- shorter duration of funding;

- frequently changing funding priorities;

- mandated collaborations with other organizations; and

- increasing requirements for financial accountability.

These changes combine to create an extremely difficult operating environment for organizations that are delivering services on behalf of government. Unstable and short-term funding makes long-term strategic planning more of a guessing game than a rational process. It also undermines the ability of organizations to develop the human and intellectual capital they require. The administrative burden associated with acquiring funding, reporting on funding, and collaborating with others has also increased. At the same time, fewer resources are available to support these activities or others that are equally important, such as the management and development of the organization's paid staff and volunteers.

CONCLUSION

Nonprofit organizations are part of the fabric of Canadian life. Most operate at the local and community level providing a broad range of services and opportunities for Canadians to express their interests. Most also rely on modest resources driven by the energies and talents of volunteers. At the same time, significant numbers command substantial human and financial resources in pursuit of their missions. Although the important social impact that nonprofit organizations have on Canadian life is often acknowledged, the sectors' economic impact is not well recognized. However, the contribution of nonprofit organizations to the nation's economy far outstrips those of a number of more well-recognized for-profit industrial sectors. Without doubt, these contributions depend heavily on the talent and skills of the Canadians who manage the country's nonprofit organizations.

Nonprofit organizations can be broadly divided into two groups: volunteer-driven organizations and those that rely to some extent on paid staff for their operations Volunteer-driven organizations tend to perform expressive functions and have relatively less in the way of financial resources. Paid-staff organizations, on the other hand, are predominantly (but not exclusively) service delivery organizations. Generally speaking, nonprofit managers are more likely to be found working within paid-staff organizations.

Just as in the corporate sector, the bulk of the revenues of the nonprofit sector are commanded by a relatively small number of large organizations. These larger organizations tend to receive substantial amounts of government funding, suggesting that there are substantial synergies between their interests and the interests of government. For nonprofit managers, the relationship with their government funders is likely to be a critical aspect of their work.

Counter to the common stereotype, nonprofit organizations do not rely extensively on donations or "charity" for their revenues. The largest source of revenue is earned income, which includes both the sale of goods and services and membership fees. This suggests that nonprofit managers require solid business skills to run their operations successfully.

Finally, the research evidence indicates that nonprofit organizations face a variety of unique and serious challenges that may tax the skills and talents of their managers. These problems revolve around the difficulty of planning in an uncertain resource environment, difficulties tapping the volunteer contributions that so many organizations depend upon, and, for those that rely on government funding, difficulties coping with a funding regime that provides little long-term stability and does not provide for the critical infrastructure that any organization requires to be effective.

Canada's nonprofit organizations are a product of the efforts of the many Canadians, both volunteers and paid staff, who have come together to pursue their common interests in communities across the country. What they have accomplished is impressive, building a collection of organizations that together comprises the second largest nonprofit sector in the world, and accounts for close to one-tenth of the nation's economy. Behind it all are the people, volunteers, members, paid staff and nonprofit managers who give their talent, skills and energy to their organizations.

REFERENCES

Febbraro, A.R., M.H. Hall & M. Pargmegianni (1999), *The Voluntary Health Sector in Canada: Developing a Typology — Definition and Classification Issues* (Ottawa: Canadian Centre for Philanthropy, Canadian Policy Research Networks, Coalition of National Voluntary Organizations, and Health Canada, 1999).

Hall, M.H. *et al.* (2003), *The Capacity to Serve: A Qualitative Study of the Challenges Facing Canada's Nonprofit and Voluntary Organizations* (Toronto: Canadian Centre for Philanthropy, 2003).

Hall, M.H. *et al.* (2004), *Cornerstones of Community: Highlights of the National Survey of Nonprofit and Voluntary Organizations* (Ottawa: Ministry of Industry for Statistics Canada, 2004), Catalogue No. 61-533-XPE.

Hall, M.H., L. McKeown & K. Roberts (2001), *Caring Canadians, Involved Canadians: Highlights from the 2000 National Survey of Giving, Volunteering and Participating* (Ottawa: Statistics Canada, 2001), Catalogue No. 71-542-XPE.

Hall, M.H., C.W. Barr, M. Eswaramoorthy, S. Wojciech Sokolowski & L. Salamon (2005), *The Canadian Nonprofit and Voluntary Sector in Comparative Perspective* (Toronto: Imagine Canada, 2005).

Hamdad, M., & S. Joyal (2005), *Satellite Account of Nonprofit Institutions and Volunteering: 1997-2000* (Ottawa: Statistics Canada, 2005) Catalogue No. 13-5015-XIE. Available on the Statistics Canada Web site: <www. statcan.ca>.

Quarter, J. (1993), *Canada's Social Economy, Co-operatives, Non-Profits and Other Common Enterprises* (Toronto: James Lorrimer, 1993).

Salamon, L.M. (1990), *America's Nonprofit Sector: A Primer*, 2nd ed. (New York: The Foundation Center, 1999).

Salamon, L.M., & H.K. Anheier, eds. (1997), *Defining the Nonprofit Sector: A Cross-National Analysis* (Manchester: Manchester University Press, 1997).

Scott, K. (2003), *Funding Matters: The Impact of Canada's New Funding Regime on Nonprofit and Voluntary Organizations* (Ottawa: Canadian Council on Social Development, 2003).

Stanford, J. (2001), "The Economic and Social Consequences of Fiscal Retrenchment in Canada in the 1990s", in K. Banting, A. Sharpe and F. St-Hilaire, eds., *The Review of Economic Performance and Social Progress — The Longest Decade: Canada in the 1990s* (Montreal: Institute for Research on Public Policy and Centre for the Study of Living Standards, 2001).

Chapter 3

MANAGING THE GOVERNANCE FUNCTION: DEVELOPING EFFECTIVE BOARDS OF DIRECTORS

Vic Murray
University of Victoria

INTRODUCTION

All registered charities in Canada as well as all organizations that are registered under provincial legislation as nonprofit societies are required to have a board of directors or trustees.[1] This chapter deals with what the role of nonprofit boards should be and how the board should operate so as to best fulfil that role.

Why are boards important? The simple answer to this question is that they are legally responsible for the actions of the organization. Their primary role is that of a fiduciary, which is to say that they are entrusted to look after the interests of the organization. In practical terms, this translates into making sure that the organization is achieving its mission, not wasting its money and not breaking any laws. For more on the legal aspects of the board's role and the all-important

---

[1] This means that an unknown, but probably large, number of all-volunteer organizations that do not register under provincial or federal legislation do not require boards, though some may have them. Even so, if they want to survive, some of their members need to fulfil, however informally, the functions normally carried out by boards, which suggests that this chapter has relevance even for them.

question of the board's legal liability if it fails in carrying out its fiduciary responsibilities, see Chapter 5 of this book.

For years, many nonprofit organization (NPO) boards were content to define their fiduciary responsibilities in a minimalist way — keeping an eye on finances and listening to reports from paid and volunteer managers that assured them everything was fine. Occasional crises might arise, such as funding cuts, a poorly performing Executive Director (ED) or bad press, in which case the board would have to get involved with details and try to sort things out.

These kinds of "rubber-stamp" boards can still be found today though they are less and less common. The reason for this is that the world of most NPOs has become much more complex and challenging. Programs supported by governments have seen their funding cut; competition has grown for all sources of funds; and the needs of clients/users of the NPO's services are growing. All these trends leave EDs feeling highly pressured. They could really use more help, so, logically, many start to expect more active assistance from their boards.

Added to this are new pressures from the outside world. The previous 10 to 15 years have seen growing public concern over the failure of the boards of *business* organizations to adequately check on the actions of their paid managers. The resulting corporate scandals have heightened the call for improved corporate governance. This trend, coupled with a few cases of blatant mismanagement in large nonprofits, has put pressure on NPO boards to pay more attention to the activities of their organizations.[2]

The problem is that this increased emphasis on board involvement has had two kinds of effects. For some, the result has been a significant improvement in the success of the organization while for others board behaviour has created even more problems than existed before. When asked to describe "boards from hell" that they have known, EDs rarely mention the passive, "rubber-stamp" boards of the

---

[2] In 1997, these pressures led several leaders of the Canadian nonprofit sector to create the Panel on Accountability and Governance on the Voluntary Sector in Canada. Its very interesting and useful final report ("Building on Strength: Improving Governance and Accountability in Canada's Voluntary Sector", Final Report, 1999), can be read online at: <http://www.vsr-trsb.net/pagvs/>. For more on what is expected of business boards see the Web site of The Directors' College created to educate corporate board members at McMaster University: <www.thedirectorscollege.com>.

past. Rather they describe "micro-managing" boards that undermine the ED's authority and want to be involved in decisions on all kinds of day-to-day operating details. They also identify "erratic boards" that behave erratically — that at some times dabble in operational detail and at others want only to "rubber stamp".

The remainder of this chapter will look at the critical dimensions of board operations and discuss how they can be managed so as to produce a "high value added" board as opposed to a strictly "watchdog" board or one that actually creates "negative value", *i.e.*, is more trouble than it is worth. Before doing this, however, it is necessary to say a word about the state of knowledge about boards.

For the past 25 years, there has been a steady outpouring of books, articles, Web sites and workshops aimed at telling those who provide leadership to boards how to do it better.[3] Over the same period, there has also appeared a much smaller body of literature reporting on empirical research into why boards actually behave as they do and the extent to which this behaviour affects the performance of the organization. With a few notable exceptions, the prescriptive literature blithely ignores the empirical literature and *vice versa*. Furthermore, though the research supports some of the suggestions of the "how to do it" literature, other studies do not and yet others raise questions about areas not even addressed by the "how to" experts. We will attempt to point out the connections between the two approaches to understanding boards as we proceed with this chapter.

THE FOUR CONTROLLABLE DIMENSIONS OF BOARD FUNCTIONING

In trying to create a high-performance board, there are only a limited number of "levers, gears and pulleys" that can be adjusted by those

---

[3]   There is not the space here to present a full overview of all the "how to" literature on boards. For example, Amazon.com recently listed 53 books under the heading "nonprofit boards of directors". One of the best examples of current Canadian books is that of Gill (2005). Another standard Canadian reference is that of the Alberta Community Development Program (1999). An excellent new (as of 2006) U.S. work is Chait, Ryan & Taylor (2005). Other recent American references are those of Block (1998), Carver (1997), Light (2001), Masaoka (2003), Robinson (2001), Scott (2000) and Widmer & Houchin (2000). There are also numerous online sources. For a list of the best of them, see the Voluntary Sector Knowledge Network: <http://www.vskn.ca/lead/gov.htm>.

tackling the problem. These have to do with: *what* the board does, *who* should be on the board and *how* they should go about their work.

The "what" dimension has to do with defining the *roles and responsibilities* of the board and differentiating what the board will be responsible for relative to the responsibilities of the ED and her or his staff.

The "how" dimension has two elements: the formal and the non-formal. The formal dimension refers to the structures and formal procedures within which boards work; such matters as the organization's constitution and by-laws, the number and nature of positions for officers and committees of the board.

The non-formal dimension refers to matters that cannot be reduced to written policies or procedures. They are the largely unspoken beliefs, attitudes and values shared by some, or all, board members and key members of staff and management. This is commonly known as the organization's culture, though boards can have cultures distinct from that in the rest of the organization. Another aspect of the non-formal dimension is the approach to leadership taken by the board chairperson and the way the organization's ED relates to the board. In other words, the non-formal dimension is all about underlying feelings and relationships in the way the board operates vis-à-vis the rest of the organization.

The "who" dimension refers to the composition of the board — how many and what kind of people make it up.

The First Dimension: Board Roles and Responsibilities

Without doubt, the single most common cause of boards contributing "negative value" to the organization they govern is a lack of clarity over what responsibilities they should take on and what role they should play in dealing with them. Lack of clarity can occur when the board members themselves are unclear or differ from one another, or when the ED and managers have one set of expectations about board roles and responsibilities and the board chair and members have another (Herman & Renz (2000); Herman, Renz & Heimovics (1997); Holland & Jackson (1998)).

For example, when one mid-sized social service agency in a large Canadian city experienced a serious reduction in government funding for one of its programs, all agreed it was necessary to try to increase funds from other sources. A problem arose because the ED and management staff expected board members to get actively involved by approaching their contacts for corporate sponsorships and donations while board members thought their role was to simply approve fundraising plans developed by staff while the actual activities would be carried out by others.

In another case, several members of the board of a small sport organization became annoyed with its one paid manager when he switched the supplier of team uniforms. The manager thought he had the authority to make such decisions but several members of the board thought he should have checked with them first.

To deal with the problem of achieving clarity regarding board roles and responsibilities, we need an understanding of what it is that boards do. The most common areas of responsibility in which boards may become involved are:

1. *Mission, Values, Goals, Strategic Priorities and Performance Assessment*: Setting the overall purpose for the organization — why it should exist, who it should serve, what services it should provide and what values and ethical guidelines it should follow in providing them. This area also includes the setting of objectives and the development of broad strategic plans for achieving them. To do this properly requires assessing how well the organization has performed in achieving the goals set for it as well as understanding the challenges and opportunities that lie ahead.

2. *Fiscal and Legal Oversight*: Ensuring that the organization behaves in a fiscally and legally responsible manner. This includes such matters as overseeing operating and capital budgets, investments, property management and compliance with various laws applying to the organization. It also includes risk assessment—attempting to identify areas in which the organization is subjected to high risk to its assets or reputation.

3. *CEO Selection and Evaluation*: Ensuring that the best person holds the position of Chief Executive Officer and performs it at a satisfactory level of competence.

4. *Community Relations (also known as "Boundary Spanning")*:

    (a) Representing the interests of the organization to its external publics; and

    (b) Ensuring that the interests of key external stakeholders are made known inside the organization.

5. *Resource Development*: Ensuring that the organization obtains adequate funds to enable it to achieve its objectives.

6. *Management Systems*: Ensuring that the organization is managed efficiently and effectively, *e.g.*, that it has the right administrative structures and policies, information systems, human resources policies, *etc*.

7. *Board Self-management*: Activities aimed at ensuring the board itself is as effective as it can be, *e.g.*, recruiting, selecting and training its members, evaluating the effectiveness of its meetings and committees.

Roles of Board Members

To list the areas in which boards should have some kind of involvement is important, but it does not indicate *how* they should be involved. This is the question of the *roles* the board can play in the organization. It is common in writing about boards to talk only about the role of members as *decision-makers*. In addition, however, they may play two other critical roles in the organization: *advisor* and *implementer*. Thus there are at least three roles that board members may play.

Decision-maker/Evaluator

The most important thing to understand about the decision-making role of the board is the concept of delegation. Except in the smallest of NPOs, the board cannot make all the decisions needed to get things done. It must trust staff and volunteers to make many decisions that it will never hear about. When the organization employs an ED, the authority to make many decisions is delegated to that position and the ED may, in turn, delegate some of that authority to others. The only decision the board makes about all these delegated matters is whether they all add up to satisfactory performance for the organization as a whole. This is the evaluation function of boards and it cannot be delegated. When the board *does* make decisions, it usually occurs only at the level of the whole board meeting in a formal session and voting on motions put forward to it. The evaluation aspect may take place in committees though the results of their assessments are used by the board as a whole.

The key issue with respect to the decision-making role of the board is what matters *it* should decide versus what it should delegate. How to resolve this issue is discussed below.

Advisor

In this role, board members provide information and expert advice to board decision-making meetings or to others such as the ED or other management staff. This role is usually played at the level of board committees who may develop recommendations for the whole board or ED. However, individual board members can also be consulted for advice in their areas of expertise by managers and others.

Implementer

In a few instances, board members may actually carry out the activities required by the decisions they (or others) make. For example, they may carry out some of the work involved in selecting future board members, approaching prospective donors for funds, or interviewing candidates for the ED position. Implementation activities are usually carried out at the level of committees charged with specific tasks such as fundraising or board recruitment. Occasionally, individual board members may get involved in implementing decisions such as approaching prospective donors to ask for contributions or presenting briefs on behalf of the organization to government bodies.

Patterns of Board Responsibility and When They Are Appropriate

Understanding the kind of matters boards might get involved in and the various roles the members can play is the first step to achieving clarity about what the board should do. However, the temptation is then to assume that there is a single pattern of board responsibilities and roles that is best for *all* NPOs. In spite of the assertions by some "how to do it" writers on boards that there is a "one best way" for all situations, the limited research on what makes for successful boards suggests that there is not (Murray (2004). Let us look at several common patterns of board roles and responsibilities and discuss when each may be appropriate.

The Working Board

There are conditions when it is quite acceptable to have board members who simultaneously participate in setting strategic directions, manage the implementation of plans and actually "do work". The term for a board like this is the "Working Board". A successful Working Board can exist when the nonprofit organization is new, small, all (or nearly all) made up of volunteers, and offers services that are not numerous or complex. For example, many self help groups, small advocacy organizations, housing co-operatives, collectives and sport organizations all operate very successfully with Working Boards.

In these conditions, board members are often the most committed and knowledgeable members of the organization and have worked up to the board as volunteers. It is not surprising, therefore, that some of them bring operational concerns to board meetings. In fact, at this stage, it may be impossible to differentiate between "the strategic" and "the operational" in any case. One botched special event fundraiser or one bad story about a mishandled client in the newspaper could end the organization's existence. Almost anything and everything has the potential to be "strategic". Getting established requires everybody with talent and energy to wear many hats.

All that is needed to create a successful Working Board is to make sure that everybody is clear about who can make decisions, who is going to do what, and that a basic agreement exists about what things are the most important. In general, whole-board meetings of Working Boards should still focus on governance issues — planning for the future, setting priorities and assessing performance. But time spent on apparent details is not necessarily wasted if the chair or others can spot the larger strategic issues that can be buried in them. In these kinds of small organizations the board can benefit by holding periodic special meetings of all active participants (such as other key volunteers and any staff) to discuss "how well are we doing in fulfilling our mission", and "where do we go from here".

The Working Board is *not* appropriate under conditions opposite to those that fit it best, that is, large organizations with a high proportion of paid staff and full-time managerial personnel who are operating many programs that take considerable skill and experience to implement. Most public institutions such as universities, hospitals and mid-to-large-sized social service agencies fit these conditions. Such organizations cannot long tolerate the confusion created by board meetings, committees or individual board members trying to "micro-manage" the organization's affairs when others are responsible, and better prepared, to do so.

The Governance-only Board

A Governance-only Board is one which restricts itself to providing broad, overall leadership to the organization by focusing primarily on issues that relate to the basic strategic question of "who is to receive what services at what cost" (Carver (1997)). This means that decision-making/evaluating becomes the key role being played and that the first four of the responsibility areas (plus number seven) discussed above become the focus of the board's attention.

The dilemma facing the large, complex institutions that need Governance-only Boards, and one of the reasons they so often become rubber-stamp boards, is that most board members are busy civic leaders who, though great supporters of the organization, have very little time to become thoroughly knowledgeable about it or the sector in which it operates (such as healthcare, education or the arts). This makes informed debate about major strategic issues very difficult. For example, it takes a lot of expertise to know whether a university should open a new faculty or whether a hospital should convert 20 per cent of its beds from active to chronic care.

The secret of creating an effective Governance-only Board lies in developing a shared understanding of basic levels of policy, deciding which of them are "strategic", and devising information systems that supply valid data on past performance and future needs in ways that clearly relate to the basic strategic issues.

"Mixed Model Boards"

Many boards in practice are neither purely Working Boards nor Governance-only Boards. They tend to be located between the two ends of the continuum. Sometimes they get involved in operational details while at other times they act more like Governance-only Boards. The movement between one state and the other can have several possible causes. Sometimes it may be due to the personalities of a few influential members who do not share a common understanding of how the board should operate. It also occurs during periods of transition or crisis. As small, new organizations grow they often employ more paid staff and acquire professional managers. Paid staff handle most of the operating duties but board members who managed many things in the past still know a lot about how the organization works. They may even be needed to perform certain functions that are not yet being performed by paid staff, *e.g.*, publicity, fundraising, government relations. These members of formerly successful Working Boards can, if the transition is not handled properly, run into increasing conflict with staff over who is to do what and who has authority to decide what.

At the other end of the spectrum, Governance-only Boards can revert to an erratic Mixed Model state during major crises such as the loss of large grants, financial mismanagement, serious labour unrest or the actions of militant client groups. Insofar as the paid managers have trouble handling these situations, the temptation on the part of board members to get involved in the direct management of operations is strong; indeed, managers may ask for it and it may be necessary. Once the crisis is over, it is easy to allow things to keep going in a confused mix of Working and Governance-only modes.

The main solution to the problem of the confused board is to push it toward clarifying its role by fully embracing one or the other of the two basic modes — "Working" or "Governance-only". However, if the conditions are too unstable or critical to allow this, *or* the organization still must use some board members as volunteers to manage certain parts of the organization's operations, it is possible to sustain a Mixed Model that can work well. In this model certain board members or committees take responsibility for managing specific functions. If these are working committees, their chairs become *de facto* operating managers and, as such, should report to the ED. The remainder of the management functions continue to be played by paid managers who, of course, also report to the ED. At the level of the Whole Board, effort must still be made to focus primarily on strategic issues. Insofar as possible, the operational committees and board members with specific operational responsibilities should work under the authority of the ED.

The Mixed Model is a difficult one to implement successfully because there are so many occasions where confusion can arise, especially as the organization's environment continues to change. The secret of success lies in exceptionally full and open communication in which all parties feel free to raise questions over gaps or overlaps in authority and responsibility. There must also be high levels of tolerance for ambiguity. For example, even though meetings of the whole board are meant to be used for discussing major issues of policy and strategy, some board members will want to talk about matters pertaining to their responsibilities as operational managers. They may thus seem to be cluttering the meetings with "managerial" details and undermining the authority of the ED. The trick is to train everybody — management and board alike — to recognize what is "strategic" and redirect the non-strategic to the ED.

In summary, there is no "one best way" of structuring the roles and responsibilities of a board of directors that fits all situations. The board cannot avoid its legal requirement of exercising "due diligence" in ensuring that the organization achieves its mission and does not get into financial or legal difficulties. However, the way it gets involved in the other responsibility areas discussed above, can be highly variable. The important thing to understand is that the board is part of the whole organizational system that includes paid mangers, staff and volunteers. All have roles to play in the process of deciding what to do and then implementing those decisions. The key to success is that everyone must be clear about who will do the deciding, who will do the implementing and what information will be obtained to assess how well the decisions have worked out (see Harris (1993)).

We will now briefly look at each of the seven responsibility areas presented at the beginning of this chapter and discuss how the board should approach each of them. We begin with the most of important of them all: the setting of the mission and strategic direction for the organization.

Confusion over What Is "Strategic"

A number of research studies have confirmed that effective boards are more likely to make regular efforts to develop and review strategic plans for the organization (Bradshaw, Murray & Wolpin (1992); Herman & Renz (2000); Herman, Renz & Heimovics (1997); Holland & Jackson (1998); Siciliano (1996, 1997)).

What, exactly, is a strategic issue and what is not? Not long ago, the United Way of America suffered a grievous blow to its image when its executive director was found to be running up gigantic expense accounts by living lavishly while ostensibly on business. One could say this happened because the organization was lax in not having clear policies regarding what should be eligible as refundable expenses. Should the board have been responsible for deciding what such policies should be? Many would say "no, this is a management matter"; yet, in the end, the inadequacy of these policies had tremendous strategic consequences for the organization.

In general terms, this issue has to do with levels of policy and each board must define what each level means for that organization. Then it must agree how far "down" the policy levels it will go in terms of what will be taken to board meetings for a vote. Finally, it must decide which level applies to any specific question. There are four basic policy levels:

(i)   *Mission and Values* — These are the questions that look at why the organization should exist and what is it trying to achieve. A mission statement must reveal in general terms who the organization is intended to serve, what services it intends to provide and the fundamental values that lie behind the way it will operate. Any issue which suggests a change in mission must be brought to the board.

(ii)   *Strategic Priorities* — There are usually many ways to achieve the mission and an organization has only limited amounts of effort and money to expend. It cannot do everything that its clients, funders, members, volunteers or staff would want. There are usually only a small number of very broad strategic directions in which it might go at any given time. They involve answering the fundamental questions of "Who are we seeking to serve?"; "What services should we provide?"; "How should we provide these services?"; and "What resources must we obtain in order to provide these services?" The answers to these questions must be identified and prioritized so everyone knows what is most important and what is less important.

For example, almost all nonprofit organizations must be concerned with getting enough money to operate. For many, raising funds is quite separate from deciding how to spend the money, and these "how to spend" decisions may have only an indirect impact on how funders decide how much to provide. Hence, most organizations these days require a clear strategic objective specifying the amount of money they need and, in general terms, how they will go about obtaining it. (Of course there are always a few with secure incomes from investments for whom this objective can assume a low priority and others who derive all their income directly from their members or clients.)

Setting priorities regarding what to spend the money on is a much more difficult task. For example, charities set up to help the victims of various diseases and disabilities must always struggle to set priorities between the broad choices of: supporting research into cures and treatments, public education about the disease, and "patient services" (activities to make the lives of victims or their families easier). Performing arts and other cultural organizations must face the classic struggle between "artistic integrity" and "audience appeal", *i.e.*, exploring new artistic frontiers that do not have mass appeal versus getting "bums on seats" by sticking with the most popular programs. International development organizations must choose between the basic options of long-term versus short-term forms of aid. Community service agencies with multiple programs have to decide which groups and social problems get what priority: for example, children-at-risk, new immigrants, single mothers, or poor and lonely seniors. Universities face continuous dilemmas in setting their admissions policies between "accessibility" and "student quality", *i.e.*, making admission equally available to students from all backgrounds (including those from deprived conditions where prior education may have been a low quality) versus an emphasis on attracting only the "best and the brightest" (which often excludes many from deprived backgrounds).

(iii) *Program and Operating Policies* — Once the strategic objectives and priorities are identified, there are the decisions surrounding what particular programs, activities, or systems will best lead to the attainment of these objectives. Human resources policies must be decided (*e.g.*, compensation levels, benefit plans, selection criteria). Accounting systems must be put in place. Actual plays must be produced by the theatre company. Specific treatments must be chosen for the family violence program in the social agency.

(iv) *Rules and Procedures* — These are the myriad specific decisions that must be made to ensure that programs and operating policies are implemented consistently and at a high level of quality and efficiency.

Most boards find that, no matter how much they might agree that at the whole board level they will only discuss issues that represent policy levels (i) and (ii), they will sometimes get into debates that seem "beneath" them. Skilled board leaders will be able to distinguish between an item that is truly an operational matter and one that is not. They will then send the latter back to operating managers for decision if the board has adopted a Governance-only model or identify it as an operational issue for another meeting of the working board or one of its committees.

Managers and committee members, on the other hand, must possess the equally special ability to spot a strategic level question in what appears to be a routine operational decision. For example, a question of whether to apply for funds from a government lottery commission may raise the much bigger question of the organization's values regarding obtaining money derived from gambling. A decision on whether to launch a pilot project for getting street kids off the street may contain the seeds of a radical reorientation of an entire agency. As Mintzberg points out in his book, *The Rise and Fall of Strategic Planning* (1994), the sources of information on strategic issues and ideas for strategic change are to be found in all parts of the organization. The great skill in leadership lies in recognizing this and knowing how to tap these sources.

When a key strategic issue does arise for the board to decide, the decision is often faulty because there is not enough of the right kind of information to assess its pros and cons in any rational way. This occurs because there are inadequate systems for gathering and synthesizing what is important to know, or because what is provided is incomplete or misleading.

Inadequate information can occur because the main (sometimes only) source of information for many boards is the chief executive. EDs may consciously or unconsciously filter what goes to the board so as to tilt the decision toward a predetermined outcome which they favour. One of the biggest difficulties for boards is finding independent sources of information and ensuring that the information they do get from "the administration" is as complete and unbiased as it can be. Public auditors may fulfil this function in the case of basic financial information. For other kinds of issues, alternative sources of information can include independently conducted client and donor satisfaction studies or information from umbrella associations of organizations in the same "business". It also behooves the board to carefully oversee the kind of information *systems* put in place for the organization, *e.g.*, ensuring that budgetary systems provide program and unit cost data; insisting on policy-oriented funding statistics and human resources information systems that monitor staff morale, absenteeism and productivity. For more on this challenge, see Chapter 9.

On the other hand, there is also the problem of too much information being presented to the board in a way that does not relate to strategic issues. The "snow job" (in which board members are buried in paper just before a meeting with no idea what parts of the pile are important) is a classic ploy of some chief executives trying to manipulate a board to "rubber stamp" a particular recommendation. In other cases it occurs because the board itself is not clear about what it wants to see, so the ED tries to cover all eventualities. Information overload may be reduced if the board chair insists that supporting information be provided in ample time to be digested before a meeting and that it explicitly connects to the issues under debate. Information not related to strategic issues would either be refused, included but not discussed unless someone has a problem with it (see "consent agendas" below), or presented in another forum outside of the board meeting.

Problems in the Fiscal/Legal Oversight Function of Boards and the Responsibility for Risk Assessment

Boards that are not capable of identifying and grappling with genuine strategic issues often fall back on an obsession with the organization's finances. If they cannot do anything else, they will make sure it does not go into debt. The problem here is that if concerns about costs are abstracted from an overall perspective of the organization's strategic priorities, they can lead to poor policy decisions. This happens when the annual budget approval exercise for the board is disconnected from the strategic priority decisions. As pointed out in Chapter 10 on financial management, all budgets contain implicit strategic plans within them in that they determine who gets what resources and the availability of money drives actions. This is the main reality for most operational managers and it heavily constrains their ability to accomplish whatever objectives may be laid out in a completely separate "strategic plan". Board chairs must insist that budgets and other financial information be presented in the context of the organization's strategic priorities.

However, guarding against financial mismanagement is only one example of risks of which boards should be aware. A comprehensive analysis of risks involves many other areas such as compliance with laws and the management of property, volunteers, client relations, investments and others.

The Responsibility for Selection and Evaluation of the Executive Director

Virtually all boards take this responsibility very seriously, at least the selection part. Yet, sometimes their choice turns out to be a poor one. Even more commonly, they fail to tackle seriously the job of perform-ance evaluation. This leads to frustrated chief executives who have no clear idea how they are doing in their boards' eyes. It also leads to major crises and lawsuits because the board fails to act on poor performance until too late, then fires the ED, who promptly sues for wrongful dismissal on the grounds of never having been told she or he was performing poorly.

For more detailed information on how to carry out a good executive search and selection process, see Chapter 11 on human resources. Suffice it to say here that, if it can possibly afford it, the board should obtain the services of experts in this area. But even this may lead to failure if the board is not clear about the organization's strategic priorities both at present and for the future. One of the major reasons that newly selected EDs do not work out is because they are chosen to lead the organization as it was, or is, but not the organization that will have to exist to succeed in the future.

As to the ED's performance evaluation, it simply must be taken seriously even though the temptation is to let it slip because leading board members and the ED often develop a close relationship so such members may feel that formally assessing performance shows a lack of trust. Nevertheless, it is a temptation that must be resisted. Doing a proper job in this area means following the basics of good evaluation practice: jointly setting, with the ED, clear and reasonable objectives; providing the resources and necessary authority to achieve these objectives; agreeing beforehand on what would be reasonable indicators of success; then meeting periodically to review progress and decide what can be done to obtain improvement if it is deemed necessary. Usually this task is best done by a committee. The choice of committee depends on the board's committee structure (see below). The whole board would come into play only in rare cases when serious performance problems persist over time and the possibility of dismissal exists; however, the board should be given an annual report from the evaluating committee summarizing the results of the performance review.

The Board's Responsibilities for Community Relations

Research on board effectiveness has shown that paying attention to community relations is one of the most important things boards can do (Herman & Renz (1997, 2000); Middleton (1988)). This area of responsibility has two components: "bringing the outside in" and "taking the inside out". The topic is discussed in more detail in Chapter 6 on government and community relations; however, a few comments are worth mentioning with respect to the specific role of the board in this area.

Problems arise in bringing the concerns of constituencies, stakeholders and the general community into important discussions on strategy when the board has no way to learn about them. This can be because no members are close to these groups or because there is no training in how to approach them or any expectation that the board will do so. Solving the problem requires:

(a)   re-examining the criteria for board membership so as to ensure that there is representation of people who know the concerns of key stakeholders;

(b)   changing the board's own management system (see below) to ensure that there are formal occasions for board members (not only staff) to meet key external groups and prior training in how to relate to such groups.

The opposite problem to inadequately representing the interests of external stakeholders during internal decision-making activities occurs when too many board members are explicitly appointed to represent such groups. The constitutions of some nonprofit organizations specify that certain board positions must be filled by appointees from designated stakeholder organizations. The difficulty occurs when such appointees pay attention only when issues arise that concern "their" interest group then contribute only that group's "line" on the issue. Such people are not willing to modify their position based on dialogue or compromise for the good of the organization as a whole.

One method for tackling this problem (not guaranteed to succeed) is to write a policy stating that all board members are expected to make decisions on the basis of what is best for the organization as a whole. Board members would be required to sign an agreement to this effect and the principle would be reinforced during orientation sessions for new members. An example of one such statement is as follows:

> Board members will be expected to make decisions based on the best interests of the institution as a whole and in keeping with its mission and objectives rather than on the basis of special interests. Members will also be expected to support the majority decisions of the board and work with fellow board members in a spirit of cooperation.

Such statements are of little use, however, unless the underlying board culture (discussed below) reinforces the value of putting the good of the organization first.

Turning to the "taking the inside out" side of community relations, the main problems are a lack of members capable of doing this
or a failure to use the resources that are there. This is usually a function best performed by individuals or a board committee (*e.g.*, community relations, government relations). If the board is made up
primarily of "insiders" such as volunteers, clients, *etc.*, they may not
have contacts with important outsiders. In other situations, members
with excellent contacts (with the media, government officials, potential
donors, *etc.*) may not be asked to do anything. "Community relations"
must be a formally recognized, and planned for, board responsibility.
If this responsibility is always an afterthought, it tends not be carried
out successfully.

The Board's Role in Fundraising

Again, for more detailed information on fundraising see Chapter 7.
Here we will concentrate on the difficult question of what role the
board should play in this very important area.

Surveys of board members and EDs assessing their satisfaction
with the board in the area of fundraising reveal that most of them
believe that boards should be "responsible" for fundraising but few
think the board does a good job of it. This is largely because of
confused expectations about what being "responsible" means. EDs
often expect board members to both "give and get", *i.e.*, donate
generously themselves and personally approach others for donations.
In Canada, many board members expect the board to be involved in
approving an overall fundraising strategy (and maybe in offering
advice as individuals when it is being developed) but do not expect to
have to "give or get" in the sense of actually donating a large amount
of money to the organization or asking their friends and associates for
donations.

Clearly, expectations of the board's role in this area must be developed and communicated without equivocation to all incoming
board members. If applicable, individual members would be informed
before they join that they may be asked on a purely individual basis to
approach people in their networks to discuss donations.

At the whole board level, however, discussion should normally
be limited to overall fundraising strategies as developed by a fundraising or development committee working in concert with whatever
experts in fund resource development the organization can afford.

Once the overall strategy is approved the fundraising committee would primarily advise and assist the actual fundraisers. Only when implementation issues have strategic implications would the committee bring them to a board meeting.

The Board's Role in the Development and Assessment of Management Systems

This refers to the processes and procedures used to manage the organization. They include the organization's systems of accounting and control, information systems that track program implementation and client demand and satisfaction, evaluation systems and human resources policies and practices. How deeply should boards become involved in decisions about these systems?

In small, mainly volunteer organizations with working boards, the board and management functions are so intertwined in any case that the board is bound to be involved. This need not be a problem provided, as always, that there is a clear understanding of who is responsible for what.

The main problems in this area tend to arise in the Governance-only and Mixed Model boards. Many of these boards contain genuine experts on various management subjects such as accounting, human resources, marketing, *etc*. Should the organization be prohibited from tapping this expertise? Not necessarily, but it should be at an individual level and in the form of advice on, or implementation of, a decision made by the designated manager.

At the whole board level, the question of management systems should come up only in the context of discussions regarding how the board is to *evaluate the performance* of the organization. The board must evaluate how the organization is doing if it wants to set future directions. To do this requires information on many matters concerning the organization's environment and current performance. Thus it is appropriate for the board to decide what information systems are needed in order to reveal to the board how well the organization is doing.

While Governance-only Boards generally should not get into debates as to whether this or that budgeting software package or program policy is best, they should insist that information of the kind they need for evaluation be provided and express their displeasure if current management systems fail to provide it. Fortunately, in recent years there has been the development of two useful tools for boards to use in guiding their efforts to evaluate the effectiveness of management systems; one American in origin (The Balanced Scorecard) and one Canadian (the CCAF-FCVI approach). A brief outline of each of them follows.

The Balanced Scorecard

This system for conceptualizing and measuring performance (<http://www. balancedscorecard.org>) was designed originally for business organizations but is currently being adapted to fit the nonprofit sector. In its original form, it assumes that the primary goal of a business is long-run profit maximization. It argues that this will be achieved through a "balanced scorecard of performance attributes" grouped around four perspectives:

- The financial perspective, which measures various financial performance indicators of primary interest to shareholders;

- The customer perspective, comprising measures of customer satisfaction;

- The internal business perspective, which measures internal efficiency and quality; and

- The innovation and learning perspective, which attempts to measure the organization's ability to adapt to changes required by a changing environment.

In the case of nonprofit organizations, their mission statement becomes the end point to be reached through these perspectives rather than profitability. The process starts with defining what that mission is and identifying outcome indicators that will reveal the extent to which it is being achieved. For nonprofits, *customers* must be replaced by *clients* or *users* of the organization's services, and the financial perspective is informed in part by the funders or potential funders.

The CCAF-FCVI Framework for Performance Reporting

This is the most significant Canadian effort at tackling the value-for-money issue in both the public and the nonprofit sectors (Leclerc *et al.* (1996), and <http://www.ccaf-fcvi.com>). The CCAF-FCVI framework puts forward 12 attributes of effectiveness suggesting that organizations can be audited in terms of how well they manifest these attributes. In this sense, it can be focused at either the organization or the program and function levels and is intended to help evaluators get a clear picture of how effectively and efficiently the mission is being achieved. It is similar in many ways to the Balanced Scorecard, although the details of implementation are more thorough. The system thus encompasses both process and outcome elements, although the former are dominant. Although there is no publicly available information on how effective this evaluation system is, there is potential in trying to merge it with the Balanced Scorecard approach. At present, the Balanced Scorecard is short on the specifics that should come under each of its four perspectives, especially with regard to nonprofit organizations. The CCAF approach offers more detail but lacks the conceptual framework that shows how their 12 attributes relate to one another.

The Second Dimension: Board Structure and Formal Operating Procedures

There is little disagreement that the board should spend time assessing how well it manages its own affairs. This means giving consideration to the remaining three basic dimensions of effective board functioning identified at the beginning of this chapter: Board Structure and Procedures, Board Composition, and Board Culture and Leadership. The following sections discuss these.

Structuring the Board

"Structures" are simply snapshots of who does what in an organization. They become frozen in time as formal policies, procedures and organization charts, which then influence subsequent actions. For boards, structural issues include such questions as:

- What is the best size for a board?

- How many, and what kind of formal positions should exist (*e.g.*, chair, vice-chair, past president, president-elect, treasurer, secretary, vice-presidents, *etc.*)?

- How many and what kind of formal board committees should exist and what authority should they have as compared to that of the whole board and the management team? Also, how large should they be and what should be the criteria for appointment to them?

"Procedures" are operating rules that govern how people ought to do their jobs. The following are typical procedural issues for boards:

- Should there be a fixed term of appointment for board members? If so, how long should it be? What rules should govern reappointment?

- Should there be rules about attendance at board meetings? If so, what should be done about members who break them?

- How frequently should the whole board meet and for how long?

- What should be the format for the board meeting agenda?

- What rules should govern the conduct of board meetings?

- What procedures should exist for orienting and training board members?

- What procedures should exist for evaluating the board's own performance and that of its members? How can board members be terminated for poor performance?

Implicit in all of the above questions is the idea that there are right and wrong answers to them. Also implicit is the belief that if the "right" answers can be found, the board's problems will be solved and it will become effective: no more rubber stamping or meddling, no more bad decisions or fundraising failures, *etc.* It turns out that none of these implicit assumptions is true.

Once again, research has found that there is no "one best way"; only structures and procedures that fit the circumstances of a given organization at a given time (see Bradshaw & Murray (1992), Herman & Renz (1997, 1998, 2000, 2002), and Sonnenfeld (2002)). The following are brief comments on some of the pros and cons to consider when looking at various answers to these questions.

Board Size

The "how to" books on boards are fairly consistent in warning against boards that exceed 15 or so people. This recommendation arises because the greater the number of people involved in the complex business of setting strategic direction (the board's #1 responsibility), the more difficult it will be to give them meaningful roles and arrive at a consensus on contentious issues. Conversely, the smaller the number involved, the more difficult it will be to get valid representation of the views of "the community" the organization is serving or, in the case of working boards, enough people to carry out the work of committees. It may also be too easy for "group think" to take hold (a shared feeling that one should not criticize if the majority share the same point of view) thus keeping out radical ideas for change.

Nevertheless, large boards (*e.g.*, 20 to 30) do exist. They often occur in part because it is believed that this is the way to gain the support of a lot of influential community leaders who will be useful in raising money and other purposes. They are also common in national NPOs who feel the need to have representation on the board from many geographical regions. Like the Canadian political scene, there is much suspicion of the agendas of other regions, hence all must be represented. However, it should be realized that it is possible to get the support of prestigious people or input from all regions without resorting to the creation of unwieldy boards. One of the more common alternatives is to create Advisory Boards or Funding Campaign "cabinets".

Even large boards may be effective, however, as long as everyone recognizes and accepts that a smaller subset of board members will probably evolve to play a leadership role. Meetings of the whole board will tend to be dominated by a "core group" and others will usually ratify their ideas. The contributions from non-core-group members will come mostly at the individual and committee-identity levels. At these levels they can provide useful advice or contacts on request though, as noted, the same thing could be provided in other ways.

More generally dangerous is the small board (fewer than six members) where there is a real risk that the board will not become aware of changing conditions that threaten the organization. They are also not very effective when the board needs to be a working board. Members tend to become overloaded with work and "burnout" can occur rapidly. However, many small boards, which are easier for a chief executive or board chair to control, are not necessarily a problem until a crisis hits. To cope in such situations requires the small board to ensure that it has independent sources of information and expert outside advice on how the organization is doing.

Formal Offices

The generally accepted recommendation is to "keep them [formal offices] to a minimum" on the grounds that many of them have no real function other than ceremonial. At minimum, however, there must be a board leader (chair, president), and someone (usually a vice-chair) to step in if the leader cannot perform her or his duties as well as learn the ropes to take over when the current leader's term is up. A skilled treasurer is a very important office with the role of taking the lead in carrying out the fiscal oversight responsibility. The office of board secretary is often created for the purpose of keeping track of board decisions and other records. In Governance-only Boards, however, where there are usually professional staff employed, the note-taking work may be delegated to administrative personnel.

The main point is that these *functions* must be performed; the actual titles used are not important. For example, in some small, simple, organizations all functions might reside in the offices of chair and vice-chair.

Other formal leadership positions are usually the chairs of the board committees discussed below. The important requirement of all formal offices is that there be clear descriptions of the duties of the office and that provision be made for training those who fill these positions. Too often office holders take up their jobs without a clue as to what is required. With luck, they can learn by osmosis before a major issue arises, otherwise they can get themselves and their organization into serious trouble.

Board Committees

At one extreme in the "how to" literature on boards are those such as John Carver (1997), who state that the correct number of committees a board should have is zero. It is argued that committees do more harm than good because they either try to dabble in operations, thereby subverting the authority of managers, or make decisions on policy issues that are the responsibility of the whole board or the ED. The board and committees therefore end up duplicating each other's work and wasting everyone's time. These are real problems, but going to zero committees is not the only approach to solving them. In fact, in the Mixed Model and Working Boards, as already pointed out, committees may be vital to the operation of the organization.

There are two basic types of committees:

(a) *Policy committees.* These are small problem-solving groups which can study important issues in depth and produce reports for the whole board with recommendations and supporting data. Note that they do *not* decide on policies, they only make recommendations to those with the authority to do so.

(b) *Working committees.* These are policy implementation groups which either assist paid staff in carrying out tasks that staff cannot do alone or are used instead of paid staff because none are available. Some argue that, strictly speaking, such operational committees should not be considered as committees of the board of directors, rather they should report only to managers. This is fine in theory but, in many organizations with Working or Mixed Model boards, the best people to head such committees are already board members. Besides, in doing their work, operational committees often must make decisions that have large-scale implications. These level (1) or (2) policy issues must be recognized and brought to the whole board for discussion. Trained and sensitive board members as committee chairs may well be the best judges of what is a major issue with strategic implications and what is not.

Even in Governance-only Boards, some working committees may be needed at times to help with new operational activities in which the management has little experience, *e.g.*, a merger with another organization, a new kind of fundraising activity, implementation of a pay equity program, property acquisition or investment decisions.

This said, there is much to support the commonly offered recommendation that *standing* committees (*i.e.*, permanent committees created by the organization's by-laws) be kept to a minimum in Governance-only Boards. Too many committees with titles such as Property Committee, Program Committee, Purchasing Committee, *etc.*, may have no clear function as either policy or working committees. Instead they waste the time of managers who have to think of things for them to do when they are not really needed, or they necessarily confuse the lines of authority of both managers and the whole board.

Many consultants urge that these useless standing committees be replaced by task forces to be created on an "as needed" basis with very clear terms of reference and deadlines for doing their jobs, after which they disappear. It is important to note that a big advantage of temporary task forces of the board is that their membership can more easily be augmented by well-qualified non-board members. At the extreme, only the chair need be a board member to bring any policy issues to the board.

Should boards using the Governance-only Board model have any standing committees, then? Since giving strategic direction is a key board responsibility, a good argument can be made for a Strategic Directions Committee to work with other strategically oriented groups in the organization (such as the management teams). It would work with these other groups to help define the issues, assemble relevant information and lay out options for the whole board to consider.

Often the role of taking the lead in strategic planning is played by the Executive Committee so it is worth saying a few words about the risks and benefits of such a committee. An Executive Committee is usually made up of those holding formal offices on the board (*e.g.*, president, vice-president, treasurer, *etc.*) and the chairs of standing committees. Its formal role is usually to look after board business between meetings and decide what matters to put before the board for decision, that is, set the agenda for board meetings. The pitfall with Executive Committees is that they can become a powerful "inner cabinet" that arbitrarily makes decisions the board should make and skews the way issues are put before the board so as to favour a predetermined position. For this reason, some board experts advise against the existence of such a committee. On the other hand, someone must perform the function of setting the board agenda and ensuring that everything that goes before it is "ready" (*i.e.*, is of sufficient importance and is well enough prepared and supported with good information). Leaving these matters solely up to the Board Chair and ED increases the possibility of just these two becoming the overly powerful "inner circle". Hence an Executive Committee with strictly limited powers as to what it can decide is probably a worthwhile entity, especially for large Governance-only Boards.

Because the board's responsibility for fiscal oversight is so critical, there is usually need for a Finance Committee, provided it can be kept from making *de facto* strategic decisions when it reviews the accounts and budgets. Organizations with unique characteristics may well identify other areas where constant operational assistance from volunteer directors is required, thereby necessitating standing committees.

Finally, most boards need help to ensure that they manage themselves well. This self help is sometimes provided in part by a standing committee of the board such as a Nominating Committee. It attempts to locate the best possible people to stand as potential board members. The trouble is that the conventional nominating committee does not go far enough. Who will arrange to have new board members oriented and trained? Who will take a lead in evaluating the board's perform-ance or deal with the cases of individual board members who fail to live up to the expectations for members? In some cases, these very important matters are the responsibility of the Executive Committee. In others, the terms of reference of the Nominating Committee are expanded and it is renamed as, for example, the "Board Development" or "Governance" Committee.

A Word about Informal Groups in Boards

Many of the "how to" writers on boards deplore the existence of "cliques" within boards. They urge that the board must speak with "one voice" and that every effort be made to give all board members equal voice in decision-making. This is unquestionably a desirable ideal. Reality, however, is something different and cliques need not be all bad. One study (Murray & Bradshaw (1992)) found that over 60 per cent of a sample of 427 Canadian nonprofit boards of all types were seen as having "core groups" within them. Of those reporting core groups, 71 per cent said they were "a positive force for change". This would suggest that boards commonly have informal groups within them based on differences in the degree of commitment and experi-ence of members. Such groups are often highly valuable advisors to both the board chair and chief executive.

This said, it must be realized that some core groups can be a strong force inhibiting needed change and a board that is broken into several competing cliques usually contains the seeds of destructive political conflict that can tear the organization apart. Leaders of boards must manage informal groups just as actively as they do other aspects of board work.

Terms of Appointment and Reappointment

It is the consensus of board management gurus that it does an organiza-tion good to get periodic infusions of "new blood" on the board to prevent the board from becoming resistant to change. This suggests that boards should have a policy of appointing members for fixed terms (*e.g.*, of two or three years) and rules as to how many consecutive terms a member can serve. Of course the number of members turning over every year must not be too great so as to provide continuity of experience. This leads to procedures such as three-year appointments with one-third of the board retiring each year. Reappointments can be made only, say, for two terms, after which the person must retire for at least one term.

Such formal procedures are potentially useful provided there is a ready pool of qualified candidates for board appointment. This may be the case either where membership on the board is eagerly sought by excellent people or where the organization has a "farm system". A farm system gets potential board members involved in the organization as volunteers and carefully develops and promotes them to the point where they become ready for board membership. It is especially useful for smaller, lower-profile organizations with Working Boards.

Some organizations persist in keeping the same people on their boards year after year and do not seem to suffer. Chances are they will not continue to be successful in the future, however, unless they are among the few nonprofit organizations with stable environments, secure funding and an unchanging and contented membership or client group OR they make vigorous efforts to continuously educate board members in the latest developments, threats and challenges facing the organization.

Attendance

Poor attendance is usually an indicator of a major problem: members who are dissatisfied with the board and their role on it. Some consultants urge compulsory attendance rules as a way of getting the members out, e.g., "Members must attend at least two-thirds of the meetings each year or resign unless a valid excuse is provided and accepted by the Executive Committee." This may get out the members but can mask the real problems behind low commitment.

Meeting Frequency and Times

There is definitely no fixed rule about the optimum frequency of official meetings of the whole board. Actual practice varies from monthly to annually. The governing criterion ought to be that the board should hold a formal meeting when it has enough business to warrant doing so. For Working Boards, this could be quite often. For many Governance-only Boards, even less often than monthly could be acceptable. Chairs and EDs can recognize if they are calling too many board meetings if they find themselves thinking: "Oh-oh, another board meeting coming up. How can we fill up the agenda this time?"

If the aim is to restrict board meetings only to the discussion of issues with implications for strategic direction as in the case of Governance-only Boards, these might well crop up only three times a year: a meeting to approve the strategic plan; an interim progress report meeting; and an evaluation meeting to assess how well the organization has performed. These, however, are *official decision-making* meetings.

Many nonprofit organizations today are finding that it is useful to differentiate between decision-making meetings and another kind of board meeting held for the purpose of becoming informed about and discussing a single important strategic issue. These meetings are usually less formal discussions and feature input from invited staff or experts from outside. Specific motions are not debated; instead, information is provided, alternatives identified and opinions sought. This is all fed to relevant board or management working groups which then develop specific policy recommendations in the context of the organization's strategic plan. Formal discussion and voting on such recommendations occurs at one of the decision-making board meetings.

The question of the *time of board meetings* is important when board membership is diverse and everyone's schedules do not fit the same period of the day, or day of the week (mothers caring for children unable to attend midmorning meetings, shift workers unable to attend evening meetings, or others unable to meet on weekdays). The organization must be conscious of the need to vary meeting times in such circumstances so all board members have an equally fair opportunity to attend.

Meeting length can be another indicator of board mismanagement. Board meeting that last longer than two hours can be an indication of problems. Either too much time is being spent on issues that do not need to be considered by the whole board or there are too many items that involve long-winded reports "for information only". Alternatively, the regular occurrence of long debates that extend meeting times may indicate badly worded motions or poorly prepared reports that do not contain enough supporting data. When these kinds of long discussions occur regularly, attention should be paid to how to improve the work of the committees or managers who prepare the agenda items in question.

One thing that has been made clear by psychological research is that the ability of a large group of people to constructively contribute to a problem-solving discussion declines dramatically the longer a meeting wears on. This leads to the common ploy used by some manipulative executive directors seeking rubber-stamp approval of their recommendations on contentious issues. They insure that these items are placed at the *end* of a long agenda. By that time, no one has the energy to think, let alone object. More commonly, however, the problem of overly long meetings exists because boards spend too much time listening to reports "for information only" or discussing matters that are not the board's responsibility. Poor committee work that places ill-thought-out recommendations on the agenda is another reason for this problem.

Conversely, short meetings that the board rushes through in, say, half an hour could be an indication of a rubber-stamp board. If this happens regularly it might suggest that the board has been conditioned not to question whatever is put before it.

Meeting Agenda Formats and Meeting Rules

One of the most common complaints of board members is that meetings are "not properly organized". Specific problems include the following:

- The agenda does not reach the board members until very shortly before the meeting so members have no time to prepare for the meeting.

- The agenda contains too much information that is irrelevant to the issues to be discussed *or* there is not enough relevant information.

- The order of the agenda items places unimportant and routine items at the top while important ones are at the end, when energy tends to run out.

- Meetings fail to follow accepted "rules of order" so are too disorganized; *or*, conversely, are too rule-bound, thereby preventing full and frank debate.

Except in rare emergency situations, there is really no excuse for not getting meeting agendas into the hands of board members at least five working days beforehand. Agendas should be organized so that items with strategic significance are put at the top. All supporting material should be directly relevant to the impending discussion.

Even the most informal working boards should adopt one of the standard authorities on "rules of order", such as Robert's Rules (<http://www.robertsrules.org/rulesintro.htm>) to be used in conducting official board meetings. This, however, does not mean that all meetings must be run in strict accordance with these rules. The rules are primarily of benefit when the items to be discussed are likely to be highly controversial with a lot of disagreement among board members. As in any emotion-laden debate, rules are needed to make it fair. These would include: how often a person can speak, how amendments to motions can be made, when and how a motion can be tabled, what constitutes being, "out of order", *etc*. In most non-crisis situations, however, a much more relaxed approach can be taken to meeting rules provided the informal culture of the board is one that values an orderly, businesslike approach.

Board Orientation, Development and Evaluation Procedures

Two of the most important reasons that boards fail to perform effectively is that their members do not know what is expected of them or lack the skill and knowledge needed to make good decisions. The most direct way to deal with this problem is through a well-planned system of board recruitment, selection, orientation, development and evaluation (Brudney & Murray (1998); Green & Gresinger (1996); Herman & Renz (1997, 2000); Herman, Renz & Heimovics (1997); Holland & Jackson (1998); Nobbie & Brudney (2003); Price (1963)). The components of such a system are:

*   A board manual which provides full background information on the organization and its current programs and plans, descriptions of the position of board members, and outlines of the responsibilities of board officers and committees.

*   A formal orientation program at which board members meet top management officials, tour facilities, and hear presentations on the organization's programs and background information on strategic issues. Also helpful here are informal "mentoring" programs which pair new members with current members. A good mentoring program will "train the trainer" by providing the mentor with a checklist of topics to discuss and the necessary information to cover.

- Periodic formal occasions at which the board assesses its own performance using feedback questionnaires covering much the same topics as the content of this paper. Additional feedback from the management team on those same topics can also be used. For an excellent example of a board evaluation tool see this one from Dalhousie University: <http://collegeofcontinuinged.dal.ca/nonprofit/governanceAndBoardDevelopment.html>.

There is also a need to evaluate the performance of individual board members. This often feels like a very awkward thing to do because members are volunteers and often have a certain amount of prestige in the community. However, it is not impossible if board members are shown when they join that there is a formal system of board evaluation and understand how the information obtained through it is to be used. Also, the board's by-laws must clearly specify what is expected of members in the way of attendance, behaviour in meetings and in the larger community. They should then specify the procedures to be followed in removing a member from the board if these responsibilities are not properly fulfilled.

The Third Dimension: Board Composition

Critical to having a successful board is getting the right people on it in the first place. The difficult part is deciding who will be "right" for the organization. Too often the tendency is to appoint members who resemble existing members or who are suitable for conditions as they were but who may not be suitable for a changing future. There is a good deal of advice available to those who are seeking to put together a successful board but there are only two universal criteria which are supported both by research and the "how-to" authors:

1. Board members must be *committed* to the organization's mission, *i.e.*, they must believe strongly in what the organization is trying to do and seriously want to help. People who agree to sit on a board as a favour to a friend or because they feel a vague "civic duty" to do "good works" will not usually be effective.

2. Prospective members must have the *time and energy* to do the board's business.

Should Boards be Composed Primarily of Prestigious People?

Having many "big name" people on the board can help in giving a nonprofit organization credibility and a high profile in the community. And some, if not all, "names" have valuable talents. The dilemma is that many of these people are so busy they do not really have time to do much more than make token appearances.

Many organizations elect to keep the percentage of "prestige" members relatively small and tolerate minimal involvement as the price that must be paid for their ability to provide contacts and credibility. The majority of the board carries the workload. Of course if the "busy names" become the majority of the board, this can often lead to a rubber-stamp board.

The other approach is to put the prestigious names on an "Advisory Board" comprising those who can give useful help with specific matters (such as fundraising) and heighten the organization's profile but who are not expected to govern. A variation of this idea is the creation of a category of "honorary" board members who may be listed as board members but do not have voting privileges.

The Diversity Dilemma

It is generally agreed that boards should represent the diversity of the people that they serve but research has established that many boards do not achieve this representation. Instead, the majority of their members have similar backgrounds (usually middle class, middle aged, well educated, with business or professional experience and of European ethnic origin). To what extent this affects the board's, or organization's, performance depends on how diverse the populations are that the organization ought to be serving. The hypothesis is that a non-representative board will increase the chances that the agency will serve the needs of non-mainstream communities poorly. Put in positive terms, the advantage of expanding a board's diversity along ethno-racial, social class, gender and other dimensions is that this will improve the board's "boundary spanning" function and lead to better strategic leadership.

On the other hand, the fear associated with a very diverse board is that these new kinds of members will not always understand how the board operates and will not be able to see what is best for the organization as a whole. Again, there is no research evidence that this, in fact, happens. Differences in background may sometimes make it more difficult to develop a comfortable, open, problem-solving climate but it is not impossible. Given careful selection of the individual nominees and an adequate board development program, a diverse board can be much more effective than a homogeneous one.

A related question is how much the board should be made up of "stakeholders" who have specific interests in the organization, as opposed to more general "community representatives". Stakeholders consist of organized interest groups, *e.g.*, on a university board of governors, there would be representation from student governments, faculty associations, government ministries, alumni associations, support staff associations and associations of potential students such as racial, ethnic or religious groups. Again, the positive side of organized stakeholder representation is the greater ease of "bringing the outside in" and "taking the inside out". Once more, the downside risk is the possibility that the representatives will feel they must act solely in what they see as the interests of the organized group they represent. Hard data on the extent to which this actually happens are very scarce. The probability is that problems arise only infrequently, but stakeholder organizations can cause major upheavals during crisis periods such as downsizing, opening or closing programs, or shifting attention from one client group to another. Again, great care in selecting the individual representatives and thorough board training can help minimize the frequency of destructive approaches to conflict during periods of change.

How Well Should Candidates Know the Organization?

Another dilemma is the extent to which the board should consist of members who already have an in-depth knowledge of what the organization does and how it operates. For boards using the Working Board model, this is quite important, at least for selection of the majority of their members. For Governance-only Boards, it may be impossible, other than by choosing internal stakeholder representatives. A majority of Governance-only Board members will not be "experts" in the organization they govern. This raises the question: how can they provide strategic leadership? As noted, the solution to this problem lies in thorough orientation and provision of at least partially independent information systems for the board.

How Much Should "Business Skills" Be Emphasized?

A related question is the extent to which board members should possess specific skills or knowledge based on their employment or training in areas such as law, accounting, marketing, human resources, public and government relations. One school of thought says this kind of talent is very useful for providing the executive director with invaluable free guidance on all sorts of management issues.[4] The other says it is overrated and runs the serious risk of creating a board which is going to be primarily interested in management issues and unable to focus on governance issues. Again, there are no data to support either of these assertions so probably there is not a universally correct mix. Organizations with Working Board and Mixed Models are, by definition, deficient in certain management skills so board members who can help fill the gaps are important. Even in large professionally managed institutions there can be certain areas of specialized knowledge that the organization cannot afford to pay for but which a board member might possess. The key in all cases is to train these useful specialists to understand that their expertise will be sought in the roles of advisors or implementers only, not as decision-makers.

What Individual Personal Qualities Should Be Sought?

Developing broad criteria for board selection such as those discussed above is important but, in the end, the most important criteria are those that are the most difficult to specify and measure in potential candidates for membership. These are the *personality characteristics* that one wants to see in board members. Everyone who has ever spent much time watching different boards come and go in an organization will agree that some years the majority of board members seem particularly quick to understand issues, creative and constructive in their handling of differences, while in other years, the opposite qualities prevail. Since most boards do not like to check carefully into

---

[4] Professional advisors, such as lawyers and accountants, may face legal restrictions and/or insurance limitations on their ability to give professional advice as a member of a volunteer board. Payment for such services is generally prohibited in the case of charities, and usually requires special approval in the case of nonprofit corporations. Accordingly, any guidance they offer should be kept general. For detailed professional advice, it is best if independent professionals from outside the organization are employed. In some circumstances, it may be possible to contract a board member to provide such advice, but care should be taken to ensure that any legal or procedural approval required has been obtained.

the personal qualities of the people they nominate, it is almost a matter of chance how well the mix works out in any particular year.

What is needed, clearly, is: (a) an attempt to articulate the kinds of personality characteristics and personal values that are being sought, and (b) a serious attempt to state how they will be discerned in any given nominee. Under heading (a), the following are some of the qualities that are important for most board members: creative imagination, ability to see "the big picture", openness to change, ability to communicate and ability to work well with others and handle conflict constructively.

Regarding (b), there is not space here to provide a full review of the most valid methods for assessing these characteristics in people; most textbooks on human resource management will do that. Suffice it to say here that the essence of the process lies in how the candidates are interviewed and how their past behaviour is checked through references. Both processes need to be systematically thought out in advance and implemented with care. The all-too-common method of nominating someone whom one other board member believes "is a wonderful person" is just not good enough.

The Special Problems of Low-profile and Non-popular Organizations

Unfortunately, for a large number of worthy but low-profile organizations that support causes that are not widely popular, the problem of board composition is not one of how to choose among a range of possible candidates. It is to find enough people of any kind who meet the basic criteria of commitment to the organization's mission and willingness to devote enough time and effort to the cause. This is a problem of recruitment, rather than selection. Solving it requires developing a focused, formal recruitment program for board members.

The usual method employed by successful nonprofits of this type is the "grow-your-own" approach. This is accomplished by concentrating on getting a lot of working volunteers to help with programs and projects. The best of these are then identified and systematically wooed and trained to accept increasing amounts of responsibility, including the leadership of others. Before long, those with skills and attitudes required on the board can be asked to join it (which, in these situations, is almost always a Working Board). In desperation, one can trust recruitment to the efforts of a few board members to pressure their friends to join, but do not expect a very effective board as a result.

A Final Word on Board Composition

Though there are no hard and fast rules about how a board should be made up, there is probably one generalization that fits all voluntary organizations that are facing rapidly changing, often threatening, environments: strive for balanced diversity. The exact *kind* of mix will vary from situation to situation, but a mix it should be. Older, younger; men, women; rich, poor; "old hands", "young blood"; business and non-business backgrounds; multi-ethnic and multi-racial — the criteria can vary. But only with a balanced mix can the organization improve its chances for getting the fresh ideas and specialized information it needs to cope with its changing world. Remember, however, that to make it all work, the board needs training in how to work together as a team and in how to discern the greater good of the organization as the basis for making all decisions.

The Fourth Dimension: Board Culture and Leadership

So far, the critical factors that shape the effective board have all been "formal": they can be the subject of written statements in board by-laws and manuals of operation. The roles and responsibilities of the whole board and its committees should be clearly set down; structures and procedures are best embodied in by-laws; and criteria for the composition of the board can be similarly published. However, even if all the "official" and "formal" policies, structures and procedures are ideal, the board may still fail to become a high value-added board. This is because, behind the formal framework is an informal one which can be called the board's "culture".

A culture is a set of attitudes, values and beliefs widely shared by a group which influences their behaviour. Taken together, they represent the shared understanding of "how we do things around here". They are often taken for granted and so deeply ingrained that group members are scarcely conscious of how they colour their individual ways of viewing the world. Not all boards have strong, widely shared cultures, especially when they are new or when there are wholesale changes in their makeup. But most do eventually evolve, in an unconscious way, ways of thinking and feeling about how the board should function. Let us look at just a few of the more important elements of board cultures.

Elements of the How-to-Run-a-Meeting Culture

A stranger observing the meetings of the boards of several organizations with similar memberships, structures and operating policies will quickly note how they can differ. In one, for example, meetings of the whole board may be stiff and formal. Discussions consist of "speeches", each of which makes little reference to previous speeches. Expressions of disagreement are few and are quickly smoothed over. There is a tendency for the meeting to be dominated by a few "senior statesmen/women". In another board, governing the very same type of organization, the meetings are much more relaxed and informal, members appear to know each other, one person's comments pick up on others, adding to or modifying their ideas. Disagreements may arise but are "talked out" until there is consensus or the parties "agree to disagree" and a vote settles the matter without lasting rancour. Though some may participate more than others, everyone usually contributes something to the discussion and the ideas of a newcomer have as much chance of influencing the debate as those of the old hands.

What we have here are cultural differences in the way meetings ought to be conducted. The important elements of the meeting culture are: the formality of discussion, the inclusiveness of participation and the management of differences. They can have a huge impact on the quality of the decisions reached by the board.

Openness to Change

Some boards come to view themselves as the "keepers of the flame". They have a strong sense of what has made the organization distinctive and successful in the past. Every proposal for change is scrutinized for evidence of a departure from tradition. At the other end of the spectrum are boards that have little or no sense of the organization's basic mission or values so are willing to opportunistically take on every new program that looks as though it might bring money or popularity. In between are those which intuitively understand the core values and mission but also appreciate that threats and opportunities in the environment require change, sometimes major change.

Acceptance of Diversity and Equity

Organizations may make official pronouncements about their commitment to increasing diversity and promoting equity in their treatment
of clients, staff and volunteers. These may even be reflected in the
board's membership as new members who represent different backgrounds are appointed; however, behind the formal are the informal
attitudes toward these others that can be reflected in a hundred ways
through tone of voice, choice of words, body language and what is left
unsaid. That message is one of non-acceptance and the newcomers
quickly pick it up. Either they leave or try to "fit in", conforming to the
others' expectations of how they ought to act.

Commitment to Action

One of the most important aspects of board cultures is the extent to
which they have an orientation to action as opposed to "just talk". In
one situation, new board members rapidly learn that the main role of
board members is simply to express their opinions in board meetings.
When it comes to taking an active role by digging up new information,
consulting outside stakeholders, raising funds, sitting on task forces,
etc., everyone gazes fixedly at the ceiling until someone suggests that
the executive director or other staff do the work. In others, the sense of
partnership with management is pervasive. Members sense when and
where they can help and step forward.

Deep-Seated Convictions about Board Roles and Responsibilities

It is quite common for boards to hold retreats at which they make firm
resolutions to change the pattern of roles and responsibilities they use
from, say, a rubber-stamp board to a Governing Board, or from a
meddling board to a clearer Mixed Model Board. Reports are written
and motions passed to this effect. Yet two or three years later they
have drifted back to their old ways of rubber-stamping or meddling.
Why is this? In all likelihood it is because the deeply held, shared
beliefs about how boards ought to operate were never touched in the
"change" exercise. The research of Chait, Holland, Taylor and Ryan
(Chait, Holland & Taylor (1993), Holland, Leslie & Holzhalb (1993),
Holland & Jackson (1998), Chait, Ryan & Taylor (2005)) is especially
useful in reminding us of how important it is for board members to

share the values of mutual trust and respect for one another and how this can develop best when they come to know one another as individuals, not just people with titles whom they sit with at meetings once a month.

What Can Be Done to Change Board Cultures? The Importance of Leadership

Students of organizational culture are far from unanimous about how board cultures (or any others) are created and what makes them change. Without doubt, the characteristics of individual board members are important which is why selection is so critical. So too are the formal policies, structures and procedures of the kind discussed throughout this chapter. But they are not sufficient to make positive changes without leadership. There are two critical leadership roles that strongly influence board cultures: those of the board chair, or president (terminology varies, but this is the volunteer head of the board) and the organization's chief executive (the paid top manager where this position exists). In all-volunteer organizations, the chair usually fills both the top board and top management roles. The way these roles are played can have a great deal of influence on the board's culture: when the two are played in complementary ways, the influence is multiplied; when they are in conflict, they can paralyze both the board and the organization.

An excellent book that summarizes the literature on leadership in nonprofits and reports research on the differences between effective and ineffective leaders in this sector is *Executive Leadership in Nonprofit Organizations* by Herman & Heimovics (1992). In condensed form, the way these two top positions influence board cultures can be described as follows:

The Chair

There is far too little research on the impact of the person who holds the board chair position but anecdotal evidence suggests that he or she can make a large difference to the way a board operates. For example, the chair is often the one who decides what will go on the agenda for board meetings, the order of the items and what will be provided as background information. This "gatekeeper" role can strongly influence the extent to which operational, rather than strategic, issues generate discussion.

Of course, one of the chair's key roles is that of actually chairing the meetings of the board. Leading meetings is very much a combination of learned skills and personal disposition. Meetings will be effective or ineffective depending on how well the chair handles the following elements:

- *Degree of Control.* Strict application of rules of order versus a looser approach. The more controlling the chair, the more likely the board climate will be formal and the greater will be the tendency to adopt a rubber-stamp model of operating. Conversely, overly loose control can lead to a confused board in which all members feel free to do and say whatever they want, for as long as they want to.

- *Degree of Organization.* Meetings start and stop on time, discussions end with clear action plans (who is going to do what and when), agendas are organized with items appearing in order of importance. The more organized the chair, the more boards will value commitment to action as opposed to "just talk".

- *Tolerance for Digressions.* This refers to how the chair handles discussions that wander off the topic. Too much tolerance breeds a "just talk" culture; too little can kill spontaneity and creativity.

- *Tolerance for Dominators and Disturbers.* If the chair cannot manage the tendency of a few members to dominate discussions by too much talk or personal attacks on the contributions of others, a culture will develop in which the majority of members (if they stay on) will feel there is no point in their saying anything.

- *Ability to Draw Out Non-speakers.* Some board members are too inhibited to contribute so must be skillfully brought out of their shells. Unless this happens, a board can evolve into two cliques — the talkers and the non-talkers. Valuable input will be lost from non-talkers and some may eventually "blow up" in damaging ways.

- *Ability to Inspire and Motivate Commitment.* By far the most important function for the board chair to play is that of helping the board to articulate its vision and find the strategic paths to achieving the goals. Some will try to do this through a form of personal charisma which inspires an unquestioning devotion on the part of followers. Without thinking too much for themselves, they buy the leader's dream and do whatever the leader suggests needs to be done to make it come true. The danger of this form of charisma is that it creates a rubber-stamp board dominated by the chair. If and when the vision fails, it is very difficult for the board to see a new way. Usually the fallen leader leaves and most of the rest of the board follows or, if they do not, it becomes paralyzed.

There is another kind of charisma, however: that of the leader who has the talent to spark creativity in others; who can synthesize and articulate the contributions of others. The result is a vision and strategic plan in which the whole board, indeed the whole organization, feels ownership. If it experiences difficulties in implementation no one runs away or blames others, rather they pull together to make the necessary changes.

The Executive Director

The results of many research studies suggest that the way EDs lead is the single most important factor differentiating successful from less successful nonprofits (for more detail on this topic, see Chapter 4). Without doubt, EDs can strongly influence the ability of boards to play their roles effectively (Herman & Heimovics (1991); Murray, Bradshaw & Wolpin (1992); Cornforth (1999); Pettigrew & McNulty (1995)).

The reason EDs are so important to their boards is because of their power to control information. Because of the amount of time and energy they put into the organization, they simply know more about what is going on both inside and outside among critical stakeholders. This gives them a tremendous advantage in determining how problems are defined and tackled. For example, "Our problem is not enough money", versus, "Our problem is that our programs don't meet the needs of our clients" — both could be offered as "explanations" for bad publicity from dissatisfied clients. They also control what information is provided to analyze issues and what solutions will be seen as "feasible".

Experienced, long-tenure EDs who want to control and manipulate their boards so they become rubber stamps, usually have little trouble doing so because they can influence who is invited to join, who is nominated to key positions as board chair and committee chairs and, as mentioned, they can control the board's agenda and its information resources.

On the other hand, EDs who want to ensure that board meetings are truly strategic will do so by involving members in information gathering and the creation of recommended actions well before complete reports and formally worded motions are put to the formal meeting for approval. They will also be very aware of contributions that board members can make in their capacity as committee members and individuals with useful skills and knowledge. Those organizations that need a Working Board or Mixed Model Board will help train the volunteer/manager board members in how to distinguish between big-picture strategic issues and operational matters so that only the former are brought before the meetings of the whole board.

CONCLUSION

The task of improving the performance of nonprofit boards of directors is still more of an art than a science. There is still a shortage of solid, oft-replicated, research "proving" that boards will cause their organiza-tions to perform better if they adopt certain structures or procedures or play certain kinds of roles rather than others. There is rather more support for the claim that boards with unclear roles that do not perform their basic "watchdog" duties and have an inability to focus on the "big picture" might well cause severe problems for the organizations they govern. Fixing these problems might move board performance from "awful" to "adequate". Getting to "outstanding", however, requires each board to adapt to the contingencies of the context in which it finds itself — the state of the organization's external environment and the mix of resources, skills and abilities within the organization itself.

As Harris (1993) and Chait, Holland & Taylor (1993) remind us, the key requirements of *all* those who have responsibility for the success of a nonprofit organization are to:

1. Decide what are the most important issues facing the organization.

2. Identify who has the skills and knowledge needed to address these issues (and acquire such people if they are not already part of the organization).

3. Ensure that they have the clear authority and resources needed to act.

4. Have in place the best possible information systems for tracking progress.

In some organizations, the board that results from this approach will look a lot like that recommended as the universal best model by Carver (1997), while in others it will look like an old-fashioned work group that simultaneously engages in operational work and major policy setting. In between can be an almost infinite combination of mixed characteristics that defy easy labelling but that nevertheless work very effectively for the particular situation the organization is in.

REFERENCES

Alberta Board Development Program, Alberta Government Ministry of Community Development (1999), *Board Development* (Series of five booklets) (Edmonton: The Muttart Foundation, 1999).

Block, S.R. (1998), *Perfect Nonprofit Boards: Myths, Paradoxes and Paradigms* (Needham Heights, MA: Simon and Schuster, 1998).

Bradshaw, P., V. Murray & J. Wolpin (1992), "Do Nonprofit Boards Make a Difference? An Exploration of the Relationships Among Board Structure, Process and Effectiveness" (1992), 21 *Nonprofit and Voluntary Sector Quarterly*, 227-249.

Brudney, J.L., & V. Murray (1998), "Do Intentional Efforts to Improve Boards Really Work? The Views of Nonprofit CEO's" (1998), 8 *Nonprofit Management and Leadership* 333-348.

Carver, J. (1997), *Boards That Make a Difference*, 2nd ed. (San Francisco: Jossey-Bass, 1997).

Chait, R.R., W.P. Ryan & B.E. Taylor (2005), *Governance as Leadership: Reframing the Work of Nonprofit Boards* (Toronto: Wiley, 2005).

Cornforth, C. (1999), "Power Relations Between Boards and Senior Managers in the Governance of Public and Non-profit Organisations". Paper presented to British Academy of Management.

Gill, M.D. (2005), *Governing for Results*: *A Director's Guide to Good Governance* (Victoria: Trafford, 2005).

Green, J.C., & D.W. Griesinger (1996), "Board Performance and Organizational Effectiveness in Nonprofit Social Service Organizations" (1996), 6 *Nonprofit Management and Leadership*, 381-402.

Harris, M. (1993), "Exploring the Role of Boards Using Total Activities Analysis" (1993), 3 *Nonprofit Management and Leadership*, 269-281.

Herman, R.D., & R.D. Heimovics (1991), *Executive Leadership in Nonprofit Organizations: New Strategies for Shaping Executive-Board Dynamics* (San Francisco: Jossey-Bass, 1991).

Herman, R.D., & D.O. Renz (1997), "Multiple Constituencies and the Social Construction of Nonprofit Organization Effectiveness" (1997), 26 *Nonprofit and Voluntary Sector Quarterly* 185-206.

Herman, R.D., & D.O. Renz (1998), "Nonprofit Organizational Effectiveness: Contrasts Between Especially Effective and Less Effective Organizations" (1998), 9 *Nonprofit Management and Leadership*, 23-38.

Herman, R.D., & D.O. Renz (2000), "Board Practices of Especially Effective and Less Effective Local Nonprofit Organizations" (2000), 30 *American Review of Public Administration*, 146-160.

Herman, R.D., & D.O. Renz (2002), "Nonprofit organizational effectiveness: practical implications of research on an elusive concept." Occasional Paper issued by the Midwest Centre for Nonprofit Leadership (April 18-19, 2002). Available online at: <www.bloch. umkc.edu/cookingham>.

Herman, R.D., D.O. Renz & R.D. Heimovics (1997), "Board Practices and Board Effectiveness in Local Nonprofit Organizations" (1997), 7 *Nonprofit Management and Leadership*, 373-385.

Holland, T.P., & D.K. Jackson (1998), "Strengthening Board Performance: Findings and Lessons from Demonstration Projects" (1998), 9 *Nonprofit Management and Leadership*, 121-134.

Holland, T.P., D. Leslie & C. Holzhalb (1993), "Culture and Change in Nonprofit Boards" (1993), 4:2 *Nonprofit Management and Leadership*, 141-156.

Leclerc, G., *et al.* (1996), *Accounting, Performance Reporting, Comprehensive Audit: An Integrated Perspective* (Ottawa: CCAF-FCVI Inc., 1996).

Light, M. (2001), *The Strategic Board: The Step-By-Step Guide to High Impact Governance* (New York: Wiley, 2001).

Masaoka, J. (2003), *The Best of Board Café: Hands on Solutions for Nonprofit Boards* (St. Paul, MI: Amherst H. Wilder Foundation, 2003).

Middleton, M. (1988), "Nonprofit Boards of Directors: Beyond the Governance Function" in *The Nonprofit Sector: A Research Handbook*, W.W. Powell, ed. (New Haven: Yale University Press 1988), 141-153.

Mintzberg, H. (1994), *The Rise and Fall of Strategic Planning* (New York and Toronto: Free Press, 1994).

Murray, V. (2004), "Prescriptive and Research-Based Approaches to Nonprofit Boards: Linking Parallel Universes". Paper presented to the annual conference of the Association for Research on Nonprofit Organizations and Voluntary Action, Los Angeles.

Murray, V., P. Bradshaw & J. Wolpin (1992), "Power In and Around Boards: A Neglected Dimension of Governance" in (1992), 3 *Nonprofit Management and Leadership*, 165-182.

Nobbie, P.D., & J.L. Brudney (2003), "Testing the Implementation, Board Performance and Organizational Effectiveness of the Policy Governance Model in Nonprofit Boards of Directors" (2003), 32 *Nonprofit and Voluntary Sector Quarterly* 571-595.

Pettigrew, A., & T. McNulty (1995), "Power and Influence In and Around the Boardroom (1995), 48 *Human Relations*, 845-873.

Price, J.G. (1963), "The Impact of Governing Boards on Organizational Effectiveness and Morale" (1963), 8 *Administrative Science Quarterly*, 361-377.

Robinson, M.K. (2001), *Nonprofit Boards That Work: The End of One Size Fits All Governance* (New York: John Wiley and Sons, 2001).

Scott, K.T. (2000), *Creating Caring and Capable Boards: Reclaiming the Passion for Active Trusteeship* (San Francisco: Jossey-Bass, 2000).

Siciliano, J.L. (1996), "The Relationship of Board Member Diversity to Organizational Performance" (1996), 15 *Business Ethics*, 1313-1320.

Siciliano, J.L. (1997), "The Relationship Between Formal Planning and Performance in Nonprofit Organizations" (1997), 7 *Nonprofit Management and Leadership*, 387-404.

Sonnenfeld, J.A. (2002), "What Makes Great Boards Great" (2002), 80:9 *Harvard Business Review*, 106-113.

Widmer, C., & S. Houchin (2000), *The Art of Trusteeship: The Nonprofit Board Member's Guide to Effective Governance* (San Francisco: Jossey-Bass, 2000).

Chapter 4

EXECUTIVE LEADERSHIP IN NONPROFIT ORGANIZATIONS

Keith Seel
Mount Royal College

INTRODUCTION

Executive management in a nonprofit organization refers to the work of the individual who has overall responsibility for the operations of the organization. While in very small, unstaffed nonprofit organizations, volunteers take on the responsibilities of the executive manager, it is typically the first paid position offered within these organizations as they grow. As Boland (2005) describes the position:

> This is the senior salaried staff position typically bearing the title, Executive Director, President, or CEO. This position reports to a Board of Directors and is accountable to the Board for the achievement of the organization's mission and goals and for the effective administration of the organization in order to meet community expectations. This position will, subject to policies, provide leadership to staff, volunteers and the community, ensure sound management of the organization and develop and maintain strong funder relationships. Other functional responsibilities *may* include financial management, fundraising, program development, and community liaison [Emphasis in original; n.p., Appendix 1.]

Put differently, Heimovics *et al.* (1993, p. 420) see executives of nonprofit organizations as being in the position of having the greatest influence on the successes and failures of the organization that they have responsibility for. Further, these executives are "at the centre of the organization's information flow" (p. 420). Because they are at the centre, nonprofit organizations often organize around the executive to "help reduce information uncertainty caused by the shifting nature of resource dependency" (p. 420). Any way you look at the role of the senior executives in nonprofit organizations, they are the focus for decision-making, information flow, accountability, responsibility, and relationships with the external world beyond the nonprofit organization.

This chapter is organized to give the reader a general overview of the executive director position within a nonprofit organization. The issues to be discussed are:

- the terminology associated with the executive position and in particular how one might understand the title "Executive Director" ("ED");

- the role of the ED and how the position is situated relative to staff, the board and the community;

- the relationship between the ED role and leadership responsibilities. The use of Canadian data from EDs provides a range of interesting perspectives on the competencies of an effective leader in the executive director role;

- the determinants of ED effectiveness;

- what shapes the effectiveness of the board-ED relationship;

- the relationship between the ED and staff;

- the financial oversight responsibilities of the ED; and

- a brief exploration of the challenges facing people in the role of ED and what might be done to meet them.

TERMINOLOGY

In the discussion that follows the term "Executive Director" refers to the senior executive position in a nonprofit organization — paid or volunteer. For smaller organizations where a volunteer or a board member may fill a similar position, the chapter will be of value in defining the broad responsibilities associated with the role. Made up of two words, the title "Executive Director" covers many functional areas and indeed this range of activities is well demonstrated in Canada's nonprofit sector, where a person having this title can, for example, run a very small organization addressing issues of street teens through to a large national organization addressing a health issue. Table 1 below looks at the two words making up "Executive Director" and provides a suggestion of the diversity of activity implied in the title.

Table 1: Definitions of the Term "Executive" and "Director"

According to the *Oxford English Dictionary*:
As a noun, *executive* has the following relevant meanings:
1. A person or group having administrative or managerial authority in an organization.
2. The chief officer of a government, state, or political division.

As an adjective, *executive* has two related meanings:
1. Of, relating to, capable of, or suited for carrying out or executing: *an advisory body lacking executive powers.*
2. Having, characterized by, or relating to administrative or managerial authority: *the executive director of a nonprofit organization; executive experience and skills.*

As a noun, *director* means:
1. One who or that which directs, rules, or guides; a guide, a conductor; "one that has authority over others; a superintendent; one that has the general management of a design or work"
2. A member of a board appointed to direct or manage the affairs of a commercial corporation or company.

These definitions provide us with the origins of what is understood to be two common characteristics of EDs:

- They hold the administrative or managerial authority in the organization.

- They are appointed by a board to direct or manage the affairs of the organization.

What is not included in these definitions is any description of the context within which EDs use their authority to realize the mission of the organization — the fundamental raison d'être of nonprofit organizations.

THE ROLE OF THE EXECUTIVE DIRECTOR

Being an ED of a nonprofit organization is arguably one of the more demanding and complicated jobs that an individual could undertake. While there are tremendous rewards that come with the job — effecting change in the community, improving the lives of people, conserving the environment, or creating theatre, for example — there are also enormous challenges that need to be addressed.

Three broad categories of stakeholders and the interplay between them are the sources of the complexity faced by EDs. The first group is the staff and volunteers working within the organization; the second is the board of directors of the organization; and the third is the community within which the organization operates and seeks funding and other kinds of support. For each one of these groups the primary point of contact is the ED.

Figure 1 below shows the relationship of these stakeholder groups to the ED. The ED is in the centre of the picture, between each stakeholder group. The teardrop shaped areas represent the staff reporting up to the ED and the board who make policy decisions to be implemented by ED. Surrounding the ED and the organization is the ring of organizations (funders, other nonprofits, government, businesses, *etc.*) that have an interest in what the organization is doing and connect through the ED to initiate some kind of action. The cones surrounding the staff and board elements represent the web of not yet connected but potential board members and employees who need to be nurtured to fill the future needs of the organization. Again, it is typically the ED who must keep contacts and networks alive and interested in the work of the organization. EDs are "sandwiched between internal and external demands, specifically: the needs of the clients they serve; the board members with whom the future of the organization and its mission resides; and, the government/funding agencies that affect their ability to carry out the work for their organization" (Seel & Angelini, 2004, p. 8).

Figure 1: Representation of the Main Stakeholder Groups in Relation to the Executive Director

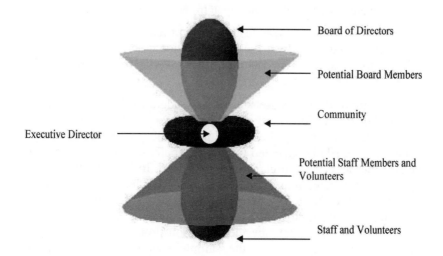

The role of the ED will now be explored using a number of different perspectives. These perspectives are intended to introduce the range of concerns faced by an ED, such as addressing board-staff relations or weighing the benefits of forming a partnership with another organization.

LEADERSHIP AND THE EXECUTIVE DIRECTOR

The question of what is leadership has many answers. To get a sense of the range of definitions consider Terry (1993), who sees leadership as something that reaches "across boundaries" to discover "what is really going on, then living the answer" (p. 9). Compare that with Bailey (1988), who finds that leadership is inherently unethical as it strives to control followers: "Leadership is a form of cultivating ignorance, of stopping doubts, and stifling questions" (p. 2). Or consider Kouzes & Posner (2002), who argue that leaders inspire a shared vision, model the behaviour they expect in others, take risks, enable others to act and to demonstrate caring and appreciation (pp. 13-20).

Leadership is often contrasted with management. Drucker (1999) succinctly defines management when he states, "It has to be *operational*" (emphasis in original, p. 34). He continues:

Management exists for the sake of the institution's results. It has to start with the intended results and has to organize the resources of the institution to attain these results. It is the organ to make the institution ... capable of producing results outside of itself [p. 39].

What the two terms — leadership and management — tell us is that while management is a focused operational activity internal to an organization, leadership is a more diffuse activity focused on creating some kind of change in the world.

Executive directors are viewed as leaders in their organizations — refining the vision, motivating people to perform effectively in realizing the vision, and being the public face of the organization. Moreover, the ED is expected to be a competent leader in the eyes of the stakeholders of the organization they lead. In Canada, the subject of the competencies required to be an effective leader were recently studied by the National Learning Initiative.[1] It generated these competencies through a first-ever "practitioner-driven voluntary sector leadership competency identification process" (p. 10). Within this action research project, the sample was peer nominated and identified 396 nonprofit sector leaders. From this list, 64 EDs participated in one of several intensive two-day workshops held across the country. Within this group of executive directors, there was representation from a number of domains including: geographic, sub-sector, organization size and service scope of organization (local through to international). Specific individuals were included to represent people with disabilities, aboriginal peoples, visible minorities, immigrants, and francophones living outside of Quebec (p. 10).

What this research showed is that leadership competencies of EDs spanned four broad domains each containing specific competencies within them. It should be noted that while the focus of the project was on leadership, several of the competencies are clearly managerial, suggesting that EDs are often both leaders and managers.[2] Table 2 summarizes the findings.

---

[1] The National Learning Initiative (NLI) grew out of the federal government sponsored Voluntary Sector Initiative to address a national skills and learning framework for the Canadian nonprofit sector. The first focus area for the NLI was leadership development. The NLI undertook Canada's first practitioner-driven leadership competency identification process. A national nomination process involved 136 nominators who identified 396 nonprofit sector leaders from which 100 individuals were invited to participate in one of seven regional two-day focus groups. Sixty-four leaders eventually participated.

[2] It should be noted that, while the following information comes from leaders believed to be effective and successful by the people nominating them, there is no claim in the project that individuals demonstrating these competencies have been proven to be effective.

Table 2: Leadership Competencies of Executive Directors in Canadian NPOs

Competency Domain	Areas of Competence
Vision and Alignment	• Vision — the leader is able to guide the development of and commitment to an inspired, achievable view of the future. • Ethical/value-oriented decisions — the leader guides the organization, individuals or community through a structured decision-making process to resolve ethical and values-based issues. • Public action — the leader guides effective and innovative action based on sound public policy. • Public policy — the leader is involved in the development of public policy. • External relations — the leader builds external relations by collaborating with individuals, organizations and communities. • Global issues — the leader is aware of and takes action on global issues at a personal, organizational and community level. • Culture of learning — the leader sustains a culture of learning in the organization such that risks are taken and innovative ideas are nurtured and valued.
Strategies and Resource Management	• Fundraising — the leader optimizes diverse, effective and ethical fundraising approaches that enhance the vision of the organization while being responsive to, and respectful of donors' wishes. • Financial stewardship — the leader is a steward of financial resources, ensuring effective use of funds towards fulfilling the mission and accepts inclusive decision-making and accountability as cornerstones of practice. • Marketing and public relations — the leader guides a variety of marketing and public relations processes to enhance the organization's ability to communicate its vision and inspire others. • Information and communication technology — the leader optimizes information and communication technology opportunities and solutions. • Research — the leader optimizes research and its application to the organization. • Planning and evaluation — the leader guides responsive and inclusive planning and evaluation processes to achieve the mission.
Relationships	• Interpersonal relationships — the leader optimizes sustains and grows interpersonal relationships and effectively negotiates relationship dynamics. • Communication — the leader is an excellent communicator in multiple media with people from diverse personal, social and cultural backgrounds. • Political acumen/savvy — the leader demonstrates political acumen by maintaining effective relationships among individuals, within the sector and beyond into the broader community.

Competency Domain	Areas of Competence
	• Public persona — the leader represents as a public figure the interests, ideas and views of the organization and its constituents to the public while being mindful of diversities and complexities. • Human resources — the leader optimizes human resources and provides a collaborative and supportive environment in which to work. • Team development — the leader employs appropriate approaches to team development enhancing the potential for creativity and productivity in the organization. • Healthy workplace environment — the leader builds and sustains a healthy workplace environment. • Collaboration — the leader encourages and supports collaboration and optimizes relationships between individuals, organizations and communities by developing shared strategies among a diversity of stakeholders.
Complexity	• Creative and innovative culture — the leader sustains a culture that celebrates creative decisions and innovative strategies, where individuals are inspired to find creative solutions to complex problems leading to long-term sustainability. • Adaptation to change — the leader guides adaptation to change by the organization and the people associated with it as well as with other organizations involved in broader change initiatives. • Interdependent perspective — the leader demonstrates interdependent perspective, recognizing the interdependence, self-organizing capacity and emergent elements of a complex system. • Multiple accountabilities — the leader ensures that multiple accountabilities are met and decisions are made with the understanding of the dynamic tensions among multiple stakeholders. • Awareness of context — the leader demonstrates an awareness of the environment and an ability to assess systems and structures. • Co-operation and competition — the leader excels at balancing the tension between co-operation / collaboration and competition / confrontation necessary to achieve the mission and sustain relationships.

Source: Adapted from NLI (2003).

This list represents the total number of competencies identified by the 64 executive directors in the research project. No one ED could be expected to have all of the competencies. For each ED and for each organization the competency mix required to generate success would vary. For example, the competencies required by an ED of a small peer support group with no staff and minimal budget would likely be different from the competencies needed in the ED of a multimillion-dollar social service agency with hundreds of staff and several locations.

Case 1

> Janet is the ED of a social service agency focusing on aboriginal issues, especially drug and alcohol addiction. The annual budget is $2.1 million and the agency employs 53 full-time and 17 part-time staff. A significant part of Janet's role is ensuring that the elders of different first nations peoples are respected, meaning that attention has to be paid to traditional lands, the traditions of the each of the first nations represented as employees and as clients, as well as herself. Without proper respect being paid to the multiple stakeholders, the support of elders for Janet's agency could be withheld, meaning that important parts of the services being provided could not be offered. Balancing those concerns with the requirements of provincial and federal government funders is a skill that Janet has had to learn. She has had to become a skilled negotiator, able to move from specific service provision concerns to global issues of substance abuse among aboriginal people, in the midst of contract negotiations. She has also become a skilled collaborator, working with affiliated aboriginal service groups to jointly sponsor projects or submit funding proposals, while at the same time ensuring that her agency remains competitive in terms of service delivery costs, funding drives, and the acquisition of skilled staff. During a recent interview Janet commented that, "No one could have explained to me how complicated this job is or what I have to be able to address in a day. I have to inspire people, fund the money to buy coffee, and oversee our finances while working within native tradition."

Case 2

> Henry is the part-time ED of an environmental agency addressing watershed issues along the East Slopes of the Rocky Mountains. The annual budget is $47,000 and Henry is the only employee. Roughly 35 volunteers stretching from the border with the Northwest Territories to the U.S. border assist with educational and advocacy initiatives. Most of Henry's time is spent working with volunteers in the field. He prepares information packages and workshop guides, and identifies political, business and other community contacts

for the volunteers. Communication has been identified as an agency issue because it is hard to keep up regular contact with a widely distributed group and because the issues vary between regions in the agency's operational area. The focus on email communications is necessary but the agency cannot afford high-speed access so Henry runs most of the agency operations from his home. A space that the agency shared with other small nonprofit groups will be closing, meaning that he will have to turn his home office into the mailing address for the agency. Henry has had one face-to-face board meeting, with monthly phone meetings scheduled as people are available. Since all of his board members are also doing volunteer work in the local community, he knows that his working board is stretched in terms of the time that they can give to the agency. Henry finds that the part-time nature of his work is a barrier to achieving the mission of the agency. He noted that, "The most stressful part of my job is knowing that we could do more if we just had the resources. There is only so much I can do on 20 hours per week."

Besides identifying competencies, the NLI project looked at how the competencies were manifested within the life of the ED. The leadership exhibited by executive directors took place at four different levels: personal (as represented by the ED's beliefs and values), organizational, community and global. Figure 2 represents the overlap of the leadership competencies and the different levels at which the competencies could be demonstrated. Further examination of these competencies is worthwhile because, in the summary that follows, we begin to understand some of the behaviours associated with being effective as an ED.

**Figure 2: Leadership Competencies and the Levels at Which
They Could Be Demonstrated**

Source: NLI (2003, p. 14).

PERSONAL BELIEFS AND VALUES

Values and beliefs are at the root of any action taken by an executive
director. The NLI project demonstrated that executive directors as
leaders acted from a personal values base that had the following
dimensions:

- social responsibility
- sustainability and self-sufficiency
- building capacity
- individual ethical and principled behaviour
- inclusion and diversity
- courage (NLI, 2003, p. 14.)

Personal beliefs and values lay behind the actions of EDs as they
attempted to shape the culture of their organizations so that it would
see itself as having a broadly conceived social responsibility to the
community. Other values fostered the organization's sustainability and

led to practical activities such as reducing the organization's reliance on single funders and more sophisticated analysis of the dynamic systems associated with exchange mechanisms within the nonprofit sector.[3]

Executive directors also needed to have personal values that made them aware of issues of power or discrimination when working with vulnerable or at-risk people in the community. Finally, at the level of values, the ED needed to have a strong sense of ethics and the courage to act properly even when such actions could disadvantage the ED or their organization.

The leadership competencies suggested by EDs in the study are unique in the Canadian literature. Kramer (1987, p. 244) observes: "Large or small, most voluntary agencies are unusually dependent on the quality of their executive leadership, and therefore, more subject to idiosyncratic rather than structural factors." In effect, the ability, skill or competency of the ED is often of more significance in the nonprofit sector than elsewhere. Considering what an ED ought to be competent in is important both for aspiring executive directors and the governors of nonprofit organizations who must hire and evaluate them. A unique combination of ED competencies will exist for each nonprofit organization. The assumption is that an ED with the right set of competencies should be effective. Are we correct in making that assumption?

EXECUTIVE DIRECTOR EFFECTIVENESS

Figure 1 portrays three major areas where executive director effectiveness could be examined:

1. effectiveness with the board of directors;
2. effectiveness with staff and volunteers; and
3. effectiveness with the community.

---

[3] The nonprofit sector, sometimes called the voluntary sector, third sector or independent sector has notably different ways of securing the resources it needs compared to either the private sector or the pubic (government sector). A fundamental difference is that many in the non-profit sector receive donations and, if registered with the Canada Revenue Agency, can issue a tax receipt to donors. Restrictions differentiating the nonprofit sector include the fact that a registered charity must be "non-distributing" meaning that, if there is money left over at the end of the year, it goes to charitable activities NOT to shareholders as might be the case in the private sector.

Before looking at these areas in greater detail, it should be stated that the question of ED effectiveness is part of the greater issue of nonprofit organizational effectiveness. Herman & Renz (1999, 1998) advance the position that nonprofit effectiveness is not only multidimensional, it is also idiosyncratic to the organization being examined. In other words, not only is the notion of effectiveness made up of many dimensions, each organization will have its own bases of effectiveness. Interorganizational comparisons of effectiveness may not be possible except in a relative sense.

How one looks at a nonprofit organization determines what one would observe when assessing effectiveness. The goal model of nonprofit organizations (Seashore, 1983) assumes that a nonprofit organization has a stated purpose and that effectiveness can be measured based on the attainment of goals. A problem with this is that, with several stakeholders, many nonprofit organizations might have several goals, some of which could be mutually contradictory (Green *et al.*, 2001). The decision-process model (Seashore, 1983) examines the relationship between ends that the nonprofit organization would like to achieve and the means by which the organization reaches those ends. This model focuses on internal processes linking means and ends. Insofar as operational processes are effective, it is assumed that the nonprofit organization will achieve its desired ends (Green *et al.*, 2001).

In both of these models, the executive director is a central figure. For many, an effective ED would also mean an effective nonprofit organization — at least within the scope covered by the models above. More specific research demonstrates particular aspects of ED effectiveness that refine our understanding.

THE BOARD AND ED EFFECTIVENESS

The relationship between EDs and their boards is a foundational one for any nonprofit organization. The ED is usually the only employee hired, evaluated and if necessary, terminated, by the board. While in practice the ED is commonly a major contributor to policy it is the board that represents the "policy" or "governance" activities of the organization and the ED is the bridge between governance and operations (the juncture of the two teardrops in Figure 1). Even though connected through the ED, the board and staff domains have been shown to be "independent and distinct factors" to which the ED must attend. (Herman & Heimovics, 2005, p. 157). Given this, how might we assess ED effectiveness with the board?

Herman & Heimovics (2005, 1990a, 1990b) after sustained work in the area of executive leadership in the nonprofit sector, conclude that effective EDs "develop their boards' abilities to carry out their duties and responsibilities" (2005, p. 157). In comparing effective executives with those who were not effective (1990) it was found that effective executives actively provided more support and leadership to their board. This characteristic was labeled as "board-centred" and meant that the executive director took on the responsibility for supporting and facilitating board work along six dimensions (Herman & Heimovics, 2005, p. 158):

1.   facilitating interaction with board relationships;

2.   showing consideration and respect toward board members;

3.   envisioning change and innovation for the organization with the board;

4.   providing useful and helpful information to the board;

5.   initiating and maintaining structure for the board; and

6.   promoting board accomplishments and productivity.[4]

Strategic planning is one area where the connection between the ED and the board is especially important. In their work with over 100 nonprofit organizations Unterman & Davis (1982) found that, among other things, an overly dominating ED can impede formal strategic planning efforts. This research supports the Herman & Heimovics findings in that a dominating ED is much less likely to be a facilitator with the board and less likely to show consideration and respect for the autonomy of the board.

While formal planning efforts of the organization should be a shared responsibility, an imbalance of responsibility, ownership or power can have dramatic results. In their review of 154 United Way affiliates, Webster & Wylie (1988) found that only half of the formal plans they produced led to any change whatsoever. Challenges such as

---

[4]   It is interesting to note that from the point of view of the ED, what makes a "good board" ranges widely. Chait *et al.* (2005, p.11) found that for some EDs a good board is a compliant board, that is, the board takes direction from the ED. On the other hand, Fletcher (1992) found other EDs felt that a good board was a board that takes its governance responsibilities seriously, chooses members carefully, participates in strategic planning, has high attendance at board meetings and has an experienced executive focused on good board behaviour.

unclear roles and responsibilities, or poor communication, between the board and the ED appeared to contribute to this lack of success.

The complexities of the Board-ED relationship were brought into greater resolution by Murray, Bradshaw & Wolpin (1992), who inquired into the relationship between power distribution and performance. They surveyed EDs of 417 health and social welfare nonprofit organizations. Most identified their organization as having either an ED-dominated board or a power-sharing board (defined as organizations in which the ED and the board shared in the making of major decisions). Power-sharing boards were strongly associated with the perception that the board was effective.

Effectiveness as something that both the board and the ED contribute to in a nonprofit organization is challenging to understand. To a large measure it is the interplay between the ED and the board that determines the effectiveness of the organization. Green *et al.* (2001) note that the primary measures of effectiveness as "focus on the activities specified in the organization's mission, goals, and objectives are often difficult to assess fully" (p. 460). Green *et al.* (2001) repeated an earlier study (Green & Griesinger, 1996) to explore how boards and EDs view each other and how they perform individually and together — that is to say, how effective they are as a team. They were able to show that:

- Boards felt that they did more than the ED gave them credit for … the reverse was also true.

- EDs believed they should have more responsibility and authority than boards acknowledged.

- EDs agreed with boards that boards needed to attend more to board performance issues and that EDs should do more to evaluate board performance.

- EDs felt that they should have more input into recruiting new board members than the board did.

- EDs wanted the board more involved in evaluating the ED.

- Boards felt they and the ED should do more to represent the organization to the community. EDs felt that they were performing this function at an appropriate level.

Throughout their research, Green *et al.* (2001) found a constant theme within ED comments: EDs wanted "more responsibility than the board members believed appropriate", and EDs believed that, "they should have more responsibility or authority than board members acknowledged" (p. 465). The research concluded that:

> Although the research has uncovered several areas of tension between board members and [EDs] in the organizations studied, they appear to be related to the overlap and lack of clarity about respective roles as well as differences in the evaluation of actual role performance. There was not a clear pattern of either the presence or absence of tension necessarily translating into effectiveness with the organization [p. 473].

THE ED-STAFF RELATIONSHIP

The National Survey of Nonprofit and Voluntary Organizations (Statistics Canada, 2004) found that only 1 per cent of the 161,000 nonprofit and voluntary organizations in Canada have budgets over $10 million. More that two-thirds have budgets under $100,000. Depending on the size of the nonprofit organization, the extent to which the ED is involved in any of the elements of the overall planning framework (see Figure 3) will vary. In a very large nonprofit, the ED will have staff or even departments responsible for such things as financial planning or human resources. In a very small nonprofit, those tasks may be the responsibility of the ED him or herself. In either case, the ED oversees the staff and volunteer resources of the organization and coordinates the overall performance of activities by employees and staff.

In an effort to give EDs ready access to human resources management information the Human Resources in the Voluntary Sector (HRVS) initiative was undertaken in 2002 by the Community Foundations of Canada and the United Way of Canada — Centraide Canada with support from by the Government of Canada. The HRVS initiative identified major human resources issues within the nonprofit sector then built an information base to improve human resource capacity of nonprofit organizations. Much of what has been collected on their Web site (<http://www.hrcouncil.ca>) is focused on the responsibility that the ED has for such things as hiring, termination and performance management. The list below is what HRVS identifies as the primary human resources management activities that one can associate with the ED role:

- Create meaningful jobs that link to the organization's mission.

- Maintain the right mix of people with the knowledge, skills and abilities to accomplish the work of the organization.

- Provide a structure that helps employees be effective at their work.

- Provide fair and consistent treatment of employees.

- Provide staff with ongoing feedback about their performance.

- Nurture an organizational culture that supports and motivates staff.

- Create a positive work environment.

- Help retain effective staff members.

- Help staff and the organization manage change (HRVS, 2005).

These responsibilities are situated within the overall strategic plan of the organization and tied to other focal areas of planning such as financial or operational plans. The diagram used by HRVS (2005) to demonstrate the areas of responsibility is shown in Figure 3, below.

Figure 3: Situating Human Resources Management within a Planning Framework

Source: HRVS (2005).

Arising out of the human resources management plan are a number of activities that can occupy a significant portion of the ED's time. The figure below categorizes these activities and suggests that to be effective in managing staff and volunteers, the ED must have considerable skill and aptitude in working with people.

**Figure 4: Human Resources Practice and Activity Areas
Requiring ED Involvement**

Human resources practice	Human resources activity
Staffing *Meeting staff requirements*	Job Analysis Job Design Job Descriptions Recruitment Selection Orientation
Training and Development *Developing effective staff*	Training Employee Development
Compensation and Benefits *Establishing fair compensation*	Job Evaluation Compensation Plan Benefits Retirement Plans
People Management *Building effective employer/employee relationships*	Work Plans Supervision Performance Management Recognition Conflict resolution Discipline Termination Day-to-Day HR Administration
Workplace Management *Creating a good place to work*	Work-life Balance Health and Safety Diversity

Source: HRVS (2005).

Executive Director perceptions of their role in the human resources function are at best mixed. In-depth work with a small group of EDs (Seel & Angelini, 2004) suggests that:

- EDs feel that they have little control over circumstances affecting personnel due to funding limitations or lack of time, for example.

- Isolation is a concern for EDs. Being the only person in that position, EDs become counsellors or confidants to all but lack that kind of support themselves. Being able to manage the concerns and issues of each staff person and board member requires tremendous personal strength.

- Many EDs do not fully understand how to delegate so as to accomplish the mission through other staff or volunteer positions within the organization. This can mean that the ED feels responsible for "doing it all themselves" and suffers the stresses of trying to live up to that expectation.

THE ED AND FINANCIAL OVERSIGHT

After oversight of the staff of the organization, financial oversight is next most important area of ED responsibility. Many might in fact argue that in terms of the time required and the significance of financial resources for the sustainability of the organization, financial oversight is *the* most important area of ED responsibility. As discussed in more detail in Chapter 10, typical areas of concern are cash and accrual accounting, financial statements (balance sheet, income statements, statement of cash flows), financial statement analysis, financial modelling and endowment management.

In principle, the ED has responsibility for overall financial management and accounting for the nonprofit. The financial responsibilities that need to be undertaken by the ED are:

- ensuring that managers have support for decision-making in financial areas appropriate to their level, role and responsibility;

- ensuring the availability of timely, relevant and reliable financial information to staff and board;

- contributing to the identification and management of risks to the organization, its employees, volunteers, and clients;

- helping the organization make efficient, effective and economical use of resources;

- enabling managers to account for their use of resources;

- ensuring the organization complies with authorities and laws and regulations; and

- safeguarding the assets of the organization through appropriate controls, processes and procedures.

It cannot be expected that every ED will have a strong financial background. What can be expected is that the ED knows how to oversee and guide the processes necessary to ensure that an appropriate degree of financial oversight is in place. Working with the board and other staff or volunteers, the ED should be supported in identifying and receiving any necessary training in how to oversee finances and/or in recruiting the needed skills into the organization. EDs with no financial experience can still be effective if they recognize what they do not know, find the needed skill sets and bring them to the table and then deploy those skills in the ways needed to ensure that the various tasks are accomplished.

As discussed in Chapter 10, financial management is differentiated from the accounting function. For EDs, it is likely that the financial management practices and activities will be of greater importance on a day-to-day basis. While the accounting and audit sides of the organization's finances are very important, the ED by law or by choice will have to involve bookkeepers and independent auditors. Figure 5 outlines common financial management practices and associated activities that are likely to be encountered by an ED.

**Figure 5: Financial Management Practices and Activities
Involving the Executive Director**

Financial Management Practice	Financial Management Activity
Management of Resources *The guidelines for managing* *finances*	Policy and procedures Process management Quality management Strategic planning Efficiency and effectiveness measures Staffing, roles and responsibilities
Risk Management and Control *Establishing risk factors and* *controlling for them*	Risk assessment Audit Insurance Organization structure and support Control mechanisms Investments

Financial Management Practice	Financial Management Activity
Information *Ensuring transparency and* *accountability to stakeholders*	Budgeting Reporting Support for decision-making Compliance Information systems
Accounting *Building effective em-* *ployer/employee relationships*	Accounting system Chart of accounts Reporting

As with financial accounting, not every ED will have financial management experience. While financial accounting requires very specific skills (*e.g.*, a chartered accountant is required to conduct the financial audit of the organization), financial management is somewhat broader in scope. The emphasis within financial management is on the oversight of processes and systems within an organization rather than the actual line-by-line work of balancing the books. As shown in Figure 5, the areas of practice and associated activities do require particular managerial skills. If EDs do not possess them they must recognize the need to obtain assistance from staff, volunteers or board members.

THE ED AND THE COMMUNITY

The community surrounds the nonprofit organization, as shown in Figure 1, and the ED is the principal point of contact with it. How the ED handles this role is influenced by a number of factors. Some EDs act like travelling salespeople, taking what their organization has to offer and bringing it to the wider community. These EDs seek out opportunities to talk about the work of their organization and may bring important information back into it for consideration. Other EDs take a much more internal role, rarely making forays beyond their organization, working on the inside, focusing on services and the systems needed to operate them. While these two examples are two ends of the continuum, they do reflect the fact that there is no one way EDs behave in their role as the point of community contact.

The work that an ED undertakes to complete the link between the organization and the community has political characteristics. In their research into the determinants of effectiveness in the ED role, Heimovics, Herman & Jurkiewicz (1993, 1995) found that effective EDs are more likely to employ a "political" view of their work as part of a more complex multiframe perspective (Bolman & Deal, 1991) than a group of executives not identified as effective. What this means is that effective EDs recognize the need to address "conflict or tension over the allocation of scarce resources or the resolution of differences" (Heimovics *et al.* (1993 at p. 421)). Such EDs respond to these issues by coalition building, mobilizing various constituencies, creating mutual commitments to future oriented goals as well as negotiating and bargaining for the resources needed to accomplish their organization's mission (p. 426).

In working with staff, board and the community, then, EDs are most effective when they are actively bargaining, negotiating, networking, building alliances, addressing conflicts between stakeholders and addressing resource allocation disputes. An ED that does not understand this political frame is "risking their organization's viability *and* its leadership effectiveness" (emphasis in original, p. 425).

CHALLENGES

Very real challenges face executive directors. Some of those have been alluded to already in this chapter. Recent research with EDs (Seel & Angelini (2004, 2005) identifies challenges as seen from the perspective of the EDs themselves. Using a peer learning circle model (Suda (2001), O'Donnell & King (1999), Wade & Hammick (1999)), Seel & Angelini worked with a diverse group of nine EDs from large and small nonprofit organizations (budgets ranged from $285,000 to $1.4 million) operating in the areas of seniors, persons with disabilities, aboriginal issues, multicultural issues, youth, and community development. Over an 18-month period, the study probed deeply into the dimensions of job satisfaction and job quality. Emerging from this research were a number of challenges commonly faced by EDs:

- *Isolation.* EDs experience isolation in two ways. First, an ED is the only person with that title and associated responsibilities in the organization and does not feel part of the staff or board team. EDs have a partial existence in both worlds but reside in neither. Second, they feel isolated from other EDs in other organizations because the opportunity to network or even just communicate with others in the same role is practically nonexistent.

- *Powerlessness to effect change.* EDs reported feeling powerless to effect meaningful organizational change because the power to do so was seen as resting primarily with the board. Whether or not this is true is immaterial since it caused EDs to behave as if they had no power to change their organization and their role in ways that would improve their job satisfaction and job quality.

- *Lack of a Clear Role.* Executive directors commonly expressed lack of clarity about the roles and responsibilities of the board and the ED. Very little relationship was reported between the EDs' written job descriptions and what they actually carried out. In large measure this is due to the board either not being familiar with the responsibilities the ED has or being unclear about what they want the ED to focus on (*e.g.*, fund development, building a stronger organization, advocacy, or outreach).[5]

- *Tunnel vision.* The demands of the job for EDs are great and very little time remains for reflection on how they are performing their jobs or on how the organization as a whole is functioning. There are many paths to achieve a goal or the mission, however, EDs can be carried along by the current of daily affairs and not have the opportunity to consider other approaches.

- *Everybody's counsellor/confidant.* Being an ED means that all interpersonal issues eventually find their way to your desk. This is especially true for smaller organizations. The ED will be sought out for support, as a counsellor when an employee needs guidance, as a confidant when personal issues emerge and so on. Board members seek out the ED for the same reasons and sometimes as a sounding board for understanding the inner workings of the board. While an ED has need for someone to act as their counsellor or confidant, it emerges as a problem should such a person be in the same organization. While it may be appropriate for a staff member to discuss a conflict with another staff member, it would not be appropriate for an ED to go to staff and divulge problems he or she was having with an employee. The lack of an outlet for personal stresses and concerns is itself a source of stress.

- *Compensation.* While pay was not a dominant determinant of whether an ED stayed or left, it had the potential for being the

---

[5] For more information on job descriptions specific to these board expectations, see the HRVS website at <www.hrcouncil.ca>.

"final straw". Other components of job quality (staff relationships, hours and scheduling, organizational structure, for example) ranked as more important aspects for EDs considering whether to stay with an organization or leave. An unsatisfying job in a low-quality workplace could not pay sufficiently to retain an ED. That said, low compensation is a very real barrier to individuals faced with yearly inflation, mortgages, and cost-of-living expenses. Reasonable pay is important to a high-quality and satisfying job.

- *Unreasonable expectations.* Internal and external stakeholders, from employees and the board to funders and the government, make claims on the ED's time. When resources do not allow for sharing these responsibilities with other staff, the ED bears the load and all of the responsibility. If there are inadequate systems or resources through which some of the work associated with these expectations could be delegated, the quality of the ED job drops. What we call "burn out" happens when well-intentioned people working hard to meet all the demands made of them have nothing left to give to the organization or themselves.

Solutions to each of the challenges identified above will be unique to each nonprofit organization. What is apparent is that open communication between the ED and all the staff, board, and community members is critical to resolving misunderstandings, clarifying perceptions and achieving the best leadership possible from the ED.

CONCLUSION

This chapter has examined executive-level management as represented by the executive director in nonprofit organizations. The role is a challenging one with broad accountabilities to multiple stakeholders combined with specific responsibilities unique to each organizational setting. There are nuances to the ED role not found in executive management in either the private or public sectors, such as the unique relationship that needs to be cultivated with volunteers both at the program level and most significantly at the governance level. While no one body of knowledge is specifically tied to becoming an ED, we can see from the literature covered in the chapter that there are skills and competencies, even predispositions, that suggest what is required for an ED to be effective.

Executive directors are unique in that they are hired by, and accountable to, the board of directors. It is the board that sets the parameters of the role and establishes the responsibilities for the ED. If boards are not up to the task of creating a reasonable position with their organizations, they should not be surprised if those hired as EDs do not perform as expected, express dissatisfaction with their job or eventually leave the organization. A board that takes the time to understand what it wants of its ED will seek to create a culture or climate within the organization that supports the work that the ED must undertake to move the organization towards achieving its mission. Therefore, success for an ED in a nonprofit organization is closely tied to board effectiveness. Conversely, as we have noted, successful EDs pay particular attention to helping boards become aware of what their responsibilities are and do not hesitate to help the board do the best job it can.

REFERENCES

Bailey, F. (1988), *Humbuggery and Manipulation: The Art of leadership* (Ithaca, NY: Cornell University Press, 1988).

Boland, P. (2005), *Survey of Not for Profit Sector Salaries and Human Resource Practices* (Calgary: Peter T. Boland & Associates Inc., 2005).

Bolman, L., & T. Deal (1991), *Reframing Organizations* (San Francisco: Jossey-Bass, 1991).

Chait, R., W. Ryan & B. Taylor (2005), *Governance as Leadership* (Hoboken, N.J.: John Wiley & Sons, 2005).

Drucker, P. (1999), *Management Challenges for the 21st Century* (New York: Harper Business, 1999).

Drucker, P. (1990), *Managing the Non-profit Organization: Practices and Principles* (Oxford: Butterworth-Heinemann, 1990).

Drucker, P. (1974), *Management: Tasks, Responsibilities, Practices* (New York: Harper & Row, 1974).

Fletcher, K. (1992), "Effective Boards: How Directors Define and Develop Them" (1992), 2(3) *Nonprofit Management and Leadership* 283-293.

Forbes, D. (1998), "Measuring the Unmeasurable: Empirical Studies of Nonprofit Effectiveness from 1977 to 1997" (1998), 27 *Nonprofit and Voluntary Sector Quarterly* 183-202.

Green, J., F. Madjid, T. Dudley & F. Gehlen (2001), "Local Unit Performance in a National Nonprofit Organization" (2001), 11:4 *Nonprofit Management and Leadership* 459.

Green, J. & D. Griesinger (1996), "Board Performance and Organizational Effectiveness in Nonprofit Social Service Organizations" (1996), 6 *Nonprofit Management and Leadership* 381-402.

Gruber, M. (1986), "A Three-Factor Model of Administrative Effectiveness," (1986), 10 *Administration in Social Work* 1.

Hall, M.H. *et al.* (2004), *Cornerstones of Community: Highlights of the National Survey of Nonprofit and Voluntary Organizations* (Ottawa: Statistics Canada, 2004), Catalogue No. 61-533-XPE.

Heimovics, R., R. Herman & C. Jurkiewicz (1995), "The Political Dimension of Effective Nonprofit Executive Leadership" (1995), 5 *Nonprofit Management and Leadership* 233-248.

Heimovics, R., R. Herman & C. Jurkiewicz (1993), "Executive Leadership and Resource Dependence in Nonprofit Organizations: A Frame Analysis" (1993), 53:5 *Public Administration Review* 419-427. Retrieved November 29, 2005, from Business Source Primer database.

Herman, R., & R. Heimovics (2005), "Executive Leadership", in *The Jossey-Bass Handbook of Nonprofit Leadership and Management*, 2nd ed. by R. Herman and Associates (San Francisco: John Wiley & Sons, 2005).

Herman, R., & R. Heimovics (1990a), "The Effective Nonprofit Executive: Leader of the Board" (1990), 1:2 *Nonprofit Management and Leadership* 167-180.

Herman, R., & R. Heimovics (1990b), "An Investigation of Leadership Skill Differences in Chief Executives of Nonprofit Organizations", (1990b), 20:2 *American Review of Public Administration* 107-125. Accessed November 29, 2005, from Expanded Academic ASAP database.

Herman, R., & D. Renz (1999), "Theses on Nonprofit Organizational Effectiveness" (1999), 28 *Nonprofit and Voluntary Sector Quarterly* 107-126.

Herman, R., & D. Renz (1998), "Nonprofit Organizational Effectiveness: Contrasts Between Especially Effective and Less Effective Organizations" (1998), 9 *Nonprofit Management and Leadership* 23-38.

Human Resources in the Voluntary Sector (2005). Available online at: <http://www.hrcouncil.ca/resources/pg001_e.cfm#cat3>.

Kouzes, J., & B. Posner (2002), *The Leadership Challenge* (San Francisco: Jossey-Bass, 2002).

Kramer, R. (1987), "Voluntary agencies and the person social services", in *The Nonprofit Sector: A Research Handbook*, W.W. Powell ed. (New Haven: Yale University Press, 1987), pp. 256-272.

Murray, V., P. Bradshaw & J. Wolpin (1992), "Power In and Around Nonprofit Boards: A Neglected Dimension of Governance", 3(2) *Nonprofit Management and Leadership* 165-182.

National Learning Initiative (September, 2003), "Voluntary Sector Leadership Competencies: Examples, Current Challenges, Complexities and Learning Outcomes." A collaborative project of the Association of Canadian Community Colleges and the Coalition of National Voluntary Organizations (Ottawa: September 2003). Available online at: <www.vsi-isbc.ca/eng/products/reports.cfm>.

O'Donnell, A. & A. King (1999), *Cognitive Perspectives on Peer Learning*. (Mahwah, NJ: Eribaum, 1999).

Seashore S. (1983), "A Framework for an Integrated Model of Organizational Effectiveness", in *Organizational Effectiveness: A Comparison of Multiple Models*, K. Cameron and D. Whetten, eds. (New York: Academic Press, 1983).

Seel, K., & A. Angelini (2004), *Strengthening the Capacity of Executive Directors* (Ottawa: National Learning Initiative, 2004). Paper presented at the annual conference of the Association for Research on Nonprofit Organizations and Voluntary Action, Novermber 21, 2004, Los Angeles, CA. Available online at: <http://www.mtroyal.ca/nonprofit/StrengtheningtheCapacityHighlights.pdf>.

Suda, L. (September, 2001), "Learning Circles: Democratic Pools of Knowledge" (2001), 12:2 *ARIS Resources Bulletin* 1-4.

Terry, R. (1993), *Authentic Leadership: Courage in Action* (San Francisco: Jossey-Bass, 1993).

Wade, S., & M. Hammick (April, 1999), "Action Learning Circles" (1999), 4:2 *Teaching in Higher Education*.

Webster, S., & M. Wylie (1988), "Strategic Planning in Competitive Environments", 10(2) *Administration in Social Work* 53-66.

Chapter 5

THE LEGAL CONTEXT OF NONPROFIT MANAGEMENT

Terrance S. Carter, B.A., LL.B. and Karen J. Cooper, LL.B., LL.L.

INTRODUCTION — DEFINITIONS AND LEGAL ENVIRONMENT

Nonprofit organizations come in many shapes and sizes and are referred to in this chapter by different names depending upon the context of the discussion, particularly with respect to the legal environment surrounding the discussion. It is important to recognize that while all charities are nonprofit organizations, not all nonprofit organizations are charities. As such, care should be taken when referring to such organizations. Additionally, despite the growth in number and size of charitable and nonprofit organizations in Canada,[1] changes to the legal framework from both the federal and provincial governments have not kept pace (Bourgeois (2002, at p. 3)), still relying heavily upon concepts developed in the seventeenth and nineteenth centuries, thereby leaving the distinction between the various types of charities and nonprofit organizations in a somewhat confused state. This is particularly so for members of the public, who often use the terms interchangeably.

---

[1] For example, Statistics Canada released the results of its survey of charitable and nonprofit organizations in 2004, which indicated that there were approximately 161,000 such organizations in Canada in 2003. These organizations had revenues totalling $112 billion ($8 billion of which came from individual donations), and they drew upon 2 billion volunteer hours and 139 million memberships. See *Hall et al.* (2004), at pp. 7, 9 and 10).

Defining Charitable and Nonprofit Organizations

Both charitable and nonprofit organizations operate on a nonprofit basis in that both must devote all of their resources to their activities and neither may distribute any of their income to their members, officers, directors or trustees. Both are exempt from tax on their income, with some exceptions for nonprofit organizations, and both will often have similar governance structures. Charitable and nonprofit organizations are, however, two distinct types of legal entities with different legal obligations and rights. An organization which has charitable objects is much more limited in the types of activities it can engage in, but, in return, receives substantial advantages in carrying out its objects by being able to issue charitable receipts for income tax purposes in response to donations that are received.

At law, charity has a specific meaning that often eludes the popular conception. For an organization to be considered charitable at law, its activities must be undertaken to achieve a charitable purpose. At present, only four categories of charity are recognized in Canadian law. In the seminal decision special *Commissioners of Income Tax v. Pemsel*,[2] Lord MacNaghten identified four "heads" or categories of charity: relief of poverty, advancement of education, advancement of religion, and other purposes beneficial to the community not falling under any of the preceding heads. This definition is mirrored in Ontario's *Charities Accounting Act*,[3] and although the *Income Tax Act* ("ITA")[4] does not make specific reference to these categories, both the Charities Directorate of Canada Revenue Agency ("CRA") and the courts rely on the same categories in regulating the sector. The Supreme Court of Canada, in *Vancouver Society of Immigrant and Visible Minority Women v. M.N.R.*,[5] clarified the Canadian approach to recognizing charities, noting that while the ITA focuses on the character of the activity undertaken by the organization, linking them to the categories established in *Pemsel*, the focus should be on the purpose in furtherance of which an activity is carried out in order to determine whether charitable status should be granted. An organization with objectives and activities that fall into one of these four categories will qualify as a registered charity for the purposes of the ITA. As we

---

2   [1891] A.C. 531 (H.L.) (Pemsel).
3   R.S.O. 1990, c. C.10 (CAA).
4   R.S.C. 1985, c. 1 (5th Supp.).
5   [1999] S.C.J. No. 5, [1999] 1 S.C.R. 10 (*Vancouver Society*).

discuss in further detail below, a registered charity may take one of three legal forms depending upon the types of activities undertaken and the relationship between the organization and its main source of funds: a charitable organization, a public foundation, or a private foundation.

Under the ITA, a "nonprofit" organization is defined as a

> ... club, society or association that ... was not a charity ... and that was organized and operated exclusively for social welfare, civic improvement, pleasure or recreation or for any other purpose except profit, no part of the income of which was payable to, or was otherwise available for the personal benefit of, any proprietor, member or shareholder ... .[6]

The ITA clearly establishes that, for its purposes, nonprofit organizations and charities are two mutually exclusive categories of organizations. As such, any organization whose objectives and activities fall exclusively within the four categories of charity discussed above is not a nonprofit organization and should seek registration as a charity under the ITA in order to avoid being taxed on its income. Although a nonprofit organization, like a charity, has tax-exempt status and does not pay tax on income or capital gains (except income from property of an organization whose main purpose is to provide dining, recreation or sporting facilities), the nonprofit organization is not able to issue charitable receipts to donors for income tax purposes. However, it is not required to disburse a specified percentage of its earnings.

L.I.U.N.A., Local 527 Members' Training
Trust Fund v. Canada

Tax Court of Canada
[1992] T.C.J. No. 466, [1992] 2 C.T.C. 2410,
47 E.T.R. 29, 92 D.T.C. 2365
July 31, 1992

The taxpayer was a trust fund established with a grant of $45,000 from L.I.U.N.A.'s existing training and recreation fund to provide retraining for L.I.U.N.A. members, and both L.I.U.N.A. and the local Construction Association ("the Association") contributed to it at a fixed rate per employee per hour

---

[6]   ITA, s. 149(1)(*l*).

worked. The CRA refused to exempt its income from tax. The taxpayer appealed to the Tax Court of Canada.

Held, the taxpayer was not a charitable trust, and therefore not a charity, since it could not meet the "public benefit" test because the recipients of its funds was too small a group — the fund was not for the general public benefit. It was, however, a special purpose trust and its entitlement to an exemption from tax on its income depended upon whether it fell within the purview of para. 149(1)(*k*) (a labour organization) or para. 149(1)(*l*) (a non-profit organization) of the ITA. Since the taxpayer was controlled by representatives of both labour and management, it could not be classified as a "labour organization". The taxpayer, however, was an "association" (within the dictionary definition of that term) organized for a purpose other than profit, no portion of whose income was available to members of the union or members of the Association. Also, although there was no evidence that the Minister had actually expressed an opinion that the taxpayer was not a charity (as required by para. 149(1)(*l*)), it clearly was not a charity. The presumption was that, if the Minister had expressed an opinion, it would have been to this effect, which was the legally correct one. For all of these reasons, the taxpayer met the criteria imposed by para. 149(1)(*l*) of the ITA and it was thus entitled to the exemption from tax on its income which it had sought.

LEGAL ENVIRONMENT

Added to the confusion of language, which is often misunderstood and misused, is a legal environment which is also confused and underdeveloped. According to Donald Bourgeois (2002, at p. 5):

> The confusion in the law and the failure to amend the statutory provisions to address and to take into account changes in society has made it more difficult for directors, officers and members to understand their legal obligations and roles. Individuals who participate in charitable and not-for-profit organizations are, for the most part, sincere in their attempts to make improvements to society, communities and institutions. They are not as often prepared for the potential legal, financial and practical consequences of their involvement. They may be "at sea" and unsure of what steps to take to address problems or issues.

Contributing to this confusion is a patchwork of federal and provincial legislation which has not been modernized. Instead, problems have been addressed through policies and practices that have developed over time. Recently, at the federal level, significant changes have been made and proposed with respect to the regulation of charities. Following years of policy development, public consultation and legislative drafting, a new *Canada Not-for-Profit Corporations Act* was introduced in Parliament in 2004.[7] The Bill, as introduced, would replace Parts II and III of the *Canada Corporations Act* ("CCA"),[8] providing a more flexible process for incorporating and governing nonprofit corporations. The future status of this legislation at the time of writing remains unknown.

For charities, the Uniform Law Conference of Canada adopted the *Uniform Charitable Fundraising Act* in August 2005, and recommended that the provinces do the same. If adopted, the *Uniform Charitable Fundraising Act* would: ensure members of the public have sufficient information to make informed decisions when contributing to charities; protect the public from fraudulent, misleading or confusing solicitations; and establish standards for charities and fundraising businesses in making solicitations.[9]

Applicable Federal and Provincial Legislation

There is a plethora of legislation that is applicable to both charitable and nonprofit organizations, whether it is at the federal or provincial level, and the directors and members of these organizations must be aware of how the legislation will impact on their operations.[10] Although space does not permit a full discussion of the applicable legislation, the following provides a brief summary of some of the more important pieces of it.

---

[7] See Burke-Robertson (2005). The new *Canada Not-for-Profit Corporations Act*, Bill C-21, was introduced in November 2004, but died when Parliament prorogued for the 2006 election. At the time of writing, there is no indication as to whether the Bill will be introduced in the new Parliament, and, if it is, whether it will be in the same form as the original draft legislation.

[8] R.S.C. 1970, c. C-32.

[9] The draft legislation and reports prepared by the Uniform Law Reform Commission are available online at <http://www.ulcc.ca>.

[10] For a useful resource in this respect, see Hoffstein, Carter & Parachin (2005).

Income Tax Act

In addition to determining whether an organization is a charitable or nonprofit organization, the ITA places certain obligations upon directors of organizations, some of which continue for a period after the individual ceases to be a director. Directors are not only liable for ensuring employee source deductions are remitted to the government, they must also ensure the charity complies with numerous reporting requirements. Directors may also face fines and imprisonment where they are involved in making false or deceptive statements in any return required under the ITA or willfully evading compliance with the ITA. To avoid liability, a director needs to show that positive steps were taken to ensure that the corporation complied with the ITA's requirements.

Canada Corporations Act

The CCA is the statute under which all federal non-share capital corporations are incorporated. The CCA sets out the manner in which the corporation is to be governed, as well as setting out the rights and obligations of directors and members.

Other Federal Legislation

- *Canada Corporations Regulations;*[11]
- *Canada-United States Tax Convention Act, 1984;*[12]
- *Charities Registration (Security Information) Act;*[13]
- *Criminal Code;*[14]
- *Cultural Property Export and Import Act;*[15]
- *Income Tax Act Regulations.*[16]

---

[11] C.R.C. 1978, c. 424.
[12] S.C. 1984, c. 20.
[13] S.C. 2001, c. 41.
[14] R.S.C. 1985, c. C-46.
[15] R.S.C. 1985, c. C-51.
[16] C.R.C. 1978, c. 945.

Provincial Legislation

Like their federal counterpart, each of the provinces have enacted legislation setting out the requirements for incorporating and maintaining a corporation. Issues concerning directors' rights and obligations are covered in detail.[17]

In Ontario, the *Trustee Act*[18] establishes that directors of a charitable corporation have the power and duty to invest the assets of the corporation as a prudent investor would. This includes the power to invest in mutual funds and the power to delegate investment decision-making to qualified investment managers, provided the corresponding statutory requirements are strictly complied with. Other provinces have similar legislation.[19]

Provincial Legislation Aimed at Regulating Charities

There are few provinces with statutes aimed at regulating the charitable sector. Some of Ontario's statutes include: the *Charities Accounting Act*,[20] the *Charitable Institutions Act*,[21] and the *Charitable Gifts Act*.[22] In addition to setting out the requirements for operating a

---

[17] See, *e.g.*, British Columbia's *Society Act*, R.S.B.C. 1996, c. 433; Alberta's *Societies Act*, R.S.A. 2000, c. S-14; Saskatchewan's *Non-profit Corporations Act, 1995*, S.S. 1995, c. N-4.2; Manitoba's *Corporations Act*, C.C.S.M., c. C225; Ontario's *Corporations Act*, R.S.O. 1990, c. C.38; Quebec's *Companies Act*, R.S.Q., c. C-38; New Brunswick's *Companies Act*, R.S.N.B. 1973, c. C-13; Nova Scotia's *Companies Act*, R.S.N.S. 1989, c. 81, and *Societies Act*, R.S.N.S. 1989, c. 435; Prince Edward Island's *Companies Act*, R.S.P.E.I. 1988, c. C-14; Newfoundland and Labrador's *Corporations Act*, R.S.N.L. 1990, c. C-36; Yukon's *Societies Act*, R.S.Y. 2002, c. 206; Northwest Territories' *Societies Act*, R.S.N.W.T. 1988, c. S-11; and Nunavut's *Societies Act (Nunavut)*, R.S.N.W.T. 1988, c. S-11.

[18] R.S.O. 1990, c. T.23.

[19] See, *e.g.*, in Alberta, R.S.A. 2000, c. T-8; in British Columbia, R.S.B.C. 1996, c. 464; in Saskatchewan, R.S.S. 1978, c. T-23; in Manitoba, C.C.S.M., c. T160; in New Brunswick, R.S.N.B. 1973, c. T-15; in Nova Scotia, R.S.N.S. 1989, c. 479; in Prince Edward Island, R.S.P.E.I. 1988, c. T-8; in Newfoundland and Labrador, R.S.N.L. 1990, c. T-10; in Yukon, R.S.Y. 2002, c. 223; in Northwest Territories, R.S.N.W.T. 1988, c. T-8; and in Nunavut, R.S.N.W.T. 1988, c. T-8.

[20] R.S.O. 1990, c. C.10.

[21] R.S.O. 1990, c. C.9.

[22] R.S.O. 1990, c. C.8. Other Ontario legislation dealing with charitable or not-for-profit organizations includes: the *Donation of Food Act, 1994*, S.O. 1994, c. 19; the *Hospitals and Charitable Institutions Inquiries Act*, R.S.O. 1990, c. H.15; the *Religious Organizations' Lands Act*, R.S.O. 1990, c. R.23; the *University Foundations Act, 1992*, S.O. 1992, c. 22; the *Approved Acts of Executors and Trustees*, O. Reg. 4/01, made pursuant to the *Charities Accounting Act*; and the *Corporations Act Regulation (General)*, R.R.O. 1990, Reg. 181.

charity, these Acts limit the activities in which a charity may participate. Failure to conform to the requirements of these Acts may result in the province cancelling the corporation's letters patent and liability for the directors. Alberta regulates the fundraising activities of charities through the *Charitable Fund-raising Act*,[23] while Saskatchewan's *Charitable Fund-raising Businesses Act*,[24] focuses its attention on fundraising businesses, not charities. Manitoba regulates fundraising activities through the *Charities Endorsement Act*,[25] requiring ministerial authorization to solicit funds. Prince Edward Island's *Charities Act*[26] makes distinctions between solicitations by charities and appeals by religious institutions (churches, synagogues, mosques, *etc.*) for financial support.

As legislation is not uniform across the country, charitable and nonprofit organizations should enquire as to the governing legislation in their own jurisdiction. These will be in addition to any laws of general application which also apply to the activities of nonprofit organizations.

LEGAL STRUCTURES FOR NONPROFIT ORGANIZATIONS

Overview of Types of Legal Structure

Just like a for-profit business, a nonprofit organization must determine the appropriate legal structure to meet its needs. Not all nonprofit organizations are created equal, and as such Canadian law provides four different legal structures for nonprofit organizations: a trust; an unincorporated association; a corporation without share capital; or a co-operative without share capital. Not only will the legal structure chosen dictate the rights and responsibilities of the organization and its directors, it may also impact on donations and grants from other bodies. When starting a nonprofit organization, the organizers must consider a number of factors in order choose the necessary structure to carry out its goals. The factors to consider include (see Burke-Robertson & Drache (2002, at p. 1-3)):

[23] R.S.A. 2000, c. C-9.
[24] S.S. 2002, c. C-6.2.
[25] C.C.S.M., c. C60.
[26] R.S.P.E.I. 1988, c. C-4.

> ... the objectives of the proposed organization, whether such objectives
> will be of short or long duration, the proposed size of membership (if
> any), whether the organization will be of national or local concern,
> whether it will be called upon to enter into contracts or hold real prop-
> erty, whether it will incur debts for which the contracting members or di-
> rectors may be personally liable, the tax treatment of the organization,
> and, of course, whether registration as a charity is desired.

Once these factors are determined, the various legal structures should
be examined in order to assess their advantages and disadvantages in
relation to the needs of the organization.

As Burke-Robertson notes, "the appropriate form of legal structure may also be dictated by the existing legislation and regulations
governing the activities of the particular type of not-for-profit organization" (p. 1-3). For example, if one is organizing an agricultural
society in Manitoba, they must refer to the requirements under the
Agricultural Societies Act.[27]

Trusts

The trust is one form of legal vehicle for nonprofit and charitable
organizations, which, because of its greater flexibility and fewer
administrative burdens, may be seen as an attractive alternative for
nonprofit organizations that are made up of only a few people. While
many academics consider the nature of a trust to be hard to define, it is
generally regarded as the relationship between the settlor (the donor)
and the trustee, where the trustee holds the trust property for the
benefit of some persons or for some objectives in such a way that the
real benefit of the property accrues to the beneficiaries of the trust
rather than the trustee. (See Waters (2005, at pp. 3-4).) While the
trustee's actions are governed by the *Trustee Act,*[28] in order for the
trust property to vest in the trustee, the trust must meet the common
law requirements. To properly be recognized as a trust, the trust
document or instrument must include what the courts refer to as the
three certainties: certainty of intention, certainty of subject-matter, and

---

[27] C.C.S.M., c. A30.

[28] *Trustee Act*, R.S.O. 1990, c. T. 23; *Trustee Act*, R.S.A. 2000, c. T-8; *Trustee Act*, R.S.B.C.
1996, c. 464; *Trustee Act*, R.S.S. 1978, c. T-23; *Trustee Act*, C.C.S.M., c. T160; *Trustees Act*,
R.N.B. 1973, c. T-15; *Trustee Act*, R.S.N.S. 1989, c. 479; *Trustee Act*, R.S.P.E.I. 1978,
c. T-8; *Trustee Act*, R.S.N.L. 1990, c. T-10; *Trustee Act*, R.S.Y. 2000, c. 223; *Trustee Act*,
R.S.N.W.T. 1988, c. T-8; *Trustee Act* (Nunavut), R.S.N.W.T. 1988, c. T-8.

certainty of objects.[29] This requires the trust document to set out the purposes or objectives of the trust, the property to be held in trust, and to identify the beneficiaries of the trust or a means by which to determine who will be the beneficiaries (Waters (2005, at pp. 132 *ff.*)).

In situations where there will be a limited number of individuals wishing to aid in the administration of a nonprofit or charitable endeavour, a trust is a useful vehicle, as involvement in the trust is limited to the trustees. For example, the Diena Family Charitable Trust is administered by two members of the Diena family, and the John H. Daniels Charitable Trust is administered by two members of the Daniels family and one arm's-length trustee.[30] Although the trust is a convenient vehicle, both statutory and common law requirements place substantial fiduciary obligations upon the trustee, including the following three fundamental duties (Waters (2005, at p. 852)):

> First, no trustee may delegate his office to others; secondly, no trustee may profit personally from his dealings with the trust property, with the beneficiaries, or as a trustee; thirdly, a trustee must act honestly and with that level of skill and prudence which would be expected of the reasonable man of business administering his own affairs.

Although there are statutory provisions governing trust documents and duties of trustees, and the common law related to the administration of trusts has developed over hundreds of years, the primary terms of a trust are to be found within the trust document itself. Apart from the general duties imposed by law, the trustee must follow the terms of the trust or risk allegations of breach of fiduciary duty.

Unincorporated Association

An unincorporated association is defined as "a group of two or more persons united together by mutual consent in order to determine, deliberate and act jointly for a common purpose" (CED (2005, at §1)).[31] In many respects, it is like a business partnership, however, it is not formed for the purposes of profit.[32] In an unincorporated associa-

---

[29] *Faucher v. Tucker Estate*, [1993] M.J. No. 589, [1994] 2 W.W.R. 1 (Man. C.A.).

[30] See 2004 Registered Charity Information Return for the Diena Family Charitable Trust and the 2004 Registered Charity Information Return for the John H. Daniels Charitable Trust, available online at <https://apps.cra-arc.gc.ca/ebci/haip/srch/sec/SrchLogin-e?login=true>.

[31] See also *Orchard v. Tunney*, [1957] S.C.R. 436.

[32] A partnership is not a structure available to either a nonprofit or charitable endeavour because, at law, a partnership requires a profit-making intention.

tion, the members may be governed by a contractual arrangement, which is commonly referred to as a "Memorandum of Association". This document sets out the purpose or "objects" of the organization and how it is to be managed or operated, providing great latitude for the creation of an organization since the only limitation is that the objects must be lawful. For example, the Dalhousie Law School Alumni Association has the following Memorandum of Association:[33]

MEMORANDUM OF ASSOCIATION
OF
DALHOUSIE LAW SCHOOL ALUMNI ASSOCIATION

1. The name of the Society is Dalhousie Law School Alumni Association.

2. The objects of the Society are:-

    (a)   to promote and encourage the active participation of graduates of Dalhousie Law School in the affairs of the School;

    (b)   to promote legal research and legal education particularly at Dalhousie university;

    (c)   to enable graduates of Dalhousie Law School to establish and maintain strong interrelationships between themselves and with Dalhousie Law School;

    (d)   to acquire by way of grant, gift, purchase, bequest, devise, or otherwise, real and personal property and to use and apply such property to the realization of the objects of the Society;

    (e)   To buy, own, hold, lease, mortgage, sell and convey such real and personal property as may be necessary or desirable in the carrying out of the objects of the Society.

    PROVIDED that nothing herein contained shall permit the Society to carry on any trade, industry or business and the Society shall be carried on without purpose of gain to any of the members and that any surplus or any accretions of the Society shall be used solely for the purposes of the Society and the promotion of its objects.

    PROVIDED, further, that if for any reason the operations of the Society are terminated or are wound up, or are dissolved and there remains, at that time, after satisfaction of all its debts and liabilities, any property whatsoever, the same shall be paid to some other charitable organization in Canada, having objects similar to those of the Society.

As is demonstrated by the above example, a Memorandum of Association must include a clause stating that no gain, dividends or income

---

[33] See Dalhousie Law School Alumni Association, *"Memorandum of Association of Dalhousie Law School Alumni Association"*, available online at: <http://law.dal.ca/law_2643.html>.

will be paid to members of the organization, and that all profits or any income must be used to promote the organization's objects. The nonprofit organization's objects cannot include the carrying on of a profit-making business.

Unlike some of the other legal structures available for nonprofit organizations, an unincorporated association does not have the legal capacity to sue or be sued.[34] The contractual nature of the organization creates a legal relationship among the members, but does not create a legal person (Bourgeois (2002, at p. 37)).

Corporation without Share Capital

A corporation without share capital (or a non-share capital corporation) is akin to the traditional corporate structure with the exception that the members (who are similar to shareholders) do not benefit financially from the organization. A corporation without share capital can be incorporated federally, under the CCA, or provincially, under the applicable corporate legislation. The decision to incorporate federally or provincially (or both) will be determined by the organization's objects, and the legislative authority under which they fall, and the scope of the organization's activities, *i.e.*, whether it is a local organization or one crossing multiple jurisdictions. It should be noted that incorporation by letters patent is a privilege and not a right and, as such, the government is able to exert more control over a corporation without share capital.

Although terminology and procedure will vary from jurisdiction to jurisdiction, in order to become a corporation without share capital, multiple persons[35] must make an application for letters patent to the appropriate authority (*i.e.*, either a Minister or Lieutenant Governor) under the applicable legislation.[36] In order to obtain letters patent, the organization must set out the objectives of the corporation, which will form its boundary with share capital's legal capacity to undertake activities. If the objectives are deficient, the only way to change them is through an application for supplementary letters patent. As such,

---

[34] See, *e.g.*, *S. (J.R.) v. Glendinning*, [2000] O.J. No. 2695, 191 D.L.R. (4th) 750 (Ont. S.C.J.).

[35] The exact number of persons required to incorporate depends on the jurisdiction. For example, to incorporate federally, three or more persons are required, whereas in British Columbia, five or more persons are required to incorporate a Society.

[36] The one exception to this is the utilization of an "unlimited liability company" in Nova Scotia, under the *Companies Act*, R.S.N.S. 1989, c. 81.

careful consideration must be given to the drafting of the objectives in order to ensure all activities will be covered. As will be discussed in greater detail below, the process of incorporation results in the creation of a separate legal person and provides the members with protection from liability.

Co-operative without Share Capital

A co-operative without share capital is a special type of corporation created under the *Co-operative Corporation Act*,[37] such as a nonprofit housing co-operative. Although co-operatives both with and without share capital are intended to be operated "as nearly as possible at cost",[38] a co-operative without share capital cannot distribute any surplus or dividends to its members, unlike a co-operative with share capital. Co-operatives without share capital must be organized, operated and administered following basic principles set out in the legislation: each member or delegate has only one vote, and no member or delegate may vote by proxy.[39] Provisions enabling a small fixed percentage of any surplus to be distributed to members do not apply to a co-operative without share capital. The legislation also places restrictions on the conversion or dissolution of such corporations; upon dissolution the remaining assets can only be distributed to similar organizations or charitable organizations.

Advantages and Disadvantages of Different Legal Structures

One of the primary advantages of organizing as a nonprofit organization, regardless of its structure, is to be exempt from income tax imposed under the ITA. The ITA provides in part at section 149(1)(*l*):

> No tax is payable … on the taxable income of a person for a period when that person was … a club, society or association that … was not a charity … and that was organized and operated exclusively for social welfare, civic improvement, pleasure or recreation or for any other purpose except profit, no part of the income of which was payable to, or was otherwise available for the personal benefit of, any proprietor, member or shareholder thereof …

---

[37] R.S.O. 1990, c. C.35.
[38] *Ibid.*, s. 1(1) "co-operative basis".
[39] *Ibid.*

A charitable organization is also exempt from income tax by virtue of paragraph 149(1) of the ITA.

Apart from the income tax benefits that accrue by obtaining non-profit status, the advantages and disadvantages of the different legal structures should be examined in order to determine if the structure is appropriate for the needs of the organization. Some of the important considerations include set-up costs, legal capacity, liability, and perpetual existence.

Set-up Costs

As would be expected, the more formal the organization's legal structure, the more expensive it will be to start up. Accordingly, a trust or unincorporated association is relatively inexpensive to set up as compared to the cost of the incorporation process for a corporation without share capital or a co-operative without share capital.

Legal Capacity

Legal capacity refers to the organization's ability to be recognized at law, *i.e.*, whether it is a separate legal entity with the capacity to commence or defend a lawsuit, enter into contracts, or own land in its own name. Without delving into legal theory, only a "person" can have rights and responsibilities, and only incorporated entities are recognized by law as "persons" capable of obtaining these rights and responsibilities. Although in some respects a trust is considered a separate entity, *i.e.*, for income tax purposes, for many other purposes the trust is not considered a legal entity (Bucknall (2002)).[40] Rather it is considered a relationship between the trust property, the trustee who holds legal title to the property, and the beneficiaries of the trust who hold equitable title to the property. As the trust property vests in the trustee, there is no trust without the trustee. As such, the trust can only sue, be sued or enter a contract through the trustee who performs these actions on behalf of the trust. An unincorporated association is also not a legal entity, and therefore is incapable of holding title to property or exercising any other legal rights. Property is held in trust and legal acts

---

[40]   See also *United Service Funds v. Richardson Greenshields of Canada Ltd.*, [1987] B.C.J. No. 1391, 40 D.L.R. (4th) 94 (B.C.S.C.).

are carried out by individual members of the group whose actions would be governed by the by-laws of the association.

The main advantage of having a separate legal entity incorporated for the purpose of carrying on charitable or nonprofit activities is that it is the entity which will enter into contracts or carry out the activities and, therefore, the entity which may ultimately be sued for any damages caused by the entity, thus providing some protection for individual trustees and members against future liability. In other words, failure to obtain legal capacity for the organization means the individual members will be personally liable for any damages resulting from the organization's activities as the organization will not have the capacity to be sued.

Liability (Organization, Directors, Officers, Members)

Liability can come in many forms, whether it is for failure to follow statutory rules, breach of contract, negligence or intentional harm. Whether individual members, directors or the organization will be held responsible will depend on the legal structure. As a separate legal entity, an incorporated corporation without share capital will be held answerable and responsible for any act, default, obligation or liability of the corporation, and the individual members are absolved of responsibility.[41] This does not mean that directors or officers can escape liability, as personal liability may arise in the execution of their duties where their conduct falls below the prescribed standard of care (Burke-Robertson & Drache (2002, at p. 6-3)): see also Bourgeois (2002, at p. 221)). Although the duties of a trustee are similar in nature to that of the director and officer, the exposure to liability is greater as the trustee is the only legal person in the trust, and is generally held to a higher standard of care, and will only be reimbursed for those expenses that are properly incurred. Expenses that are improperly incurred become the sole responsibility of the trustee (Waters (2005, at p. 1151)). Members are at greatest risk in an unincorporated association, "which has no legal status apart from that of its members". As such, an association cannot incur liabilities or be convicted of an offence; instead, the members of an unincorporated association may be held personally liable for the acts or omissions of the organization.

---

[41] See, *e.g.*, *Corporations Act*, R.S.O. 1990, c. C.38, s. 122.

Perpetual Existence

As a separate legal entity, the incorporated corporation without share capital can, theoretically, have perpetual existence, so that changes in the membership will not affect its continuity. Similarly, there are provisions in the *Trustee Act* to appoint successor trustees when a trustee dies, retires, refuses to act or is incapable of acting.[42] An unincorporated association on the other hand cannot have perpetual existence as it is indistinguishable from its members. When the members no longer exist, neither does the association.

As a result of the advantages noted above, specifically relating to the protection from liability and perpetual existence, incorporation is generally preferred.

National Nonprofit Corporate Structures[43]

The business sector has utilized multiple corporations for years to contain liabilities and to protect assets. Charitable and nonprofit corporations, though, have been generally slow to establish and implement multiple nonprofit corporations to the same end. The traditional use of a corporation by charities has been focused almost exclusively on obtaining limited liability protection for its members, and very little thought has been given to the benefits associated with carrying on operations within a separate corporation in order to contain liabilities and to protect charitable assets while addressing the common nonprofit purpose or objective that may be found on a national or multi-jurisdictional basis. Such an organization can be based on one of two models: the national association model or the centralized chapter model.

National Association Model

The national association model involves multiple legal entities that are organized at various levels, such as incorporated provincial associations or incorporated local organizations. The national association model will have a governing body, normally established as a federal corporation, to act as the umbrella body over its member organiza-

---

[42]   *Trustee Act*, R.S.O. 1990, c. T.23, s. 3.
[43]   See Carter (1998; 2001).

tions, whether those members are corporations or unincorporated associations. A member organization will normally have either a name or nonprofit purpose that is similar to that of the governing national association.

The primary benefit of utilizing the national association model is that of reduced liability exposure for the organization by containing the liability attributable to each member organization within a separate corporate entity. As such, the claims made against a member organization do not necessarily affect the assets of other member organizations or that of the governing body.

The most obvious problem with the national association model is that a governing body can easily lose control over its separately incorporated member organizations if appropriate steps are not implemented to ensure that the member organizations are subject to appropriate contractual and/or licensing control mechanisms. As such, the national organization can lose goodwill and such intangible assets as trademarks through the actions of the local member.

Centralized Chapter Model

The centralized chapter model involves one legal entity acting as a single nonprofit organization across Canada, normally involving multiple divisions at either the provincial, regional or local level, as is the case with the Canadian Cancer Society. Those divisions are often referred to as chapters or branches. However, none of the chapters or branches are themselves separate legal entities. Instead the chapters or branches are a part of a single monolith legal entity.

The most significant benefit of the centralized chapter model is that by requiring only one corporation, it is much easier to maintain a higher degree of control over chapters or branches without the necessity of contract or licence agreements that are otherwise required with the national association model. In addition, by utilizing only one corporation to carry on operations on a national basis, there is generally more symmetry and coherency to day-to-day operations and control of personnel. This model also avoids the risk of losing its assets, goodwill, donor base, or trademarks to a "renegade" member organization, since everything is legally owned by the single national corporation. A chapter or branch would have no legal right to take any assets on its own if it were to leave the national organization.

The most fundamental problem inherent in the centralized chapter model is that by having only one corporation, the liabilities that occur in the operations of one chapter will expose all of the assets of the national organization to claims arising out of activities of that one chapter even though other chapters may have had nothing to do with the incident in question. Similarly, even if the incident involves a national program involving all chapters, there is no ability to protect specific assets of the national organization, since all assets are owned by the national organization.

Association Agreements

An association agreement is often referred to as a "chapter agreement", an "affiliation agreement" or a "membership agreement". The content of the agreement, not the terminology used to describe it, is what is important. The agreement sets out the contractual relationship between the governing association and its member organizations. Some of the more important considerations include:

- a recognition that despite the similar purposes, the two organizations are recognized at law as being separate and distinct corporate entities with separate boards of directors and that they are to remain independently responsible for the management and governance of their respective operations;

- an indication that the contractual relationship contained in the agreement does not constitute either a partnership or a joint venture arrangement between the parties;

- the term of the agreement;

- the basic requirements of the association relationship;

- the rights that flow from the association relationship;

- the actions by the member organization that would terminate the association relationship and the consequences that flow from termination; and

- a mechanism for conflict resolution.

REGISTERED CHARITIES UNDER THE INCOME TAX ACT

Types of Registered Charities

As discussed above, there is an important distinction between nonprofit organizations and registered charities in Canada. The definition in the ITA of a nonprofit organization is a negative one in the sense that a nonprofit organization is one that is not a charity within the meaning of section 149.1(1) of the ITA.[44] If an organization has charitable purposes, it must be a charity and should seek registration under the ITA. Next, a charitable nonprofit organization has to determine what type of registered charity will best suit its objectives: a charitable organization, a public foundation or a private foundation. Recent proposed amendments to the ITA seem to be blurring the distinction between the types of registered charities, particularly between a charitable organization and a public foundation (see, *e.g.*, Man & Carter (2005a; 2005b)). However, the choice of charitable structure is important because it will determine which rules in the ITA will apply. The following general discussion of the differences between the types of registered charities will be followed by a more detailed summary of the specific rules affecting registered charities.

Charitable Organization

Under the ITA, a charitable organization is an organization which devotes all of its resources to charitable activities carried on by the organization itself[45] — it is generally considered to be a "doing"

---

[44]   ITA, s. 149(1)(*l*).

[45]   The definition of "charitable organization" in s. 149.1(*l*) provides as follows:

"charitable organization" means an organization, whether or not incorporated,

(a)   all the resources of which are devoted to charitable activities carried on by the organization itself,

(b)   no part of the income of which is payable to, or is otherwise available for, the personal benefit of any proprietor, member, shareholder, trustee or settlor thereof,

(c)   more than 50% of the directors, trustees, officers or like officials of which deal with each other and with each of the other directors, trustees, officers or officials at arm's length, and

(d)   ... not more than 50% of the capital of which has been contributed or otherwise paid into the organization by one person or members of a group of persons who do not deal with each other at arm's length and, for the purpose of this paragraph, a reference to any person or to members of a group does not include a reference to Her Majesty in right of Canada or a province, a municipality, another registered charity that is not a private foundation, or any club, society or association described in paragraph 149(1)(*l*).

organization. A charitable organization may be established as a corporation, an unincorporated association or a trust. It cannot be controlled by a group of related directors/trustees,[46] and, like a non-profit organization and the other types of registered charities, no part of its income may be payable to or otherwise available for the personal benefit of a proprietor, member, shareholder, trustee or settlor.

Charitable Foundation

The ITA provides that a charitable foundation is an entity which is constituted and operated exclusively for charitable purposes,[47] which may be either a public foundation or a private foundation. While a charitable foundation may itself carry on a limited amount of charitable activities, charitable foundations generally provide funds to other charitable organizations or "qualified donees" so that those organizations may carry out their charitable activities — commonly considered a "spending" or "funding" organization. A charitable foundation may be established as either a corporation or a trust — it cannot be an unincorporated association.

There are two types of charitable foundations: a public foundation and a private foundation. Like a charitable organization, a public foundation cannot be controlled by a group of related directors/trustees. A private foundation is defined in the ITA as simply a foundation which is not a public foundation. Generally, a private foundation is an entity established for philanthropic and/or tax planning purposes by a wealthy family or corporation which may be controlled by them.

Specific Rules Affecting Registered Charities

Relationship between Directors/Trustees and Control

Apart from the distinctions based on the difference between "doing" and "funding" entities, the most important requirement distinguishing

---

[46]   The details of this requirement are discussed below.

[47]   The definition of "charitable foundation" in s. 149.1(1) is as follows: "'charitable foundation' means a corporation or trust that is constituted and operated exclusively for charitable purposes, no part of the income of which is payable to, or is otherwise available for, the personal benefit of any proprietor, member, shareholder, trustee or settlor thereof, and that is not a charitable organization".

a charitable organization and public foundation from a private foundation is the relationship between the directors/trustees and control of the entities. The Act currently provides that more than 50 per cent of the directors or trustees of charitable organizations and public foundations must deal with each other and with each of the other directors or trustees at arm's length.[48] The Act also currently requires that not more than 50 per cent of the capital contributed or otherwise paid to a charitable organization or public foundation be contributed by one person or members of a group of such persons who do not deal with each other at arm's length, save and except some organizations, *i.e.*, the federal government, provincial governments, municipalities, other registered charities that are not private foundations, and nonprofit organizations. This is usually referred to as the "contribution" test.

As a result of inquiries from the public, the Department of Finance has proposed to amend[49] the definition of both "charitable organizations" and "public foundation" in order to ensure that in certain circumstances large donations are not prohibited by replacing the "contribution test" with a "control test" in section 149.1(1) of the Act, whereby it would be permissible for a person, or a group of persons not dealing with each other at arm's length, to contribute more than 50 per cent of the charity's capital as long as such a person or group does not control the charity in any way or represent more than 50 per cent of the directors, trustees, officers and similar officials of the charity.

The rationale for amending the definitions is to permit charitable organizations and public foundations to receive large gifts from donors without concern that they may be deemed to be private foundations by

---

[48] Section 251(1) provides that related persons do not deal at arm's length with each other and s. 251(2) provides that persons may be related by blood, marriage or adoption. There are also detailed rules in ss. 251 (am. S.C. 1994, c. 7, Sch. II, s. 195; S.C. 1998, c. 19, s. 242; S.C. 2000, c. 12, ss. 140, 142; S.C. 2001, c. 17, s. 192), and 256 (am. S.C. 1994, c. 7, Sch. II, s. 198; S.C. 1994, c. 21, s. 114; S.C. 1995, c. 3, s. 55, S.C. 1995, c. 21, s. 44; S.C. 1998, c. 19, s. 246; S.C. 2001, c. 17, ss. 194, 231; S.C. 2005, c. 19, s. 55), dealing with factual non-arm's length and factual control which are relevant for the determining whether corporations deal at arm's length with individuals or other corporations, but are beyond the scope of this text.

[49] These amendments were first introduced as part of Draft Technical Amendments to the Act released on December 20, 2002. Those changes were included in the Revised Draft Technical Amendments released by the Minister of Finance on February 27, 2004, with the addition of minor wording in subpara. (*d*)(ii) of both definitions for clarification. The wording of the proposed amendment was further revised in a package of draft technical amendments released by the Department of Finance on July 18, 2005. These amendments have not been introduced in Parliament for enactment. However, once enacted, these amendments will become generally retroactive to January 1, 2000.

virtue of such gifts. However, funds received from the federal government, provincial governments, municipalities, other registered charities that are not private foundations, and non-profit organizations are not subject to the "control test". As a result, in relation to the application of the control test and the contribution test, there is no difference between charitable organizations and public foundations.

There is no change proposed to the current definition for "private foundations" — there is no requirement that more than 50 per cent of the directors/trustees/officers of a private foundation must be at arm's length and more than 50 per cent of the funds a private foundation receives may come from a donor or donors who do not deal at arm's length with it.

Under the proposed rules, when applying the "control test", some registered charities may find that they no longer fit under their current designation. Registered charities that wish to apply under section 149.1(6.3) to change their designation as a result of the amendments described above will be required to apply within 90 days of when the July 2005 amendments receive Royal Assent.[50] These registered charities will then be deemed to be registered as charitable organizations, public foundations or private foundations, as the case may be, in the taxation year that the Minister specifies.

As a result of the introduction of a "control" test, the convoluted rules under the Act in relation to "control" will become applicable, specifically due to the inclusion of the phrase "controlled directly or indirectly in any manner whatever" in the new definitions.[51] However, the application of the rules concerning "control" in the charitable context is unclear, since these rules are premised upon application to commercial arrangements in a business context rather than for registered charities. (See Couzin (2005); Loukidelis (2004).) As such, directors and officers of registered charities will need to carefully review these rules when establishing charitable organizations and public foundations involving a major donor or when receiving a

---

[50]   At the time of writing, the proposed amendments had not yet received Royal Assent.

[51]   Section 256(5.1) provides as follows:

> For the purposes of this Act, where the expression "controlled, directly or indirectly in any manner whatever," is used, a corporation shall be considered to be so controlled by another corporation, person or group of persons (in this subsection referred to as the "controller") at any time where, at that time, the controller has any direct or indirect influence that, if exercised, would result in control in fact of the corporation ...

donation from a major donor who contributes more than 50 per cent of the capital of a charity in order to ensure that the charity in question will not inadvertently be caught by these rules, which might otherwise lead to the unintended result of a charity being deemed a private foundation. As well, the current relationships between entities in multiple corporate structures should also be reviewed in order to assess whether this new control test may have an undesirable effect, particularly where the boards of directors of various related organizations are composed of substantially the same individuals, *e.g.*, a university or hospital with a parallel foundation.

Disbursement Quota Rules

All registered charities are required to expend a portion of their assets annually in accordance with a disbursement quota ("DQ"), which is a prescribed amount that registered charities must disburse each year in order to maintain their charitable registration. The purpose of the disbursement quota is "to ensure that most of a charity's funds are used to further its charitable purposes and activities; to discourage charities from accumulating excessive funds; and to keep other expenses at a reasonable level".[52] New DQ rules were enacted in Bill C-33 on May 13, 2005,[53] and apply generally to taxation years beginning after March 22, 2004, except that, for charitable organizations registered before March 23, 2004, the 3.5 per cent DQ will only apply to their taxation years beginning after 2008. Prior to Bill C-33, the disbursement quota rules for charitable organizations and public foundations were significantly different. However, the new disbursement quota rules contained in Bill C-33 generally apply to registered charities retroactively to March 23, 2004, such that the disbursement quota rules for charitable organizations and public foundations are now the same, subject to some transitional provisions.

The new rules are too complex to detail here,[54] but the calculation of the DQ occurs in accordance with a complicated formula consisting of two parts: the 80 per cent disbursement requirement aimed at

---

[52] See Information Circular RC 4108, *Registered Charities and the Income Tax Act*, updated May 7, 2002, and available at <http://www.cra-arc.gc.ca/E/pub/tg/rc4108/rc4108eq .html>.

[53] The *Budget Implementation Act, 2004, No. 2*, S.C. 2005, c. 19 (Bill C-33).

[54] Provided for in the definition of "disbursement quota" in s. 149.1(1) of the ITA. See Man & Hoffstein (2005). See also *Charity Law Bulletin* Nos. 59, 61, 67, and 69, available online at <www.charitylaw.ca>.

limiting administrative expenses and the 3.5 per cent requirement aimed at preventing accumulation of funds. The main features of the new disbursement quota for charitable organizations and public foundations may be summarized as follows:

The 80 per cent disbursement quota is equal to (1) 80 per cent of gifts receipted in the immediately preceding year (except gifts of enduring property and gifts received from other registered charities), plus (2) 80 per cent of enduring property expended in the year and 100 per cent of enduring property transferred to qualified donees in the year, less the optional reduction by the amount of realized capital gains on enduring property, plus (3) 80 per cent of gifts received from other charities in the immediately preceding year (except property that was received as a specified gift or as enduring property). The primary concern for most organizations with respect to changes to this part of the DQ will be ensuring that it clearly identifies what may be considered enduring property in accordance with the new definition in section 149.1(1): gifts by way of bequest or inheritance; 10-year gifts; life insurance proceeds, registered retirement income funds and registered retirement savings plans as a result of direct beneficiary designation; and gifts received by the charity as a transferee of an enduring property from either an original recipient charity or another transferee charity.

In addition to the 80 per cent DQ requirement, organizations will also be required to expend at least 3.5 per cent of their assets that are not used directly in its charitable activities or administration (commonly referred to as "investment assets").[55] The value of the assets in this regard is based on the average value of the charity's assets that are not used directly in its charitable activities or administration in the 24 months immediately preceding the taxation year.[56]

The disbursement quota rules for private foundations are very similar to those for charitable organizations and public foundations, except that private foundations must expend 100 per cent (rather than

---

[55]   The reduced 3.5 per cent disbursement quota applies to public and private foundations for taxation years beginning after March 22, 2004. For charitable organizations registered before March 23, 2004, the 3.5 per cent disbursement quota applies to their taxation years that begin after 2008. For charitable organizations registered after March 22, 2004, the 3.5 per cent disbursement quota applies to their taxation years that begin after March 22, 2004.

[56]   The 3.5 per cent DQ does not apply if the amount of property owned by the charity in this regard is $25,000 or less. The detailed method for the calculation of the 3.5 per cent DQ is set out in ss. 3700, 3701, and 3702 of the *Income Tax Regulations*, C.R.C. 1978, c. 945 (am. SOR/87-632, s. 1; SOR/94-686, ss. 22(F), 51(F), 73(F), 79(F)).

80 per cent) of all amounts received from other registered charities in the immediately preceding taxation year, other than specified gifts and enduring property.

Related Business

Charitable organizations[57] and public foundations can carry on related businesses.[58] If charitable organizations and public foundations carry on *un*related businesses, their charitable status may be revoked.[59] Private foundations, however, may not carry on any business activity, otherwise their charitable status may be revoked.[60]

Charitable Activities

As noted above, charitable organizations primarily carry on their own charitable activities. They may give funds to other qualified donees but may not disburse more than 50 per cent of their income annually to qualified donees,[61] unless the qualified donees are also associated

---

[57] Paragraph 149.1(6)(a) of the ITA.

[58] See Canada Revenue Agency Policy Statement CPS-019 entitled "What is a Related Business?" dated March 31, 2003, for a discussion of what CRA considers to be a related business, available online at <http://www.cra-arc.gc.ca/tax/charities/policy/cps/cps-019-e.html>. See also *Alberta Institute on Mental Retardation v. Canada*, [1987] F.C.J. No. 286, [1987] 3 F.C. 286 (F.C.A.) and *Earth Fund v. Canada (Minister of National Revenue)*, [2002] F.C.J. No. 1769 (F.C.A.).

[59] Paragraphs 149.1(2)(a) and 149.1(3)(a) of the ITA.

[60] Paragraph 149.1(4)(a) of the ITA.

[61] Paragraph 149.1(6)(b) of the ITA. Section 149.1(1) of the ITA provides that qualified donees are organizations that can issue official donation receipts for gifts that individuals and corporations make to them under ss. 110.1(1)(a) and (b) and 118.1(1). These consist of registered charities in Canada, registered Canadian amateur athletic associations; housing corporations resident in Canada constituted exclusively to provide low-cost housing for the aged; Canadian municipalities; the United Nations and its agencies; universities that are outside Canada that are prescribed to be universities the student body of which ordinarily includes students from Canada; charitable organizations outside Canada to which Her Majesty in right of Canada has made a gift during the fiscal period or in the 12 months immediately preceding the period; and Her Majesty in right of Canada or a province. In July 2005, it was proposed to amend ss. 110.1 (am. S.C. 1994, c. 7, Sch. II, s. 79; S.C. 1994, c. 7, Sch. VIII, s. 46; S.C. 1996, c. 21, s. 20; S.C. 1997, c. 25, s. 22; S.C. 1998, c. 19, s. 20; S.C. 2001, c. 17, s. 85; S.C. 2005, c. 19, s. 19) and 118.1 (am. S.C. 1994, c. 7, Sch. II, s. 88; S.C. 1994, c. 7, Sch. VIII, s. 53; S.C. 1995, c. 3, s. 34; S.C. 1995, c. 38, s. 3; S.C. 1996, c. 21, s. 23; S.C. 1997, c. 25, s. 26; S.C. 1998, c. 19, s. 22; S.C. 1999, c. 22, s. 32; S.C. 1999, c. 31, s. 136; S.C. 2001, c. 17, s. 94; S.C. 2005, c. 19, s. 23) of the Act by expanding the list of qualified donees to include municipal or public bodies performing a function of government in Canada.

charities.[62] Public foundations, however, are required by CRA to give more than 50 per cent of their income annually to other qualified donees. This requirement is not explicitly set out in the Act, but implied by virtue of the requirement in section 149.1(6)(*b*) of the ITA that charitable organizations may not disburse more than 50 per cent of their income annually to qualified donees and the definition of "charitable foundation" in section 149.1(1) of the ITA, which provides that a charitable foundation is "not a charitable organization" (Man & Carter (2005b)).

Private foundations may carry on their own charitable activities, and may give funds to other qualified donees. It is not clear from the Act whether there is any requirement on private foundations to give more than 50 per cent of their income annually to other qualified donees. As explained above, CRA takes the administrative position that the language in the definition for "charitable foundation" implies that public foundations must disburse at least 50 per cent of their income to qualified donees. CRA also takes the administrative position that since the definition of "private foundation" in section 149.1(1) of the ITA provides that a private foundation is a charitable foundation that is *not* a public foundation, private foundations are not required to give at least 50 per cent of their income annually to other qualified donees.

Borrowing

Public and private foundations are prohibited from incurring debts other than debts for current operating expenses, the purchase and sale of investments or the administration of the charitable activities.[63] These restrictions do not apply to charitable organizations.

Control of Other Corporations

Public and private foundations are prohibited from acquiring control of any corporation.[64] Failure to comply with this restriction may lead to revocation of a foundation's registration. Generally, control occurs when the foundation owns 50 per cent or more of a corporation's

---

[62]   Paragraph 149.1(6)(*c*) of the ITA.
[63]   Paragraphs 149.1(3)(*d*) and 149.1(4)(*d*) of the ITA.
[64]   Paragraphs 149.1(3)(*c*) and 149.1(4)(*c*) of the ITA.

issued share capital, having full voting rights under all circumstances. However, a foundation that has not purchased more than 5 per cent of these shares but is given a block of shares that brings up its total holding to more than 50 per cent will not be considered to have acquired control of the corporation.[65]

The restrictions that apply to foundations do not apply to charitable organizations. This means that, for purposes of the Act, charitable organizations are permitted to acquire control of a corporation. As such, CRA suggests that a charitable organization may operate a business through a taxable share capital corporation with the charitable organization retaining control over the taxable corporation "through share holdings or a power to nominate the board of directors".[66] However, this option is not available to charities in Ontario as a result of the application of the Ontario *Charitable Gifts Act.*[67]

The following table summarizes some of the specific rules affecting registered charities, including recently enacted amendments and proposed amendments released in July 2005 (Man & Carter (2005a)).

---

[65]   *Ibid.*

[66]   See CRA Policy Statement CPS-019 entitled "What is a Related Business?" dated March 31, 2003 at paras. 47 and 48, available online at: <http://www.cra-arc.gc.ca/tax/charities/policy/cps/cps-019-e.html>.

[67]   Section 2(1) of the *Charitable Gifts Act*, R.S.O. 1990, c. C.8, provides that a charity is not permitted to own more than ten per cent (10%) of an "interest in a business that is carried on for gain or profit is given to or vested in a person in any capacity for any religious, charitable, educational or public purpose". A charity, however, is permitted to invest in a business as a minority owner, provided that it does not "own", either directly or indirectly, an interest in excess of 10 per cent. If the charity is found to own more than 10 per cent of an interest of a business, it would have to dispose of any interest in excess of 10 per cent within seven years, although it might be possible to obtain a court order to extend the seven-year period.

Table 1: Rules affecting Registered Charities

Characteristics	Types of Registered Charities		
	Charitable Organizations	**Public Foundations**	**Private Foundations**
(1) Relationship between directors/trustees and control	Currently, more than 50% of the directors of charitable organizations and public foundations must deal with each other and with each of the other directors or trustees at arm's length. Further, not more than 50% of the capital contributed or otherwise paid to a charitable organization or public foundation can be contributed by one person or members of a group of such persons who do not deal with each other at arm's length (except some organizations, i.e. the federal government, a provincial government, a municipality, other registered charities that are not private foundations, and non-profit organizations). This is usually referred to as the "contribution" test. Proposed amendments will replace the "contribution test" with a "control test", such that a person or a group of persons not dealing with each other at arm's length may contribute more than 50% of the charity's capital as long as such a person or group does not control the charity in any way or represent more than 50% of the directors, trustees, officers and similar officials of the charity (amendment retroactive to January 1, 2000).		No requirements — may be closely held.
(2) Disbursement quota rules	The disbursement quota rules for charitable organizations and public foundations are now the same, subject to a transitional period for charitable organizations registered before March 23, 2004 in that the 3.5% disbursement quota will apply to their taxation years that begin after 2008. To summarize: • 80% disbursement quota: generally 80% of gifts receipted in the immediately preceding year (except gifts of enduring property) • 3.5% disbursement quota: 3.5% of investment assets with possible encroachment on capital gains to satisfy the 3.5% disbursement quota		The disbursement quota rules for private foundations are very similar except that private foundations must expend 100% (rather then 80%) of all amounts received from other registered charities in the immediately preceding taxation year (other than specified gifts and enduring property).
(3) Related business	Can only carry on related businesses		Cannot carry on any business

Characteristics	Types of Registered Charities		
	Charitable Organizations	**Public Foundations**	**Private Foundations**
(4) Charitable activities	Primarily carry on their own charitable activities, may give funds to other qualified donees, may not disburse more than 50% of their income annually to qualified donees, unless they are associated charities.	Public foundations must give more than 50% of their income annually to other qualified donees.	Private foundations primarily fund other charities.
(5) Legal structure	Must either be corporations, unincorporated associations or charitable trusts.	Must be either corporations or trusts.	
(6) Borrowing	No restriction.	Cannot incur debts other than debts for current operating expenses, the purchase and sale of investments, or the administration of the chartable activities.	
(7) Control of other corporations	No restriction.	Cannot acquire control of any corporation. Generally, control occurs when the foundation owns 50% or more of a corporation's issued share capital, having full voting rights under all circumstances. There is an exception where a foundation has not bought more than 5% of these shares and is given a bloc of shares that brings up its total holding to more than 50%, it will not be considered to have acquired control of the corporation.	

New Regulatory Regime

In addition to changes to the DQ, Bill C-33 introduced a new regulatory regime for registered charities. The amendments implement new rules concerning the taxation and administration of charities, including new intermediate sanctions and a more accessible appeals regime. The introduction of new intermediate sanctions and a new appeals regime are important changes for charities, providing more appropriate recourse for unintended or incidental breaches.

Interim Sanctions

Prior to the 2004 Federal Budget, the only sanction available to CRA in regulating registered charities was the revocation of a charity's registration (Canada, Department of Finance (2004, at p. 338)). Revocation occurred sometimes inadvertently as a result of a failure by the charity to file an information return or because the charity was being discontinued, and was only invoked rarely by CRA in situations of serious non-compliance and only after a lengthy audit process. To provide an alternative to the revocation of charitable status for minor or unintended infractions, the ITA now provides for intermediate sanctions.[68] In the situation of a failure to file an information return on time, the registered charity will be subject to a monetary penalty of $500 (Canada, Department of Finance (2004, at p. 352)). A registered charity may also face a suspension of its ability to issue tax receipts and to receive funds from other charities for one year if it fails to comply with certain verification and enforcement provisions of the Act (*e.g.*, fails to keep proper books and records) (at p. 353). Private foundations, public foundations and charitable organizations which carry on certain business activities will be subject to a monetary penalty equal to 5 per cent of their gross revenue from such business activities and a repeat offence within five years of the first infraction will carry a monetary penalty equal to all of the charity's gross revenue from the offending activities as well as a suspension of its ability to issue tax receipts (at p. 353).

Similarly graduated monetary penalties will be applied to registered charities if:

- a charitable foundation acquires control of a corporation;

- a registered charity confers on a person an undue benefit (essentially, transfers resources of the charity for the personal benefit of a member, director or trustee of the charity which could include excessive salaries or board compensation);

- a registered charity issues improper receipts;

- a person provides false information for the purposes of a tax receipt, which could include incorrect valuation information of either the property gifted or the advantage received by the donor when making the donation; or if

- a registered charity makes a transfer to another registered charity for the purpose of delaying expenditures on charitable activities (at p. 353).

---

[68]   For a complete list of sanctions, see "Penalty Chart" in Canada Revenue Agency, Policy Statement CSP-S18, available online at: CRA <www.cra-arc.gc.ca/tax/charities/policy/csp/penalties-e.html>.

In addition, if a charitable foundation acquires control of a corporation a second time within the span of five years, if false information has been provided and the amount of the penalty imposed is in excess of $250,000, or if a charity has received a gift and issued a receipt on behalf of a registered charity under suspension the registered charity will also face suspension of its ability to issue tax receipts and to receive funds from other charities for one year (at p. 353).

Appeals Process

The new appeals regime is intended to make the appeal process more accessible and affordable for registered charities and unsuccessful applicants for charitable status. Previously, the only avenue for challenging CRA's decisions on charitable matters was through the Federal Court of Appeal. The amendments have extended CRA's existing internal objection review process to notices of a decision by CRA regarding the revocation or annulment of a charity's registration, the designation of a charity as a private or public foundation or a charitable organization, the denial of applications for charitable status, suspension of tax-receipting privileges, and the imposition of monetary penalties or revocation tax against a registered charity. Filing a notice of objection is now a required step before an appeal may be brought to the courts.

If a charity disagrees with CRA's decision resulting from an objection, appeals in respect of decisions concerning refusals to grant registered charitable status and revocation of registered charitable status will continue to be made to the Federal Court of Appeal. However, with respect to the imposition of the new monetary penalties and/or the revocation tax or suspension of its tax receipting privileges, a charity may appeal the decision to the Tax Court of Canada under either the informal procedure (expected to apply if the amount of penalties or tax is less than $12,000) or general procedure.

RISK MANAGEMENT AND LIABILITY

Black's Law Dictionary defines "risk" as the "chance of injury, damage or loss", and it defines "risk management" as the "procedures or systems used to minimize accidental losses".[69] Although the levels

---

[69] *Black's Law Dictionary* (1999), *s.v.* "risk" and "risk management".

of risk are subjective and difficult to quantify for such a diverse sector as the nonprofit sector in Canada, it is important for directors and members to understand the impact of risk on the operation of their organizations. As most directors and managers already understand, risk cannot be completely eliminated, but it can be managed through conscientious and careful planning and organization. Liability and risk management must be reviewed from many different standpoints, including from the level of the organization or corporation and from the level of directors and officers.

Level of the Organization/Corporation

Choice of Nonprofit or Charitable Structure

As was discussed above in the section "Legal Structure for Nonprofit Organizations", the choice of the appropriate nonprofit or charitable structure is a primary consideration for risk management and liability. Depending on the choice of legal structure, risk and liability will rest with different parties. An unincorporated association has no legal capacity to sue, be sued or to contract, and only derives its existence from its members. As such, the unincorporated association can bear no liability for the acts or omissions of its members; instead it is the individual members who will ultimately be liable (Bourgeois (2002, at p. 49)). An incorporated corporation without share capital, on the other hand, is a separate legal entity from that of its members, and therefore has the legal capacity to sue, to be sued and to contract with other parties. With the legal capacity, the incorporated corporation without share capital bears the liability for breach of contract, negligence or other sueable actions of its directors, officers, members, staff, volunteers and agents. Like the unincorporated association, a trust has no legal personality. Thus, all actions are carried out by the trustee, who must bear the liability for any acts or omissions. However, the trustee acting in accordance with its obligations and authority as trustee is entitled to be reimbursed for reasonable expenses, so the trust and/or the beneficiaries may ultimately bear the financial liability for any claim (Waters (2005)).

Standard of Care

The standard of care is a legal concept referring to the degree of care expected of an individual in relation to a duty to other individuals. An individual will only incur liability where his or her conduct falls below that which is expected by the community. Texts and case law generally do not discuss the standard of care expected of a business corporation, let alone a nonprofit corporation. As such, any discussion of standard of care will generally relate to that which is expected of directors and officers. This is likely because the corporation is a fictionalized person while a trust or unincorporated association has trustees and members standing in front of them. Conceptually, it is difficult to apply a standard of care to a fictional person, but the courts will hold a corporation both directly and vicariously liable for the acts or omissions of its directors, officers, staff and volunteers. In assessing liability against a corporation, the court will apply the "reasonable person" standard; that is, whether the corporation acted in the same manner as a reasonably careful person in the circumstances (Osborne (2003)). For example, a court (and therefore an effective risk manager) would ask: "Did the nonprofit corporation exercise reasonable care in training its staff?"

Vicarious Liability (Directors, Officers, Staff, Volunteers)

Vicarious liability imposes liability upon an employer or principal for the conduct of an employee or agent, on the grounds that the employer or principal should be held accountable for losses to third parties that arise from the actions of the employee or agent. Unlike the principle of personal liability, vicarious liability does not require that the employer or principal actually cause the loss sustained by the third party. Liability is imposed on the employer or principal with the rationale that the loss is the result of a reasonably foreseeable risk and attributable to the employer's or principal's activities, and that it is reasonable that the employer or principal should be liable for the risk.

From a public policy point of view, vicarious liability is designed to ensure that parties undertaking risky enterprises take all reasonable measures to reduce the risk. It is a form of risk allocation, in keeping with the logic behind tort law in Canada; namely, losses will be suffered in our modern world, and we should be aware of the losses we cause, and should try to reduce the risks of such losses, or compensate for them when appropriate.

The Supreme Court of Canada provided in the case of *Bazley v. Curry*[70] a two-part approach to determining whether and when vicarious liability should be imposed on an employer, such as a nonprofit corporation. The two-part approach involves a court determining if there are any precedents which determine whether vicarious liability should be imposed under the circumstances in the case, and if the wrongful act can be sufficiently connected to the conduct authorized by the employer or principal. The court rejected arguments that nonprofit or charitable organizations should be shielded from tort liability. Recently, the Supreme Court of Canada again rejected the use of the old doctrine of charitable immunity to shield a religious organization from liability arising from sexual abuse in a residential school,[71] as well as confirming the need for a nexus between the wrongful act and the job.[72]

Bazley v. Curry

Supreme Court of Canada

[1999] S.C.J. No. 35, [1999] 2 S.C.R. 534,
174 D.L.R. (4th) 45, 62 B.C.L.R. (3d) 173,
43 C.C.E.L. (2d) 1, 46 C.C.L.T. (2d) 1,
99 C.L.L.C. 210-033, [1999] 8 W.W.R. 197,
124 B.C.A.C. 119, 241 N.R. 266, 203 W.A.C. 119
June 17, 1999

A not-for-profit foundation operated two residential care facilities for the treatment of emotionally troubled children. The Foundation's employees were to do everything a parent would do, from general supervision to intimate duties like bathing and tucking in at bedtime. Unbeknownst to the Foundation, they hired a pedophile to work in one of its homes. After investigating a complaint about the employee, and verifying that he had abused a child in one of its homes, the Foundation discharged him. The employee was convicted of 19 counts of sexual abuse, two of which related to a party to this case. The

---

[70] [1999] S.C.J. No. 35, [1999] 2 S.C.R. 534 (S.C.C.) (hereinafter "Bazley").
[71] *Blackwater v. Plint*, [2005] S.C.J. No. 59, [2005] 3 S.C.R. 3 (S.C.C.).
[72] *E.B. v. Order of the Oblates of Mary Immaculate in the Province of British Columbia*, [2005] S.C.J. No. 61, [2005] 3 S.C.R. 45 (S.C.C.).

individual sued the Foundation for compensation for the injury he suffered while in its care. The parties stated a case to determine whether the Foundation was vicariously liable for its employee's tortious conduct. The chambers judge found that it was and the Court of Appeal upheld that decision.

Held, the Supreme Court of Canada determined that employers are vicariously liable for both employee acts authorized by the employer and unauthorized acts so connected with authorized acts that they may be regarded as modes (albeit improper modes) of doing authorized acts. In determining whether an employer is vicariously liable for an employee's unauthorized, intentional wrong in cases where precedent is inconclusive, courts should be guided by the following principles:

1.   Courts should openly confront the question of whether the employer should be found liable.

2.   The fundamental question the court should ask is whether the wrongful act is sufficiently related to conduct authorized by the employer to justify the imposition of vicarious liability. Vicarious liability is generally appropriate where there is a significant connection between the creation or enhancement of a risk and the wrong that results, even if unrelated to the employer's aims. Incidental connections to the employment enterprise, like time and place (without more), will not suffice. Once engaged in a particular business, it is fair that an employer be made to pay the generally foreseeable costs of that business. In contrast, to impose liability for costs unrelated to the risk would effectively make the employer an involuntary insurer.

3.   In determining the sufficiency of the connection between the employer's creation or enhancement of the risk and the wrong complained of, subsidiary factors may be considered such as the following: (a) the opportunity that the enterprise afforded the employee to abuse his or her power; (b) the extent to which the wrongful act may have furthered the employer's aims (and hence be more likely to have been committed by the employee); (c) the extent to which the wrongful act was related to friction, confrontation or intimacy inherent in the employer's enterprise; (d) the extent of power conferred on the employee in relation to the victim; and (e) the vulnerability of

potential victims to the wrongful exercise of the employee's power.

Anti-terrorism Legislation Compliance

A discussion of anti-terrorism legislation compliance may seem odd in a work about nonprofit organizations, yet they, with charities and non-governmental organizations ("NGOs"), have been identified as a "crucial weak point" (Financial Action Task Force (2002a)) in money laundering and terrorist financing initiatives in the international community, and are thus subjected to increasing scrutiny by government.[73] The fear remains that "non-profit organizations that engage in raising or disbursing funds for charitable, religious, cultural, educational, social or fraternal purposes, or for the carrying out of other types of 'good works' [will be] ... misused or exploited by the financiers of terrorism".[74] In addition to sham organizations, the international community has witnessed instances where terrorist organizations were supported without the knowledge of the donor or directors of the organization.[75]

Although nonprofit and charitable organizations were not the primary target of the far-reaching counterterrorism legislation that was introduced in Canada following the terror attacks on New York and Washington, D.C., on September 11, 2001, the organizations and directors of those organizations have much to fear should they become the unwitting assistants of terror organizations. Nonprofit organizations should be aware of some of the key pieces of legislation that were affected by Canada's *Anti-terrorism Act*,[76] including the *Criminal Code*[77] and the *Proceeds of Crime (Money Laundering) and Terrorist Financing Act*.[78] Of particular note in the *Criminal Code* amendments is the introduction of offences for "facilitating" a terrorist activity or organization.[79] Despite government claims to the contrary, these poorly

---

[73] An important resource in this respect is <www.antiterrorismlaw.ca>. In particular, see, *e.g.*, Carter (2005).

[74] Carter (2005).

[75] See, *e.g.*, Financial Action Task Force, *Report on Money Laundering Typologies 2001-2002* (2002). The FATF Report provides a number of examples of activities that were found to be in support of terrorist activities, whether it be providing financial assistance or providing shelter.

[76] S.C. 2001, c. 41 (proclaimed in force December 24, 2001).

[77] R.S.C. 1985, c. C-46.

[78] S.C. 2001, c. 17.

[79] See, *e.g.*, *Criminal Code*, R.S.C. 1985, c. C-46, at ss. 83.18, 83.19, 83.21 and 83.22 (all enacted 2001, c. 41, s. 4).

drafted sections may ensnare otherwise innocent organizations that unknowingly assist terrorist organizations. The extent to which the government will enforce these provisions against unwitting organizations remains to be seen. The *Proceeds of Crime (Money Laundering) and Terrorist Financing Act* also places a heavy burden on organizations that deal in large financial transactions to retain detailed records and report information to the Financial Transactions & Reports Analysis Centre of Canada ("FINTRAC"). Failure to do so carries significant penalties and the possibility of seizure of funds.

These provisions highlight the need for due diligence on the part of the nonprofit organization. Not only should there be strict controls on the financial operations of the organization, but the operational side of the organization needs to be carefully managed. Policies demonstrating intent to comply with anti-terrorism legislation should be in place and nonprofit organizations should be able to document their administrative, managerial and policy control over their operations. This necessarily includes auditing or investigating other organizations with which the nonprofit organization works, overseeing activities conducted and accounting for funds expended.

Level of Directors and Officers

Role and Duties of Directors and Officers

The most basic role or duty of a director of a nonprofit organization is to manage the affairs of the corporation.[80] In essence, the directors are the guiding minds of the corporation, while the officers and staff manage the day-to-day operations. Managing the affairs of the corporation encompasses a broad spectrum of duties, including: ensuring the organization adheres to and carries out the goals of the corporation; setting long-term objectives in accordance with these goals; ensuring financing stability; assessing the corporation's performance; establishing policies; and being the public face of the corporation (Burke-Robertson & Drache (2002, at pp. 5-1 and 5-2)). Any or all of these duties may be limited by the organization's by-laws; however, the directors must

---

[80] See, *e.g.*, *Corporations Act*, R.S.O. 1990, c. C.38, s. 283(1). A useful reference tool in this respect is a publication from Industry Canada, *Primer for Directors of Not-for-Profit Corporations (Rights, Duties and Practices)* (Ottawa: Industry Canada, 2002).

always be able to demonstrate that they "manage the affairs" of the corporation in accordance with the governing legislation.

In managing the affairs of the corporation, a director has a number of fiduciary duties, including: a duty to act honestly; a duty of loyalty; a duty of diligence or to act in good faith; a duty to exercise power; a duty of obedience; a duty to avoid conflict of interest; a duty of prudence; a duty to continue. Many of these duties are self-explanatory, but some comments are warranted. The duty to exercise power is essentially a requirement that the director fulfils his role, pursues the organization's objectives and does not fail to supervise delegated tasks. Similarly, the duty to continue requires a resigning director to ensure there is an adequate replacement. Resignation will not avoid liability and may constitute breach of fiduciary duty where the director put his or her own interests ahead of those of the corporation.

Liability of Directors and Officers

As Burke-Robertson notes, although the applicable standard of care for directors of business corporations is statutorily defined, most jurisdictions do not provide the same for corporations without share capital (at p. 6-3). Only British Columbia, Newfoundland, Manitoba and Saskatchewan have codified an objective standard of care (at p. 6-4).[81] In the absence of a codified standard of care, one must look to the common law, which has set the standard of care as "conduct that may reasonably be expected from a person of such knowledge and experience as the identified director".[82] This subjective standard of care means that a director who is, for example, a lawyer or business executive may be held to a higher standard of care than a director who is a factory worker. Although Bourgeois notes that the courts have historically been "reluctant to enforce the standard too rigorously in circumstances where, for example, the director was not involved in managing the affairs of the corporation" (Bourgeois (2002, at p. 223)), there has been a noticeable change in tide in the wake of the collapse of Enron and Worldcom. Enhanced corporate governance is a popular slogan for both business corporations and nonprofit corporations. Good governance, which includes such principles as participation in

---

[81]   See *Society Act*, R.S.B.C. 1986, c. 433; *Corporations Act*, R.S.N.L. 1990, c. C-36; *Non-profit Corporations Act, 1995*, S.S. 1995, c. N-4.2; and *Corporations Act*, C.C.S.M., c. C225.

[82]   At p. 6-4.1, referencing *In re City Equitable Fire Insurance Co.*, [1924] All E.R. Rep. 485 (Eng. C.A.).

decision-making; accountability and transparency; responsive, effective and efficient performance; and sound rule of law, is the responsibility of the directors, who have the duty and power to manage the affairs of the corporation. In the absence of a limitation on liability for directors (which is available only in Saskatchewan), acting in good faith will be not be sufficient to avoid liability. As such, directors who do not perform to the expected standard of care may be liable for the damages that result from their actions.

Additionally, both provincial and federal statutes impose liability on directors in specific circumstances. For example, directors of nonprofit corporations are jointly and severally liable to employees for unpaid wages to a maximum of six months.[83] On a related issue, they are liable for the corporation's failure to remit an employee's source deductions to the tax authorities, along with interest and penalties.[84] Directors will also be held liable for the corporation's failure to meet reporting, record keeping or filing requirements under various pieces of legislation.[85] As such, directors are subject to both pecuniary and criminal liabilities.[86]

Rights and Powers

It goes without saying that directors would be unable to effectively carry out their duties without concomitant rights and powers. Given the heavy burden directors carry with respect to liability for their actions and the actions of the corporation, directors have a right to unimpaired access to all resources of the corporation in order to effectively perform their duties. This necessarily requires access to books and records, notice of meetings, an equal right to vote at the

---

[83] See, *e.g., Canada Corporations Act*, R.S.C. 1970, c. C-32, s. 99 (am. 2004, c. 25, s. 189); Ontario *Corporations Act*, R.S.O. 1990, c. C.38, s. 81 (am. 1992, c. 32, s. 6(6); 2002, c. 24, Sch. B, s. 31).

[84] ITA, s. 227.1(1).

[85] See, *e.g.,* CCA, s. 114.2(5) (am. 1985, c. 26, s. 36); or ITA, s. 238.

[86] Although there are no statistics on the number of directors that have had pecuniary and criminal liabilities imposed upon them, there are some interesting examples. In *Ontario (Public Guardian and Trustee) v. National Society for Abused Women and Children*, [2002] O.J. No. 607 (Ont. S.C.J.), the three directors of the charitable organization were ordered to repay the nearly $1 million they funnelled into non-arm's length fundraising corporations and were prohibited from acting as directors of any other charitable organization until the funds had been repaid. Noting that only $1,365 of the nearly $1 million raised made its way to charitable work, the court stated: "A distinct odour emanates from the facts of this case."

meetings, and a right to inspect and approve or disapprove the minutes of previous meetings of the board.

Like the director's rights, the powers complement their duties. In this respect, directors have the power to manage the affairs of the corporation, the power to borrow money in accordance with statutory procedures, the power to make investments on behalf of the corporation and the power to dispose of property.

Statutory Protection

Unlike their business counterparts, there is little in the way of statutory protection for directors of nonprofit organizations. In fact, the CCA only provides two forms of statutory protection. First, in respect of contracts with third parties, directors will not be liable to those parties so long as they are acting within the scope of their authority as agents of the corporation (Carter (2002, at p. 74)). The second statutory protection deals with conflicts of interest. There is a common law rule prohibiting directors of nonprofit organizations from profiting or benefiting directly or indirectly from their position. Should any benefit accrue, the director would be in breach of his or her fiduciary duty and would be held accountable to the organization for the benefits received. This translates into a practice of avoiding conflicts of interest or even the appearance of a conflict of interest. However, the CCA enables a director to avoid liability for receiving a benefit if the director declares his or her conflict of interest and abstains from any discussion or vote on the matter (Carter (2002, at p. 74)).

Other Means of Reducing Risks

Indemnification and Insurance

Indemnification and insurance are key considerations for both the nonprofit organization and any individual considering being a director. Indemnification is the process by which the corporation agrees to cover the cost of, or compensate the director for, any loss or damage sustained as a result of the acts or omissions of the director in his capacity as a director of the organization.[87] Of course, this would not cover illegal acts or omissions, or directors who are in breach of their

---

[87]   *Black's Law Dictionary* (1999), *s.v.* "indemnification" and "indemnify."

fiduciary duty. In order for a nonprofit corporation to provide indemnity for its directors, such a power must be included in the organization's by-laws. This provides a measure of protection for the director, thereby enabling the organization to attract capable individuals to the position. However, such an indemnity is worthless if the organization does not have sufficient assets to cover significant claims, such as is likely the case if there is a sexual abuse claim.

Insurance, on the other hand, could prove to be an important safety net if the nonprofit corporation is involved in risky operations which could result in significant claims made against the organization and its directors. There are a variety of types of insurance an organization should consider obtaining, depending on the size and type of its activities. In addition to general liability insurance, directors and officers liability insurance ("D&O") is one type that is appropriate for all nonprofit organizations, as it provides protection in relation to the board's acts or omissions, and any activities conducted under the auspices of the board of directors.

Regardless of the type of insurance obtained, directors should review the policies in order to determine any limitations. These limitations may be in the form of the type of activity covered, the number of claims permitted in a time period, or the timeframe in which an action will be covered (*i.e.*, whether the policy will provide coverage in 2005 for an incident that occurred in 1995, or if a policy purchased in 2005 will cover any claims made in 2015 as a result of incidents occurring in 2005).

Due Diligence in Operations (Maintaining the Corporation)

Exercising due diligence is the most effective way for directors to protect themselves from liability. Due diligence includes utilizing the rights and powers of the director and seeking professional advice when necessary. However, it will not provide a defence for all statutory violations, *i.e.*, failure to comply with the anti-terrorism legislation. As Bourgeois notes (2001, at p. 17):

> Due diligence is both a question of fact and of law. What is due diligence will depend on the circumstances, the type of organization and the activities undertaken. In general, directors or officers will meet their obligations if they act *reasonably, prudently and sagaciously* and within the law, including the objects of the organization and the scope of their position or office.

(Emphasis added.)

As such, directors will be exercising due diligence in circumstances in which they fulfil their primary duty of managing the affairs of the corporation. As noted above, this necessarily includes ensuring that meetings are held as required, that the director attends the meetings and is prepared to discuss matters, that corporate records are duly maintained, and that reports are submitted as required. There is the accompanying need for ongoing training and education in order to ensure directors maintain and enhance their skills and knowledge in the area of the organization's operation, as well as the applicable legislation and case law. In certain circumstances, it will be necessary for the directors to obtain advice from qualified professionals, which can assist in insulating directors from liability. Such circumstances include situations requiring legal, accounting or financial expertise.

Legal Risk Management Committees

Another means of reducing risk is through establishing legal risk management committees to conduct the reviews of the organization's policies, activities and associations, and identify risk areas. These committees should conduct a comprehensive audit of the corporation's assets, structure, legal relationships (contractual and non-contractual), and particularly activity-related risks, and the committee should advise the board on implementing due diligence and risk management procedures.

Independent Legal Advice

Directors should obtain independent legal advice in situations where they may be facing a high degree of exposure to personal liability. As noted above, simply resigning is not necessarily a measure that will insulate a director from potential liability. As such, before considering resigning from the board, a director should obtain independent legal advice.

Size of the Board

Careful consideration should be given to the appropriate number of directors required to effectively operate the nonprofit corporation. A smaller board will give directors more effective control over the management of the corporation's affairs, and will help reduce the number of individuals who will be exposed to liability.

Transfer of Assets

No proactive or due diligence steps can completely shield a director from all potential liability. In circumstances where the organization participates in high-risk activities, *i.e.*, work with children, it may be advisable for the director to transfer his or her personal assets to the director's spouse in advance of joining the board in order to aid in shielding the assets in the event of a finding of liability. However, such an action is not advisable after the director has joined the board as it may be viewed as a fraudulent conveyance in order to avoid creditors.

Checklists

The use of a checklist in order to ensure the nonprofit corporation has complied with all legal requirements is an effective tool in any corporation's risk management strategy. Whether it is prepared by the directors or available through professional advisors, a checklist can guide the board through its duties to ensure all bases are covered. A sample Legal Risk Management Checklist for Charities is available at <www.charitylaw.ca>.

REFERENCES

Black's Law Dictionary (1999), 7th ed. (St. Paul, MN: West Publishing, 1999).

Broder, P. *et al.*, eds. (2002), *Primer for Directors of Not-for-Profit Corporations (Rights, Duties and Practices)* (Ottawa: Industry Canada, 2002).

Bourgeois, D.J. (2001), *Charities and Not-for-Profit Administration and Governance Handbook* (Toronto: LexisNexis Canada, 2001).

Bourgeois, D.J. (2002), *The Law of Charitable and Not-for-Profit Organizations*, 3rd ed. (Toronto: LexisNexis Canada, 2002).

Bucknall, B. (2002), "Conventional and Unconventional Parties: How Documents Are Engrossed and Executed", in P.M. Perell and S.H. Troister, eds., *LSUC Special Lectures, 2002: Real Property Law* (Toronto: Irwin Law, 2002).

Burke-Robertson, R.J. (2005), "Life After Bill C-21: How Will It Affect Your Organization?" Paper presented to the Canadian Bar Association 3rd National Symposium on Charity Law, May 2005.

Burke-Robertson, R.J., & A.B. Drache (2002), *Non-Share Capital Corporations* (Toronto: Thomson Carswell, 2002).

Canada, Department of Finance (2004), *The Budget Plan, 2004* (Ottawa: Department of Finance Canada, 2004).

Canadian Encyclopedic Digest (CED 2005), "Associations and Non-profit Corporations" (Toronto: Thomson Carswell, 2005).

Carter, T.S. (1998), "Fit to Be Tithed 2: National and International Charitable Structures: Achieving Protection and Control" (Toronto: Law Society of Upper Canada, 1998).

Carter, T.S. (2001), "Pro-active Protection of Charitable Assets: A Selective Discussion of Liability Risks and Pro-active Responses". Paper presented to the Law Society of Upper Canada, November 20, 2001.

Carter, T.S. (2002), "Risk Protection" in P. Broder *et al.*, eds., *Primer for Directors of Not-for-Profit Corporations (Rights, Duties and Practices)* (Ottawa: Industry Canada, 2002).

Carter, T.S. (2005), "The Impact of Anti-terrorism Legislation on Charities: The Shadow of the Law", September 27, 2005. Available online at: <www.antiterrorismlaw.ca>.

Couzin, R. (2005), "Some Reflections on Corporation Controls" (2005), 53:2 *Canadian Tax Journal* 305-332.

Financial Action Task Force (2002a), *Combating the Abuse of Non-profit Organisations: International Best Practices* (Paris: FATF Secretariat, 2002). Available online at: FATF-GAFI <http://www.fatf-gafi.org/dataoecd/39/19/34033761.pdf>.

Financial Action Task Force (2002b), *Report on Money Laundering Typologies 2001-2002* (Paris: FATF Secretariat, 2002). Available online at: FATF-GAFI <http://www.fatf-gafi.org/dataoecd/29/35/34038006.pdf>.

Hall, M.H. *et al.* (2004), *Cornerstones of Community: Highlights of the National Survey of Nonprofit and Voluntary Organizations* (Ottawa: Ministry of Industry for Statistics Canada, 2004).

Hoffstein, E., T.S. Carter & A.M. Parachin, eds. (2005), *Charities Legislation & Commentary, 2006 Edition* (Toronto: LexisNexis Canada, 2005).

Loukidelis, J. (2004), "Comments on Certain Proposed Tax Rules Applicable to Charities: Gifts to Foreign Entities, Large Gifts and 'Split Receipts'" (2004), 18:4 *The Philanthropist* 261-302.

Man, T.L.M., & T.S. Carter (2005a), "A Comparison of the Three Categories of Registered Charities", *Charity Law Bulletin* No. 73, July 21, 2005. Available online at: <www.charitylaw.ca>.

Man, T.L.M., & T.S. Carter (2005b), "How do Charitable Organizations and Foundations Differ Under Income Tax?" (September 2, 2005), 25:16 *Lawyers Weekly*.

Man, T.L.M., & M.E. Hoffstein (2005), "New Disbursement Quota Rules Under Bill C-53". Paper presented at the Canadian Bar Association/Ontario Bar Association 3rd National Symposium on Charity Law, May 6, 2005. Available online at: <www.charitylaw.ca>.

Osborne, P.H. (2003), *The Law of Torts*, 2nd ed. (Toronto: Irwin Law, 2003).

Waters, D.W.M. (2005), *Waters' Law of Trusts in Canada* (Toronto: Thomson Carswell, 2005).

Chapter 6

GOVERNMENT AND COMMUNITY RELATIONS

Kathy Brock
Queen's University

INTRODUCTION: MANAGING UP AND OUTWARDS

Change is a constant in the world of nonprofit organizations, particularly in their relations with other organizations and the public. Citizen demands shift according to population trends and preferences, causing nonprofit organizations to frequently reassess their programs, services and methods of operation. All this may cause nonprofit organizations to build new alliances, merge or reconsider existing relationships.

In many cases, changes in government underlie these societal shifts but governments may also impose new demands or pressures through new contracting, funding or accountability arrangements, by re-evaluating current services or program delivery, or by requiring nonprofit organizations to fulfil new roles in either the policy process or society. Managers of nonprofit organizations are expected to balance these shifting requirements. The most successful managers will respond positively to the new environments, ensuring their organizations are flexible in operations yet remain true to their missions and founding ideals.

This chapter will examine the changing world of nonprofit organizations and the challenges affecting managers as they position their organizations to survive and thrive in this inconstant environment. Managers are increasingly expected to build more effective alliances within the nonprofit sector but also with the public and corporate sectors if they are to serve Canadians in an efficient and satisfying manner. To function effectively in this increasingly integrated world, an understanding is required of four dimensions of the changes.

First, both the federal and provincial levels of government are moving away from traditional "command and control" models of government to what is known as a "governance model". This requires more reliance upon external organizations to advise on policies and deliver services and programs to the public. This shift requires the movement from traditional hierarchical relationships in which the government actors define the nature of the relationship to negotiated arrangements between the two sectors. However, in spite of this trend, tensions abound as governments often still attempt to retain control and enforce accountability requirements that are not negotiated but imposed and at variance with the nature of the service or program. Defining the relationship between the two sectors in largely instrumental terms, that is, according to what the two sectors can do for each other, further complicates the role of nonprofit organizations in the policy process by leaving the questions of advocacy and critical analysis of public policies in abeyance. Managers must cope with this ambivalence in the relationship and strive to negotiate flexible arrangements that meet citizen requirements.

Second, pressures are building on nonprofit managers to look to the corporate and business sector as allies in serving Canadians. Traditionally the two sectors have been viewed as more competitive and even antagonistic towards each other, pursuing objectives that are at variance. The "market failure" theory of nonprofit organizations characterized them as providing programs and services where the private sector had failed to offer a commercial variant of those goods or where public needs were created as a byproduct of the operation of the private sector.[1] In both cases, the nonprofit organizations were often critical of the operation of the private sector and profit motive. However, as public resources to nonprofit organizations have become increasingly constrained and as the corporate sector is engaging in more socially responsible endeavours and shifting towards more

---

[1] The "market failure" theory of the nonprofit sector has been largely developed by economists and posits that nonprofits arise where the private sector fails to meet needs due to insufficient market incentives. For a discussion of some of the major theories explaining nonprofit, private and public sector relations see Young (1999); *cf.* Weisbrod (1988).

strategic investment in the nonprofit sector,[2] managers of nonprofit organizations must strive to develop relations with private sector actors that benefit both partners and enhance their operations but remain loyal to their principles. This is not an easy task.

Third, nonprofit organizations are building relations, both wanted and unwanted, with other nonprofit organizations. Increasingly, both public and private funders of nonprofit organizations are exerting pressure on their managers to look to creative means of co-operating with other organizations in order to reduce overlap or duplication in services or to rationalize management structures. The ultimate objective is to use funding dollars more efficiently and effectively. At the same time, many managers of nonprofit organizations are identifying benefits in partnering at the subsectoral level and reaching out to other organizations, independent of their funding situations.

A critical factor affecting the ability of organizations to forge strong alliances is the cost both in terms of dedicated monetary and personnel resources to nurturing the relationships and the time required. However, relationships between individual organizations, networks at the community level, and sectoral alliances and multisectoral coalitions at the provincial and federal levels are all becoming increasingly necessary to the vibrancy and sustainability of the nonprofit sector.

Fourth, as nonprofit organizations exercise more influence in policy design, development and delivery, they have come under more scrutiny. The governance and accountability scandals affecting a small minority of nonprofit organizations in Canada and the U.S. in the 1980s and 1990s created a new attentiveness in the media that has only been fostered with the increasing role of nonprofits in delivering services to needy portions of the population both home and abroad. As the level of public donations to nonprofit organizations increases, this scrutiny is intensified. Not only is the office of the Auditor General examining the relationships established between nonprofit organizations and government departments more closely and providing a source of material to the media, the media are tracking nonprofit organization performance on a more sustained and regular basis. Managers must adapt to the sometimes capricious but more often

---

[2] For comments on this trend in Canada, see Cunningham and Cushing (1988); *cf.* Parker (2000). For a study of current U.S. trends, see *Philanthropy Journal Corporate Giving: A Special Report* (9.19.2005) at <http://philanthropyjournal.org/>.

insightful and thoughtful world of investigative journalism. This requires developing good media relations skills — quick judgment, clear soundbites and sensible responses to probing questions, among others.

The requirements imposed on managers of nonprofit organizations by the shifts in these relationships cannot be underestimated. Already coping with heavy workloads, managers must develop new skills and adapt to unstable environments. The first step, in not just coping but thriving amidst these challenges, is to understand the nature and significance of these shifts. This chapter begins that process but focuses primarily on relations with governments owing to their importance.

GOVERNMENT TO GOVERNANCE: TRENDS IN GOVERNMENT–NONPROFIT RELATIONS

Nonprofit organizations are being increasingly drawn into the orbit of government. At the most sustained and complex level, these bisectoral arrangements involve multiple nonprofit organizations in delivering advice and engaging in policy development in areas ranging from international affairs and trade to childcare, to sports policies, to railway safety, to emergency response preparedness, right up to redefining the overall relationship between the two sectors.

In many cases, nonprofit organizations execute government policies through the provision of services to citizens. These relations tend to draw specific organizations into direct relations with specific government departments through contractual arrangements. In other cases, organizations may consider themselves independent of the governments and quite rightly may not be engaged in policy advice or service delivery. However, they are still increasingly affected by governments through the myriad of legislative arrangements and regulations governing their daily operations.

Relations between the two sectors are further embedded as public funding of nonprofit endeavours grows and nonprofit organizations become more dependent on public sources of revenue. Finally, the identification of the nonprofit sector as an entity and important force in the Canadian economy has meant that the operation, capacity, reach and impact of the sector is being more carefully monitored than ever before with manifold policy implications that this data will yield.

As a result, senior officials and managers in the nonprofit world must pay increasing attention to trends and shifts in government and in legislation affecting them or the sector as a whole. While the main responsibility for monitoring the relationship may be efficiently relegated to larger, well-resourced nonprofits or to umbrella organizations, managers of nonprofits are advised to keep abreast of new developments as they affect their particular organizations and to ensure that their interests are not overlooked or adversely affected. To perform this monitoring role effectively, nonprofit managers should have an understanding of:

- the pressures on government towards change and engagement of the nonprofit sector;

- the types of relationships being forged; and

- the challenges facing the two sectors as they strive to cooperate, including the recent attempt to redefine the parameters of governmental–nonprofit sector collaboration and co-operation. Each topic is addressed below.

Accountability, the Westminster Model of Government and Nonprofit Services

In a globalized and more competitive environment, governments are increasingly expected to build community, position their countries economically and ensure national security in all its forms, all while their capacity is being diminished through reorganization, streamlining and reducing expenditures (Reich (2001), pp. 207-10). The devolution of powers to external agencies and other governments has become a normal process of operation. The result is the increased need of government departments for collaboration with external agencies in the private and nonprofit sector and special operating agencies (Webb, (2005)). The role of government becomes one of surveillance and monitoring to a greater extent and less of direct action and involvement as a service provider with the citizenry.

The paradox is that government not only remains answerable for these policies, services and the quality of life enjoyed by citizens, but also must confront new expectations that are being formed. The emergence of an audit society, a citizenry that is more aggressive and less deferential, involves

> demands for greater transparency in the conduct of public business by political and administrative officials, increased public access to govern-

ment information, more explicit standards of public service entitlements and rights, enhanced citizen consultation and engagement in policy development and in the design and delivery of public services, and, among other things, public reporting on the performance of government

(Aucoin & Heintzman (2000), p. 245).

The result is a system that is measured less in terms of process and inputs and more in terms of outputs and outcomes. Efficiency and performance evaluation become the hallmarks of government action. Accountability is the new buzzword.

What is accountability in government? The constant is that accountability literally means "to hold to account", or "capable of explanation". In a political system like the Canadian one characterized by the Westminster parliamentary model of government, accountability translates into: the ability of citizens to hold governments responsible for their policies and programs through elections; the ability of politicians to oversee and ensure the responsiveness of the administrative branch of government to the public; and the power of the courts and tribunals to ensure that elected and non-elected public officials act in conformity with the powers of their offices. While the first two forms of accountability have traditionally operated in a hierarchical authority structure, the latter has imposed a horizontal check on the actions of government.

The notion of accountability within government is changing as governance becomes the new mode of operation (Sutherland (1991); Peters & Savoie (1999); *cf.* Thomas (1998)). Aucoin and Heintzman identify three central tenets of accountability within the parliamentary system as: "to control for the abuse and misuse of public authority"; "to provide assurance in respect to the effective use of public resources and adherence to public service values"; and, "to encourage and promote learning in pursuit of *continuous improvement* in governance and public management" (Aucoin & Heintzman (2000), pp. 244-45). They suggest that there is an inherent tension between these purposes of accountability but that improved performance and measurement (read efficiency) are not necessarily antithetical to improved accountability. The hierarchical models of control and the objective of assurance can be balanced with efficiency and more horizontal modes of governance. Decentralization does not always equate with improved efficiency, just as hierarchy, uniformity and central control may be efficient and responsive to public need.

Similarly, managing to outcomes and outputs may become just as ossified as a system of accountability measured on inputs and process. Good governance requires a certain fluidity and the right balance of the three purposes.

This change in government operations has had an impact on the relationship between the nonprofit sector and government as well as on the internal operations of the sector and organizations. To justify funding nonprofit organizations to provide services and programs previously administered by the public sector, governments must provide public assurances that the organizations will be held accountable for the efficiency and quality of those services and programs. Thus, while governments might be attracted by the flexibility enjoyed by nonprofit organizations in delivering goods and services, they will require certain operational methods to remain standard, such as financial management and accounting practices, key policy objectives including equity, forms of program evaluation and measurement, and adherence to human rights and environmental objectives. Public scandals involving nonprofit organizations in various Western nations have caused governments to impose more stringent public accountability requirements than in the past.

Government requirements for accountability have been largely accepted by nonprofit organizations but do cause consternation for five principal reasons. First, greater accountability to the public sector is not uniformly embraced across the nonprofit sector. While many nonprofit organizations have generally been improving their accountability mechanisms, others have eschewed transparent and public accountability in favour of retaining their status as private organizations and adhering to internal codes of good practice consistent with their missions.

Second, stricter public sector reporting requirements can increase bureaucracy within agencies at the cost of flexibility, informality, internal control over operations and responsiveness to members or beneficiaries.

Third, dependence on government funding and entering into shared arrangements with government departments may compromise an organization's independence and its ability to serve as an advocate for the sector or to criticize government policy in that area. Organizations may become stakeholders in policies instead of agents of change and improvement.

Fourth, in the quest for efficiency, governments have imposed upon nonprofit organizations principles of "new public management" including the market ethos,[3] transforming citizens into consumers and beneficiaries of services into clients. And yet, this designation may obscure the more meaningful and personal relationship between the nonprofit organizations and their members or community served.

Fifth, to meet the externally driven notions of accountability and efficiency, nonprofits may be obliged to move away from its traditional strengths such as diversity and a democratic (or grassroots) ethos. Professionalism instead of responsiveness becomes the standard.

These concerns are valid and require vigilance among organizations as they adapt to the changing environment. However, there are key benefits for organizations in improved and closer relations between the nonprofit and public sectors. For example, public funding provides a measure of financial security for organizations to achieve their goals, particularly after an organization establishes a good reputation with a department. Recent federal government improvements to contracting-out procedures and clarification of performance measures enhance the desirability of such contractual arrangements. Further, meeting public sector requirements for accountability and establishing a record with public partners, improves organizations' chances of securing funding from or collaborating with other nonprofit or private sector organizations. Finally, these relationships may result in closer harmonization of public and nonprofit objectives and definitions of public service, to the benefit of both, and most of all, to the Canadian public.[4] How to maximize the benefits of relationships and minimize the tensions is the focus of the rest of this section.

Understanding the Nature of the Relationship with Government

Traditionally, relationships between nonprofit organizations and governments have been characterized as conflictual or competitive. In this

---

[3] "New public management" refers to a new paradigm in government operations. It embraces: providing high quality services valued by citizens; increasing the autonomy and decision-making authority of public managers; measuring and rewarding organizational and individual performance; investing in the necessary human and technological resources to enhance performance; and valuing competitiveness and openness with regards to the delivery of public services by the nonprofit, private and public sectors. For a discussion of these values, see Blakeney and Borins (1998), esp. at pp. 156-58.

[4] For an excellent guide on introducing and improving accountability measures in nonprofit organizations, see: <http://www.vsi-isbc.ca/eng/funding/financial_guide/index.cfm>.

view, organizations were cast as critics of the state or as being threatened by state intervention. However, in a seminal study of the relationship between the state and the nonprofit sector, Benjamin Gidron, Ralph Kramer and Lester Salamon refuted this depiction in favour of a much more complex characterization of it (Gidron, Kramer & Salamon (1992)). They argue that the relationship between the state and the nonprofit sector will be influenced by the functions each side performs, the method of financing, the historical context, as well the political culture and social context of the relationship. In Canada, this would mean that, while some generalizations about the relationship might be made for the nonprofit sector at the federal level, these assumptions would not hold for the relationship between the state and sector in each province. Indeed, variations would even occur at the local or municipal level.

The relationship is even more complex. Since both governments and organizations have multiple roles, it is "quite possible for third sector organizations to have one set of relationships with government with respect to their service functions and another with respect to their representational or advocacy functions" (Gidron, Kramer & Salamon (1992, at p. 11)). While organizations might be critics of government policies and attack the very departments that fund them, governments may be equally torn between supporting organizations that deliver their programs and enforcing regulations. In the case of the federal government — Voluntary Sector Initiative (VSI), which brought together senior representatives from both sectors to redefine their relationship for the future, officials found themselves negotiating as equals at the VSI table but then dealing with each other in contractual arrangements at the level of department-to-organization with all the tensions implicit in those relations.

To make sense of the complexity in these relations, Gidron, Kramer and Salamon offer four basic models of the types of relationships that can exist between the state and sector but then distinguish between two types of functions involved in service delivery, namely, the financing and authorization of services, and the delivery of services. Figure 1 captures these models and their variations.

Figure 1: Models of Government–Nonprofit Sector Relations

Function	Model			
	Government Dominant	Dual	Collaborative	Third Sector Dominant
Finance	Government	Government/Third Sector	Government	Third Sector
Delivery	Government	Government/Third Sector	Third Sector	Third Sector

In the Government Dominant model, typical of modern welfare state arrangements, the government is the main provider of both funding resources and services to the public, with the nonprofit sector playing a largely supplementary role determined by the state. In the case of the Third Sector Dominant model of relationships, typically found where there is opposition to a large role for the state in social welfare provisions, organizations play the key role in financing and delivering services.

In the Dual model, the state and sector operate relatively autonomously of each other, both providing services and financing their operations. The sector might be either supplementary or complementary to the state but will be principal in its areas of operation.

In the Collaborative model, both act but tend to work together and most often with the state as funder and sector organizations as service providers. The degree of autonomy and shared functions will be dependent on negotiations. The political appeal of organizations combined with the difficulty of governments in monitoring sector organizations means that the collaborative arrangements are more common than is usually assumed (Gidron, Kramer & Salamon (1992, at pp. 16-19)).

In their study of state-sector relations in Canada, Susan Phillips and Katherine Graham accept that collaborative arrangements have become more common (Phillips & Graham (2000)). They suggest that it is useful to distinguish among the types of collaborative arrangements by placing them on a continuum as Figure 2 does.

Figure 2: Types of Collaborative Arrangements

Insular ➡➡ Collabitation ➡➡ Partnership ➡➡ Merger

At one end of the continuum, organizations operate autonomously with little or no collaboration with government, other organizations or the private sector. In the second phase, "collabitation",[5] organizations co-operate in some areas of the relationship but are competing for resources. The third phase foresees more co-operative relations with greater sharing of resources, risk, information and decision-making authority between the state and organizations. While equality is an ideal in a partnership, it cannot be assumed and the degree of equal authority in the relationship will depend on the negotiated terms. In the extreme form, collaboration can lead to mergers. State-imposed accountability requirements have meant that organizations are locked into the collabitation model of relations predominantly.

In positioning itself with the state, a nonprofit organization should understand the fundamental nature of the relationship. What is the best possible funding arrangement? Is the sector influential enough to negotiate more autonomy? How much does the state require its services? Are there other organizations that are likely to be competing for the same contract or resources? If so, are they better positioned? Is collaboration among competing organizations possible or desirable? Questions like these will determine the parameters of the funding negotiations.

The second step in understanding the nature of the relationship is to examine the service or function involved. Is it one the state has traditionally provided? If so, more state control might be expected. Is it new? Does the organization have expertise needed by government? If so, the organization can assume more dominance in the relationship and negotiate for more autonomy. Is it an area better shared by both state and sector organizations? If so, the lines of decision-making and the scope of authority of both actors must be clearly delineated to ensure lines of responsibility are clear and conflict is minimized.

The third step in an organization's calculations concerns its advocacy or representational role. Where the state is dominant and the

---

[5]   The authors constructed this term to capture the idea of both collaboration and competition.

organization is more dependent on state funding and authorization, or where the organization has become a stakeholder in policies through shared authority, the organization will need to be more circumspect in its public criticism of government. As autonomy increases, organizations have more latitude to criticize government policies and programs, bearing in mind that positive relationships are more likely to develop in future when the criticisms are judiciously and discreetly offered and, on the state side, capable of acceptance.

The nature of the relationship between the state and organizations, and in particular the ability of organizations to perform an advocacy role, is heavily influenced in Canada by the federal regulatory regime in operation. A. Paul Pross and Kernaghan Webb document the regulatory reach of the federal government on the nonprofit sector in a groundbreaking study (Pross & Webb (2003)). They argue that viewing federal authority over the nonprofit sector as largely determined by its constitutional jurisdiction over taxation is misleading and too narrow. Instead, they identify a more comprehensive but often conflicting regulatory regime that encompasses seven areas of authority over charities and nonprofit organizations:

• Accountability

• Regulation of access to policy formulation

• Corporate status

• Direct funding

• Tax expenditure funding

• Regulation of lobbying

• Regulation of participation in elections

Each can impact on organizations and affect their operations in important ways.

The first two forms of regulatory measures range from the requirement for filing a tax form each year, to the obligatory audits and evaluations associated with government grants and programs, to adherence to criteria to maintain access to policy formation, to more informal requirements to ensure trust and co-operation between nonprofit and public officials. Corporate status for nonprofit organizations is desirable, especially to limit directors' liability, facilitate legal transactions, secure government contributions funding or raise the level of public donations by establishing a reputable form, and to ensure organizational stability and structure. However, acquiring such status may be expensive, confusing and time-consuming for many organizations while yielding few direct benefits (Pross & Webb (2003, at pp. 77-79)).[6]

Similarly, obtaining recognized status under the *Income Tax Act*[7] may result in direct benefits for organizations, including the ability to issue tax receipts for donations in addition to being exempt from paying taxes (this latter provision applies to registered nonprofit corporations whether or not they are charities under the *Income Tax Act*). However, as with corporate status, obtaining charities status may be time-consuming, expensive and confusing, and imposes restrictive standards on the expenditure of funds, including the obligation to spend money as promised when raised, and the duty to spend a majority (usually 80 per cent) of funds on charitable activities, the restriction on nonpartisan political activities (10 per cent of resources), and the need to meet a public benefits test.

Some of the burdens of charitable status have been eased by recent federal activity flowing out of the VSI, including streamlining of the tax form, making the process for application and appeals of charitable status more transparent, and creating a nonprofit advisory board to the Canada Revenue Agency.[8] However, more work is required to enable nonprofits to obtain the full benefits of this tax expenditure. It should be noted too, that size of a charity or nonprofit organization will affect the application of these regulations.

The other three federal regulatory measures can circumscribe the behaviour of charities in important ways. While the impact of contribution agreements is discussed below under challenges facing nonprofits, it is important to mention the impact of regulations on electoral participation and lobbying.

The federal *Lobbyists Registration Act*[9] requires the formal registration of lobbyists who are attempting to influence government policy and who are either employees of an organization with a significant amount (20 per cent) of their time dedicated to that purpose or consult-

---

[6] *Ibid.*, pp. 77-79. Federal attempts to introduce a *Nonprofit Corporations Act* have only mitigated these problems somewhat.

[7] R.S.C. 1985, c. 1 (5th Supp.).

[8] For a discussion of changes to federal regulations affecting corporate and tax status, see: <http://www.vsi-isbc.ca/eng/regulations/index.cfm>.

[9] R.S.C. 1985, c. 44 (4th Supp.).

ant lobbyists acting on behalf of an organization. However, as Pross and Webb point out, the requirements for registration are ambiguous and do not affect activities like "responses to government requests for consultation or in the form of appearances before inquiries, parliamentary committees, and so on" (Pross & Webb (2003, at p. 98)). Given the limited amount of "pure lobbying" done in the sector and the ambiguity around the need to register, the legislation has limited effect on organizations. However, managers of nonprofit organizations would be well advised to consult the registrar about the need to register if they do wish to influence government policy on contentious or important political issues.

In a similar vein, electoral regulations affecting the ability of nonprofit organizations to advertise during elections or engage in partisan activities do not apply to the vast majority of nonprofits (Pross and Webb (2003, at pp. 101-04)). While advocacy organizations might see a benefit in direct partisan engagement in an election, most organizations would value their nonpartisan status. The regulations on partisan activities do not impede the ability of organizations to track issues during campaigns and conduct public awareness campaigns of party positions and issues. However, the caution is for nonprofits to remain objective not critical or partisan lest they run afoul of election guidelines.

While federal regulations are significant and may be considered to constitute a "regime" governing nonprofits as Pross and Webb conclude, most nonprofit organizations will have more daily interaction with provincial/territorial and municipal levels of government. For example, the *National Survey of Nonprofit and Voluntary Organizations* found that: "Most organizations rely more on provincial government funding than they do on funding from federal or municipal sources" (Hall *et al.* (2004, at pp. 25, 23).) Further, most organizations provide their services locally (about 64 per cent), regionally (about 19 per cent) or province-wide (about 9 per cent), thus necessitating more contact with the provincial and local levels of government (Hall *et al.* (2004, at p. 15)). While the variations among these jurisdictions are too numerous to allow a summary, nonprofit managers should inform themselves of the regulatory policies and practices within their jurisdictions and government themselves accordingly. Most governments at the provincial and territorial level have branches that deal with the nonprofit sector and can direct organizations to other areas of government that will affect their operation in most areas of nonprofit activities.

Challenges in Developing and Maintaining Relationships with Governments

The challenges in developing and maintaining relationships with governments will depend largely on the nature of the relationship. Is it primarily a policy, service delivery, funding or advocacy relationship? In many cases, organizations may have multiple relations with government departments and may have to manage competing sets of requirements. This section reviews some of the challenges in each type of relationship briefly.

There are three main challenges in developing and maintaining a policy relationship with government.

(1)   An organization must gain access to the relevant government actors in a policy field. While access to politicians may help place an issue on the policy agenda, to maximize influence over the longer term, organizations should build relations with senior officials in the departments. Obtaining access involves establishing an organization's legitimacy and policy research and development capacity in the area of interest. In an environment where there are a number of organizations operating, influence will be diluted by conflicting advice to officials. In these cases, organizations are most effective if they co-ordinate policy advice.

(2)   The second challenge involves maintaining policy access. This is critical to long-term policy influence since legislative or regulatory changes can be ongoing or take place over a number of years and through a number of changes of government. Maintaining good policy relations with senior officials involves adequate resources to track changes and monitor government activity and to conduct research, to deliver reliable advice, and to understand what is negotiable and what is not in any policy discussions. While most of the relationship will occur in private or semi-private meetings, organizations should be prepared to make submissions to parliamentary committees or inquiries, and, when necessary, to use the media responsibly to build support on an issue.[10]

(3)   Finally, organizations must assess the quality and extent of their influence on a policy issue when determining whether to engage. Are they merely being brought into policy discussions by officials

---

[10]   The use of media or public lobbying tactics requires discretion since embarrassing officials is likely to produce resistance or resentment in government officials towards the organization. If an organization releases any information officials consider private, then trust will decline, eroding the relationship.

to legitimize a chosen policy route or is their advice genuinely sought? The answer will determine whether and how they allocate resources to a policy relationship.

The types of relationships constructed and maintained between the public and nonprofit sector to deliver services are as varied and intricate as the nature of services available to Canadians. The nature of the relationship will depend on the funding relationship, the type of service, the relative strengths of the bureaucracy and nonprofits, the importance of the issue to the political agenda, and the working relationships established between the public and nonprofit actors. However, three areas are especially important.

First, who is in control? Is the organization an agent of the public sector or is it an actor with decision-making authority? Which role is more acceptable and desirable for solid or improved service delivery?

Second, when agreeing to engage in service delivery, an organization must provide a realistic assessment of its strengths and capacity. Can it manage the service without overtaxing its resources or detracting from service provision in another area of operation? Are the public sector resources adequate to sponsor the service, including the internal costs to the organization? The terms must be carefully negotiated.

Third, organizations must learn to say no when arrangements are not adequately resourced or the mission and objectives of the nonprofit will be compromised unduly. Before refusing contracts, however, organizations should consider whether changes could be negotiated to make an arrangement more acceptable. In this case, a strong policy relationship with the relevant department and officials will be important.

The funding relationships between the federal government and nonprofit community have undergone significant changes in recent years. As the Canadian Council on Social Development has documented, funding matters. It is not just the amount of funding that makes a difference, but the type of funding regime (Scott (2003 and 2003 Summary)). In this seminal work, Scott tracks the shift from core funding to project funding, noting the impact that this change has on the ability of organizations to maintain operations and their missions as their administrative functions are starved of resources. Instability of funding, shorter funding terms, increased reporting requirements and the need to collaborate with other organizations to secure funding add to the operation costs of organizations which are not compensated in the contracts gained. Although the sector is resilient and has adapted remarkably well to the pressures, all things considered, Scott names some worrisome trends including: volatility of resources which affect an organization's stability and capacity to provide consistent quality in services; mission drift as organizations vie for funding; a loss of infrastructure that sustains the organizations; reporting overload caused by the concurrent loss of staff and multiple reporting requirements and forms by multiple funders; precarious financial structures and dependence on maintaining multiple funding sources to survive; an advocacy chill as organizations attempt to maintain good relations with multiple funders with divergent directives; and human resource fatigue in an increasingly competitive and onerous environment. The pressure of the new funding regime identified by Scott constrains the creative and longer-term work that has characterized the sector.

A key point of tension in the funding relationship between the federal government and the nonprofit sector has been the move towards contribution agreements and away from sustaining grants. Contribution agreements are favoured within the public sector as a means of ensuring stricter performance measures and reporting requirements consistent with the Auditor General's guidelines. These contracts involve specified terms and outputs and strict reporting requirements (usually quarterly progress reports, financial reports and an independent assessment). Eligibility requirements for organizations are also strict. Protracted negotiations and public sector approval of the agreements, heavy reporting requirements (often disproportionate to the amounts involved), lapses or delays in funding as reporting documents are filed and approved, monitoring of contracts and inconsistent standards for approval, as well as changing requirements in the agreements, have produced frustration for both public and nonprofit sector officials whose common objective is to ensure funds are available for the provision of reliable, stable and worthy services and causes. However, the auditor's chill in the public sector has meant that these accountability measures are likely to remain despite efforts made in the VSI to streamline negotiations and provide more flexibility in funding arrangements.

How can nonprofit managers cope in this increasingly volatile, competitive and unpredictable funding environment? Marilyn Struthers advises organizations not just to cope with change and strive for stability but to accept change as the constant and recognize it as an opportunity to thrive. She identifies four main characteristics of organizations that enable them to obtain financial vibrancy, defined as "the capacity of an organization to transition from one sustainable moment to the next" (Struthers (2004, at pp. 2-3)). First, organizations must build an organizational culture and architecture that allows for fluidity in roles that can be adapted to build links with other organizations without losing identity or mission focus. These linkages may include umbrella organizations, networks of information sharing, global ties with similar organizations, strategic alliances, in-kind exchanges, joint ventures and collaborative planning in addition to developing a long-term, networking relationship with funders. Second, they must engage in strategic planning with multiple stakeholders, including reflection upon and learning from past experiences, and focusing their missions. Third, they should pursue funding sources that "further their mission while generating revenues such as fee-for-service projects, developing research capacity or marketing training" rather than developing adjunctive activities that raise funds (Struthers (2004, at p. 8)). In short, they must focus on the creation of social value through revenues consonant with their missions and organizational strengths. Finally, they should "have a strong and creative understanding of organizational financial management and accountability", that results in a deliberate resourcing strategy consonant with missions and values (Struthers (2004, at p. 9)). Developing these traits will prepare organizations to enter into a more creative and productive alliance with funders.

Nonprofit organizations must be innovative and active in the new funding regime. This includes monitoring government department Web sites for new funding opportunities, foundations and granting agencies for changes in programs and requirements, and sharing possible funding opportunities with other organizations. Given constrained resources in organizations, collaboration among organizations in sourcing and applying for funding maximizes opportunities for securing new streams of funding. It can also include risk-taking and innovation in structure. For example, when public sector funding to the arts community was becoming more constrained and less dependable in Alberta in the 1990s, the Glenbow Museum undertook the innovative step of moving to nongovernmental organization status, which allowed it to compete for international funding and broadened its activities to include international co-operative endeavours. This strategy has been successful and resulted in new and exciting art exhibits but is not without its own complications.

In all of the relations built between nonprofits and governments or between nonprofit and government funders, one ingredient is critical to success. Nonprofit organizations must be true to their mission and purpose but flexible in the means of obtaining their objectives.

Sector Wide Relations: The Significance of the Voluntary Sector Initiative

The Federal Government – Voluntary Sector Initiative (VSI) was a five-year, $94.6 million initiative launched jointly by the voluntary sector and the federal government in 1999. Born out of two reports issued in 1999 (Panel on Accountability and Governance for the Voluntary Sector (1999); Government of Canada/Voluntary Sector Joint Initiative (1999)) the VSI was intended to bring together senior officials from both sectors to redefine and strengthen their relationship. The work was carried out by the seven joint tables, named the Joint Coordinating Committee (JCC), the Accord Table, the Awareness Table, the Capacity Table, the Information Management and Technology Table, the Regulatory Table and the National Volunteerism Initiative Table (Phillips (2001a); Brock (2001); *cf.* Brock (2003). In addition, the sector created two working groups to address the issues of funding and advocacy while the federal government kept its participation on these topics in-house.

Voluntary sector participation was led by a steering group of senior representatives from national organizations and the members on the joint tables were selected from a wide range of national, provincial and local organizations through an open process (Brock (2002)). The federal process was more closed and appeared more closely directed. The federal government created a Voluntary Sector Task Force (VSTF) housed within the Privy Council Office to support the development of a new relationship with the voluntary sector. Most of the $94.6 million flowed through other departments to the Joint Tables and those departments provided support to those tables. Within government, a Reference Group of Ministers, headed by the President of the Treasury Board and including eight Cabinet ministers, provided political leadership. A corresponding group of assistant deputy ministers provided executive direction. Subsequently, oversight of implementation of the work of the VSI was handed to Heritage Canada and now resides with Social Development Canada.

The VSI vision document reveals five major outcomes with specific deliverables (outputs) (Joint Coordinating Committee (2002). First, the VSI was intended to improve and sustain a dialogue or collaboration between the federal government and voluntary sector in areas of mutual interest with the broader goal of improving quality of life for Canadians. The specific deliverable was an *Accord* signed by representatives of both sectors on December 5, 2001, with subsidiary implementation agreements in the form of codes of good practice in the areas of policy dialogue and funding, annual reporting requirements, and ongoing mechanisms to ensure a continued relationship (Voluntary Sector Initiative (*Accord*)).

Modelled upon the United Kingdom idea of compacts, the *Accord* is a framework agreement intended to set the tone of future relations between the two sectors (Voluntary Sector Initiative (*Accord*)). The document outlines a shared vision and common principles, and a mutual commitment to future collaboration, and is intended to strengthen the relationship between the two sectors by encouraging better partnering practices, fostering consistent treatment of voluntary organizations across government and promoting a better understanding within each sector of the constraints, operations and practices of the other.[11] The *Accord* underscores the separate accountability requirements of each sector and then promises transparency, high standards of conduct and sound management as they work together, as well as monitoring and reporting on the results (Voluntary Sector Initiative (*Accord*, at p. 9)). A narrow construction of this section of the *Accord* could justify limited performance evaluations and just good management practices. However, a more robust reading would impose evaluation standards consistent with the values identified as underlying the *Accord* — democracy, active citizenship, equality, diversity, inclusion, and social justice (Voluntary Sector Initiative (*Accord*, at p. 7)).

The *Codes of Good Practice*, attending the *Accord*, are operational documents. So, for example, the *Code on Policy Dialogue* is intended to fulfil the *Accord*'s commitment to implement its provisions by establishing an ongoing dialogue between the sectors in the development and design of policies and programs (Voluntary Sector Initiative (*Code on Policy*, at p. 2)). To facilitate this, "Both sectors will provide feedback to their respective constituencies on the full range of views expressed, and clearly communicate how this input has been considered in the public policy process" (Voluntary Sector Initiative (*Code on Policy*, at p. 7)). In addition, the voluntary sector is expected to provide feedback to

---

[11] For detailed analyses of the birth and content of the *Accord*, see Phillips (2003) ("In Accordance"); and Phillips (2001a).

government on policies and processes with an eye to improving performance (Voluntary Sector Initiative (*Code on Policy*, at pp. 8-9)). Similarly, the *Code on Funding* pledges to sustain the capacity of voluntary organizations to serve Canadians through direct funding as well as indirect mechanisms such as taxation measures (Voluntary Sector Initiative (*Code on Funding*, at pp. 2-4)). The *Funding Code* commits the voluntary sector to sound financial, board, ethical, administrative and monitoring practices and the federal government to flexible application and accountability standards subject to effective protection of public money, consideration of alternative monitoring mechanisms, agreement on measurable results and clear roles, and respect for diversity in imposing accountability requirements.

The second intention of the VSI was to strengthen the capacity of the voluntary sector to serve Canadians well. This was realized in the development of strategic approaches to building human resources, financial management and information technology and management capacities with the necessary resources, and in the experimental Sectoral Involvement in Departmental Policy Development (SIDPD), which aimed at building policy and research capacity in the sector by flowing funds through departments to selected voluntary sector partners to enhance their capacity to collaborate with government, develop, implement and evaluate policy, represent citizens more effectively, mobilize participation in the sector, and ensure accountability. SIDPD was limited in scope but represented an opportunity for changing the policy-making process and ensuring that the principles of the VSI penetrated to the operational levels of government activity.

Third, the VSI was intended to increase awareness of the contributions made by volunteers and role of the voluntary sector in Canadian society. The VSI was much more successful in recognizing volunteer activities during the International Year of the Volunteer (2001). The media and awareness campaigns for the voluntary sector have been more limited in effect.

Fourth, the VSI addressed the need for more information about the sector and its role in Canadian life with the creation and funding of ongoing mechanisms such as the Canadian Survey on Giving, Volunteering and Participating, the Statistics Canada Satellite Account to the System of National Accounts, and the National Survey of Nonprofit and Voluntary Organizations (NSNVO).[12] These data collection

---

[12] The results of both the CSGVP and the NSNVO are available at: <www.nonprofitscan.org>.

devices will provide the longitudinal data so desperately required to map the sector and its trends, and to inform policy decisions about the sector, as well as provide more exact information on the contribution of the sector to the nation's social and economic life. They coincide with the Capacity Table funding for the inclusion of Canada in the high-profile Johns Hopkins comparative country studies of the third sector — a significant omission over the past 20 years. Further, the NSNVO provides insight into the collective state of financial, human and administrative capacity of organizations for the first time.[13]

Finally, the VSI envisioned a streamlined regulatory framework, revised tax form with clarified definitions of allowable activities for charities, and a review of liability for members of the board of directors of organizations. A further objective of achieving clarity, consistency and transparency in the funding relationship between the sector and state was undertaken through the federal funding review, the code of funding practice and a strategic funding approach. Although the federal government consulted the sector on these reforms, it retained control over the final shape of them. While the federal government has reviewed the definition of "charities" and shortened the tax form, further regulatory reforms continue to be discussed between the two sectors. The VSI did not come to terms with the funding and advocacy issued posed by the sector.

Preliminary assessments are divided on the effectiveness of the VSI. More time is needed before any definitive conclusions can be formed as to its impact on relations between the sectors (See Brock (2005, 2004)).[14]

---

[13] Consortium members include Canadian Centre for Philanthropy, Alliance de Recherche Universités-Communautés en Economie Sociale at UQAM, the Canada West Foundation (CWF), the Canadian Council on Social Development (CCSD), the Capacity Development Network at the University of Victoria, the Community Services Council of Newfoundland and Labrador (CSC), Queen's University School of Policy Studies, the Secretariat on Voluntary Sector Sustainability of the Manitoba Voluntary Sector Initiative, and Statistics Canada.

[14] In late 2005, the VSI Joint Evaluation Committee released "The Voluntary Sector Initiative Process Evaluation: Final Report available at: http://www.vsi-isbc.ca/eng/relationship/evaluations.cfm; and "An Evaluation of the Sectoral Involvement in Departmental Policy Development (SIDPD)" at: <http://www.vsi-isbc.ca/eng/policy/sidpd_report.cfm>.

PARTNERING WITH THE CORPORATE SECTOR: FROM ANTAGONISTS TO ALLIES

The relationship between the nonprofit and for-profit sectors has never been a simple one. On the one hand, nonprofit organizations have often found themselves in operation to serve the very people that private enterprise has "failed". Thus, some nonprofit leaders have emerged as trenchant critics of the corporate sector for its failure to engage in sustained and positive community action and for the social costs of doing business. On the other hand, traditionally, many nonprofit organizations and businesses have worked together, sometimes warily, to provide services and benefits to Canadians. Examples of these partnerships include corporate donations to nonprofits enabling them to conduct their work, joint partnerships in activities such as the Royal Bank Run for the Cure, and corporate promotion of charitable activities.[15] But much of their relationship has been predicated on independent coexistence.

These relationships are currently in transition. As governments have shifted from hierarchical modes of operation towards governance and horizontal relations, nonprofits and businesses have had to re-evaluate and re-orient their policy and public roles. Nonprofits and businesses have moved towards viewing each other as allies more than antagonists with the urging of governments.

The Shift Towards Partnerships

Corporations and nonprofit organizations are increasingly moving to more co-operative and sustained arrangements. The pressures towards greater nonprofit and corporate co-operation derive from different sources. As forces of globalization have increased economic pressures domestically, corporations and nonprofits have realized the need to work together to ensure national competitiveness and to mitigate the fallout from corporate failures. New technologies have encouraged citizens to expect more not just of their governments but also of corporations and nonprofits in addressing social problems. Citizens increasingly expect seamless services requiring the three sectors to

---

[15] In the first case, the relationship is monetary. In the second case, officials from both sectors will be involved in planning, running and participating in the event. In the third case, a corporation will take an active role and have a vested interest in the promotion of a cause, much like The Body Shop does with respect to women's health.

work together. Social activists, environmentalists and the Aboriginal community have all engaged in sustained action against corporations to impress upon the public and the corporations the costs of doing business and the need for co-operation with community organizations.

Each sector is re-evaluating its relationships as well. Governments have been reducing funding for nonprofits, requiring them to look to the corporate sector for more sustained sources of revenue while encouraging corporations to accept more responsibility for social ills. Corporations have found that mere association with good causes through cheque-book charity or through occasional alliances is no longer sufficient to ensure a positive public image (Dunham & Pierce (1989); Forcese (1997); Global Business Responsibility Resource Centre; Selley (1998); Verschoor & Entine). Socially conscious employees and shareholders increasingly expect corporations to engage in building community relations.

For their part, nonprofit organizations have realized that the relationship is not just one of dependence on businesses for funding, but a mutual one in which they can provide businesses with community knowledge and more legitimacy as creators of social value. Cross-sectoral co-operation is also necessary to begin to address increasingly complex, polycentric public policy issues that affect all segments of society.

Two examples illustrate the increasingly intertwined relationships and roles of the three sectors. When confronted with more frequent and alarming shootings and gang violence in Toronto in 2005, Mayor David Miller called on nonprofits to provide more youth services and counselling, and on large corporations to provide educational and employment opportunities to youths, as well as on public sector agencies such as the police and the courts to enforce coercive measures, and social services to reinforce support systems.

When a tsunami hit Southeast Asian countries at the end of 2004 and when Hurricane Katrina struck New Orleans, military and state aid agencies teamed with nonprofit organizations that had valuable local knowledge and networks, and with businesses that had necessary technologies and skills, to provide relief in a more effective and immediate manner than any sector alone could provide. Despite differences and tensions, the three sectors are learning to act together to serve citizens better.

The Types of Relationships

Co-operation among the sectors can take various forms. Given that public–nonprofit relations have been addressed extensively above, this section will concentrate on the main types of relationships emerging between the private and nonprofit sectors. Three main categories of relationships have emerged: competitors, partners or allies, and dependants. Each has its strengths and its points of caution for the sector.

First, nonprofit and for-profit organizations may still operate as competitors in key areas of public service as well as in new areas as the public sector devolves responsibilities. For example, in recent years the provision of home care services to the elderly and sick has been the locus of increasing competition between the nonprofit and for-profit sectors. In one case study in which the Victorian Order of Nurses faced competition from for-profit organizations for public contracts, the nonprofit experienced lowered efficiency and higher costs in providing services to a smaller, more dispersed community. The agency was forced to seek commercial opportunities and charge fees for services, thus fundamentally altering the culture of the organization in the eyes of its employees (Tindale & MacLachlan (2001, at pp. 199, 200-01, 204-08)). In another study of nonprofits and for-profits providing homecare services in the same community, Luc Thériault and Sandra Salhani noted the emergence of a two-tier structure of services: poorer service recipients could not afford the costlier and often more extensive services offered by private care firms. They emphasized that nonprofits could maintain their organizational culture and level of services if they did not overstep their capacity to provide services and developed extensive networks with other providers. This study concluded that co-operation between all three sectors is developing as the need for home care services increases (Thériault & Salhani (2001, at pp. 232-23, 243-45)). Even competitive relations may produce opportunities for co-operative and productive relations.

Partnerships and alliances between the two sectors can assume a wide range of forms. Martha Parker, then Executive Director for Volunteer Calgary, observed in her study of partnerships between nonprofits and for-profits that corporate involvement may ascend from arm's length to full engagement, as Figure 3 illustrates (Parker (2000, at p. 37)).

Figure 3: Partnerships between Nonprofits and For-profits

Cheque Book ➡️➡️	Strategic ➡️➡️	Community ➡️➡️	Corporate ➡️➡️	Corporate
Philanthropy	Philanthropy	Investment	Social	Citizenship
			Responsibility	

Cheque book philanthropy is the "old" style of corporate interaction with worthy causes in the sector. Strategic philanthropy is becoming more prevalent. Corporate dollars are targeted with investment strategies to build corporate image, and employees may volunteer for good causes as a formal or informal part of their corporate duties. Cause-related marketing, where a corporation attaches its logo to a nonprofit cause to publicly associate sympathy for the issue with its products as a means of market retention or expansion, is an example of strategic philanthropy. Community investment is the next stage, where corporations identify causes that are related to their business objectives, are proactive in the investment strategies by seeking out partners, are more closely involved in the activities undertaken within the partnership, and expect greater accountability and performance results. In the areas of corporate social responsibility and corporate citizenship, corporations integrate social values into business functions, adopt social audits, implement sound social, environmental and ethical practices, and demonstrate leadership working in tandem with the other sectors.

Nonprofit partnering develops along a parallel continuum according to Parker, as Figure 4 demonstrates (Parker (2000, at p. 38)).

Figure 4: Nonprofit Partnering

Service ➡️➡️	Strategic ➡️➡️	Partnerships ➡️➡️	Nonprofit ➡️➡️	Nonprofit
Provider/	Positioning	&	Social	Citizenship
Entitlement		Collaborations	Responsibility	

At the lower end of the spectrum, nonprofits operate in isolation and are dependent on key funders while focusing on their missions and performing good works. At the level of strategic positioning, nonprofits begin to diversify their funding needs and compete for corporate dollars. They may engage in some sectoral collaborations but will maintain a focus on their missions and markets. At the level of partnerships and collaborations, nonprofits demonstrate knowledge of community issues valuable to corporate partners, are proactive, engage in enterprising thinking including brand equity, build business capacity, supportive organizational culture and cross-sectoral partnerships, and adopt more accountability measures. They adapt business practices to serve their causes. In the cases of social responsibility and citizenship, nonprofits develop and share best practices, adopt value-added strategies, contextualize their narrower organizational interests within broader social issues, commit to building community capacity and promoting civil society, and demonstrate leadership while working with the other sectors. Nonprofits emerge from positions of dependency and isolation to equality with the other sectors in serving citizens.

Finding the Right Partner

Partnerships can be beneficial to nonprofits when right, and disastrous if poorly chosen. Some cautionary notes must be sounded in reviewing relations between nonprofits and for-profits. Nonprofits need to develop and maintain a clear understanding of both their mission and their capacities before engaging with for-profits. In some cases, a dependent funding relationship may serve the needs of the nonprofit and its clients. To engage in a more extensive relationship might jeopardize the existing quality of services. However, suspicion of the corporate sector or its motives should not hamper an organization from developing better or closer ties with for-profit funders or partners when the ability of the organization to execute its mission will be improved. As nonprofits engage more closely with corporations, though, they will need to research the relationship for their interests in more depth and engage in discussions with other stakeholders about the terms of the partnerships. A critical part of the analysis is the benefits that the nonprofit brings to the relationship: too often these aspects are undervalued and underexploited. And, as in any relationship, know your partner and the skeletons in the closets. The better prepared the nonprofit is to engage with corporations, the better the alliance will fit its objectives. This means learning to say "no" when the fit is wrong. Alliances may turn sour because of personalities, mission drift, conflicting objectives and interests or changes in circumstances. In these cases, nonprofits must be prepared to cut ties. Corporations can be seductive but if enticing incentives to partner distort the culture, mission or operation of the nonprofit in unacceptable ways, nonprofits must remain virtuous and cultivate other more satisfying, even if less exciting, relationships.

A critical ingredient for building relationships between for-profits and nonprofits is mutual self-interest. From their extensive involvement with these alliances in the United States, Shirley Sagawa and Eli Segal conclude that:

> In working more closely together, organizations need not, and should not, abandon their central missions. Over-commercialization of nonprofit organizations could undermine their legitimacy, discourage donors and volunteers, and cause them to neglect those who are hardest, and costliest, to serve. Businesses that put social change ahead of profits risk losing shareholders and customers, and ultimately, threaten their own survival. The key is for business and social sector organizations alike to strike the right balance as they move in these new directions.

(Sagawa & Segal (2000, at p. 238))

Instead, by identifying their self-interests and then finding common interests with partners that embrace them, the most successful relationships will be formed. Sagawa and Segal go on to remind nonprofit and for-profit organizations of several elements that have to be watched in order to sustain their joint ventures all captured by the acronym "COMMON": Communicate with each other and internally; seek out new Opportunities and grow in the relationship; ensure both sides Mutually contribute to and benefit from the relationship in ways appropriate to their organizations; engage at Multiple levels and identify champions of the relationship and cause in both organizations; keep the relationship Open-ended with the termination point when it is not longer working or with the possibility of renewal if a termination date has been set for a specific exchange; and, create New value for both partners (Sagawa & Segal (2000, at pp. 213-33)).

Corporate and nonprofit partnerships face a serious challenge in Canada. Globalization has resulted in two challenging trends. First, corporate restructuring and consolidation have meant that smaller and rural communities have lost many of their immediate ties with the business community. Head offices often make decisions on partnering and levels of donations, with the discretion of regional managers increasingly diminished.[16] The personal faces of nonprofit and for-profit organizations are lost in this new world. Thus, to a greater extent

---

[16] This fact emerged twice during the interviews Jan Elliott, David Brook and I did with voluntary sector leaders on globalization (Brock, Brook & Elliott (2003, at pp. 18-20)). In addition, work with voluntary sector boards in Kingston has revealed that the discretion of regional managers in banks and corporations is limited to under $5,000, thus limiting local control over dollars spent.

than ever before, nonprofits need to engage in proactive partnering strategies involving *other* nonprofit organizations when they approach for-profit partners with potential common interests.

Second, globalization has witnessed the movement of more corporate headquarters out of the country (Brock, Brook & Elliott (2003, at pp. 18-20)). Again, this increases the competitiveness of the donor and partnering pool. However, in these relationships, nonprofits can offer valuable local knowledge not available as readily to corporate headquarters to ensure more effective use of corporate resources. Nonprofits should not discount partners from "away".

BUILDING WITH OTHER NONPROFITS: THE CHALLENGES OF FORMING ALLIANCES

Nonprofits can form alliances with each other. These relationships may take the form of umbrella organizations, coalitions to lobby funders or policymakers, strategic alliances, joint endeavours, and even mergers. The previous sections of this chapter have indicated that the incentives for nonprofits to ally with other nonprofits are growing. Katherine Scott explains what is old and new in these pressures (Scott (2003, at p. 51)):

> Increasingly, public and private funders are encouraging nonprofit and voluntary groups to form partnerships or coalitions to advance their work. Nonprofit and voluntary groups have always worked with a variety of partners — including community representatives, other nonprofit and voluntary organizations, local business and funders — to develop and implement programs. As well, nonprofit and voluntary organizations have a long history of joint advocacy, working with various communities of interest to promote change, such as alleviating child poverty or expanding public support for the arts. What is new is the call by funders to submit joint funding proposals in an increasingly wide range of areas.

Nonprofit organizations are using past techniques to adapt to the new funding environment but the "forced" alliances are not always the best arrangements for citizens being served. For example, if two agencies have similar missions but serve different populations, the alliance might result in compromises in service delivery that disadvantage some of the recipients. This is particularly the case with respect to ethnic and racial minority services versus services provided to the general population. Similarly, two organizations might provide services which appear similar but are different in operation. Public choice is reduced and quality of service delivery might suffer as operations are rationalized. Finally, two organizations in a region might provide the same service but the geographic and cultural needs of the recipients might be different. This is particularly apt in the case of rural and urban organizations.

The ingredients for successful alliances have been outlined in the sections on government and corporate relations. However, some characteristics of relationships among nonprofits should be mentioned before examining some of the questions surrounding these alliances.

First, nonprofits co-operate. As the National Survey of Nonprofit and Voluntary Organizations documented (Hall *et al.* (2004, at p. 25)):

> A substantial amount of funds is transferred among nonprofit and voluntary organizations. The primary function of some registered charities is to provide funding to other organizations. In addition, organizations may operate as part of a larger network of organizations and may, for example, transfer funds to the national arm of their organization. Finally, organizations may also transfer funds to pay for services provided by other organizations. Twenty-seven per cent of all nonprofit and voluntary organizations transfer or disburse funds to other organizations. These transfers make up almost $4.7 billion ... or 4% of total revenues.

Second, while about one-quarter of organizations identify collaborating with other organizations as a problem, this does not rank as a serious concern very often (only 2 per cent) for organizations and remains relatively low on the list of problems and challenges facing organizations (Hall *et al.* (2004, at pp. 43-44)).

How well are these relationships working? In a survey of civil society leaders, Don Embuldeniya reflected on the quality of these relationships. Since the 1980s, organizations have increasingly been forming umbrella and networking organizations to support and promote volunteerism, fund development and leadership. However, civil society leaders have questioned the capacity of these organizations to represent members effectively. Only 57 per cent of leaders suggested that umbrella organizations have the capacity (financial and human resources, knowledge, information technology) to represent the interests of their members. On the positive side, approximately 65 per cent believe that these organizations integrate members into decision-making (Embuldeniya (2001, at pp. 11-12)).[17] Similarly, while leaders realized the benefits of alliances among organizations, they were skeptical of the ability of organizations to form those alliances. About

---

[17] This was a targeted survey of 104 key leaders.

three-quarters of leaders said that organizations "seldom or only sometimes collaborate across different subsectors to further social and community well-being", over 50 per cent believe organizations seldom or only sometimes join alliances with other organizations and almost 50 per cent believe organizations join with citizens (Embuldeniya (2001, at pp. 12-13)). And as the National Survey discovered, these alliances are most problematic for organizations whose primary activity areas include international aid (40 per cent), law, advocacy and politics (35 per cent), universities and colleges (39 per cent), health (32 per cent) and social services (30 per cent). The least problematic for collaboration were the areas of development and housing (14 per cent) and religion (14 per cent) (Hall *et al.* (2004, at p. 46)).

One noticeable effect of the VSI has been the increase in regional, provincial and national coalitions. Their sustainability and effectiveness have yet to be determined.

Forced arrangements raise more concerns than voluntary partnerships. Nonprofit leaders recognize and acknowledge the benefits of sharing information and best practices especially as resources are more constrained and the strategic value of alliances in achieving policy or practical changes or delivering services. Where time and resources are available to prepare and build these alliances, they tend to be more successful. While territorial or personality clashes may impede the formation of alliances among nonprofits, generally the culture is one of co-operation.

However, in the case of funder-imposed partnerships, more problems arise. While such alliances may be useful for leveraging funders' dollars, in many cases what appear to be logical alliances among organizations may be costly in execution or inefficient in operation.[18] Rarely do funders cover the real costs of building partnerships or merging organizations. In some cases, organizations need to resist forced arrangements but to explain their reasons to funders. While organizational differences are unlikely to be compelling, inefficiencies and cost arguments may be persuasive. Where resistance to proposed alliances is strong, funders should be prepared to re-evaluate their reasons for promoting the alliance. Is it in the best interests of the community or are the reasons ones of administrative convenience for

---

[18] For a discussion of nonprofit concerns with forced partnerships, see Scott (2003, at pp. 51-52).

the funder? In any case, Struthers' recommendation for a sustained dialogue between funders and organizations is important in assessing the value of consolidation in the sector.

PUBLIC AND MEDIA RELATIONS: WITH INFLUENCE COMES SCRUTINY

Nonprofit organizations are subject to a higher level of public scrutiny than ever before in the history of the sector. Media are regularly tracking the performance of organizations, particularly in the aftermath of large-scale fundraising. International and domestic agencies track donations to organizations and the expenditure of those funds. For example, after the tsunami disaster in Southeast Asia, the United Nations created a monitoring agency to track donations made to provide relief efforts. Media outlets reported extensively on donations, expenditures and the state of relief efforts at both the six-month and one-year anniversaries of the tsunami. And the public is watching: direct access to information about organizations is increasingly accessible through convenient technologies. Organizations need to build their media and public profiles.

One tendency that organizations need to struggle against is the perception that the media are a threat. The qualitative portion of the National Survey of Nonprofit and Voluntary Organizations reported that organizations worry about fair media coverage (Hall *et al.* (2003, at p. 18)):

> Media coverage of nonprofit and voluntary organizations often focuses on problems rather than the contributions of these organizations. Many participants suggested that a broad-based public relations campaign could counteract bad press, raise awareness of the value of the sector, and educate the public about the actual cost of, and need for, basic administration. A number of participants, often from smaller communities, reported difficulties in fundraising because of negative media depictions of fiscal inefficiencies and mismanagement.

Negative media reports contributed to public misperceptions about the needs and work of the sector, thus discouraging donations and volunteers.

Despite these fears, the sector is beginning to understand the potential of the media as an ally in delivering the good news of the sector to the public. This is occurring at two levels. As participants suggested, a sector-wide public awareness campaign is being mounted under the aegis of the VSI. In October 2005, the Awareness project released its discussion paper inviting organizations to contribute to a broad-based media and public awareness strategy that would extol the variety and extent of ways in which the sector contributes to the quality of life in Canada.[19]

This strategy will unfold in 2006 and into 2007. Similarly, the national surveys are released to maximize media attention to the contributions of the sector. At the organizational level, nonprofits are also learning to use the media to their benefit. While larger organizations have traditionally had strong public relations campaigns, smaller and medium-sized organizations are increasingly realizing the need to reach the public beyond featured events like fundraisers. A sustained event such as Volunteer Week is one method, but other tactics include keeping interested media reporters informed of organizational activities, goals and contributions, and exemplary volunteers. Boards often include a public relations expert to ensure a positive media presence and to track media coverage.

There are three immediate benefits to sustained media relations. First, media reports tend to be better informed and more accurate. Organizations can provide often harried reporters with good leads or ideas for feature or human interest stories, thus saving them time. Second, trust is built between the media and the nonprofits. Third, if a relationship has been established between an organization and the media, then reporters are more likely to call that organization when negative or "hot" stories surface about that organization or the sector. This provides organizations with a critical opportunity to offer needed commentary or refutations of any inaccuracies. In these cases, nonprofit leaders must be careful not to appear defensive or too aggressive, or to avoid the media, but must respond with honest answers that reinforce the positive image of the organization and sector. The "right spin" is one that treats the topic in a fair and practical manner. When handled well, the relationship can be a positive and mutually beneficial one.

Finally, nonprofit organizations need to develop a strong public presence through new technologies. The recent development of Web portals and the provision of information on Web sites is a positive development in this regard. However, to be effective, Web sites must be kept up to date and as accurate as possible. Further, organizations

---

[19] The Voluntary Sector Awareness Project's Discussion Paper, "Greater Than the Sum of Our Parts" (October 19, 2005), is available at: <http://www.vsi-isbc.ca/eng/whatsnew.cfm>.

must strike a balance between providing public information available to all interested parties and select information available only to members. If a Web site or public information is too readily available, the incentive for membership in an organization may be less compelling. Well-used, new technologies can be effective means of publicizing organizational goals and leaders' messages to the public and, when interactive, can keep leaders informed of changes in public opinions or member preferences.

And the new technologies are critical for reaching youth. This is a "turned on" generation who are more likely to access information through cell phones or computers than newspapers. Organizations must deliver in the way they expect. And finally, it means that organizations would do well to cultivate "e-volunteers" — those volunteers that might not be willing to be present physically but will make substantial contributions over the Internet. It is just a matter of tracking the times.

CONCLUSION

Building government and community relations requires nonprofit organizations to use their resources strategically and wisely in an increasingly complex world where the roles and responsibilities of the three sectors are eroding and blurring. While larger organizations will have more capacity to respond to challenges and adapt to changes, smaller and medium-sized organizations can target their efforts and create alliances to support their work. Dialogue, clarity of mission, knowledge of the broader community, and flexibility in action will be traits that allow organizations to take advantage of the opportunities embedded in the changing relations between nonprofits and the external world.

One last word of caution. On a sombre note, Robert Reich, looking at the changing world of community relations in the U.S., warns that (Reich (2001, at pp. 208-09)):

> Nonprofit leaders, likewise, are immersed in continuous efforts to lure talent and money. "To direct an institution nowadays you have to be an opportunist," says Marcia Tucker, former director of the New Museum of contemporary art in New York. "You have to use every social situation to think about fundraising and social contacts." While university deans busily court faculty stars (increasingly, as has been observed , in ... bidding wars), most college presidents are consumed by the task of raising funds. "One has to be a beggar, a flatterer, a sycophant, a court jester," notes

Leon Botstein, president of Bard College. The great visionary university presidents who once changed America's thinking on weighty matters ... have been replaced, for the most part, by a generation of leaders whose vision is focused on raising large donations.

Positioning an organization, whether a university or a health agency or a small social service provider, for dollars and donations may take precedence over developing a vision. When organizations focus on developing relations to build donations and image instead of using their vision to drive their relations, the community suffers.

REFERENCES

Aucoin, P., & R. Heintzman (2000), "The Dialectics of Accountability for Performance in Public Management Reform", in B.G. Peters & D.J. Savoie, eds., *Governance in the Twenty-First Century: Revitalizing the Public Service* (Montreal and Kingston: McGill-Queen's University Press, co-published by Canadian Centre for Management Development, 2000).

Blakeney, A., & S. Borins (1998), *Political Management in Canada*, 2nd ed. (Toronto: University of Toronto Press, 1998).

Brock, K.L. (2003), "A Final Review of the Joint Coordinating Committee of the Voluntary Sector Initiative 2000-2002 by the Official Documentalist and Occasional Advisor" (Ottawa: VSI, March 2003).

Brock, K.L. (2002), "Accountability, the Westminster Model and Government through Partnership with the Voluntary Sector", a paper presented to the ARNOVA annual general meetings, Miami (November 2002).

Brock, K.L. (2005), "Judging the VSI: Reflections on the Relationship Between the Federal Government and the Voluntary Sector" (2005), 19:3 *The Philanthropist* 168-91.

Brock, K.L. (2001), "State, Society and the Third Sector: Changing to Meet New Challenges" (2001), 35:4 *Journal of Canadian Studies* 203-20.

Brock, K.L. (2004), "The Devil's in the Detail: The Chrétien Legacy for the Third Sector" (2004), 9 *Review of Canadian Studies* 263-82.

Brock, K.L., D. Brook & J. Elliott (2003), "Globalization and the Voluntary Sector in Canada (Ottawa: Public Policy Forum, 2003).

Cunningham, P., & P.J. Cushing (1988), "Cause-Related Marketing: A Restructuring Alternative", in *The Ethics of the New Economy*, L. Groarke, ed. (Waterloo, Ont.: Wilfred Laurier University Press, 1988) (pp. 95-109).

Dunham, R.B., & J.L. Pierce (1989), "Social Responsibility and Managerial Ethics", in *Management*, R.B. Dunham & J.L. Pierce, eds. (Glenview, IL: Scott, Foresman and Co., 1989) (pp. 96-113). Available online at: <http://instruction.bus.wisc.edu/obdemo/readings/DP_ethics.htm>.

Embuldeniya, D. (2001), *Exploring the Health, Strength and Impact of Canada's Civil Society* (Toronto: Canadian Centre for Philanthropy, 2001).

Forcese, C. (1997), *Putting Conscience into Commerce* (Montreal: International Centre for Human Rights and Democratic Development, 1997).

Gidron, B., R.M. Kramer & L. Salamon (1992), "Government and the Third Sector in Comparative Perspective: Allies or Adversaries?", in *Government and the Third Sector: Emerging Relationships in Welfare States*, B. Gidron, R.M. Kramer & L. Salamon, eds. (San Francisco: Jossey-Bass, 1992).

Global Business Responsibility Resource Centre, *Corporate Citizenship*. Available online at: <www.corporatecitizenship.net>.

Government of Canada/Voluntary Sector Joint Initiative, *Working Together: Report of the Joint Tables* (Ottawa: Privy Council Office, 1999).

Hall, M.H. *et al.* (2004), *Cornerstones of Community: Highlights of the National Survey of Nonprofit and Voluntary Organizations* (Ottawa: Ministry of Industry for Statistics Canada, 2004).

Hall, M.H. *et al.* (2003), *The Capacity to Serve: A Qualitative Study of the Challenges Facing Canada's Nonprofit and Voluntary Organizations* (Toronto: Canadian Centre for Philanthropy, 2003).

Joint Coordinating Committee (2002), "Progress to Plan Report", Ottawa, September 5, 2002.

Panel on Accountability and Governance in the Voluntary Sector (1999), *Building on Strength: Improving Governance and Accountability in Canada's Voluntary Sector* (Ottawa: PAGVS, 1999).

Parker, M. (2000), *Partnerships: Profits and Not-for-Profits Together* (Edmonton: Muttart Foundation, 2000).

Peters, B.G., & D.J. Savoie, eds. (1995), *Governance in a Changing Environment* (Montreal and Kingston: McGill-Queen's University Press, 1995).

Phillips, S.D. (2001a), "A Federal Government-Voluntary Sector Accord: Implications for Canada's Voluntary Sector", a paper prepared for the Voluntary Sector Initiative Secretariat (February 2001).

Phillips, S.D. (2001b), "From Charity to Clarity: Reinventing Federal Government-Voluntary Sector Relationships", in *How Ottawa Spends 2001-2*, L.A. Pal, ed. (Toronto: Oxford University Press, 2003) (pp. 145-76).

Phillips, S.D. (2003), "In Accordance: Canada's Voluntary Sector Accord from Idea to Implementation", in *Delicate Dances: Public Policy and the Nonprofit Sector*, K.L. Brock, ed. (Montreal and Kingston: McGill-Queen's University Press, 2003).

Phillips, S.D., & K. Graham (2000), "Hand-in-Hand: When Accountability Meets Collaboration in the Voluntary Sector", in *The Nonprofit Sector in Canada: Roles and Relationships*, K.G. Banting, ed. (Montreal and Kingston: McGill-Queen's University Press, 2000) (pp. 149-90).

Pross, A.P., & K.R. Webb (2003), "Embedded Regulation: Advocacy and the Federal Regulation of Public Interest Groups", in *Delicate Dances: Public Policy and the Nonprofit Sector,* K.L. Brock, ed. (Montreal and Kingston: McGill-Queen's University Press for the School of Policy Studies at Queen's, 2003) (pp. 63-122).

Reich, Robert B. (2001), *The Future of Success* (New York: Alfred A. Knopf, 2001).

Sagawa, S., & E. Segal (2000), *Common Interest, Common Good: Creating Value Through Business and Social Sector Partnerships* (Boston: Harvard Business School Press, 2000).

Scott, K. (2003), *Funding Matters: The Impact of Canada's New Funding Regime on Nonprofit and Voluntary Organizations* (Ottawa: Canadian Council on Social Development, 2003).

Scott, K. (2003 Summary), *Funding Matters: the Impact of Canada's New Funding Regime on Nonprofit and Voluntary Organizations — Summary Report* (Ottawa: Canadian Council on Social Development, 2003).

Selley, D. (1998), "Social Accounting and Auditing: Has the Time Come at Last?", *Management Ethics* (December 1998). Available online at: <www.ethicscentre.ca/html/resources/december1998.html>.

Struthers, M. (2004), "Supporting Financial Vibrancy in the Quest for Sustainability in the Not-for-Profit Sector", a paper prepared for the Community of Inquiry Symposium, Toronto (July 2004).

Sutherland, S. (1991), "The Al-Mashat Affair: Administrative Responsibility in Parliamentary Institutions" (1991), 34 *Canadian Public Administration* 573-603.

Thériault, L., & S. Salhani (2001), "At the Loose End of the Continuum: Two Saskatchewan Nonprofit Organizations Delivering Preventive Home Care Services in Saskatchewan", in *The Nonprofit Sector and Government in a New Century*, K.L. Brock & K.G. Banting, eds. (Montreal and Kingston: McGill-Queen's University Press, 2001).

Thomas, P.G. (1998), "The Changing Nature of Accountability" in *Taking Stock: Assessing Public Sector Reforms*, B. Guy Peters & Donald J. Savoie, eds. (Montreal and Kingston: McGill-Queen's University Press, 1998) (pp. 348-93).

Tindale, J.A., & E. MacLachlan (2001), "VON 'Doing Commercial': the Experience of Executive Directors with Related Business Development", in *The Nonprofit Sector and Government in a New Century*, K.L. Brock & K.G. Banting, eds. (Montreal and Kingston: McGill-Queen's University Press, 2001).

Verschoor, C.C., & J.H. Entine, "Social Auditing: Oxymoron or Wave of the Future?", in *Values: A Publication of US Trust*. Available online at: <http://www.jonentine.com/articles/social_auditing.htm>.

Voluntary Sector Awareness Project's Discussion Paper, "Greater than the Sum of Our Parts" (October 19, 2005). Available online at: <www.vsi-isbc.ca/eng/whatsnew.cfm>.

Voluntary Sector Initiative (*Accord*), *An Accord Between the Government of Canada and the Voluntary Sector* (Ottawa: Voluntary Sector Task Force, Privy Council Office, 2001).

Voluntary Sector Initiative (*Code on Policy*), *A Code of Good Practice on Policy Dialogue* (Canada: Joint Accord Table, 2002).

Voluntary Sector Initiative (*Code on Funding*), *A Code of Good Practice on Funding* (Canada: Joint Accord Table, 2002).

Webb, K. (2005), "Sustainable Governance in the Twenty-First Century: Moving Beyond Instrument Choice", in *Designing Government: From Instruments to Governance,* P. Eliadis *et al.*, eds. (Montreal and Kingston: McGill-Queen's University Press, 2005) (pp. 242-80).

Weisbrod, B. (1988), *The Nonprofit Economy* (Cambridge, Mass.: Harvard University Press, 1988).

Young, D.R. (1999), "Complementary, Supplementary, or Adversarial? A Theoretical and Historical Examination of Nonprofit-Government Relations in the United States", in *Nonprofits and Government: Collaboration and Conflict*, E.T. Boris & C.E. Steuerle, eds. (Washington: Urban Institute Press, 1999) (pp. 31-67).

FURTHER RESOURCES

Suggested Readings:

Boris, Elizabeth T., & C. Eugene Steuerle, eds. *Nonprofits and Governments*: *Collaboration and Conflict* (Washington: Urban Institute Press, 1999). This collection of essays explores the tensions and history of relations between the government and nonprofit sectors as they attempt to work together to deliver policy and programs in the United States.

Broad, Dave, & Wayne Antony, eds. *Citizens or Consumers? Social Policy in a Market State* (Halifax: Fernwood Publishing, 1999). This collection of essays explores the impact of the adoption of private sector values in the Canadian state on the citizens and their services.

Brock, Kathy L., ed., *Delicate Dances: Public Policy and the Nonprofit Sector* (Kingston and Montreal: McGill-Queen's University Press for the School of Policy Studies, Queen's University, 2003). The essays in this collection explore the changing symbiotic relationships between the state and the nonprofit sector in Canada as they face new challenges.

Brock, Kathy L., & Keith G. Banting, eds., *The Nonprofit Sector in Interesting Times: Case Studies in a Changing Sector* (Kingston and Montreal: McGill-Queen's University Press for the School of Policy Studies, Queen's University, 2003). These essays explore how the nonprofit sector is adapting to change and responding to pressures imposed by the state, society and the market in Canada.

Parker, Martha. *Partnerships: Profits and Nonprofits Together* (Edmonton: Muttart Foundation, 2000). Martha Parker studies the evolving relationship between the nonprofit and private sector to discern the most effective means of collaboration in the seice of Canadians.

Phillips, Jim, Bruce Chapman & David Stevens, eds., *Between State and Market: Essays on Charities Law and Policy in Canada* (McGill-Queen's University Press for The Kahanoff Foundation Non-Profit Sector Research Initiative, 2001). This collection of essays explores the intricate and changing world of charities law in Canada.

Sagawa, Shirley, & Eli Segal, *Common Interest, Common Good: Creating Value through Business and Social Sector Partnerships* (Boston: Harvard Business School Press 2000). Sagawa and Segal reflect upon the ingredients for successful partnerships between the nonprofit and private sectors.

Salamon, Lester M., *The Resilient Sector: The State of Nonprofit America* (Washington: Brookings Institute, 2003). Salamon captures the ability of the nonprofit sector in the United States to adapt to changing times by re-engineering themselves and creating new alliances.

Vaillancourt, Yves, & Louise Tremblay, *Social Economy, Health and Welfare in Four Canadian Provinces* (Halifax and Montreal: Fern-wood and LAREPPS, 2002). Vaillancourt and Tremblay compare the vitality and contribution of the social economy sector to crucial areas of policy across Canada.

Web Sources:

General:

For helpful and practical advice on managing relations with the government, other organizations, the private sector and the media, see:

<http://www.vskn.ca/commune.htm>
<http://www.envision.ca/>
<http://www.nonprofitscan.ca/>
<http://www.vsf-fsbc.ca/>
<www.charityvillage.ca>
<http://www.sdc.gc.ca/en/hip/sd/06_vsi.shtml>

Other Useful Sites:

<http://www.vsi-isbc.ca/>
<http://www.literacy.ca/govrel/role.htm>
<http://www.axi.ca/>
<http://www.law-nonprofit.org/bib/full7.html>

Chapter 7

RESOURCE DEVELOPMENT BASICS

Andrea McManus, CFRE
The Development Group, Calgary

WHAT IS "RESOURCE DEVELOPMENT"?

The changes in the nonprofit sector over the past 15 years or so, and particularly the decrease in government funding and the significant growth in the number of nonprofit organizations, has forced organizations to look at diversifying their funding bases. A dramatic outcome of this shift has been the way organizations both think about and approach the development of new funding resources and, in particular, their philanthropic-based revenue.

This chapter provides an overview of non-government funding with primary focus on an organization's fundraising and philanthropically based activities.

Clarifying Terminology

Broadly termed as "resource development", the pursuit of new funding sources can include everything from fees for service to numerous forms of fundraising to more entrepreneurial ventures. The terminology can differ from organization to organization and, while there are more overlaps and similarities than differences, it is worth clarifying these various terms.

The most commonly used terms found in Canadian nonprofits are "resource development", "fund development", "institutional advancement" and "fundraising".

Resource development is the broad umbrella under which a variety of non-government funding sources are collected and pursued. According to the Association of Fundraising Professionals (AFP) Dictionary, resource development refers to *"the practice of identifying, cultivating, and securing financial and human support for an organization"*. AFP/Wiley Fund Development Series, 1996.[1]

Organizations that call their function resource development will typically utilize a broad approach that includes both philanthropically based revenue and more entrepreneurial methods such as fees-for-service, gift shops, cause marketing (alignment of a corporate brand or product with a cause for marketing purposes) or social enterprise (a business within the nonprofit that promotes mission awareness and/or raises financial revenues).

Fund development refers to a system that raises philanthropic and sponsorship support for an organization. It is a process, certainly part art and part science, but one that moves in an orderly and logical sequence. It starts with preparation and planning, moves to execution, is controlled at various points throughout, is tracked, evaluated and measured, and then moves back to renewal of the plan. This "cycle" is not haphazard, nor is it reactive (although crisis fundraising, by its nature, is reactive to such things as natural disasters). Rather, it is a thoughtful, relevant connection of activities in a program that raises financial and human support for a nonprofit organization. Fund development is by far the most commonly used name for this function in Canadian nonprofit organizations and, by and large, resource development and fund development are used interchangeably and usually referred to as "development".

Institutional advancement is a term most commonly used to refer to fundraising in post-secondary education organizations such as universities and colleges. Advancement is "a systematic, integrated method of managing relationships in order to increase an institution's support from its key outside constituents, government policymakers, the media, members of the community and philanthropic entities of all types".[2] The primary core disciplines of educational advancement are alumni relations (in educational organizations), communications,

---

[1]   AFP Fundraising Dictionary Online: <www.afpnet.org/content_documents/AFP_Dictionary_A-Z_final_6-9-03.pdf>.

[2]   Council for Advancement and Support of Education (CASE): Web site <www.case.org>.

marketing and development. Communications and marketing usually also include public relations, external relations and government relations.

In this model, the department is generally referred to as the "advancement office" or "the external relations" department. The use of the term "advancement" is enjoying increased use outside of the post-secondary world as more and more nonprofits understand that, if they wish to maximize their potential, an integrated model delivers better results. However, this integrated philosophy is also key in both of the previous two models.

Fundraising is one outcome of all three models that describes the actual activities directly involved with raising resources for the work of the organization and can be done by professional staff or by volunteers. There are different fundraising methodologies (direct mail, telemarketing, sponsorships, major gifts) in a fund development program and each of them has its own targeted constituents, strategies, measurements and cycles.

UNDERSTANDING THE DIFFERENCES BETWEEN NON-PROFITS AND REGISTERED CHARITIES

The 2004 study *Cornerstones of Community: Highlights of the National Survey of Nonprofit and Voluntary Organizations* (Hall *et al.* (2004)) indicates that there were about 161,000 nonprofit and voluntary organizations operating in Canada in 2003. Of these, about 81,000 are registered charities and the remainder have nonprofit status. The distinctions between the two types of organizations are important for resource development.

A nonprofit organization can be created through a variety of statutes at either the provincial or federal level. Registered charitable status can only be given at the federal level through application to the Canada Revenue Agency (CRA). Once a nonprofit is given registered charitable status and a registered charitable number, it is then able to provide tax receipts for philanthropic gifts that donors can use for personal tax credits. Unregistered nonprofits cannot issue a tax creditable receipt.

There are a few important things to know about the issuance of charitable receipts:

- Charitable tax receipts can only be issued for a contribution that meets the conditions of a "gift" as defined under tax legislation.[3]

  - The gift must be transferred by a donor to the registered charity.

  - The gift must be given voluntarily by the donor.

  - No consideration can be provided in return for the gift.

- Charitable tax receipts can be issued for in-kind contributions of product or materials (the donation of an item for an auction, a building, or a piece of art) but cannot be issued for the gift of services (contribution of 10 hours of consulting time, labour to install new flooring). Charities will typically handle this kind of situation through a simple cheque exchange; the services are provided and billed for, the charity pays the bill and the provider donates the same amount back in exchange for a tax receipt.

- Corporate gifts that sponsor an event, name a building, or for which public recognition is a condition of the gift do not qualify for a charitable tax receipt. According to CRA this constitutes a marketing benefit and does not meet the gift definition. If a corporation takes a general business (non tax-creditable) receipt, the gift is then exempted from the gift receipting limitations.

There are other considerations that charities must take into account, such as the format and content of tax receipts as well as other kinds of contributions that do not meet the gift standard, and charities should be aware of all of these requirements. These can all be obtained from the CRA Web site at: <www.cra-arc.gc.ca/tax/charities/menu-e.html>.

While there are certainly advantages that nonprofits with registered charity status enjoy when it comes to philanthropic fundraising, this in no way precludes other nonprofits from successfully diversifying their revenue base. In fact, not having the limitations that come with charitable status allows nonprofit organizations to be more entrepreneurial and market-driven in expanding their resources.

---

[3] "Registered Charities and the *Income Tax Act*", Canada Revenue Agency, RC4108, at p. 5.

TYPICAL SOURCES OF INCOME

The National Survey of Nonprofit and Voluntary Organizations
provides us with a good picture of how organizations are funded (Hall
et al. (2004 at pp. 23-25)). Forty-nine per cent of all revenues reported
by nonprofit organizations come from governments. Of that, 40 per
cent is from provincial sources, 7 per cent is from federal sources and
2 per cent is from municipal sources. Earned income from non-
governmental sources accounts for 35 per cent of revenues and
includes such items as charitable gaming (1 per cent), membership fees
or dues (11 per cent), fees for goods and services (20 per cent) and
earnings from endowments or investments, including interest income
(4 per cent).

The remaining 13 per cent (9 per cent excluding religious wor-
ship organizations) of all revenues comes from gifts and donations and
breaks down as shown in Table 1.

Table 1: Sources of Gifts and Donations for all Canadian Charities

Source	Percentage
Individual donations	8%
undraising organizations and family community foundations	1%
Disbursements from other nonprofit organizations	3%
Corporate sponsorships, donations or grants	3%

These numbers apply to all 161,000 nonprofit organizations and within
this group there are some common generalizations (Hall *et al.* (2004, at
pp. 23-25)):

- Smaller organizations rely more upon gifts and donations for
  revenues than do larger organizations.

- Larger organizations, particularly hospitals and universities, rely
  more on government funding but get a far greater share of the total
  value of gifts and donations than do the smaller organizations.

- Registered charities rely more on government revenues (54 per
  cent of their total revenues) than do other organizations (39 per
  cent) but also depend more on gifts and donations — 18 per cent
  compared with 4 per cent for non-charities.

- Other organizations rely more on earned income from non-government sources (53 per cent of revenues vs. 25 per cent for charities).

There are a number of different sources for earned income other than fundraising.

Fees for service — Many nonprofit organizations are able to charge their clients a service fee. This can be on a sliding scale, as often found in social service organizations, or a flat rate more common to sports groups and community associations and fees like university tuition.

Gaming — Gaming includes raffles, bingos, casinos and lotteries of all sizes. Gaming is sometimes included as part of the development function and sometimes as part of the volunteer management function. Bingos and casinos are often found in the volunteer management function and raffles and lotteries in the development function. Raffles, bingos and casinos are all fairly labour intensive, relying heavily on volunteers, to resource the event. While smaller lotteries can be handled by volunteers, the larger ones should be professionally managed.

The proliferation of lotteries, particularly large-scale ones, has been very evident since the mid 1990s. While they have potential to raise significant sums, possibly millions, for an organization, they are not for everyone and should be carefully researched before a commitment is made. Joan Black, of Black Fund Development Inc., is one of the leading consultants for large lotteries in North America. She says that an organization needs to be one of the top three in its market, that the target market needs to be large enough to sustain a minimum of $6 million in ticket sales (60,000 tickets at $100) and that health care organizations are best positioned to successfully sell lottery tickets because their cause touches so many people in the community.[4]

Black also says that research conducted by her firm after lotteries they have managed are completed, consistently shows that 50 to 60 per cent of people buy tickets to support the cause first, to win second. Hence, the natural reach of the organization is a critical factor. She also cautions that there is a significant upfront investment in marketing and the purchase of prizes and no guarantee that comes with ticket

---

[4]   Interview with Joan Black, January 9, 2006.

sales. The upfront risk and investment is usually a minimum of $500,000 and a lottery needs to sell 60 to 70 per cent of tickets just to break even.

Auxiliaries/Guilds — Auxiliaries are typically found in health-related and cultural organizations and can range from an unstructured "friends of" group to a legally constituted, separate charitable organization. Historically, auxiliaries and guilds are female-run organizations that take ownership of specific initiatives. They may operate a gift shop, hold bazaars and fairs, and conduct other special events. Typically, and particularly if they are separately constituted organizations, their fundraising revenue does not just automatically flow through to the related nonprofit but is disbursed either upon request or on a regular (annual) basis for specific projects. There are also "friends of" groups in the arts and health sectors that raise money for specific aspects of a charity's mission, *i.e.*, acquisition of art or a piece of medical equipment.

Membership Fees and Dues — Many nonprofit organizations are member-based and these members can play an active role in the organization's affairs. Some organizations, such as the YMCA or volunteer centres, charge annual member fees that provide access to reduced fees for some of their services and other member-only benefits. Others, such as social service agencies or sports groups, offer membership more as a way to generally support the organization's mission. Either way, membership fees can be not only a source of revenue but, because they usually come from the people closest to your organization, a source of future philanthropic support.

Social Enterprise — Entrepreneurial ventures, such as thrift shops, consulting services and other "for profit" ventures within the nonprofit sector have become increasingly utilized as a way of balancing the demand for service and funding needs of nonprofit organizations. While most Canadian social enterprise ventures are relatively recent, the opportunity for growth and adoption by all types of nonprofits is significant though not without risk.

Shelley Williams, Executive Director at the Bissell Centre in Edmonton, researched social enterprise in 2004 with the support of The Muttart Fellowship Program. Her 2005 book *Social Enterprise: The Three P's: Philosophy, Process, and Practicalities* provides a guide for nonprofit organizations considering social enterprise as a means of increasing revenues or furthering its mission. Williams defines social enterprise as: "A venture/business/activity within a nonprofit organization providing financial and/or social benefits that further its mission" (Williams (2005 at p. 4)). She goes on to outline the three different models of social enterprise (at p. 8):

Business (or profit-based) — where an organization operates a business that is not related to its mission but does meet the statutory requirements of provincial and federal bodies. This model is not allowed by CRA for charities that want to maintain their charitable status. In this model, while the business does in the end provide benefit to the nonprofit, the business itself is set up as a separate limited company, pays taxes, and is subject to all business laws and regulations. An example would be a women's support and counselling organization that operates a property management company under a separate legal entity.

Social Service (needs-based) — where a nonprofit creates a venture that is directly linked to and helps fulfil its mission, vision and/or mandate. This type of venture is typically directly linked to its target population and can be an offshoot of existing programs or services. In this model, the important criterion is that the venture is providing social benefit and it may not be making any money. An example of this model is an organization that provides support to youth in the inner city and offers contract services to the municipal government.

Hybrid (profit and social benefit-based) — Williams describes this model as one that meets the organizational mission (social benefit) while also generating net revenue (profit). While it may not be directly linked to the organization's target population, it is linked to its mission and generates revenue that can be used for other services and programs. Examples would be an agency that provides support to immigrants and also sells language-interpreting services to businesses, other agencies and the public; a hospital that runs a parking lot (serving its target population and generating revenue); and the YMCA and YWCA, which for many years have provided fitness facilities to their target population and the general public.

Social enterprise projects can evolve from one model to another. For example, Developmental Disabilities Resource Centre (DDRC) in Calgary provides a variety of programs, services and resources to people with disabilities and the public to integrate people with disabilities into the community and to promote inclusion of all people. DDRC started Bow Catering, a full catering company that provides services to the public, as an opportunity to provide both training and meaningful work for its clients. At this point it was a needs-based model. The venture eventually grew into a revenue generator for DDRC, evolving into the hybrid model.

There are, of course, both advantages and disadvantages to social enterprise. Table 2 outlines the most commonly considered ones that nonprofits may encounter (Williams (2005, at p. 23)):

Table 2: Social Enterprise Advantages and Disadvantages

Advantages	Disadvantages
<ul><li>May bring in more revenue to the overall agency</li><li>The agency may become more self-sufficient</li><li>Financial diversification</li><li>Increases the agency's visibility</li><li>Expansion of contacts within community including donors</li><li>Develops skills and knowledge within the organization</li><li>Opportunity to be innovative in developing services/programs</li><li>Puts the agency on the same playing field as the other sectors giving more credibility and power to influence policy change</li><li>Will not have to always dance to the funders' tune</li></ul>	<ul><li>Lose focus or change mission and philosophy of the agency</li><li>Level of human resource expenditure</li><li>Level of financial start-up expenditures</li><li>Too much — not only an expert in running an organization, but now also need to be expert as an entrepreneur</li><li>Internal philosophical conflicts</li><li>Risk of financial loss if the venture is not successful</li><li>Risk of increased financial expenditure if the venture requires unanticipated subsidization</li><li>Board liability</li><li>It is a big structural change</li><li>It is a big cultural change (changes relationships with all stakeholders)</li><li>Just another phase, wait it out until the next flavour of the decade</li></ul>

Whichever model a nonprofit chooses, it should make that choice after in-depth consideration of what will work for that particular organization, in terms of risk, support to target population, mission, mandate and values. In 2003 CRA changed the *Income Tax Act* to allow charitable organizations and public foundations to carry on related businesses that accomplish or promote their charitable objectives. A related business is a commercial activity (*i.e.*, revenue generating) that is either related to a charity's purposes or substantially run by volunteers.[5] Registered charities need to take CRA requirements into account when considering social enterprise as a revenue generating opportunity.

There are numerous other sources of income that fall under the umbrella of fundraising. These include grants from foundations, corporate gifts, special events, direct mail, door-to-door campaigns and telemarketing, to name a few. They are discussed in more detail later in this chapter.

RECENT TRENDS IN FUND DEVELOPMENT

Understanding the environment in which you are operating is key to strategic planning for any organization. For nonprofit organizations, understanding their giving and fundraising environments, both from a trend and a competitive perspective, is critical to assessing what your fundraising potential is and how best to achieve it.

Giving is steadily increasing in Canada. Charitable giving in Canada has been on an upward trend since 1996. Between 1996 and 2002, the value of charitable gifts claimed by tax filers increased by 62.5 per cent. In 2003, 24.9 per cent of Canadian tax filers claimed $6.5 billion in charitable donations, a further 11 per cent increase over 2002. The average gift was also up 10 per cent from 2002 to $1,160 — the highest ever recorded.[6] Additional research conducted by the Association of Fundraising Professionals (AFP), an international association that represents fundraisers around the world, presented in its annual State of Fundraising review, reveals that fundraising revenue in Canada increased by 10 per cent in 2003 and an additional 7 per cent in 2004. Further, 62 per cent of Canadian organizations raised more money in 2004 than they did in 2003 and 69 per cent reached their goal (AFP (2003)).

---

[5] CRA, CSP-R05. Available online at: <www.cra-arc.gc.ca/tax/charities/policy/csp/csp-r05-e.html>.

[6] CRA and Hall *et al.* (2000).

However, there is also a decreasing trend in the number of tax filers (donors) who are claiming charitable gifts on their return. Giving, both in number of tax filers and percentage of income, varies by province or territory and this information is available through organizations such as Imagine Canada. KCI (Ketchum Canada Inc.), one of the largest fundraising and philanthropy consultancies in Canada and a leader in philanthropic research, estimates that total giving (tax-receipted and other) in 2003 is better estimated at $9.105 billion (KCI (2005)). According to The Fraser Institute, Canadians donated 0.70 per cent of their aggregate income to charity, a generous amount, but one that falls short of the giving habits of Americans who give 1.57 per cent of their income to charity (Fraser Institute (2005)). (The differences between the countries might be because Canada has a long tradition of government (tax) supported social services, health care and education and thus many Canadians believe they support these services through their taxes, which are generally higher than in the U.S.)

Individuals provide by far the largest portion of charitable gifts. Every year, approximately 74 per cent of total donations come from individuals, 14 per cent comes from corporations and 12 per cent comes from foundations. According to KCI estimates, individual giving grew by 11 per cent in 2003 and is a critical factor in the overall growth of giving in Canada. This is often surprising news to the leadership of many organizations, who assume that corporations and foundations are the best prospects for major sources of funding. It should be noted that it is difficult to assess the true value of corporate contributions because it can be sourced from so many pots within the corporate structure (community investment budget, marketing and executive). Nevertheless, it is generally accepted that, even if we were able to identify the total amount, it would not vary the picture by much more than 1 to 2 per cent.

The fundraising profession is growing. There has been a huge growth in the fundraising profession itself. In 1995, 214 Canadian fundraisers were members of the AFP. By 2005, this had grown to 2,683, an increase of over 1,150 per cent. Fundraisers are better educated, have greater training and have more ongoing professional development opportunities. Organizations are responding to the increased competition for funds and the retreat of government funding by hiring professional fundraisers. As a result, more people are coming into the profession from all walks of life, many as a second career. There are also far more educational opportunities for fundraisers available in both Canada and the United States. An individual interested in fundraising as a career can take a certificate course at a local community college, a degree at a university or, in the United States, a Master's degree in philanthropy. Within the profession there is also a certification process. The "CFRE" (Certified Fund Raising Execuive) benchmarks the achievements and expertise of fundraisers with a minimum of five full years in the profession. The ACFRE (Advanced Certified Fund Raising Executive) is an advanced credential for professional fundraisers with a minimum of 10 years' experience. Additional information about credentialling and educational opportunities can be accessed at <www.afpnet.org> (the oversight body for the ACFRE credential); <www.cfre.org> (the oversight body for the CFRE credential and for information about U.S.-based educational opportunities); and <www.vskn.ca/fund/fund_edr.htm> for information about Canadian educational opportunities.

Nonprofit fundraising activities show increased strength and professionalism. Over the past decade in particular, nonprofit organizations have become more strategic and professional in the way in which they plan and implement their development activities, the way they staff and resource their programs and also in the way in which they work with donors. Cultivation of donors and solicitation methods have become more personalized, more strategic and more professionally conducted. Organizations better understand the value of research and the importance of stewardship.[7]

More organizations are also hiring professional fundraisers to lead and manage their development activities. A 2002 study conducted by the Association of Fundraising Professionals (AFP) and Canadian Policy Research Networks (CPRN) found that almost a quarter (24 per cent) of its respondents (fundraising professionals) were working for organizations that had been involved in fundraising for less than 10 years (McMullen (2003, at p. 13)). This was most common in organizations in the social services sub-sector. While there are no statistics on the number of Canadian nonprofits that employ professional fundraisers, extrapolation of the membership numbers of various professional associations (AFP, AHP, CASE) cross-referenced with the number of nonprofits that actually have staff (a very small percentage) would lead us to believe that there may be about 10,000 profes-

---

[7] Stewardship focuses on the whole relationship and recognizes that a donor has invested in your organization. Donor recognition is a part of stewardship as is accountability and trust.

sional fundraisers in Canada working for about 12 to 15 per cent of the 81,000 registered charitable organizations.

There is a greater focus on leadership. A demonstration of internal leadership has always been an important factor in an organization's ability to raise philanthropic revenue. With the increasing sophistication of donors and professionalism of fundraisers, this has become even more paramount. Donors expect an organization's key leadership (staff and board) to be visible, engaged and a part of their relationship.

At the same time, it has become more challenging to recruit volunteer leadership. People have busy lives and, when they do volunteer for an organization, they want that experience to be meaningful. They expect to be strategically used and professionally supported.

SIX KEY FUNDRAISING PRINCIPLES

Fundraising can be a new and unfamiliar area for those nonprofit leaders who do not come into their positions with much experience in raising money either through fundraising or by more entrepreneurial means. Establishing a fundraising focus within a nonprofit, or enhancing a program that is already in existence, can be a challenging, and sometimes intimidating, undertaking. Assessing your strengths and weaknesses, your competitive position in the community and what is going to work for a particular nonprofit organization are all factors for consideration. The following six key fundraising principles apply across the board to all fundraising and are important to recognize as your program develops:

People give to people. People give for all kinds of reasons but individuals in particular give for specific reasons. While there is no quantitative research available on this subject, anecdotal and experiential evidence tells us the following:

- The number one reason people give to a particular organization is because they or someone close to them has been touched by the cause that organization represents. For example, they or a family member, had cancer, they have a child with a disability, they attended a particular university or their mother/father/husband/wife/child/friend received exemplary care at a particular hospital.

- People give to other people, not to organizations. Too many organizations make the mistake of telling potential donors about how great their organization is. What donors want to hear about are the people your organization helps, how effective your organization is at providing services to them and the benefits to the community as a result of what your organization does. People want to give to the people for whom your organization is there to provide help and services. How your organization recognizes the gift and stewards the donor relationships (use of the gift, effectiveness, accountability) will help that donor to make the gift to your particular organization — usually after the donor has decided to make a gift to your general cause.

- People give because they are asked. All too often nonprofits make the mistake of not asking people to give to their organization. Whether this is board members, volunteers, prospects, clients or current donors, if you do not ask you will not likely receive. People are generous and like to help others, but they need to be directly asked.

- People do not make donations primarily because of the tax credit they receive. The tax credit is a bonus. They give to help, or build, or care for, or invest. However, the tax benefits are often a factor in determining the size of a gift, particularly when an individual is making a planned gift such as a bequest or a gift from assets, such as securities, real estate or life insurance.

Much comes from few. The Pareto Principle, or 80/20 rule, created by Italian economist Vilfred Pareto in 1906 and later expanded upon by American Dr. Joseph Juran, is an accepted mathematical formula that describes how 20 per cent of something is always responsible for 80 per cent of the results. The 80/20 rule can be applied to just about anything: 20 per cent of the people in a business make 80 per cent of the decisions; 20 per cent of the people hold 80 per cent of the wealth; and 20 per cent of the work consumes 80 per cent of your time. The 80/20 rule is equally applicable to fundraising and is a key principle of fund development upon which goals and strategies are based. A successful fund development program will receive 80 per cent of its donations from 20 per cent of its donors. This is true pretty much across the broad spectrum of any fund development program and particularly so in major gift and campaign fundraising. An analysis of the 2003 CRA data on charitable contributions reveals that 25 per cent of all donors gave 82 per cent of the value of all donations. And this breakdown is consistent from year to year. In large capital campaigns, the trend is to an even wider ratio with 90 per cent or more of the gifts coming from 10 per cent or fewer of the donors.

Wealth is not always obvious. Too many organizations spend too much time trying to secure donations from the "usual suspects", *i.e.*, the high-profile community individuals who are known to have both influence and affluence. Again, a look at CRA data for 2003 provides a different reality — 94 per cent of individuals with incomes over $75,000 claimed a charitable donation in that year and, on average, gave .32 per cent of their income to charities. In contrast, 76 per cent of individuals with incomes of less than $25,000 made a similar claim and, on average, gave 1.38 per cent of their income to charities. Clearly, there is generosity at all levels.

There is also wealth in less than obvious places. The high-profile community leaders (the "usual suspects") may well be doing good works for many other organizations in the community but you can be sure that there are an even greater number who are trying to get them on their board, as a donor, or to head up their campaign. Charities need to take a broader view. There are many generous individuals with less, or less obvious, wealth but who still have the means and the interest to support your organization, and businesses that may not be the corporate leaders but still have a strong sense of community. The challenge for a nonprofit is to identify its potential donors and then find an approach to them.

It's not about the money, it's about building the relationship. With the growth of the fundraising profession, its increasingly professional approach to the discipline, and the greater knowledge and expectations of donors, organizations have realized that they need to pay more attention to donors and to building relationships with them in order to sustain their support. Donors are an organization's friends and play a large and vitally important role in organizations in which they invest. They contribute to an organization because they believe in the cause. At the same time, they do not always understand or accept the professional approach to fundraising and, in fact, can be suspicious of it. Getting to know and understand your donors, particularly at the higher giving levels, is key. Relationship, or donor-centered, fundraising is now a hallmark of successful programs that requires a nonprofit to look beyond the money transaction and respect donors as stakeholders in your mission.

Fundraising is not a stand-alone activity. One of the biggest mistakes a nonprofit can make is to treat fundraising as if it operates in a silo, separate and distinct from everything else that happens in your organization. Henry Rosso, in his groundbreaking and authoritative book, *Achieving Excellence in Fundraising*, says (Rosso (2003, at p. 27)):

> Fundraising cannot function apart from the organization; apart from its mission, goals, objectives and programs; apart from a willingness to be held accountable for all of its actions ... Fundraising by itself and apart from the institution has no substance in the eyes and heart of the potential contributor.

In order to achieve success, fundraising must work in synergy and collaboration with strategic planning, governance, and program planning and execution. And, it will involve and engage other staff, volunteers and the board in all of these activities. The fundraiser is the professional manager, but the whole organization has a role to play in ensuring the cause is worth investing in and providing the opportunity for donors to make that investment.

Philanthropy is something to be proud of, and fundraising enables philanthropy. Philanthropy is often defined as "the gift of time, talent and resources", in the dictionary as "love of humankind" and also as "voluntary action for the public good through voluntary action, voluntary association, and voluntary giving" (Payton (1988)). People who give to organizations do so because they believe in something. They are proud of their act of philanthropy and consider it a privilege to be able to help and to make change. Ethical fundraising is the process that enables philanthropy, the presentation of the opportunity to make a gift. It is the responsibility of the nonprofit organization, board and staff, to approach its fundraising activities by seeking to match a prospective donor's interests with the needs of the organization and to do so in a way that does not demean the act of asking but presents the opportunity to support the cause with pride.

OVERVIEW OF A DEVELOPMENT PROGRAM

Nonprofit organizations come in all sizes and shapes. So too do development programs. Clearly, what is necessary in terms of staff, resources, volunteers, planning, evaluation and communication to reach the large financial goals of a major university is not going to be what is required, let alone even feasible, for a small, grassroots nonprofit that has much smaller goals and no staff. Nevertheless, good and ethical fundraising is a component of all development programs, no matter the size of the organization or its financial goals.

In order to be successful and sustainable over the long term, to have renewal and growth, to develop mutually beneficial relationships with donors and to be accountable to those donors, a development program must integrate a diversified funding base with a number of fundraising vehicles rather than relying on just one method such as special events or direct mail or major gifts.

Donors can be grouped into broad categories, *i.e.*, individuals, corporate/business, foundations, groups/associations, for the purposes of broad strategies and evaluation. An integrated development program recognizes that there are different motivations for giving and preferred vehicles for giving. Some people prefer to handle their philanthropic giving by buying tickets or donating auction items to special events, some prefer giving at the door, some via direct mail, some like to give monthly and others once a year. The onus is on the nonprofit to offer a diverse number of vehicles that appeal to a broad base of donors.

CATEGORIES WITHIN AN INTEGRATED DEVELOPMENT PROGRAM

Organizational needs are typically classified into four specific categories: ongoing annual needs, special purpose needs, capital needs and endowment needs. The corresponding fundraising programs are typically the annual fund, major gifts program, capital campaigns and planned giving. The "donor pyramid" is a conventional model that illustrates how an organization uses these fundraising programs to move a donor up the ladder in terms of both involvement and level of giving. It is also a key underpinning for all development planning. With the emergence of major giving it has become more common for donors to come into the pyramid at any level. Nevertheless, the concept of the pyramid still has value to demonstrate the inter-relationships between the various pieces of a development program.

Figure 1: Pyramid of Giving

Estate, Planned and Endowment Giving

Bequests and Other Planned Gifts

Investment

Donor Commitment

Major Gifts
Endowment Campaigns
Capital and Special Campaigns
Major Gifts from Individuals
Major Gifts from Corporations and Foundations

Involvement

Interest

Donor Growth

Annual Giving
Support Group Organizations
Specials Events and Benefits Events
Annual Giving Campaign/ Direct Mail Program
Selected Publics
All the Public – Everyone in the Area

Information

Identification

Donor Contact

Annual Giving

Ongoing annual financial needs arise out of the annual budgeting process and relate to that portion of a nonprofit's annual programs, services and operating costs that are not covered by core grants or other forms of earned revenues. Some programs and services may need to be fully funded through fundraising revenues, others partially funded and others may not require any philanthropic support. In many organizations, core operating costs are not fully funded and fundraising is also required just to pay staff, buy copier paper and keep the lights on.

An annual gift is one that is reasonably expected to be given year after year. Most annual gifts are small but the important thing for the annual giving program is that there are gift renewal mechanisms in place. Like anything else, it costs more to get the gift in the first place than it does to renew that gift. An annual development program that does not include a planned and proactive renewal program is neither cost-effective nor strategic.

A *successful* annual fund can provide several benefits such as:

• A reliable base of funding on an annual basis

• A foundation for all other fundraising

• Support for annual operating and program needs that are not funded by other means

• A source for "undesignated" gifts that can be used by the organization where most needed

• An excellent way to attract greater numbers of new donors into the organization with potential to move up the giving pyramid toward the major gift status

• An increase in the profile of your organization in the community on a mass-market basis.

Most annual giving occurs in non face-to-face activities such as personalized mail, special events, door-to-door campaigns, telephone solicitation, e-philanthropy or other mass promotional opportunities such as organizational newsletters. Although face-to-face fundraising is by far the most effective, it can also be the most expensive, particularly in human resources (staff and volunteers). Since annual gifts tend to be much smaller, the mass-market appeals can make sense from a cost versus benefit perspective.

Typical annual giving vehicles include:

Direct Mail — Direct mail is one of the most commonly used fundraising vehicles by large and small organizations alike. FLA Direct, a Canadian direct marketing firm, measured the Canadian direct mail market for two years in 2003 and 2004 and found that:[8]

• 35 per cent of Canadian adults (8.5 million donors) gave to charity through the mail, and

---

[8]   FLA Direct research, available online at: <www.theflagroup.com>.

- direct mail donations accounted for more than $1 billion in charitable revenue.

Regular, targeted solicitation mailings can be an effective way to bring in new donors, upgrade or renew current donors and past donors who have not given to your organization for a few years, and create awareness for your cause.

The two key aspects of any individual direct mail piece are having a compellingly written letter and making sure it is sent it to the right people. Nonprofits can create their direct mailings in-house or with the aid of a direct marketing specialist. Lists can be bought from list vendors or drawn up internally. This can be as simple as identifying the key stakeholders for your nonprofit (volunteers, suppliers, names supplied by volunteers) or purchasing lists from list vendors according to very specific criteria relevant to your particular cause. There are also mailing vendors who are able to take care of the actual distribution of a direct mail piece.

Direct mail can be undertaken by any size organization, from large hospitals who do grateful patient mailings and universities who do alumni direct mail marketing, to much smaller organizations who may only mail at Christmas or for special appeals. Many organizations, particularly those that are organ or disease related, choose a particular month around which to create awareness (April is the Canadian Cancer Society's Cancer Awareness Month, January is Alzheimer Awareness Month sponsored by the Alzheimer Society of Canada) and will then conduct a number of events in that month that might include a special acquisition appeal (to acquire new donors), events, phone and door-to-door solicitation.

Direct mail can be expensive, particularly in the early stages, and organizations need to thoughtfully consider the risks and rewards. Direct mail is about building a long term relationship with donors so they become annual contributors. To achieve success, nonprofits have to make a long-term commitment. The first year of any direct mail program may only break even or it could lose money. The second year is likely to be marginally better but it may take five years or more until the program reaches its maturity both in scope and revenues.

The age-old question about direct mail is: *how often is too often?* Charitable organizations may be concerned that by mailing a solicitation to their donors more than one or twice a year they might be seen as intrusive and this could result in turning donors off. However, what many organizations find is that frequency of approach during the year actually increases the annual renewal rate of existing donors. This stands to reason since a donor is being given more one opportunity during the year to make a gift — at a time when it is more convenient or to an appeal that resonates more with them. Furthermore, there tends to be a direct correlation between the frequency of giving during a calendar year and donor loyalty over time. Those donors who make multiple gifts during the year are self-identifying themselves as ones who feel more connected to the cause and are possible candidates for personal giving options. And if you did not ask more than once, you would not know this.

However, when conducting a direct response program where there will be multiple "asks" during the year, it is essential that the donor data system be structured in such a way as to honour donor requests such as not sending mail, mailing only once per year, or even, where possible, mailing at a preferred time of year. Those donors who may be offended by too many mailings should be given an option to join a monthly giving program. This could be the right solution for them and a big win for the organization.

Special Events — Special events can figure prominently in many development programs and not at all in others. What they should not be is the primary or sole method of raising funds. Events can be expensive and labour-intensive, requiring both significant volunteer and staff time, and have no guarantee of success. They are one of the least cost-effective ways of raising money but can also be one of the most effective at raising profile and, if directly mission-related, awareness of the cause. Events tend to be more about raising friends than raising money.

Events come in all sizes and shapes and include everything from runs/walks to gala dinners and balls to the newer on-line auctions. Many organizations may use an annual signature event to define themselves with the public and to raise dollars. Key considerations for event fundraising include:

- Know why you are having an event. Is it to raise money or raise friends and awareness? Or a combination and, if so, in what mix?

- Have a clear understanding of who your event is targeted to. An event targeted towards twentysomethings is going to be much different from an event targeted to an older, more sedate crowd.

- Clearly outline the roles and responsibilities between staff and volunteers;

- Have an event plan and a timeline for key activities to keep everyone on the same page and on track.

- Have an event budget so both staff and volunteers know what resources are available and what the net financial goal is.

- Make sure the event is appropriate for your organization. Creativity and innovation can make or break an event but it must be aligned with your organization's values and not offend your key stakeholders in any way.

The two main sources of revenue for events are ticket sales and sponsorships. In order to maximize results it is often a good strategy to target one or the other as the source of revenue that will cover all of the event costs, leaving the other as net profit.

Telemarketing/Phone Solicitation — Telephone solicitation remains a vital component of many development programs and is particularly effective for renewal and upgrading of current donors, for membership associations, for donor clubs, and for recapturing lapsed donors. A combined mail/phone campaign can yield even better results. Using phone solicitation for acquiring new donors through cold calls can be both expensive and inefficient. Privacy has become more of a concern to people and many dislike being called at home; the increased use of voice mail and call display makes impersonal phone solicitation challenging. Nevertheless, thousands of nonprofits of all sizes raise millions of dollars each year by telephone solicitation.

Historically, a telephone solicitation program was conducted by volunteers but the majority of nonprofits now hire telephone canvassers or use a professional telemarketing company. A common exception to this is phone-a-thons, used by causes that have wide public appeals, such as those often conducted by community partners for children's hospitals. Universities have long used student canvassers to solicit support from alumni. They are paid for their services but the function is overseen internally.

There are advantages and disadvantages to both models but, in most cases, in-house programs should only be considered if a nonprofit is willing to invest the time and resources to ensure success.

Table 3: Telephone Solicitation

	Advantages	Disadvantages
Conducted in-house	• Can recruit, train and supervise callers yourself • Offers more day-to-day control over activities • Can write your own script • Less costly • Highly interactive and personal	• Can be difficult to recruit trainers • Need to have staff to train and supervise callers • Recruitment is ongoing • Need equipment and space for call centre
Conducted by outside vendor	• Vendor hires, trains and supervises callers • Vendor will take care of all administrative functions, tracking and reporting data • High cost efficiency (technology, technique and experienced staff)	• Less control on day-to-day basis • Can be more costly, particularly in the early stages • Less commitment to your cause

Selection of a vendor needs to be done carefully and involves checking references, quality control processes, pricing, reliability and success rates. It is helpful to talk to other clients. Pricing is a key factor. In the past many vendors billed on a percentage of dollars raised and this often resulted in the vendor taking an unreasonably high portion of the funds raised. (See the section of ethics and percentage-based fundraising for additional information.) Flat-fee contracts are now the norm and provide safety nets for nonprofits and assurance to donors that a greater percentage of their donation will go to the cause (depending, of course, on how much is raised). Commercial telemarketers will charge the same rate regardless of how much is pledged and ultimately collected so a phone campaign could cost 20¢ for every dollar raised or 45¢ for every dollar raised, depending on the purpose of the campaign and the targeted list.

Door-to-door Campaigns — There are far fewer door-to-door campaigns in the 2000s than there were in the 1980s. The major challenge with a door-to-door campaign is finding the volunteers to do the canvassing, and many nonprofits are not comfortable with hired canvassers. A few organizations such as Canadian Cancer Society and Heart and Stroke, continue to be able to canvass with volunteers but many, such as the Salvation Army, have discontinued their door-to-door campaign because of this issue. Safety of canvassers has also become of increasing concern.

Nevertheless, door-to-door campaigns remain solid fundraisers, particularly for many smaller, community-based organizations, such as local sports groups, that have the capacity to draw from an invested group of volunteers within a localized geographic area. In larger urban areas door-to-door campaigns are now almost solely conducted by larger organizations but in smaller communities they are still feasible for many organizations.

E-philanthropy — The advent of the Internet has had a significant impact on fundraising in a number of ways. One of these is the emergence of e-philanthropy, or the use of the Internet to build donor relationships with supporters of a nonprofit organization. Ephilanthropy can include the ability to make an online contribution or to purchase product or services. Web sites are now key information tools for the nonprofit to communicate its cause and its needs and for donors who want information about an organization or a particular cause. Now widely used for ticket sales and disaster relief,[9] online giving is particularly favoured by younger donors and is becoming a staple of many development programs.

There are a number of online giving portals that charities can register with as a cost-effective alternative when it does not make sense to establish an online giving mechanism through its own Web site. CanadaHelps.org is one such portal. Established in 2000, by 2005 CanadaHelps was facilitating over $10 million in donations to Canadian charities annually.[10]

---

[9] In 2005, the American Red Cross reported that it received nearly 50 per cent ($762.5 million) of the total donations ($1 billion +) in the first two weeks after Hurricane Katrina online.

[10] CanadaHelps.org Web site <www.canadahelps.org>.

Major and Special Giving

There has been an explosion of major gift fundraising in Canada and of the number and value of major gifts given. Rather than relying on many small gifts from a large number of donors, major gift fundraising focuses on strategically identifying and cultivating donors with the potential to contribute significantly greater amounts to an organization. The University of Toronto launched the largest campaign ever held in Canada in 1997 with a goal of $400 million. By the time the campaign was over in 2004 it had raised and achieved its goal of $1 billion. While the vast majority of charities would never have the need or capacity to set a goal of that size, goals have steadily increased in campaigns across the country.

KCI estimates that in 2002 alone there was more than $1 billion donated to charities across the country in gifts of $1 million or more and 74 per cent of this was from individuals, with 20 per cent from corporations and 6 per cent from foundations. While the 2003 numbers are only about half of that ($500 million) what is noteworthy is that 24 per cent of it came from foundations. Since the majority of foundations are family foundations we can draw the conclusion that individuals are using foundations as giving vehicles for legacy and tax purposes.

There are a variety of financial needs that a nonprofit has that are most suitable to a major gift program. Current programs and services, special projects, seed money for new projects, research and capital needs are examples. Characteristics of major gifts include:

- They are one-time gifts as opposed to gifts that an organization can reasonably expect to receive annually.
- They are almost always designated, *i.e.*, one that the donor is making for a specific purpose, and the gift the nonprofit is morally obligated to use according to the donor's intent.
- They can be made from cash or assets (gifts of appreciated securities, real estate, art).
- They are almost always the result of a face-to-face cultivation and solicitation.
- They are generally the top 10 to 20 per cent of gifts received.

Major gift programs have become a critical component of non-profit development programs of all sizes for two main reasons. First, they are the most effective way of building what could be long-term relationships with donors to an organization and, second, because major gift fundraising is an individual, face-to-face exercise, it is the most cost-effective way of raising money.

What constitutes a major gift varies from organization to organization. In smaller organizations they could start at $1,000 and in larger institutions at $50,000. Historically, major gifts tended to come from donors who had made several smaller annual gifts to a nonprofit over time. Today, however, major gifts can come from current donors or first time donors. Current donors are still the best prospects for greater giving and individuals, corporations and foundations are all potential prospects for major gifts.

There are a number of vehicles through which major gifts are solicited and received.

Major Gift Program — A major gift program is a seamless, on-going series of activities that is specifically focused on identifying potential major gift prospects, cultivating their interests, and matching them to a nonprofit's needs before soliciting them for the gift.

Major Gift Campaign — A major gift campaign utilizes the same series of activities as a major gift program but it is packaged as a time-sensitive campaign. This may be for a special project such as research, a new program or programs, or expansion of current activities.

Capital Campaign — A capital campaign is a one-time, intensive effort to raise a specific dollar goal for a specific bricks and mortar project. It could be a new building, renovation of an existing building, a new wing of a hospital or a combination of capital and program needs. A capital campaign is a focused project in and of itself that is strategically planned and executed, generally relies heavily on volunteers, and has a beginning and end.

An organization considering a capital campaign is generally wise to first conduct a feasibility or planning study into the community's interest and willingness to participate. Feasibility studies are a worthwhile investment that test the goal, the potential leadership, the case and the timing, and should be conducted by an outside consultant to ensure objectivity.

Endowment Giving — An endowment fund is a self-sustaining funding source based on the interest from invested money. It can be extremely helpful in providing long-term financial stability in the present and future. Gifts to an endowment are not subject to a charity's regular disbursement quota and are invested in stocks, bonds and other vehicles. With the exception of a small percentage of assets as required by the *Income Tax Act*,[11] the principal remains intact in perpetuity and the interest is spent on charitable purposes.

An important method of creating an endowment fund is by utilizing the resources of Community Foundations. These organizations exist in many areas of Canada. They solicit donations from many individuals and then provide grants to causes specified by the donors or by the foundation itself. Most community foundations are willing to talk to specific nonprofit organizations about housing and administering endowment programs for them.[12]

Typical endowments are endowed chairs at universities, which can be set up with a lead donor and then many other smaller donors (*e.g.*, an endowed research chair in pediatric oncology). Another example is an operating endowment, which a nonprofit would hold for long-term sustainability purposes and for which it would solicit donations from a variety of sources. (Often undesignated bequests will go directly into an operating endowment.)

An endowment can also be created for a fixed term — until a specified period of time elapses or until a specified event occurs. In the meantime, it functions as a true endowment as discussed above. Some nonprofits choose to set up a quasi-endowment, or a reserve fund that, while they treat it is an endowment, it is not subject to endowment tax regulations.[13]

Endowments are largely derived from gifts from individuals. Corporations and foundations will usually exclude this type of giving from their guidelines because of their long-term nature and, particularly with corporations, the difficulty in providing recognition.

Endowments can be held and managed internally but many organizations prefer to have them managed externally by a community foundation, private foundation or private investment firm where the expertise and capacity to do so already exists.

---

[11] R.S.C. 1985, c. 1 (5th Supp.).

[12] See Community Foundations of Canada Web site at: <www.cfc-fcc.ca> for additional information.

[13] For information on 10-year gifts and endowments see the CRA Web site at: <www.cra-arc.gc.ca>.

Planned Giving — Frank Minton and Lorna Somers define planned giving as " ... the process of designing charitable gifts so that the donor realizes philanthropic objectives while maximizing tax and other financial benefits" (Minton & Somers (1997)). Planned gifts are either current or deferred major gifts. Current planned gifts are given from current assets such as securities or real estate and timed to minimize any capital gains tax and obtain full benefit of the tax credit. Deferred gifts are gifts that are committed to in the present but the value of the gift is not received by the charity until some time in the future. Deferred gifts can be through bequests, charitable remainder trusts, life insurance policies or gifts of residual interests.

There has been much discussion about the transfer of wealth between generations over the next several decades, with some estimates as high as one trillion dollars. This, combined with a change in Canadian tax law that made tax treatment of capital gains on gifts of appreciated securities more favourable, has fuelled a steep rise in the incorporation of planned giving into development programs. A 2001 study conducted by six Canadian philanthropy-related organizations and Deloitte & Touche found that the dollar value of gifts of publicly traded securities increased as a percentage of receipted donations, rising from 0.9 per cent in 1996 to 11.1 per cent in 1999. In just three short years, gifts of appreciated stock went from being a minimal factor to accounting for, on average, more than 10 per cent of a charity's receipted donations. While the results varied depending upon the type and size of the organization, the percentage increased in every category.

The surge of planned giving activity has resulted in a sub-specialty of the professional fundraiser, the gift planner, within the development office. However, all nonprofits can incorporate some element of planned giving into their fund development program without a specialist on staff. Bequests and gifts of securities are easily handled by most organizations. The more sophisticated vehicles call for outside legal or financial expertise and are usually proactively promoted by organizations with specialized gift planners on board.

There are several resources available for nonprofits interested in implementing a planned giving program. The Canadian Association of Gift Planners (CAGP)[14] has numerous resources available and operates

---

[14] <www.cagp-acpdp.org>.

Leave a Legacy Councils in many communities. These councils provide a professional resource for nonprofit gift planners as well as public activities such as Wills Workshops to educate donors on making bequests. Many of these Wills Workshops are hosted in conjunction with local community foundations which are also good resources for planned giving information.

IDENTIFYING DONORS

Successful fundraising is predicated on the building of relationships with donors who have the most potential to support your organization. While there is a whole universe of potential donors for nonprofit organizations, identifying the donors who are going to be interested in your particular cause, have both the ability to give to you and the connections to your organization is something that must be done in a focused, thoughtful and strategic manner. Broad categories of donors include individuals, corporations/business, foundations and other groups/associations. Within each of these categories there are sub-categories that apply to individual nonprofits, as shown in Table 4.

Table 4: Identifying Donors

Individuals	• alumni (universities, colleges, private schools) • clients and potential clients (social service agencies) • members (religious organizations, environmental groups, membership-based organizations, professional associations, sports and recreation) • patients (health care) • current and former staff • current and former volunteers • parents/family of clients, members, students, patients
Corporate/Business	• corporations that operate in the area • small and medium-sized businesses that operate in the community • businesses with which someone connected to the organization may have a relationship, *i.e.*, business owned by a board member or volunteer

	• businesses that provide supplies, equipment or services to the organization
Foundations	• the local community foundation • private family foundations • foundations set up by other nonprofits that may grant outside of their connected institution
Groups/Associations	• United Ways and other federated funding organizations • service clubs • employee groups • professional associations • community groups

This list is not exhaustive by any means. Individual nonprofits will each have their own stakeholder groups. The key is to identify them from the inside out. Start with those closest to your organization, the prospective donors who have the greatest potential for your own organization.

Figure 2: Constituencies and Energy of an Organization

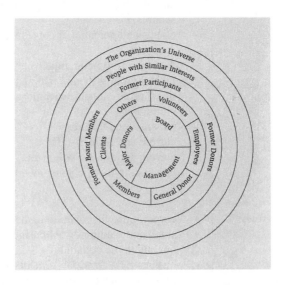

Source: © 2002, The Fund Raising School at the Center on Philanthropy at Indiana University. Reprinted by permission.

The concentric circles developed by The Fund Raising School[15] illustrate the constituencies and energy of an organization. The closer a person is to the organization (the middle of the circle) the greater the energy, the stronger the bond and the greater potential for obtaining donations. As one moves outwards, the energy and the bonds weaken and the potential for recruiting donors is lessened.

Individual Donors

Individual donors are the mainstay of almost all development programs. From small annual donors to major gift donors, individuals consider their gifts to be investments in the cause of the organization. The *2004 Canadian Survey of Giving, Volunteering and Participating* reveals that 89 per cent of donors gave because they felt compassion for those in need and that 86 per cent gave because they personally believed in the cause. On the other hand, only 20 per cent (or one in five donors) gave because of the tax credit they would receive.[16] For the most part, experience confirms these statistics and tells us that the vast majority of people give to organizations they believe in or by whose cause they have been personally touched.

In 1994 Alan Prince and Karen File studied more than 800 individuals and developed seven basic profiles for major givers (Prince & File (2001)).

The Communitarians — people who give to charities because of a strong sense of community and a desire to help build or enhance that community.

The Devout — people who generally give to their church or for other religious or spiritual reasons.

The Investors — people who give because it is good business to do so. Often corporate leaders and people to whom the charity's cost-effectiveness will be an important factor.

The Socialites — people who give through their leadership and attendance of special events.

---

[15]   The Fund Raising School, 2002, p. 2-17.
[16]   CSGVP, 2004, available online at: <www.givingandvolunteering.ca>.

The Altruists — people who give because of a strong moral sense that it is the right thing to do.

The Repayers — people who give because they have benefited from a cause, a program or an organization's services.

The Dynasts — people who give through family foundations or from a strong family tradition.

These profiles are helpful in understanding why people give and how they should be approached, but for each nonprofit identifying the potential group of donors in the community who might be interested in the specific organization and then identifying their individual motivations is the key to success. Simply meeting and talking to them, possibly utilizing such techniques as focus group interviews, is the best way to learn about these motivations.

Donors are also more knowledgeable and sophisticated about their giving. The accessibility to information through the Internet, the increase in natural disasters and media coverage on the sector have all resulted in a higher sector profile and more information for donors to use in deciding where to contribute and in planning their giving.

Corporate Donors

Corporate giving has changed dramatically in the past 15 years from simple donations to a more marketing-driven model. Donations programs are now a part of strategically focused community investment programs and come under the banner of corporate social responsibility initiatives. Many companies have strict guidelines about what they will give to and where their interests are, or are not, and these are tied to its "triple bottom line" (economic, social and environmental returns on investment). Many companies also realize that community involvement is important to their employees and so has value in the recruitment and retention of their workforce. It also has a positive impact on their public image and can be used to support the company's marketing efforts. As a result, corporate philanthropy has by and large merged with the marketing and community relations functions and is tied much more closely to the company's bottom line.

For the nonprofit organization, this necessitates a much more strategic approach to securing corporate support. Research is a must — the lack of homework on the part of an organization will be clear to the company's community investment staff. Like individuals, corporate donors now have clearly defined outcomes they expect the nonprofit to achieve and will scrutinize the use of their funds to a greater degree. Figure 3 and Figure 4 illustrate the continuum of corporate philanthropy and the framework within which corporate giving tends to occur today.

Figure 3: Continuum of Corporate Philanthropy

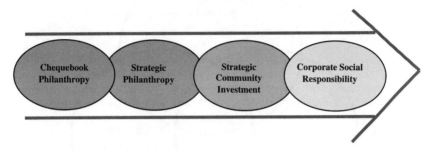

- Financial donations
- Traditional causes/approaches

- Focus area
- Employee volunteerism
- Image

- Linked to business
- Proactive
- Stakeholder involvement

- Integrated
- Value add strategies
- Social vision

Source: The Strategic Giving Group, The United Way of Calgary and Area: www.calgaryunitedway.org. © 2006 United Way of Calgary and Area. Reprinted by permission.

**Figure 4: Community Investment —
A Convergence of Key Elements**

Source: Petro-Canada internal document. Reprinted by permission.

To identify potential corporate donors, a nonprofit needs to have a clear understanding of what the opportunities for each partner are.

**Table 5: Identifying Opportunities for Companies
and Nonprofits**

What Companies Might Be Looking For:	What Nonprofits Might Need:
• Build brand awareness • Enhance image or reputation • Increase profits • Increase employee morale and attract and retain employees • Attract investors • Create public trust and goodwill now and in the future • Gain competitive advantage	• Secure needed revenue • Diversify revenue base • Enhance reputation • Increase public awareness of the organization and the cause • Attract volunteers and donors • Gather in-kind resources or services • Build capacity

Corporations are more likely to give to specific program or capital projects and much less likely to give undesignated operating support money. There are a number of ways in which they may make contributions.

Sponsorships — A rapidly growing form of corporate giving, companies sponsor everything from special events to special projects. Sponsorship is a pure marketing endeavour for which a company will require public recognition. Nonprofits should look for companies that align with their cause, where their cause may support a company's brand and where there are natural synergies between the nonprofit and the company.

In-kind Donations — In-kind giving is one of the largest forms of support by companies. Everything from furniture to media buys to personnel secondments can provide a source of non-financial but needed resources that assist a nonprofit in fulfilling its mission.

Matching Gifts — Many companies have programs that will match the contributions that employees make to nonprofits up to a certain amount.

Cause Marketing — The phrase "cause-related marketing" was first used by American Express in 1983 to describe its campaign to raise money for the restoration of the Statue of Liberty. Every time someone used an American Express card, the company made a one-cent donation to the Statue of Liberty. The result was a sizeable donation to the project as well as a significant growth in both cardholders and card usage.

Since that time, cause marketing has come into its own and become a viable part of many nonprofit fund development programs. Today, it annually raises over $4 billion (Daw (2006)) in marketing support (cash and awareness) for North American nonprofit organizations through creative, innovative and mutually beneficial partnerships.

In her 2006 book, *Cause Marketing for Nonprofits: Partner for Purpose, Passion and Profits*, Jocelyne Daw, Vice-President Enterprises at The Glenbow Museum in Calgary, defines cause marketing as "… a corporate-nonprofit partnership that aligns the power of a company's brand, marketing and people with a nonprofit cause's brand and assets to create shareholder and social value and to publicly communicate values" (Daw (2006, at p. xvii)).

Cause-related marketing initiatives come in many forms. Traditionally, cause marketing referred to a for-profit company associating itself with a nonprofit organization by promoting a product and raising money for the nonprofit at the same time. Most common are agreements to donate a percentage of the purchase price of a specific object to a specific organization or project. An example is McDonald's McHappy Day®, which invites local celebrities and community leaders to serve on a specific day and $1 of certain products sold on that day is donated to charity. McHappy Day® has raised more than $22.5 million for children's charities since its inception in 1977. Other initiatives include affinity credit cards, long distance telephone services and special offers of services by professionals (dentists, lawyers).

Cause marketing has continued to evolve and to build on the brand and assets of both the nonprofit and the business to achieve greater awareness, enhance mission fulfilment and raise revenues by working together. The CIBC Run for the Cure is one such cause marketing initiative. Started in 1992 by a small group of volunteers who wanted to raise awareness for breast cancer, it now involves over one million participants and raises in excess of $21 million each year to support breast cancer research and educational initiatives.[17] CIBC aligned itself with the run from the start and has brought its considerable assets, marketing power and reach, staff support (the CIBC team is 10,500 strong) and funding to promote the run, the breast cancer cause, and CIBC as a community-minded and caring company.

Cause marketing can bring many benefits to a nonprofit but also comes with challenges and risks. *Cause Marketing for Nonprofits* points out that there are benefits beyond just dollars, including validation of a nonprofit's activities, help in achieving its mission, the creation of brand awareness, the dissemination of information, the opportunity to change behaviour and attitudes, the bringing of valuable corporate expertise and finally, the leveraging of additional resources.

For corporations, as Daw says, "the more active cause-marketing relationships give the company a competitive advantage by creating tangible value and increasing their profitability by helping them attract employees; selling products; managing their reputations; increasing their bottom line; appealing to employees, customers, and stake-

---

[17] Canadian Breast Cancer Foundation, available online at: <www.cbcf.org>.

holders; and securing the license they need to operate in many markets" (Daw (2006, at p. xvii)).

While cause-related marketing can be an excellent source of long-term returns with minimal long-term effort, the nonprofit must still think carefully about whether or not such a partnership will work for it. Questions to consider include:

• What is it you have to offer a potential cause marketing partner?

• Who are good potential partners for your organization?

• Is there a good alignment of values between the organizations so that the nonprofit's vision, mission and values are not undermined?

• What is required in terms of internal infrastructure to support the relationship?

• How much time will it take?

• Are there staff in place to support and manage the program?

Foundations

Foundations exist to contribute financial resources to charitable organizations. They are almost always governed by strict guidelines that define their areas of interest, the types of programs they will and will not fund, their geographic scope of giving, and their application process. Grant applications are typically detailed in nature and differ from foundation to foundation. Foundation fundraising can be a time-consuming undertaking and, in order to maximize results, thorough research into potential foundation funders is critical. There are a number of databases available as a good resource for researching foundations and their giving records. Imagine Canada's *Directory to Foundations* (<www.imaginecanada.ca>) and Metasoft's *The Big Database* (<www.bigdatabase.ca>) are two that provide a good first overview of potential funders. Additional research is strongly recommended so that only those foundations with demonstrated potential for interest in the organization's cause are targeted. A broad, mass appeal to foundations is not recommended nor is it a good use of resources.

Groups and Associations

Every community has its share of Kinsmen Clubs, Rotary Clubs, Lions Clubs and a good variety of community groups that can provide both financial and volunteer resources to a nonprofit. As these groups are largely volunteer run and managed, access to them is best achieved by volunteers from the nonprofit. While many of these groups provide small grants, some have the potential and preference for larger grants. For example, more affluent Rotary Clubs will often make a smaller number of larger grants to fewer organizations and Kinsmen Clubs will often tend to align themselves with a particular cause.

There are also federated funding agencies in most communities across Canada such as the United Way/Centraide that run annual campaigns to raise funds from a broad community base and then invest it back into that community. United Ways typically limit their funding to social service agencies, and the more progressive ones will also identify key community issues and fund solutions-based initiatives that draw on a diverse number of community partners.

FUNDRAISING FOR CORE OPERATING NEEDS

Fundraising for core costs can be extremely challenging because they are not as exciting to donors as special projects and programs. They are, however, essential and legitimate components of the projects and programs that donors do like to fund. While fundraising for undesignated dollars helps to cover the lights, heat or rent, the better way to approach core costs is to ensure that they are fairly allocated across the spectrum of programs and services a nonprofit offers. Rather than operating with a line item budget, nonprofits are better positioned if they operate with project-oriented budgets. Project accounting is widely used by business and government and is completely ethical and legal for use by a nonprofit. The goal is not to trick donors but to present the true costs of a program. For further discussion of this form of budgeting and accounting, see Chapter 10.

IDENTIFYING WHAT WORKS FOR YOUR NONPROFIT

Identifying the development approach that offers the best return on investment and is suitable for a particular organization is the key to success. While diversity is always important, each fundraising vehicle needs to be designed in a way that capitalizes on the organization's strengths and its financial and human (staff and volunteer) resources. While not exhaustive, the following table outlines the financial and human resources generally required for each type of fundraising and how they might apply to different sized nonprofits.

Table 6: Identifying What Works

Type of Fundraising	Financial Resources	Human Resources	Suitable for
Annual Giving			
Direct Mail	Significant upfront investment of dollars over multiple years with no guarantee of ROI in early years.	Small, irregular mailings can be done by volunteers. Larger programs require staff to either run in-house or manage an out-sourced campaign; no volunteer involvement necessary.	All sizes of nonprofits but difficult for all-volunteer organizations to conduct a program with regular mailings.
Telemarketing	Significant investment in equipment, space, and administrative infrastructure. Hired callers add to costs.	Recruiting volunteers to make calls can be challenging. Staff to run in-house program or monitor outsourced one. Outsourcing requires no volunteers.	Volunteer phone solicitors effective way to thank and renew donors. All nonprofits can run an out-sourced telephone solicitation if budget allows.
Door-to-door Campaign	Investment in materials and administrative infrastructure. Hired canvassers add to costs.	Recruitment of volunteers can be challenging. Safety is an issue. Require staff to plan program, recruit and monitor, and do follow-up.	Small organizations typically depend on volunteers. Larger nonprofits can handle volunteer or hired canvassers.
E-philanthropy	Investment in Web site capability and administrative infrastructure.	Staff to monitor; minimal volunteer involvement.	All organizations, either through their own Web site or a giving portal.

Type of Fundraising	Financial Resources	Human Resources	Suitable for
Major gifts			
Major Gift Programs and Campaigns	Materials, research, cultivation activities.	Volunteers play a key role in identifying, opening doors and cultivating prospects. Can be volunteer only or staff/volunteer mixed.	Suitable for all organizations tailored to size.
Capital Campaigns	Can require significant costs in materials, training, campaign counsel, recognition.	Staff and volunteers together. Difficult to do all-volunteer campaign (will take longer and may flounder without staff direction).	Suitable for all organizations tailored to size.
Endowment Giving	Financial costs are generally associated with other vehicles.	Same as for major gifts.	Same as for major gifts.
Planned Giving	Start-up costs in materials, information, available technical expertise. The more complex the offerings the more costly the program.	Same as for major gifts.	Same as for major gifts. Being more proactive in encouraging bequests a good starting point for smaller nonprofits.
Sponsorships	Recognition, event planning. Costs are part of event budget.	Can be volunteers or staff or mix. Sponsor support should usually be staff.	All sizes. Sponsor/nonprofit alignment and clear goals are key.

Type of Fundraising	Financial Resources	Human Resources	Suitable for
Cause Marketing	Research, cultivation, negotiation, travel, administrative oversight.	Requires staff to implement and monitor on a larger scale.	Appropriate to size. Small organizations on a local level; larger nonprofits have regional and national potential.
Social Enterprise	Research, start-up costs, administrative oversight.	Generally requires staff to implement and monitor.	Medium to larger organizations.
Foundations	Research, grant preparation.	Generally staff though volunteers ok on small scale.	All organizations.
Groups/Associations	Minimal financial costs.	Staff and volunteers.	All organizations.

RESOURCING THE DEVELOPMENT FUNCTION

Organizational Structure

There are two possible frameworks within which the development function can take place on behalf of a nonprofit. The function can operate as a separate department within the organizational hierarchy or it can function within a separately instituted organization or foundation. A nonprofit can opt to establish a parallel foundation for a variety of reasons. These are the pros and cons to be considered:

Table 7: Parallel Foundation Pros and Cons

Pros	Cons
• Can help make fundraising happen faster • Provides the opportunity to recruit a separate set of influential leadership just focused on fundraising, particularly when the governing board does not have profile or does not consider fundraising part of its job • Recruitment can be easier because leaders do not need to be consumed by other governance issues • Formalizes the separation between operating, endowment and/or capital funds • Places the funds out of sight of government encroachment • Eliminates bureaucratic restrictions • Protects assets in the event of a legal suit	• The establishment of a separate legal entity requires by-laws, separate board meetings, minutes, annual meetings, financial statements, tax returns and other government-related documents • Requires recruitment, orientation and support of a completely different set of volunteer leaders • It can be challenging to ensure that the mission, goals and objectives of the two organizations do not diverge over time • There is a more stringent disbursement quota applied to parallel foundations than there is to a registered charity • A foundation does not always increase fundraising results. Commitment and planning are still a prerequisite

Some nonprofits choose to set up a small "f" foundation that is not legally constituted, but nevertheless operates as a foundation with a separate leadership group and single focus. Others utilize Community Foundations as the home for certain kinds of funds.

Staffing

The growth in fundraising and of the fundraising profession has resulted in staffing challenges for nonprofit organizations. The 2003 CPRN Study (McMullen (2003, at p. ix)) found that slightly more than 40 per cent of the fundraisers surveyed had 10 or more years of experience while 29 per cent had less than five years. This correlated to organizational size with 43 per cent working for small organizations that generated less than $250,000 annually and having less than five years' experience. Even though 60 per cent worked for organizations that had increased their fundraising staff in the previous two years, the majority (60 per cent) worked in establishments with fewer than 25 paid staff (McMullen (2003, at p. 13)). Of these, we can reasonably assume that a strong majority are working in one-person development shops, likely with no or part-time administrative support. In the current climate, the number of job opportunities far outstrips the number of experienced and qualified fundraisers and this, along with a number of other factors, has led to a high level of transience in the profession and escalating salaries, often higher than program heads.

Professional staff are essential if an organization wants to build a long-term, sustainable development program. Almost equally as important is the need for support staff. Development is a labour-intensive undertaking where quality and timeliness of data and attention to detail are crucial. Receipting, recording, reporting and supporting donors are time-consuming activities that are most cost-effectively done by including qualified administrative support in the staffing plan in order to ensure that the professional fundraiser is spending time on the initiatives designed to bring in revenue rather than the details that support it.

Non-staff Resources

In addition to staff resources, a development budget should include a realistic level of expense to support the function. In addition to the standard operational expenses, fundraising materials, prospect and donor research resources and databases, cultivation activities, volunteer support and training, postage, meetings, marketing and community relations, and professional development and training all need to be included in the expense budget.

Technology is an essential management tool for development. There are many fundraising software programs available at various price ranges. While small organizations may be able to use programs such as Excel or Microsoft Access to manage their information, most will eventually grow out of their capacities, requiring a specialized database program. The purchase of a fundraising software program should be done after a thorough assessment of an organization's development program and its data management needs and, most importantly, should be considered as a necessary investment that will produce a future return. Individual software packages will have their own Web sites but information about assessing an organization's needs and identifying the right package can be obtained through the AFP Resource Centre (<www.afpnet.org> — there is a nominal fee for non-members) or in the archives of Charity Village (<www.charityvillage.ca>).

Fundraising Costs

Donors and the public expect that most of the money they contribute will be spent on a charitable purpose. While this is a reasonable assumption, it is complicated by the fact that there is such limited awareness as to the true cost of either the programs they are supporting or the reasonable costs of fundraising itself. The bottom line is that, like any other for-profit or government enterprise, it costs money to make money and nonprofits need to be transparent and realistic about how they present these costs. Fundraising cost effectiveness is a very complex issue and there are many factors involved for individual organizations: the age and size of the organization; the size of its donor base; its mix of fundraising programs and the maturity of individual programs; the maturity and effectiveness of its staff; the time it takes to see returns; and anomalies of giving such as the receipt of a large bequest. This, and the fact that there are a variety of different kinds of funding models used by organizations, often results in comparing apples and oranges and making it very difficult to establish a set of guidelines that are reasonably applicable to all organizations. Organizations also have different cost issues and may treat revenue streams differently. Large endowment investment returns may be included or may be held in a separate foundation. Office space can be provided or not. Nevertheless, the sector does need to develop better benchmarks and standards to communicate to donors that it is fundraising in an efficient and effective manner. There are a number of things nonprofits should do to provide a more realistic picture:

- Establish targets that are appropriate and achievable (based on track record and resources), not just numbers that make up a gap in the budget.

- Implement project accounting to capture the true cost of programs.

- Report on individual programs rather than on fundraising as a single entity.

- Evaluate, measure and report fundraising costs on a three-year rolling average as opposed to an annual basis.

- Report on other things besides the "cost of dollar raised" such as fundraising achievements, historical trends, and the acquisition and retention of donors.

Fundraising costs can range from as low as $.12 to $1.50 per donation for individual methodologies and anywhere from 5 per cent to 35 per cent of overall fundraising revenue. James Greenfield, one of the leading authorities on fundraising cost-effectiveness, provides the following guidelines for fundraising programs that have been active for a minimum of three years. (Note: these are based on U.S. studies and experience but are also applicable to Canadian practice.) These guidelines are the result of a number of national studies and from Greenfield's own considerable years of experience (Greenfield (1996, at p. 281), and additional sources).

Table 8: Reasonable Cost Guidelines for Solicitation Activities

Solicitation Activity	Reasonable Cost Guidelines
Direct mail (acquisition)	$1.25 to $1.50 per $1.00 raised
Direct mail (renewal)	$0.20 to $0.25 per $1.00 raised
Membership associations	$0.20 to $0.30 per $1.00 raised
Activities, benefits and special events	$0.50 per $1.00 raised (gross revenue and direct costs only)[18]

---

[18] Event revenues should be reported as net revenues.

Solicitation Activity	Reasonable Cost Guidelines
Donor clubs and support	$0.20 to $0.30 per $1.00 raised
Volunteer-led personal solicitation	$0.10 to $20 per $1.00 raised
Corporations	$0.20 per $1.00 raised
Foundations	$0.20 per $1.00 raised
Special projects	$0.10 to $0.20 per $1.00 raised
Capital campaigns	$0.10 to $.20 per $1.00 raised
Planned giving	$0.20 to $0.30 per $1.00 raised

PLANNING AND EVALUATING DEVELOPMENT ACTIVITIES

Philanthropic Culture

As outlined earlier in this chapter, a development program should be integrated within your organization and not function in isolation. Development is an organizational process that involves just about all aspects of the nonprofit. Growing your mission, leadership at all levels and strategic planning are all impacted by your success at fundraising. A respect for the philanthropic process, an awareness of the fundraising requirements and activities, and an appreciation throughout the organization of its (not the fundraiser's) need for support enable development to flourish.

Planning and Implementation

Successful fundraising is not about a quick hit. It is about thoughtful planning and meticulous execution and, in fact, the planning is where most of the activity happens. Development needs to be part of the larger organizational system as the workings of one function affect what happens in other functions. In *Strategic Fund Development*, author Simone Joyaux lists of number of initiatives for a chief executive to ensure a philanthropic culture and a development program that is integrated throughout the organization (Joyaux (2001, at p. 7)):

- Help board and staff to see the links between fund development and other institutional functions, to identify and resolve systemic issues at various points.

- Make sure the fundraising staff understand the program and relate well with the program staff.

- Involve your fundraiser in board selection, recruitment and development.

- Insist that fundraising staff work with all other staff, including program and marketing, to identify the agency's constituents, find out their interests and needs, and brainstorm how the agency can respond.

- Show your staff — janitor, receptionist, direct service personnel, trustees, chief executive, book-keeper — the role they play in fund development.

- Listen to your fundraiser's thoughts about program quality and community perception.

- Expect your fundraiser to be actively involved in the community, serving on boards and exploring community issues, trends, and solutions.

The CPRN/AFP study revealed that fundraisers were more likely than other Canadian workers to be considering a job change. Overall, 42 per cent reported that they had looked for a job in the previous year and these numbers held across the sub-sectors. Further, 46 per cent of these cited frustrations with the work environment, 36 per cent cited a lack of recognition, and almost 30 per cent said that it was because they faced unrealistic expectations or their workplace was unsupportive (McMullen (2003, at pp. 68-70)). Clearly, the quality of the work environment plays an important role.

Strategic and Annual Planning

A healthy nonprofit that knows the direction it is heading is one that embraces strategic planning. Development should be a part of the organizational strategic planning process from the outset. It only makes sense that if the direction involves programs, services or buildings that require philanthropic revenue, development should be included. Development staff provide a touchstone to the community, can most effectively represent the views of your donors and feed external views and information back into the process.

In addition to strategic planning, development requires a clearly written plan complete with goals, strategies, tactics, target markets, cultivation, communication and solicitation strategies, the case for support, benchmarks of success, evaluation mechanisms, timelines, resources and responsibilities. The annual development plan is based on past results, current and future trends (internal and external) and future goals. A growth in goals will likely entail a growth in staffing and/or other resources. The planning cycle will generally start mid-year in concert with the budget planning process and be completed prior to the commencement of the next year, providing the framework for the development program. Like the strategic planning process, a sound development plan is developed with the input and participation of the whole organization.

Evaluation and Measurement

The annual development plan should be measured and evaluated on a regular, ongoing basis separate and apart from the financial reporting of the organization. Key performance measurements include gross revenues, net revenues, number of new donors, percentage rate of renewed donors, percentage rate of lapsed donors, cost of fundraising, average gift sizes, and expense versus income. These measurements should be conducted across the program as well as by individual program. There is much more to development than the dollars raised and future performance is dependent on solid information about the past.

ROLES AND RESPONSIBILITIES

Fundraising can be completely done by volunteers (as in many smaller nonprofits), by a combination of staff and volunteers, or solely by staff (generally in bigger organizations with larger development offices). The majority of Canadian nonprofits have no professional staff and rely heavily on volunteers to raise money through their community networks. In most other organizations, fundraising can be led either by volunteers with support from staff, or, less common but increasing with the professionalization of fundraising, staff led with support from volunteers. Characteristics of these two models are shown in Table 9.

Table 9: Roles and Responsibilities of Volunteers and Staff

Volunteer Led/Staff Supported	Staff Led/Volunteer Supported

• Volunteers fulfil governance and leadership roles that determine vision, direction and broad strategies for fundraising activities such as:
  • Approve annual financial and non-financial goals
  • Lead and own strategic planning process
  • Define and redefine mission, vision
  • Annual joint retreat.
• Volunteers play a lead role in external championing of organization, opening doors, cultivation initiatives and solicitation of larger gifts.
• Staff provide professional expertise and management of fundraising process.
• Volunteers and staff share ownership for success of program.
	• Volunteers operate in service volunteer capacity only (no governance or leadership).
	• Staff set goals (with appropriate internal collaborations), define program initiatives, set budgets, manage and direct the process.
	• Staff are responsible for program growth, vision, development and policies.
	• Staff provide professional expertise and management of fundraising process.
	• Volunteers involved selectively and appropriately with key asks. Includes developing cultivation and solicitation strategies collaboratively with staff. Solicitation generally conducted jointly.
	• Staff own and manage program success. Volunteers contribute to success.

The development professional, the Chief Executive Officer or Executive Director and volunteer leadership all play key roles in successful fundraising.

Table 10: Key Roles in Fundraising

Development Professional	• Sets strategic direction • Responsible for planning and execution • Leads, enables and supports volunteers • Maintains infrastructure • Conducts evaluation and reporting • Identifies strategic issues for board discussion and action • Proposes and tests goals and directions

Chief Executive Officer	<ul><li>Sets strategic direction</li><li>Ensures resources are in place</li><li>Champions program</li><li>Participates in cultivations and solicitations</li><li>Chief representative of the organization</li></ul>
Board as a Whole	<ul><li>Ensures the nonprofit is worthy of investment by donors</li><li>Endorses goals and direction</li><li>Adopts plan as part of budget process</li><li>Participates in strategic discussions regarding strength and weaknesses, progress, trends and implications</li></ul>
Individual Board Members	<ul><li>Carry out specific activities such as identification of potential donors, cultivation and solicitation of donors</li><li>Are accountable for fulfilling commitments made</li><li>Make personal gifts</li></ul>

There is always much debate about the role of boards in fundraising. The CPRN/AFP study reveals that almost half of all respondents (47 per cent) said that their board members did not play an active role in fundraising while only 37 per cent agreed that their board members were active. As well, 30 per cent did not think that board members had realistic expectations of fundraising activities, with goals being set too high (McMullen (2003, at p. 44)). Clearly, for many managers and fundraisers in organizations the lack of board engagement is an issue.

The expectations are fairly widespread that board members have a responsibility to lead by example (give personally), provide contacts, open doors and cultivate others, and generally to act as an ambassador for the organization. The way this is done varies with different sizes and types of organizations and the model of governance used. Each organization needs to set expectations and responsibilities that work for it. The key is to have these discussions in advance of major fundraising and particularly during board recruitment, not after an individual has joined the board.

The role of volunteers and board members may also change over time. A nonprofit that has never had the need to raise money may now find itself facing that requirement. Or a nonprofit that has done all of its fundraising at the staff level and is facing a large expansion or building campaign will likely need to reconsider its model. These are discussions that are held at the board level. The result could be that the board changes its fundraising responsibilities or finds other leadership volunteers to do the job. Some board members may leave the board as a result.

Giving by board members can be another controversial topic. While we do not know what percentage of nonprofit board members actually give to their organization, common wisdom holds that you start with those closest to you and then go out to the community. But is this reality? We at least know from experience that there is a moral authority attached to a nonprofit that can say that 100 per cent of its board contributes to the organization on an annual basis. And, a request for support by a board member or campaign volunteer who has given himself or herself clearly carries more weight than from one who has not contributed. There are several other compelling reasons supporting board engagement (both time and money):

- Board members are usually better positioned in the community to open doors and make contacts than just relying on the development professional or the Executive Director.
- Board members can extend the reach of the development activities into broader networks.
- Commitment by board members demonstrates a belief in the cause, *i.e.*, walking the talk.
- It is usually very de-motivating for other fundraising volunteers if they are volunteering their own time and money and board members are not.

Development Committees

Some nonprofit boards choose to have a standing development committee that is responsible for leading fundraising activities. This can work well as it provides focus and clear lines of responsibility for reaching the goals. However, it can also be detrimental to overall success if it means that fundraising is delegated to a small group that ends up working in isolation from the rest of the board. Development committees are also known to have become mired in minutiae rather than focusing on the identification, cultivation and solicitation of donors. Strong leadership and clear responsibilities, supported by firm staff direction (if applicable) are necessary to ensure a development committee lives up to its potential benefits.

ACCOUNTABILITY, STEWARDSHIP AND ETHICS

Accountability and Stewardship

The 2000 study *Talking About Charities: Canadians' Opinions on Charities and Issues Affecting Charities*, found that 84 per cent of Canadians think charities are honest about how they spend their donations and 76 per cent of them trust charities "some" or "a lot".[19] Notwithstanding that these are impressive numbers, the issue of accountability has increased in public awareness, particularly as it relates to governance and fundraising activities. The increased competitiveness for funds combined with the more knowledgeable donor has raised expectations and guaranteed that accountability is no longer optional. Donors are asking more questions before and after making their gifts and have higher expectations of the organizations which they choose to support. They increasingly consider their contributions to be an investment in the mission of the organization and, as such, view themselves as stakeholders in that organization.

Nonprofits are the stewards of the philanthropic dollars contributed by its donors and, as a result, have a responsibility to maintain that relationship and that trust through ethical fundraising and accountability to its donors.

Stewardship presupposes that as soon as a donor makes a gift that donor immediately becomes another prospect and the organization must earn the donor's trust and prove itself worthy of future investment. Good stewardship includes:

- The policies that govern investment practice

- The use of sound financial and management practices

---

[19] *Talking About Charities: Canadians' Opinions on Charities and Issues Affecting Charities*, The Muttart Foundation, 2000. Available online at: www.muttart.org/surveys.htm>.

- The honouring of donor intent
- The acknowledgement and recognition processes for gifts
- Transparent and accountable financial reporting

Ethical Fundraising

Ethical fundraising is a fundamental underpinning of trust, donor relationships and long-term success. Regardless of the size of the community, the donor sphere is small. A perceived or actual unethical act by the nonprofit can have long-term and severe consequences for fundraising. Fundraising is about relationships; ethical fundraising is about building and maintaining trust.

There are a number of codes that an organization can adopt and operationalize into policy as Step 1. Step 2 is to ensure that all staff and volunteers are aware of these policies and of the organization's commitment to ethical fundraising. Some of the codes and principles governing ethical fundraising are as follows:

- *The Code of Ethical Conduct and Standards of Practice* of the Association of Fundraising Professionals applies to individual professional fundraisers and commits them to serving the ideals of philanthropy. Among other things, it places the responsibility for ensuring that all solicitation materials are accurate and truthful, that contributions are used according to a donor's intent, that confidential and privileged information will be protected and that gift conditions will not be altered without donor permission, squarely on the fundraiser. This code can be found at <www.afpnet.org>.

- *The Ethical Fundraising and Financial Accountability Code* of Imagine Canada outlines the commitment of charities and their boards to fundraising practices that respect donors' rights to truthful information and to privacy. It also commits board to managing responsibly the funds entrusted to them by donors and to report their financial affairs accurately and completely. This code can be found at <www.imaginecanada.ca>.

- *The Accountable Not for Profit Organization* is a statement of principles that outlines the operations and procedures a charity takes to show it is accountable to donors, the people it serves and the general public. This code can be found at <www.afpnet.org>.

- *The Donor Bill of Rights* sets out commitments to donors' rights and can also be found at <www.afpnet.org>.

In addition, there are codes governing prospect research, planned giving, and e-philanthropy, all of which can be obtained from different Web sites or through links from the above-noted sites.

Percentage-based Fundraising

A key tenet of all codes is the prohibition of percentage (or commission) based fundraising. First promulgated by the AFP Code, this ban is based on the belief that for professional fundraisers charitable purpose, not self-gain, is paramount and that if percentage-based compensation is used:

- charitable mission can become secondary to self-gain;

- donor trust can be unalterably damaged; and

- there is incentive for self-dealing to prevail over donors' best interest.

AFP also believes that percentage-based compensation produces reward without merit and can encourage abuses, imperil the integrity of the voluntary sector and undermine the philanthropic values on which the sector is based.[20]

In 2005, the Uniform Law Commission of Canada developed a proposed Uniform Charitable Fundraising Act that, if adopted by individual provinces, will regulate fundraising activities. The proposed act includes a ban on percentage-based fundraising.

Privacy Legislation

In 2000 the Canadian Government enacted PIPEDA, the *Personal Information Protection and Electronic Documents Act*,[21] to guide the use of personal information. Several provinces have enacted their own legislation which complies with the federal legislation. In provinces that do not have provincial legislation the federal Act applies. The Privacy Commissioner subsequently ruled that fundraising is not a

---

[20] AFP Position Paper: Percentage-Based Compensation, available online at: <www.afpnet.org/ethics/ethics_papersarticles>.

[21] S.C. 2000, c. 5.

commercial activity within the definition of the Act and is therefore exempt from most of its provisions. However, there are still implications for the collection and use of data that nonprofits must comply with.

FUTURE TRENDS

The face of development has changed significantly in the past 10 years and indicators lead us to believe that the pace of change will not only continue but will likely increase. Three trends that will have impact on a nonprofit's ability to earn revenues and fundraise effectively in the future include:

Human Resource Challenges — Professionalization of fundraising is occurring at a rapid pace. The number of organizations involved in fundraising and requiring professional fundraisers will continue to outstrip the availability of experienced individuals even as the profession itself continues to grow. This places pressure on the organization to offer competitive compensation packages (including salaries, benefits and professional development opportunities) and a quality of work environment (realistic expectation, organizational support and leadership) to recruit and retain fundraisers.

A Growing Awareness of Philanthropy — The sophistication and expectations of donors will continue to grow. Access to more information fuels the expectation that information will be forthcoming, transparent and readily available. The Canadian nonprofit sector is proactively working to increase awareness of its role in our society. As the sector profile rises, Canadians will continue to become more knowledgeable, ask more questions and develop deeper bonds with the organizations in which they invest. They will have a greater sense of the role of philanthropy and the philanthropic process. The onus will be on the development program to respond to these expectations and retain donor loyalty.

E-philanthropy — This is already a rapidly growing vehicle, and nonprofits will have to embrace e-philanthropy to remain competitive. Still in its relative infancy in Canadian organizations, e-philanthropy offers wider reach and the opportunity to retain donors as they become more mobile in a global world.

REFERENCES

AFP, *State of Fundraising 2003 Report* (Alexandria, VA: Association of Fundraising Professionals, 2004). Available online at: <www.afpnet.org>.

Daw, J. (2006), *Cause Marketing for Nonprofits: Partner for Purpose, Passion, and Profits* (Hoboken, NJ: John Wiley and Sons, 2006).

Fraser Institute (2005), *Charitable Giving in Canada and the US: The 2005 Generosity Index* (Vancouver: The Fraser Institute, 2005).

Greenfield, J.M. (1996), *Fund-Raising Cost Effectiveness: A Self-Assessment Workbook* (New York: John Wiley and Sons, 1996).

Hall, M. *et al.* (2000), *Highlights from the 2000 National Survey of Giving, Volunteering and Participating* (Ottawa: Imagine Canada, 2000).

Hall, M. *et al.* (2004), *Cornerstones of Community: Highlights of the National Survey of Nonprofit and Voluntary Organizations* (Ottawa: Ministry of Industry for Statistics Canada, 2004).

KCI (2005), *Philanthropic Trends*, Ketchum Canada Inc. (Spring 2005). Available online at: <www.kciphilanthropy.com/english/explore/trends.html>.

McMullen, K. (2003), *A Portrait of Canadian Fundraising Professionals* (Canadian Policy Research Networks Inc./Association of Fundraising Professionals, 2003). Available online at: <http://cprn.org/en/doc.cfm?doc=347>.

Minton, F., and L. Somers (1997), *Planned Giving for Canadians*, 2nd ed. (Waterdown, ON.: Somerville, 1997).

Payton, R.L. (1988), *Voluntary Action for the Public Good* (New York: American Council on Education/Macmillan Publishing, 1988).

Prince, A.P., & K.M. Maru (2001), *The Seven Faces of Philanthropy: A New Approach to Cultivating Major Donors* (San Francisco: Jossey-Bass, 2001).

Rosso, H.A., & Associates (2003), *Achieving Excellence in Fund Raising*, 2nd ed. (San Francisco: Jossey-Bass, 2003).

Joyaux, S.P. (2001), *Strategic Fund Development: Building Profitable Relationships that Last*, 2nd ed. (Gaithersburg, MD: Aspen Publishers, 2001).

Williams, S. (2005), *Social Enterprise: The Three P's: Philosophy, Process and Practicalities* (Edmonton: The Muttart Foundation, Fellowship Series, 2005).

ADDITIONAL RESOURCES

Web-based Resources

Canada Revenue Agency (CRA) <www.cra-arc.gc.ca>

Association of Fundraising Professionals (AFP) <www.afpnet.org>

Association of Healthcare Philanthropy Canada (AHP) <www.ahpcanada.com>

Council for Advancement and Support of Education (CASE) <www.case.org>

Canadian Association of Gift Planners <www.cagp-acpdp.org>

Community Foundations of Canada <www.cfc-fcc.ca>

Charity Village <www.charityvillage.ca>

Imagine Canada <www.imaginecanada.ca> and <www.givingandvolunteering.ca>

Print Resources

Social Enterprise

Williams, S., *Social Enterprise: The Three P's: Philosophy, Process, and Practicalities* (Edmonton: The Muttart Foundation, 2005).

Cause Marketing

Daw, J., *Cause Marketing for Nonprofits: Partner for Purpose, Passion and Profits* (Hoboken, N.J.: John Wiley and Sons, 2006).

Steckel, R., *Filthy Rich: How to Turn your Nonprofit Fantasies into Cold, Hard Cash*, 2nd ed. (Berkeley, CA: Ten Speed Press, 2001).

Fundraising

Burnett, K., *Relationship Fundraising: A Donor-Based Approach to the Business of Raising Money*, 2nd ed. (San Francisco: Jossey-Bass, 2002).

Greenfield, J.M., *Fundraising Cost Effectiveness: A Self-Assessment Workbook* (New York: John Wiley and Sons, 1996).

Joyaux, S.P., *Strategic Fund Development: Building Profitable Relationships That Last*, 2nd ed. (Gaithersburg, MD: Aspen Publishing Inc., 2001).

Rosso, H.A. and Associates, *Achieving Excellence in Fundraising*, 2nd ed. (San Francisco: Jossey-Bass, 2003).

Planned Giving

Minton, F., & L. Somers, *Planned Giving for Canadians*, 2nd ed. (Waterdown, ON: Somersmith, 1997).

Chapter 8

PLANNING AND ORGANIZING FOR RESULTS

Thea Vakil
University of Victoria

INTRODUCTION

This chapter discusses how nonprofit organizations should decide on which strategic direction they should take and how they can best be organized for optimal performance. The chapter is concerned with those organizational characteristics that are separate from the people populating the organization yet are indispensable for meeting the organization's objectives. Organizational characteristics refer to aspects of the nonprofit organization that describe its form, structure and strategy as well as the subcomponents of strategy: planning, programs and projects. Each of these topics will be addressed in this chapter to assist nonprofit leaders in deepening their understanding of organization strategy and structure and enhancing their ability to consciously use organizational attributes to achieve the organization's vision.[1]

The chapter begins with a general discussion about the importance of strategy, strategic thinking and the need to create a strategic vision for the nonprofit organization. It then moves to the strategic planning process, its major components and the steps involved in putting a strategic plan in place, including project management. Planning strategically may have significant consequences for the

---

[1] The term "nonprofit leader" denotes executives responsible for the operations of the nonprofit. This chapter uses the titles Chief Executive Officer and Executive Director interchangeably.

organization's operations, structure and processes, so the second part of the chapter provides an overview of the more common structures and processes in nonprofits in order to inform a possible redesign of the organization flowing from the strategic direction of the organization.

STRATEGIC MANAGEMENT

Nonprofit organizations are created to achieve a specific purpose. The purpose may be modest and small scale, *e.g.*, establishing a neighbourhood safety program, or large and ambitious such as the Red Cross or UNICEF. Nonprofits articulate their purpose in mission statements and it is this mission that guides their programs and activities. But mission alone may not be enough. Nonprofits also need to make sure that mission connects to strategy so one does not lose sight of the other. For example, the mission of SOS Kinderdorf, a nonprofit established in Austria in 1949, was "to provide orphaned, abandoned and destitute children with a new and permanent home, and to lay a sound foundation for a useful and productive life". Kinderdorf created children's villages all over the world to provide shelter and care. However, because in developing countries no schooling was available and shelter alone would not have been enough to lead to a useful and productive life for children there, the organization established kindergartens and schools. By 1990, about 40 per cent of its budget was being spent on schools and medical centres. While these activities were consistent with the mission, the organization now only dedicated 60 per cent of its budget for its original purpose of providing homes (Rangan (2004)).

Another way mission and strategy can become disconnected is when they shift their core services as they pursue available funding. Governments and foundations provide funding consistent with their own objectives and cash-strapped small nonprofits may find themselves applying for programs that only marginally fit with their mission. Nonprofit organizations thus need to protect and support their mission through well-integrated strategies.

Strategy is central to successful decision-making in the private sector. Business strategy and its principles were famously articulated many years ago by Michael Porter in his book on competitive strategy. Porter recommended that firms make conscious decisions about how to position themselves in the market by selecting one of three competitive strategies: low-cost leadership, differentiation and focus (Porter (1980)). More recently, the development and execution of strategies have been conceptualized as "strategic management". Strategic management consists of two different components: strategic thinking and strategic planning. Mintzberg explains that strategic thinking involves synthesis — encouraging intuitive, innovative and creative thinking at all levels of the organization; strategic planning concerns analysis — establishing and formalizing systems and procedures (Mintzberg (1994a)). Tim O'Shannassy has proposed a model that shows the breakdown of strategic management into strategic thinking and strategic planning. He has also connected the two processes in a continuous feedback loop. The model has been reproduced in Figure 1.

Figure 1: Strategic Management Process

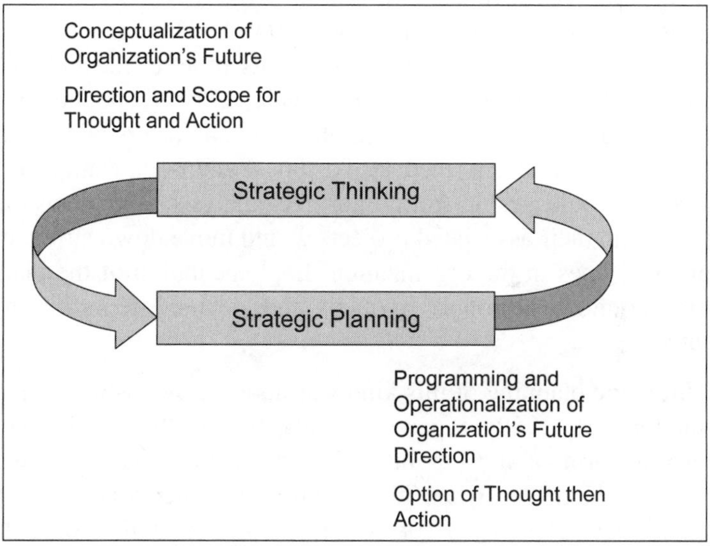

Source: Adapted from Tim O'Shannassy, "Modern strategic management: Balancing strategic thinking and strategic planning for internal and external stakeholders". *Singapore Management Review*, (2003)25, 1, p. 55.

Similar models have been developed by Liedtka (1998) and Graetz (2002). Liedtka (1998) has identified five major attributes of strategic thinking that should be of interest to nonprofit leaders. They are generic and can be equally applied in the private and nonprofit sector.

1. Strategic thinking is holistic in that it looks at all parts of the organization and their inter-relationships.

2. Strategic thinking is characterized by strategic intent, which is the force that mobilizes leaders to think beyond the current capacity of the organization.

3. In addition to future oriented strategic intent, strategic thinkers make connections between the past, present and future.

4. Strategic thinking involves asking "what if" questions. Strategic thinkers develop hypotheses about different scenarios and are prepared to test them.

5. Strategic thinking requires leaders to be intelligently opportunistic. They will remain open to alternative strategies even after they have developed a strategic path for the organization (Liedtka (1998)).

To some extent, research on strategic thinking has been influenced by critiques levelled at constraints imposed by rigid strategic planning processes (*e.g.*, Mintzberg (1994b)). This is not surprising since, historically, strategic planning has its roots in the military and referred to the management of large-scale military operations. As a result, early efforts at strategic planning were characterized by a highly controlled process determined at the top of the organization. Formal documents would result from intensive analysis, and decisions on strategies and their associated projects would move down strict vertical hierarchical lines in the organization. Implementation of the plan was closely monitored through frequent and detailed reporting to the executive.

Strategic planning of this kind was adopted by business organizations in the early 1950s. It gained popularity until the mid-1970s, after which this form of it went into a steady decline. This decline was reversed in the 1990s when globalization and increased competition presented new challenges for business and the notion of strategic thinking began to replace the creation of formal long-term plan documents. This was also the period during which public sector organizations and nonprofit organizations started to plan "strategically". Now, because newer models of strategic planning include a certain amount of "visioning" as part of the planning process, nonprofit leaders are able to apply their strategic thinking to strategic planning. More and more nonprofit organizations formalize their vision in a strategic plan which in turn provides the framework for initiatives and projects.

Strategic Planning

One of the major challenges of strategic planning is how to prevent strategic plans from languishing on the shelf in well-designed binders that nobody ever looks at! Strategic planning demands executive involvement, employee commitment and, above all, should be relevant to the organization's day-to-day functioning. Nonprofit leaders also need to pay attention to the "political" dimension of strategic planning. The Board of Directors must be convinced, politicians' requirements must be met, stakeholders' sensitivities must be respected and employees must be persuaded to buy in to the process. The formal creation of a strategic plan is a technique, but the development of an effective strategic planning process is an art

Most nonprofits in Canada, however, are small organizations, with the majority of them employing less than 10 people. As a result, they often lack the expertise in developing and implementing a strategic plan and so have to rely on outside expertise. In doing this, executive directors may ask advice from other nonprofits or may turn to consultants to help them with various components of strategic planning. Consultants may be hired as:

- Facilitators: to prepare for and manage strategic planning retreats or other key meetings;

- Researchers: to carry out time-consuming, highly specialized work such as environmental scans;

- Writers: to prepare successive drafts of the strategic plan and;

- Coaches/guides: to help participants become more effective in the strategic planning process by providing individual support.

- Good consultants can be beneficial because they are able to dedicate their full attention to the planning process, something which is usually not possible for people within the organizations of all sizes. They can also provide an objective perspective on the process and mediate between people with divergent opinions. Management consultants are also well versed in techniques used to help groups make complex and difficult decisions. Of course, hiring outside consultants also means that the organization does not develop its own in-house expertise, nor will there be a corporate memory of the process. CEOs will have to weigh this loss of knowledge against the advantages of bringing in someone with experience.

A visual representation of the strategic planning process appears as a linear journey through a process that is anything but linear. Strategic planning is circular, often circuitous, iterative and problematic. For the sake of expediency, the model is presented as if it were a straight line with step-by-step logic which proceeds systematically through the strategic planning process. Bryson (2004) has done seminal work in strategic planning for the nonprofit sector and much of the discussion that follows is based on his model. A modified version of the model is shown in Figure 2.

Figure 2: Strategic Planning Process

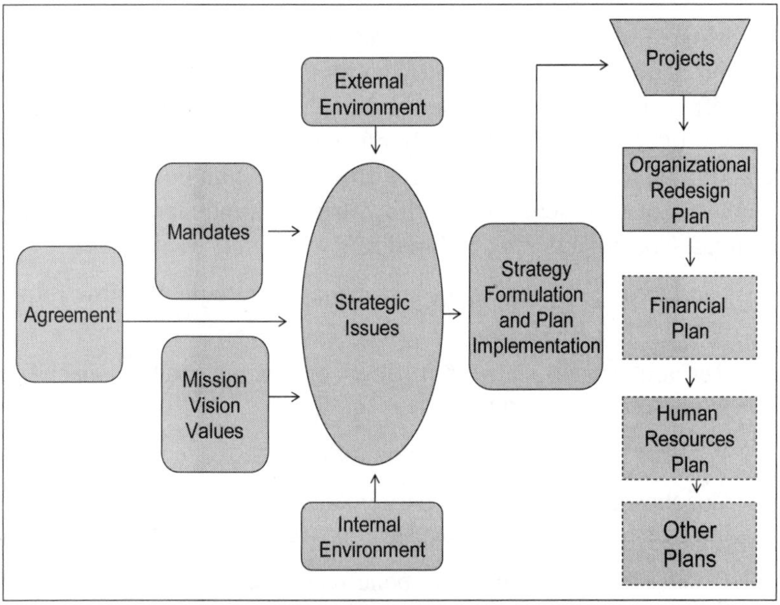

Source: Adapted from John M. Bryson (2004), *Strategic Planning for Public and Nonprofit Organizations* (San Francisco: Jossey-Bass, 2004), p. 33.

The model shows a number of discrete stages, starting with the agreement and ending with a series of projects that flow from the strategies and goals that are to be implemented. The first part of the framework is primarily concerned with information collection, strategic thinking about mission, vision and values, and the creation of strategic issues. The second part is mainly concerned with giving form to the strategic issues, translating them into "doable" strategies in a strategic plan and implementing the plan through an appropriate set of projects or programs. Depending upon the nature of the plan there may be many projects or just a few. In this chapter, we will concentrate on a project that involves the redesign of the organization.

Get Agreement on the Strategic Planning Process

It is useful to start the planning process by formally agreeing to do so. Agreements are likely to have different forms and different names. They may be called charters, contracts or planning documents. They may be very detailed or consist of simple letter of intent, indicating that strategic planning will take place, what its objectives are and who will be involved. Not all agreements need be very specific. However, the greater the specificity, the more guidance it can provide for the process. A formal document of agreement provides legitimacy and authority for the planning effort, demonstrates that the CEO is committed to the process and will assist in getting buy-in from the employees.

Nonprofit leaders will need the dedicated support of a team to create the strategic plan, even if the organization is supported by an outside adviser. If possible, team members should be appointed at the agreement stage and should be held directly accountable to the CEO.

Confirm Mandate and Conduct Stakeholder Analysis

The first step in the actual planning process itself should consist of those involved formally confirming the organization's mandate (even though the executive may be crystal clear about it). The mandate states what the organization is, what the limits are within which it is legally allowed to function and what it is required to do. In addition to its formal mandate, nonprofit leaders need to consider the organization's informal mandate. Informal mandates relate to the — often unspoken — expectations that stakeholders have, including internal stakeholders.

Stakeholders are "any person, group, or organization that can place a claim on an organization's (or other entity's) attention, resources, or output or that is affected by that output" (Bryson (2004, p. 35)). Internal stakeholders, *e.g.*, the Board of Directors and the staff and volunteers working in the organization, have their own ideas about the informal mandate of the organization. Their views may be more restricted than the official mandate or they may believe that the organization's tasks go beyond that mandate and are looking to broaden the agency's range of activities. Outside stakeholders too, may expect an organization to take on responsibilities that, strictly speaking, do not fall within its mandate. An internal and external stakeholder analysis will assist nonprofit leaders in assessing their mandate as perceived by the stakeholders.

A stakeholder analysis should identify each stakeholder, describe the relationship between the stakeholder and the organization (and, if applicable, the relationship between the stakeholders and other stakeholders), and group stakeholders in accordance with their relative importance to the organization. In addition, it is important to describe, as precisely as possible, the expectations that the stakeholders have of the organization. Internal stakeholders may have very different expectations than external stakeholders. It is advisable to create a simple diagram that shows the relative importance of the stakeholders. The diagram could show for example, that funders and clients (members, service recipients, and the community) are key stakeholders by showing them in large boxes and in close proximity to the organization.

Stakeholders are key to an organization because it is they who must be satisfied if the organization is to continue a successful existence. Attention to stakeholders has been common in the private sector but has received greater attention in the nonprofit sector only in the past decade. For example, Fletcher *et al.* (2003) reported on the results of an empirical investigation of the stakeholders of the Australian Red Cross Blood Service. Using a methodology of value contribution they were able to aggregate a large number of stakeholders' priorities with respect to the agency. This allowed the agency to reconsider its mandate, mission and vision.

Review Mission, Vision and Values

Mission

Once the organization has established (or redefined) its mandate and has carried out a stakeholder analysis, it is ready to review its mission. Of course, most nonprofits already have a mission before they undertake a strategic planning exercise. However, leaders need to review the existing mission to ensure that it still meets both the organization's mandate and stakeholders' expectations. Compare for example the mission statement published on the Internet by the U.S.-based St. Charles County Department of Community Health and the Environment in 1999 with that of 2004.

1999 Mission Statement

The St. Charles County Department of Community Health and the Environment is committed to the protection and enhancement of health and the quality of life for all members of our community by assessment of health and environmental status, development of policies and priorities, and assurance that there is appropriate response to needs.

2004 Mission Statement

We are committed to the protection and enhancement of the quality of life for all members of our community through good health that comes from education, disease prevention and from promoting and upholding good healthcare and environmental standards and practices.

The difference between the two mission statements is subtle but meaningful. The former specifies what the Department will do (*i.e.*, assessment of health, development of policies and assurance of responses), whereas the latter is much more general in stating what will occur. It is no longer immediately obvious where the responsibility rests, and accountability will be diffused. The new mission statement may have been the result of a change in government policy, a change in mandate or a change in financial resources available to the organization.

Vision

Recently, the author of this chapter reviewed about 50 strategic plans of nonprofit organizations and was surprised to find that about 15 per cent of them did not include a vision statement. It is hard to imagine a strategic planning exercise without having a vision for the organization in place. An organization's vision is the beacon directing and guiding the nonprofit organization towards its desired future. The development of a vision for the organization comes closest to the realm of "strategic thinking" discussed earlier. Executive directors must be able to provide a description of what a successful organization should look like once it has reached its full potential. The vision statement should "emphasize purposes, behaviour, performance criteria, and decision rules that service the public, rather than the organization, and create public value" (Bryson (2004, at p. 226)). This conception of success should be widely shared within the organization to mobilize in employees a sense of commitment to the organization's goals. It should also be shared with the stakeholders to ensure a thorough understanding of the organization's objectives by interested outsiders.

Values

Mission and vision statements are often accompanied by explicit statements of values and principles. Values are those conditions that the Board of Directors considers it desirable for the organization to meet in executing its mandate. For example, a social service agency might hold as a value "unconditional respect for all our clients" or "transparency in all our operations". Values can be stated as principles that become the rules or standards that guide employee behaviour. The value of "respect" in a social agency, for instance, might dictate a number of principles which will lead staff to refrain from such actions as asking personal questions unless absolutely necessary for the provision of service. "Respect" in a half-way house could translate into a principle of zero tolerance for drugs. An organization's mission and vision should be strongly supported by values and principles that are more than just lofty statements. Nonprofit leaders should make an effort to create meaningful values and principles that are directly relevant to the mission and vision to guide the organization.

External and Internal Environmental Analysis

External Scan

The next step in the planning process is to carry out an analysis of the internal and external environments (referred to as an environmental scan). Environmental analyses can be quite extensive and many small organizations who attempt strategic planning prefer to engage a consultant for this work. Outside assistance might also be helpful when the organization attempts an environmental scan the first time. Ongoing and routine scanning can then be taken over by employees.

Conceptually, the environmental scan be broken down into three components: scanning for emerging issues, monitoring priority issues and forecasting trends. *Scanning for emerging issues* consists of picking up (sometimes quite weak) signals of the first expression of new ideas or pressures. An example in the nonprofit sector would be an increased emphasis by funders on accountability requirements for community service agencies. Such requirements may lead to demands for such things as quality assurance through accreditation. Ideas around accountability might have been "out there" for quite a while before they became articulated as new requirements for measuring and reporting on inputs, outputs and outcomes. The idea of scanning the external environment is to identify such issues early enough to determine whether a future strategic response may be needed.

Monitoring occurs after scanning activities have identified emerging issues. It involves keeping track of them and clarifying them in sufficient detail to actually formulate a strategic response.

Forecasting trends is based on scanning and monitoring but goes beyond the capacity of scanning and monitoring by projecting different scenarios into the future.

In addition to these three phases of environmental analysis, it is also important for nonprofit leaders to assess the complexity of the environment and the risks it poses to the organization. The larger the scope of its programs, the greater is likely to be the complexity of its environment. For example, a national program operates in a more complex environment than a local or regional program. Likewise, the more heterogeneous the programs, the greater the complexity of the environment within which the programs operate. Finally, the greater the rate of change in the environment, the greater the risks it creates for the organization. Historically, many in the nonprofit sector enjoyed relative environmental stability and consequently operated in a low-risk environment for a long time. However, the late twentieth century heralded a period of accelerating change that has made the environment in the much more uncertain.

Internal Scan

While the external environment is extremely important, CEOs and other nonprofit leaders should not ignore the organization's internal environment. An internal scan involves the assessment of the organization's people and financial resources. Leaders should determine its current information technology, the competencies that staff possess and the prevailing culture. An assessment should also be made of the current overall strategy and, in the case of large organizations, their departmental and unit strategies. Finally, an internal scan includes examining current performance using existing indicators, history or specially prepared reports such as a balanced scorecard. Small, voluntary organizations or large nonprofits that rely to some degree on volunteer labour should also complete an assessment of volunteers.

Strength, Weaknesses, Opportunities and Threats (SWOT)

The result of external and internal information gathering is a SWOT analysis. A SWOT analysis might best be presented in a table. A possible SWOT table for an agency promoting literacy in a medium-sized city is presented in Table 1.

Table 1: Partial SWOT Analysis

External		Internal	
Opportunities	**Threats**	**Strengths**	**Weaknesses**
Seen as a municipal resource	New or increased competition by other providers of literacy services	Central geographic location in populated area	Lack of space for volunteers and information collections
Good internet connections — access, connectivity	Internet connections — access, connectivity	Well connected with other agencies	High staff turnover
Culturally diverse population	Culturally diverse population	Expertise in locating resources	No fundraising strategy

From this example it can be seen that opportunities may be a threat but that threats may also be opportunities. A culturally diverse population is an opportunity because it creates a rich environment in which clients learn about each other's culture. At the same time, a culturally diverse population may be a threat because the methods that the organization uses may not be universal enough to support multiple cultures. Clients may experience loneliness and even alienation if they cannot relate to the mode of operation the agency employs.

A potential problem with SWOT analysis is that tables, such as in Table 1, may be very large and contain a great many boxes. Priorities are not always obvious and sometimes CEOs and their strategic management team feel overloaded with information and unable to make the best use of the analysis. The key is to remember that whether something is an opportunity or a threat is directly related to the organization's strengths and weaknesses. For example, good Internet connections are only an opportunity if the organization has computer-literate staff or volunteers. Otherwise, it will likely be a threat.

Definition of Strategic Issues

We have now come to the central point in the strategic planning process: determining the organization's strategic issues. As Figure 2 on page 280 indicates, all foregoing activities are completed in the service of this important step. Strategic issues are key questions facing the organization that most fundamentally affect its policies, programs and services. In the Canadian nonprofit sector for example, one of the key strategic issues over the past several years has been "how to ensure continued participation by volunteers in the organization". This strategic issue is the result of a number of factors that an environmental scan would readily reveal. For example:

- Volunteers are moving from long-term volunteering with a single organization to short-term commitments to several organizations. More and more volunteers will commit for a specific, limited period of time but may or may not do so repeatedly.

- The volunteer pool has become increasingly diverse. New Canadians may not be familiar with the concept of volunteerism, leading to a reduction of total number of volunteers.

- Increased sophistication and education levels of volunteers have resulted in individuals seeking more meaningful, challenging and interesting volunteer opportunities. Nonprofits may not be aware of this shift or do not have exciting jobs to offer.

- The majority of volunteers today are working people and likely to come from families where both parents are employed. As a result there is an increasing interest in opportunities that can include or involve the entire family.

- With the advent of personal computers and the Internet come opportunities to change the way volunteering is managed and the programs being offered. The use of technology can impact volunteer job design and activity through home-based involvement (sometimes known as "virtual volunteering") (Renz (2005)).

The continuing reduction in volunteer hours since 1997 and the fact that volunteer labour is equivalent to about one million jobs in the nonprofit sector makes this a strategic issue for the sector as a whole. It is also a strategic issue for the leadership of individual nonprofit organizations because they have an opportunity to do something about it by responding creatively to the issue. The degree to which volunteers are a strategic issue for any one nonprofit organization however, will depend on more than the external environmental scan. Nonprofit leaders need to take into account the organization's internal strengths and weaknesses with respect to volunteers, the role envisioned for volunteers in the mission and vision statement and the relationship between volunteers and major stakeholders.

The identification and definition of strategic issues should be firmly connected to the vision statement. A collective picture of the future in which the organization has successfully met its mission will provide a clear point of reference for framing strategic issues. Within this context leaders have to ask a number of questions. Not surprisingly, the first one is: "What is the issue?" For example, if the organization does not use volunteers or anticipate using them in the future (*i.e.*, volunteers are not part of the vision of success), changes in the volunteer population will be of no consequence. Strategic issues should be framed as questions the organization can do something about. If the answer to the strategic issue is beyond its control, it does not qualify as a strategic issue.

The next question asks what factors (mandates, stakeholders, and environmental forces) make this a strategic issue. Sometimes, but not always, it is useful to ask the additional question: "What happens when the strategic issue is *not* addressed?" The answer to this question would be most helpful if there are numerous strategic issues and the CEO and the strategic management team have to rank them in order of importance or urgency or both.

An alternative method to approaching strategic issues is called "scenario building" or "scenario planning". Scenario building is a technique that allows leaders to imagine and build on different possible futures (Schwartz (1991)). It introduces a new step between the environmental scan and the final identification of strategic issues. One of the three components of environmental scanning is the forecasting of trends. Forecasting is based on informed guesses and implied probabilities of events occurring. Scenario planning makes these probabilities explicit by imagining and articulating mutually exclusive, relevant futures. It involves a number of steps that start with an initial strategic question. For example, an agency providing shelter to homeless adults may wonder about its current strategy of relying on government grants and contracts to fulfil its mandate. The question might be whether this strategy should be replaced with a more market-based strategy that sees the organization securing mortgage financing to build revenue-generating apartment buildings. The revenue would be used to finance the shelters. In order to flesh out the scenario, next steps would involve the identification of trends in the housing market, the rate of increase in the homeless population and current government funding strategies. This information would be available from the environmental scan. Then, different scenarios could be developed on the basis of possible trends being realized. For example, real estate prices may increase, decrease or stay the same. The effect on the alternative financing strategy will vary with each scenario. Other driving forces expected to be related to each of these price variations will be added to the scenarios until the scenarios are complete. Finally, each of the scenarios will form a specific strategic issue for the organization. Scenario planning techniques answer "what if" questions and enhance the nonprofit leaders' ability to add strategic thinking to the strategic planning process.

Strategy Formulation and Plan Implementation

Once the strategic issues have been identified, the next step in the strategic planning process is to design a strategic plan to address these issues. The strategic plan is a blueprint for realizing the organization's vision. It formulates the specific goals and objectives to be achieved. The Canadian Mental Health Association of Ontario (CMHAO), for example, has identified "knowledge transfer" as one of the strategic issues its 2005-08 strategic plan. Within the knowledge transfer area, it has identified three major strategies one of which is "public education and health promotion". Key activities within this category are:

*   Continue CMHA Ontario involvement in the Making Gains conference, in partnership with three other organizations, and the national CMHA conference in 2007.

*   Work with branches to strengthen their capacity to deliver public education in their local communities, by facilitating the sharing of information and resources.

- Establish a link with the Ontario Ministry of Education and explore partnership opportunities with educational institutions to raise mental health awareness and improve support in the elementary, secondary, and post-secondary school system, by developing key messages for schools and creating public education programs around such themes as bullying, self-esteem and parenting.

- Participate in public mental health awareness events, such as Mental Health Week and Mental Illness Awareness Week.

- Work to ensure mental health training for service providers, including physicians and other health care providers, teachers, police, and others.

- Increase actual and virtual opportunities for dialogue with the public, including people with mental illness, family members, employers, and professionals, in order to raise the organization's profile and credibility.

- Guide and support consumers and family members in telling their own stories through CMHA Ontario for the purposes of public education.

- Include addictions content in our public education and health promotion activities.

(Canadian Mental Health Association (2005)).

These strategies are to be implemented over the next three years, which brings us to the topic of implementation. Plan implementation is qualitatively different from the process of arriving at the strategic plan and its rate of success tends to be rather low (Mintzberg (1994b)). Implementation is an entirely new undertaking. It is the point where planning ends and reality starts. Implementation is also the most vulnerable stage since much of the excitement that went into putting the plan together and coming up with creative ideas and strategies to deal with the organization's future diminishes as the planning phase draws to a close.

Implementation requires nonprofit leaders to provide new energy and possibly new players who can invigorate the process of realizing the strategic plan. Also, the skills associated with plan implementation are quite different from those needed for planning. Good implementers are people who take a highly structured approach to their work and pay sufficient attention to detail without losing sight of the larger picture. Their talents will include the management of sometimes very large teams from different parts of the organization who may have their own objectives for the plan's implementation. Most small nonprofits do not have employees with the requisite range of skills but, on the other hand, their involvement with complex organizational issues will be less demanding. Successfully implementing strategic plans also demands solid budgeting, scheduling, monitoring and evaluation skills. In short, nonprofit leaders who take strategic planning to the implementation stage must possess competencies that have a broad range as well as significant depth.

Implementation is also the point of transition between strategic planning and project management as shown in Figure 2 on page 280. A project, whether resulting from a strategic planning process or existing independently, is defined as "a unique complex of activities aimed at achieving a jointly predetermined, unique result that must be realized with limited means" (Kor & Wijnen, (2000, p. 17)).

The literature on strategic plan implementation and project management contains many articles about the failure to implement plans successfully. Indeed, according to Raps (2004) only 10 per cent to 30 per cent of all implementation efforts succeed (p. 49). Nonprofit leaders need to be particularly vigilant during the project management phase or all the efforts to create an exciting strategic plan will have been in vain.

Project Management

There are two types of projects: those that flow from a strategic planning effort and those that are undertaken independently. In the private sector, emergent projects may come in the form of, say, large engineering assignments such as building a tunnel under the English Channel or dealing with the implications of a natural disaster. In the public sector, projects may emerge from government decisions in response to crises such as the 2003 SARS outbreak in Canada, or in response to otherwise unanticipated circumstances. In the nonprofit sector projects may be the result of changes in governments' fiscal, economic or social policies. In British Columbia, for example, the provincial government recently made several attempts to consolidate nonprofit organizations involved with delivering family services — a large project. Other changes in the funding environment may result in different networks having to be established. New accountability regimes may require the capturing of additional electronic information from more sources. Technological change may also drive projects as computer systems may no longer be supported by vendors and may need to be replaced. Clearly, nonprofit leaders are often faced with projects other than those following from the strategic plan and one of the ongoing challenges is to sustain the focus on strategic projects rather than constantly "putting out fires". It seems appropriate therefore to briefly review the main components of project management (Kor & Wijnen (2000)).

Project Life Cycle

A project life cycle is the sequence of stages that a project might progress through, from the time that it emerges from a strategic plan to the point that its objectives have been accomplished.

Feasibility Study. A feasibility study is an early, high-level assessment of whether it would be practicable and worthwhile to pursue an opportunity or a solution to a problem and, if so, how. It should identify and evaluate optional solutions, their justification and viability, and how one might implement each. The study needs to provide sufficient information to justify any recommendations on whether and how to proceed. Feasibility studies would normally precede a business case. When there are limited resources, feasibility studies will assist in selecting from among competing strategies.

Business Case. The business case is the documented justification for setting up a project, defining the benefits being sought, the likely investment, the constraints and the timescales, all of which go to answer the question: "Why should we do this project?"

Risk Management. A project risk is a possible future event or situation that, if it happens, will affect the ability of a project to arrive at its intended outcome. Procedures should be put in place to identify those factors that might throw the project off-course, and result in measures to deal with them.

Terms of Reference. Written terms of reference are used to indicate the parameters of a particular project. They are important for defining the expectations of those working within the project and for accountability purposes.

Scope. This is the definition of what the project needs to deliver (in terms of specific outputs) to identified stakeholders for a pre-defined purpose within a pre-defined period. It is often helpful to explicitly state in advance what is in and out of scope so that expectations about deliverables remain within the parameters of the project.

Sponsor. In the project environment, a sponsor describes a senior individual in the organization, normally a person who will see his or her part of the organization benefit from the project's outputs. Usually the CEO is the ultimate authority on a project but this may be delegated depending on its scope and importance.

Communication Plan. A communication plan is that part of the project plan designed to ensure that internal and external stakeholders know what is going on, when and why, and enabling feedback from them. Large, lengthy and complicated projects are particularly in need of a communications plan since much of a project success depends on the level of satisfaction of many stakeholders, not just the sponsor.

Impact Analysis. An impact analysis is conducted to understand the effect of requested changes to the project. It is used to forecast the possible effects of any proposed or imposed changes and the justification, schedule, budget, risks and issues. This will allow the board of directors the opportunity to consider the full implications before committing to a course of action.

Post-project Review. A post-project review is an appraisal to determine whether the expected benefits, as documented in the business case (or any other authorized documents showing expected results) have been achieved. The business case should also have identified how the benefits should eventually be measured, so this is a vital input to any review process.

There are quite a few similarities between the strategic planning process and project management. All projects can be broken down into five distinct phases:

1. **Initiating** — the development of a vision for a project and the establishment of overall project goals.

2. **Planning** — definition of financial and human resources, development of a schedule, specification of detailed project objectives.

3. **Executing** — management and co-ordination of the project team and the resources allocated to the project as agreed to in the terms of reference or project charter.

4. **Controlling** — monitoring the project for deviations from the plan and taking remedial action as and when required.

5.   **Closing** — bringing formal closure to the project through completion of all deliverables, disbanding of the team and the production of final reports.

In the nonprofit sector strategies and projects are for the most part formulated within the current structure of the organization. Organization structures constrain the type of strategies that the CEO may wish to pursue, *i.e.*, those strategies that flow logically from the strategies issues. It may therefore be desirable to redesign the organization to achieve those ends. The next section of this chapter examines elements of organizational form and organizational design.

ORGANIZATIONAL FORM

This volume is dedicated to nonprofit organizations in Canada and to the nonprofit *form*[2] of organization, *i.e.*, governance by a voluntary board of directors, use of volunteers, and benefits that accrue to either the membership or the community. However, this is not the only form traditionally "pure" nonprofit organizations can take. Reductions in funding, increasing social and economic pressures, greater competition within the nonprofit sector and the encroachment of the private sector have pushed some into the realm of "social entrepreneurship", which is another form of organization.

Social entrepreneurship occurs when nonprofit organizations establish or enter into profit-making ventures to finance their nonprofit operations. Nonprofits may use their expertise to sell their services to other nonprofit organizations. For example, an organization that manages a large number of properties may use its expertise to assist other nonprofit organizations with property financing and management. Others may have special expertise in communications which they offer in the community on a fee-for-service basis. The benefits appear to be mutual; the service-providing organization gains even greater expertise and the service-receiving organization does not have to develop its own expertise and obtains services at relatively low prices.

Nonprofits may offer services by employing their clients and selling their labour, *e.g.*, mental health clients. Clients may provide

---

[2]   Organizational form refers to the legal status of the organization; it is different from organizational design, which denotes the configuration of structures and processes. Organizational design is discussed in the next section.

landscaping services, manufacture products for sale or cater events. Provider clients gain because they get work experience and increase their ability to function independently, and receiving organizations benefit because they obtain services at a reduced cost. Other entrepreneurial activities may include organizing events such as conferences, workshops and training programs.

What these activities have in common is that they are intended to create revenue in the form of profit for the nonprofit organization. In order for such activities to be successful, the social entrepreneur has to build capacity, *i.e.*, acquire employees with business skills that are not necessarily aligned with the organization's mission and vision.

Social entrepreneurship may also lead to nonprofit organizations entering into subcontracts to provide programmatic expertise with private sector firms that have won government contracts through privatization. They may enter into partnerships with the for profit sector through the creation of new (for-profit) companies. Some cases may even convert to for-profit status in order to carry out their mission.

As a result of these kinds of social entrepreneurial activities, nonprofit organizations may adopt non-traditional organizational hybrid forms. Holding companies and joint ventures are new forms that allow the nonprofit organization to generate additional funding while at the same time remaining true to its mission. An example of a holding company would be a university operating a real estate company or a hospital owning parking lots. A hospital could also restructure by "creating a nonprofit parent, a nonprofit hospital subsidiary, and for-profit ambulatory surgery centers and diagnostic laboratories" (Tuckman (1998, at p. 188)). In other words, joint ventures may be created between nonprofit organizations for the purpose of making a profit but the organizations would remain structured as nonprofits.

The strategic vision and key strategic issues in a strategic plan may contemplate a deviation from the traditional nonprofit form through entering into social entrepreneurial initiatives. In this case, leaders should be prepared to operate in a paradoxical environment. Staff and volunteers will have to be trained to become more business-focused in one area while upholding the organization's mission, values and principles at the same time. This is particularly important in small organizations where the skills of organizational members are usually related only to the organization's service objectives.

ORGANIZATIONAL DESIGN

Organizational design refers to the grouping of organizational functions within an organization. An organization's basic design is the backbone of its structure, which comprises "the various processes technologies, systems, and coordination and control mechanisms necessary to allow individuals to perform tasks in an integrated manner" (Shoichet (1998, at p. 77)).

One of the most common designs is the functional grouping. "Functional grouping places employees together who perform similar function or work processes or who bring similar knowledge and skills to bear" (Daft (2004, at p. 97)). Thus some nonprofits may be designed around the primary functions served by the organization. They may have a nursing department staffed by nurses and nurse assistants and a social work department that houses probation officers, counsellors and child protection workers.

More often, however, nonprofits are organized by programs. A social service agency for example, may be organized around a shelter program, an addiction program, a half-way house and an employment program. Each program is headed by a program manager who has employees reporting to him or her. Programs may be in the same building or may be physically separate and located in special centres to be closer to the clientele. Program managers usually have their own budget, goals and objectives for the program. In small organizations functions and programs may be organized around individuals. For example, one nurse may be employed who, by definition, fulfils the nursing function. But she or he may also be responsible for a program that includes home visits, addiction counselling and a small recreation unit.

Regardless of whether a nonprofit is organized by program or function, if it is large enough, it usually has separate (functional) departments responsible for finance, information systems, human resources and public relations. Again, in small organizations these functions may be bundled and carried out by one or two people. These departments or individuals perform what are known as "staff" functions *i.e.*, they provide services to other parts of the organization. Programs and functions directly concerned with meeting organizational objectives are called "line" functions. Line functions are carried out by employees who directly serve the purpose of the organization and staff functions are carried out by employees who support line managers in doing their job.

Nonprofit leaders may have to deal with conflicts between line and staff functions when, for example, the financial manager attempts to influence the way a particular program is delivered because he or she feels that money can be saved by serving clients differently. Disputes may also arise when the person responsible for human resources puts severe restrictions on a line manager in terms of attracting staff or when the systems analyst puts the efficiency of the system before the ease of managing the system by field staff.

Tensions may occur as a result of confusion about the authority and responsibility of staff and line positions or may be the result of poor organizational design. For example, groupings of staff functions and line programs may be overlapping, reporting relationships may be unclear or bottlenecks may exist that prevent efficient decision-making. Organizational design may either facilitate or obstruct efficient and effective operations. However, there is no perfect design that will work for all organizations, nor will an organization's design guarantee successful outcomes. Of course, size may limit the flexibility of the organization in assigning individuals to either a staff role or a line role. The important point for CEOs is to ensure that a clear distinction is made between the line and staff responsibilities and authority.

Mechanistic and Organic Design

The very existence of organizations depends on the nature of their environment. In the private sector this environment is primarily framed by technological advances and competition. Political, legal and regulatory regimes have traditionally been the environmental forces that most strongly influence the existence of nonprofit organizations. However, over the past 20 years competition from other nonprofits, economic and social conditions, and technological developments are having an increasing effect.

In 1961, Burns and Stalker observed that for-profit organizations tended towards either mechanistic or organic structures as a function of the relative stability of their environment. In stable environments with high levels of certainty, structures tended to be *mechanistic*. Mechanistic structures exercised strict hierarchical control, *i.e.*, were highly centralized. Employees' tasks were strictly circumscribed and employees had little or no flexibility or discretion in carrying out their work. In unstable, uncertain environments however, organizations tended to be more flexible and their structure became more *organic*. In organic structures authority is decentralized, communication happens across the organization rather than from the top down and employees have more discretion in decision-making and work more in interdependent teams. The characteristics of mechanistic and organic structures are compared in the table below.

Table 2: Mechanistic versus Organic Structures

Mechanistic	Organic
Tasks are broken down into specialized, separate parts.	Employees contribute to the common tasks of the organization.
Tasks are rigidly defined.	Tasks are adjusted and redefined through employee teamwork.
There is a strict hierarchy of authority and control, and there are many rules (high formalization).	There is less hierarchy of authority and control, and there are few rules (low formalization).
Knowledge and control of tasks are centralized at the top of the organization.	Knowledge and control of tasks are located anywhere in the organization.
Communication is vertical.	Communication is horizontal.

Source: Adapted from Gerald Zaltman, Robert Duncan, & Johnny Holbeck, *Innovations and Organizations* (New York: Wiley, 1973), p. 131.

It would probably be fair to say that today most Canadian nonprofit organizations exist within a dynamic and changing environment where nothing much is certain and the future is anything but predictable. In addition, many nonprofits are greatly affected by public policy and must deal with highly charged and politicized environments. Given these conditions, it is suggested that the characteristics of organically structured organizations would appeal to the leaders of such organizations. It is also the case that smaller nonprofits would be more conducive to organic designs simply because they lack the resources to build extensive specialized staffs and heirarchies. Conversely, executives who run their organizations based on more traditional mechanistic principles may discover that that they need to rethink the organization's structure to bring it in line with the prevailing forces in the environment. Again, there is no perfect structure but organizations that fail to align themselves with the demands of their environment will be less successful than those that do.

Vertical and Horizontal Structures

Vertical Structures

An organization's design can be further analyzed (and managed) by looking at its vertical and horizontal structures. The vertical structure comprises two major (control) mechanisms: hierarchy and formalization. The horizontal structure includes two central (co-ordination) devices: information systems and cross functional teams and task forces.

Hierarchy

The chain of command emanates from the top (CEO or Executive Director), and flows down through the management layers to the front-line workers who provide services to the clients, community or members. This chain of command is expressed in organization charts (sometimes called organigrams), showing the employee names and titles in boxes connected by lines to other boxes below them. The lines indicate the reporting relationship within the organization's hierarchy. The Board of Directors is usually shown on the organization chart but the Board is (or should be) concerned with governance, not operations.[3] The organization chart illustrates who is "in charge". Directions flow from the top of the organization, and problems and queries are referred to upwards for resolution. Therefore the lines of authority also reflect the organization's communication channels.

The number of employees who report to a particular position constitute that position's *span of control*. The span of control at the top is usually narrow, *e.g.*, in midsize organizations three or four senior managers may report to the Executive Director. At the lower end of the organization the span of control tends to be wide. Each senior manager may be responsible for five to seven different programs or functions and program managers may have a dozen or more professionals reporting to them. This is also the reason why organization charts typically take the form of a pyramid. The number of direct reports may

---

[3]   This separation of governance and operations may be difficult to achieve in very small operations where board members tend to do volunteer work. See Chapter 3.

vary from organization to organization depending on the complexity of the work being done. Organizations that have an overall narrow span of control (few people reporting to individual managers) have a *tall* hierarchy. The greater the number of layers between the CEO and the lowest employee in the hierarchy, the taller the organization. Organizations that have an overall wide span of control (many employees reporting to individual managers) have a *flat* hierarchy. Many small nonprofits are very flat, in that most employees report directly to the executive.

One of the ways in which medium and large nonprofit organizations can become more efficient is through increasing spans of control, thereby reducing the number of managers in the organization. This "flattening" may reduce costs since fewer people have to be employed to do the same amount of work, but may negatively impact effectiveness since managers will have less time to deal with problems that need resolution and may generally feel overworked and undercompensated.

It is possible to find different organizations with the same hierarchy and span of control but with different loci of authority. Organizations in which the top executive makes most of the decisions without involving staff have highly centralized authority; they are *centralized*. In organizations where employees at the lower levels are permitted (and sometimes actively encouraged) to make the day-to-day decisions, authority is *decentralized*. The ability and willingness of the CEO to delegate authority to lower levels in the organization is mainly dependent on the real or perceived competency of employees, the personality of the CEO and the programs delivered by the organization. The degree to which authority is centralized is an indicator of organizational control.

Not all nonprofit organizations are structured in a pyramidal fashion. Some nonprofit leaders strongly believe in non-hierarchical structures. Such organizations are set up and managed in accordance with broad democratic principles, decisions tend to be made collectively and active participation by all staff is encouraged. In terms of organizational structure such organizations are very flat and decentralized. In small organizations operating on these principles everyone reports to the Executive Director. Medium and larger organizations may appoint team leaders rather than managers and staff may rotate in and out of these positions.

Formalization

The number of rules, regulations and operational procedures in place in an organization represents how formalized its structure is. One of the most commonly used sets of formal procedures is the departmental or program budget. A well-structured budget will allow employees to carry out their responsibilities within clear parameters. Other examples of formalization are detailed job descriptions, protocols for the treatments of clients, health and safety regulations, disciplinary procedures, and many more.

Nonprofit organizations that employ large numbers of professionals, such as museums and research organizations, usually have a low degree of formalization. This is based on the premise that professionals are assumed to have been trained before they joined the organization and so do not require a high level of control. They are believed capable of setting their own goals and objectives within the parameters set out in the organization's vision and mission statement. On the other hand, very large nonprofits with many programs staffed by a wide range of occupational groups would likely need a high degree of formalization to co-ordinate them and to ensure a standard level of performance in all parts of the organization.

Formalization may also be directly related to the type of nonprofit organization. A study by Hillel Schmid (2002), for example, showed that residential boarding schools for troubled children were characterized by a moderate to high degree of formalization which "substantiates the argument that boarding schools are committed to formal patterns that dictate the life of the professional staff and children" (p. 388). On the other hand, home care service organizations tended to have low levels of formalization combined with strong centralized management control. Schmid concluded that the high degree of control "is appropriate for the type and level of staff in home care organizations, which rely almost exclusively on an unskilled, non-nursing, female labor force"(p. 389). In other words, plans, rules and procedures provide less control than direct oversight by those in authority. Leaders of nonprofit organizations must match the amount and type of control needed in the organization with the capacity of its employees and the nature of the organization's programs.

Horizontal Structure

The horizontal structure of an organization refers to the formal linkages *across* the vertical hierarchy. They are the means used by leaders to co-ordinate work and overcome gaps and barriers that arise from the hierarchy and the division of labour by organizational functions or programs. For example, the exhibit unit, the outreach department and the marketing department in a cultural organization may all serve the same objectives, but unless they co-ordinate their work and communicate their ideas to each other, objectives may not be achieved. Information systems that cross functional teams and task-forces are the major tools used in the private sector and can be used to advance the objectives and strategic issues of nonprofits.

Information Systems

It is probably fair to say that today electronic information systems permeate all aspects of Canadians' personal and professional lives. In organizations, information systems have taken on different meanings over time. Today, information systems typically refer to computerized data processing for programmatic, financial or other purposes. Computerized information systems play a central role in an organization's structure and operations, not just to collect, store and retrieve information but also to provide linkages across departments and programs. In addition to serving vertical communication, tools such as electronic mail create the opportunity for employees (and volunteers) at all levels of the organization to communicate with each other. Electronic message boards allow employees to stay in touch on emerging issues. Employees are also able to create communities of practice using Web-based technology in order to share information about problems they face in their professional area. Organizations can also use personnel databases (subject to confidentiality provisions) to bring people together with common backgrounds and interests.

Program databases can provide information on clients (again subject to confidentiality provisions) to be used by managers who are responsible for different programs but who service the same group of clients. In this way managers can stay in touch to ensure integrated services are provided to clients even though clients make use of different programs. Information systems can also be used as a central co-ordinating mechanism to link activities within the organization's strategic plan, thereby ensuring appropriate and timely input and the dissemination on the progress of the strategic plan and its related activities. For more on the use of information technology in nonprofit management, see Chapter 12.

Task Forces and Cross-functional Teams

Task forces or work teams fall under the general rubric of "committees". They are created for a specified time and are usually charged with the responsibility for completing a large project or dealing with an important problem that affects the organization across functional and program units. For example, a library can put a taskforce together to deal with a recurring problem of theft and vandalism. Taskforce members may be drawn from librarians, support staff, volunteers and technical staff. The taskforce may be led by one of the representatives or by a member of the executive and would be required to present options to management to reduce theft while maintaining an open and welcoming atmosphere in the library.

The creation of a taskforce to address a particular problem acknowledges that solutions should be created though different parts of the organization working together. In the case of strategic planning, the taskforce would be the employee team supporting the CEO in putting the strategic plan together.

Cross-functional teams can be seen as permanent taskforces. Again, they are similar to committees. They are highly task directed and consist of members from different programs and will sometimes include line and staff representatives. Cross-functional teams may be charged with the responsibility for projects that require strong co-ordination over a long period of time. In the case of a three-year strategic plan they would be responsible for the implementation and maintenance of the plan during the three years. Or, they may be responsible for the co-ordination of client services across different programs. Another example would be creating a cross-functional team to attract and manage volunteers and review volunteer policies to ensure the volunteer population continues to serve the mission of the organization. Cross-functional teams do not take the place of the CEO; rather they support the organization by providing a bridge between organizational components at the employee and managerial level.

CONCLUSION

Strategy and structure are closely related concepts. Strategic planning gives form and content to the strategic vision of nonprofit leaders. A well-constructed and carefully implemented strategic plan will enable the achievement of the organization's future vision of success.

However, in order to successfully achieve strategic objectives the nonprofit organization needs a structure that is aligned with the strategy. If strategic goals cannot be achieved with the current structure, then structural redesign is called for. The description of the different features of organizational structure presented in this chapter is intended to assist nonprofit leaders in redesigning structures to meet the goals of the organization.

REFERENCES

Burns, T., & G.M. Stalker (1961), *The Management of Innovation* (London: Tavistock Publications, 1961).

Bryson, J.M. (2004), *Strategic Planning for Public and Nonprofit Organizations: A Guide to Strengthening and Sustaining Organizational Achievement*, 3rd ed. (San Francisco: Jossey-Bass, 2004).

Daft, R.L. (2004), *Organization Theory and Design*, 8th ed. (Mason, OH: Thomson/South-Western, 2004).

Canadian Mental Health Association, Ontario (2005), *Strategic Plan 2005-2008*. Available online at: <www.ontario.cmha.ca/content/inside_cmha/strategic_plan.asp>.

Fletcher, A., J. Guthrie, P. Steane, G. Roos & S. Pike (2003), "Mapping Stakeholder Perceptions for a Third Sector Organization" (2003), 4 *Journal of Intellectual Capital* 505-527.

Graetz, F. (2002), "Strategic Thinking Versus Strategic Planning: Towards Understanding the Complementarities" (2002), 40 *Management Decision* 456-462.

Kor, R., & G. Wijnen (2000), *50 Checklists for Project and Programme Managers* (Brookfield: Gower, 2000).

Liedtka, J. (1998), "Linking Strategic Thinking with Strategic Planning" (1998), 26:4 *Strategy and Leadership* 30-35.

Mintzberg, H. (1994a), "The Fall and Rise of Strategic Planning" (1994), 72:1 *Harvard Business Review* 107-114.

Mintzberg, H. (1994b), *The Rise and Fall of Strategic Planning: Reconceiving Roles for Planning, Plans, Planners* (Toronto: Maxwell Macmillan, 1994).

O'Shannassy, T. (2003), "Modern Strategic Management: Balancing Strategic Thinking and Strategic Planning for Internal and External Stakeholders" (2003), 25:1 *Singapore Management Review* 53-67.

Porter, M.E. (1980), *Competitive Strategy: Techniques for Analyzing Industries and Competitors* (New York: Free Press, 1980).

Rangan, V.K. (2004), "Lofty Missions, Down-to-Earth Plans" (2004), 82:3 *Harvard Business Review* 112-119.

Raps, A. (2004), "Implementing Strategy" (2004), 85:12 *Strategic Finance* 49-53.

Renz, H. (2005), "The Changing Nature of Volunteerism in the 21st Century". Unpublished paper.

Schmid, H. (2002), "Relationships Between Organizational Properties and Organizational Effectiveness in Three Types of Nonprofit Human Service Organizations" (2002), 31:3 *Public Personnel Management* 377-395.

Schwartz, P. (1991), *The Art of the Long View: Planning for the Future in an Uncertain World* (New York: Doubleday/Currency, 1991).

Shoichet, R. (1998), "An Organization Design Model for Nonprofits" (1998), 9:1 *Nonprofit Management and Leadership* 71-88.

Tuckman, H.P. (1998), " Competition, Commercialization, and the Evolution of Nonprofit Organizational Structures" (1998), 17 *Journal of Policy Analysis and Management* 175-194.

Zaltman, G., R. Duncan & J. Holbek (1973), *Innovations and Organizations* (New York: Wiley, 1973).

Chapter 9

FROM CONTROL TO LEARNING: ACCOUNTABILITY AND PERFORMANCE ASSESSMENT IN THE VOLUNTARY SECTOR

Susan Phillips and Tatyana Teplova
Carleton University

INTRODUCTION

Accountability is a central concern and growing pressure for voluntary sector organizations. But the issue for most of them is not a lack of accountability, but an over-abundance of it. In a narrow sense, accountability is the exercise of control over and the provision of assurances for how a mandate is being achieved (see Aucoin & Heintzman (2000); Aucoin & Jarvis (2005); Perrin (2002)). Such control may be driven externally or internally. Funders, for example, want to ensure that the money they provide is spent on the purposes intended in ways that conform to their requirements, and that those responsible answer for the expenditures and accept responsibility for fixing any problems encountered.

Boards of directors who hold such responsibility, and considerable personal liability, want internal control systems in place so that they get accurate financial reporting as well as good assessments of how well the organization is achieving its mission. Users of the organization's services want assurances that there is quality control over the services provided and members expect to have democratic control over the direction an organization is taking. So they should. There is an important place for accountability as control and assurance in the voluntary sector. With multiple sources of funding, the contracting out of public services that occurred over the past two decades, declining public trust and rising expectations about transparency, the multiple accountabilities faced by voluntary organizations have increased quite dramatically in recent years.

If accountability were only about control, however, it would seriously impair innovation and strategic direction setting. In a broader sense, accountability is about learning (Aucoin & Heintzman (2000)). It can and should be a strategic management tool for better performance, better results and continuous improvement (PAGVS (1999); Taylor (1996); Perrin (2002)). In contrast to the largely rules-based regimes that support accountability as control, accountability as learning has to be infused into the governance, operations, management styles and cultures of voluntary organizations.

This chapter takes a critical look at accountability and performance assessment as a strategic management tool and explores some of the key challenges involved. It focuses specifically on assessing the performance of programs and the organization as a whole, rather than on the details of broader accountability and regulatory regimes — *e.g.*, rules governing registration of charities, political activities, and funding — that are discussed in Chapters 5 and 6 of this volume.

The main challenges of performance assessment as accountability for learning do not lie in finding the "right" measurement tools or management techniques. There are a plethora of methods available and, indeed, the branding and selling of an array of new techniques to voluntary organizations has built a substantial evaluation consulting industry. So, we will not be extolling the virtues of, say, the balanced scorecard over the Drucker Foundation self-assessment tool, or any of the other helpful and not-so-helpful techniques that are available and marketed to voluntary organizations these days. Rather, we argue that the tough issues of performance assessment for voluntary organizations involve addressing the meta-questions, such as when and why to evaluate what, dealing with the political implications of performance assessment, making effective use of evaluation results, and building the capacity to become a self-improving, learning organization. These meta-issues are the focus of this chapter.

The notion of accountability as learning is evolving quite quickly in the voluntary sector, as it is in the public and private sectors. The fact that even the language we use to describe such measurement has changed in the past few years demonstrates that not only are new tools for measurement being adapted, but the very foundations of thinking about the rationale, focus and benefits of accountability are also shifting. Only a few years ago, we would have referred to *evaluation*, usually in reference to evaluation of programs or projects. Program evaluation has now been displaced by the concept of *performance assessment*. The latter is meant to emphasize the measurement of results rather than activities. It implies that assessment is an ongoing process rather than an episodic snapshot, and that it encompasses a broader focus that includes the assessment of entire organizations rather than just specific programs. More recently, the language of *performance management* is being recycled to encompass even broader issues of institutional design, co-ordination and organizational culture that enable assessment to be not only a driver of change, but a common language for achieving collective goals (Kettl (2005)).

The chapter begins with a brief overview of the current state of performance assessment in Canada's voluntary sector, as indicated by a recent national survey, and of the shifting language used to describe such assessment. We then focus on the meta-questions and challenges involved in using performance assessment as a management tool with an eye to providing some practical guidance to those working in the voluntary sector. Performance assessment is not without its darker side, however, and the conclusion gives a glimpse of some of this darkness. It also offers some suggestions for ways of enhancing performance assessment and accountability as a process of learning rather than control.

A TIDE OF RISING EXPECTATIONS: EVALUATION PRACTICES IN CANADA'S VOLUNTARY SECTOR

> Accountability in the voluntary sector is multi-layered — to different audiences, for a variety of activities and outcomes, through many different means.

(PAGVS (1999, at p. 14)).

The pressures for accountability and performance assessment have grown significantly over the past decade or so. These pressures for both more *and* better performance assessment are driven both internally, by boards, staff and volunteers concerned about making effective use of scarce resources, and externally, mainly by a variety of funders and by the need to demonstrate value in a somewhat crowded public space. Although most Canadian voluntary organizations conduct performance assessments of their own volition and as part of their routine operations, rather than because they were required to do so by funders, it is difficult to clearly differentiate internal and external drivers because the environment for both has changed rather dramatically in recent years.[1] In this section, we take a brief look at the current environment and state of practice for performance assessment in Canada's voluntary sector.

A Changing Environment

The introduction of New Public Management (NPM) with its emphasis on consumers, privatization, contracting out and market-based policy instruments, created an "explosion" (Power (1994); Phillips & Levasseur (2004)) in auditing in Canada as elsewhere. Across large parts of government at all levels, the role of managers shifted from supervising and delivering programs directly to managing contracts for services now provided by third parties — both voluntary organizations and private-sector firms. Assurances of quality in the expanded contracting culture created under NPM were provided by extended reporting requirements and by increased demands for evaluation of programs and projects. Performance assessment was by no means a new thing for NPM. Indeed, waves of budgeting and public sector reform over several decades had advocated different systems for assessing and managing performance, creating a virtual alphabet soup of techniques. What changed was the controlling role of government as a funder and contractor of services over the evaluation activities of a wide range of third parties.

   With concomitant funding cuts and the increased demand for services that occurred in the late 1980s and early 1990s, voluntary organizations needed to make tough decisions among programs, sometimes rationalizing or even closing programs (Toronto Agency Survey (2004)). Evaluation took on new importance in this context, although the extent to which it was actually used for decision-making varied enormously.

---

[1]   As noted in the discussion of the results of a 2003 national survey of performance assessment practices in Canada, three-quarters (73 per cent) of voluntary organizations indicated that the evaluations were part of their routine processes and were internally driven (Hall *et al.* (2003)). Only 4 per cent of evaluations were conducted solely in response to funders' requirements.

The focus of what to evaluate also changed over the course of the 1990s with the rise of outcome or results-based measurement. Whereas evaluation had tended to focus on activities and *outputs* (what was produced), the new demands were for evidence of *outcomes* (what actual changes were realized in the lives of users and beneficiaries). Although the interest in outcome measurement emanated in part from the field of evaluation itself and flowed through internationally connected networks, such as the United Way movement,[2] the real pressures set in when provincial and federal governments began to adopt results-based management.

In March 2000, the federal government adopted a comprehensive management framework known as *Results for Canadians* that committed departments to be more results-oriented and was dedicated to responsible spending. As indicated in this Treasury Board document, the new management framework meant that "public service managers are expected to define strategic outcomes, continually focus attention on results achievement, measure performance regularly and objectively, learn from this information and adjust to improve efficiency and effectiveness".[3] Several provinces, notably Alberta, were already ahead of the federal curve. By the mid-1990s, they had already begun to incorporate business planning and performance measurement into their budget planning processes and develop "results-based cultures".[4]

Outcome measurement and the production of performance indicators thus became closely tied to budgeting and to program reviews within Canadian governments, as it had elsewhere. It took on a particular saliency in Canada, however, as a result of the development of a mode of "instrumental federalism" in the late 1990s under the Social Union Framework Agreement (SUFA) and associated accords (Phillips (2003)). From the federal government's perspective, an instrumental approach to federalism involved solving problems for Canadians, without being hampered unduly by jurisdictional barriers,

---

[2] Several large American funders, notably the United Way of America and the Kellogg Foundation, produced handbooks for evaluation that circulated and were used quite widely in Canada. In particular, see Hatry *et al.* (1996).
[3] From the Treasury Board Secretariat Web page: <www.tbs-sct.gc.ca>.
[4] Alberta was the leader in developing a government-wide performance measurement system in the early 1990s. For example, its 1995 report, *Measuring Up*, reported on 22 core government performance measures. See Ogata *et al.* (1998).

and enhancing learning through evaluation (Saint-Martin (2004, at p. 31; Phillips (2003)).[5]

At all levels, then, the policy environment became enamoured with a results focus and with the production of standardized population-level performance indicators. The fact that relatively few of the indicators produced by governments were actually outcome measures was irrelevant: the policy and political environment — and the expectations created for the voluntary sector — had shifted considerably.

Leaders in Canada's voluntary sector were cognizant of the potential impact of the growing concern with accountability and performance assessment. In addition to pressures for greater performance measurement, there was an active campaign in the early 1990s by a federal Liberal backbench MP to severely tighten the regulatory regime. The vicarious effects of several major scandals among nonprofits south of the border illustrated both the importance and the fragility of public trust. In 1997, the Voluntary Sector Roundtable, an unincorporated group of national associations or networks that broadly represented all parts of the sector and that had formed to provide policy leadership, commissioned a panel of six (volunteer) experts to review and make recommendations on issues of accountability. The Panel on Accountability and Governance in the Voluntary Sector (PAGVS), chaired by Ed Broadbent, was charged with reviewing, consulting and making recommendations on how the sector could improve its own practices.

The Panel took a very broad perspective on accountability, considering both internal and external accountabilities and giving significant attention to the sector's relationship with government, particularly the federal government, which holds the main responsibility for the regulation of charities. Its 1999 report is best known for paving the way for the creation of the Voluntary Sector Initiative (VSI), a process established by the Government of Canada in 2000 to encourage a better relationship and enhance capacity in the sector. It was concerns over evaluation, however, that dominated the Panel's consultations

---

[5] However, in transferring block funds to the provinces that are nominally designated for particular policy fields, such as health care or early childhood initiatives, the federal government has no authority to require that they be spent on the initiatives they were designated for. The only means of securing accountability for these federal transfers is by requiring public reporting on policy outcomes and, according to the logic of SUFA, having the public and voluntary sector organizations serve as watchdogs by identifying which provincial and territorial governments are not up to "standard".

with voluntary organizations.[6] Of all the briefs submitted and the discussions held, the Panel probably heard more about outcome measurement and how voluntary organizations feared being carried away by a tidal wave of unrealistic expectations about performance measurement than any other topic.

The report of the PAGVS recognized that results-based perform-ance assessment was here to stay, at least for the foreseeable future, and it encouraged voluntary organizations to begin to develop their own sets of appropriate indicators before less appropriate ones were imposed on them. The Panel also noted, however, that better perform-ance measurement had to be a joint effort with funders, with a strong supporting role played by intermediary organizations (the federations, umbrellas and research organizations that serve the sector). In this regard, it called upon funders to use more multi-year funding, cover the costs of evaluation and consider more core funding, which helps build the capacity for performance assessment, and, perhaps most importantly, to begin a sustained dialogue with voluntary organizations related to evaluation.

Serious follow through on sector-wide or collaborative actions related to performance measurement was derailed by two things, one more positive than the other. When the VSI was established in 2000, sector leaders became consumed with that process, leaving little time for other issues. The five-year VSI program advanced understanding of the voluntary sector through better research,[7] laid a foundation for a better relationship between the federal government and voluntary organizations with the creation of the Accord (VSI *Accord* (2001)) and the Codes of Good Practice on Funding and Policy Dialogue (VSI *Code on Funding* (2002); VSI *Code on Policy Dialogue* (2002)), and made modest steps in regulatory reform. It did not, and was not explicitly mandated to, advance the state of performance assessment and accountability. But neither did it hurt.

---

[6] Personal observation. S. Phillips was Research Director for the Panel and attended many of the consultations held across the country.

[7] These include the National Survey of Nonprofit and Voluntary Organizations (NSNVO); the Canada Survey of Giving, Volunteering and Participating (CSGVP); the Canada Volunteer-ism Initiative (CVI) Knowledge Development Centre; *Funding Matters: The Impact of Canada's New Funding Regime on Nonprofit and Voluntary Organizations* (Canadian Council on Social Development, June 2003, online: <www.ccsd.ca/pubs/2003/fm/>); and *Satellite Account of Nonprofit Institutions and Volunteering: Final Report* (online:< www.vsi-isbc.ca/eng/knowledge/satellite.cfm>).

A second development — the establishment of a very stringent, control-based accountability regime related to contribution agreements that came as a response to a scandal over grants and contributions at the largest federal department in 2000 — was a major setback to accountability as learning (Good (2004)). The new accountability requirements have had a serious negative impact on the voluntary sector: delaying approvals for projects, stifling innovation, increasing micro-management and auditing of projects, and consuming enormous time and administrative staff with the minutiae of reporting (Phillips and Levasseur (2004)). The shift to control-based accountability centred on financial accounting became *the* consuming focus of accountability while simultaneously doing little to encourage better evaluation of programs and their impacts. Although concerns about the impact of these accountability measures were raised with government officials during the VSI, there was no movement to address them (SDC, 2004 Process Evaluation). The impact of the Gomery Inquiry of 2005-06 into inappropriate contracting (with the private sector) under the sponsorship program is likely to further tighten controls and audit, and to leave even less room for the innovation or risk-taking that is essential in a learning environment.[8]

A Survey of Current Practices

What impact have all these changes had on the voluntary sector? How have voluntary organizations responded? Although the responses vary widely depending on size of organization and locale, a recent national survey points to come consistent trends and themes. The Voluntary Sector Evaluation Research Project (VSERP) was formed in 2000 as a partnership of national and community organizations, led by the Centre for Voluntary Sector Research and Development at Carleton University and Imagine Canada, and funded by a Community University Research Alliance grant from the Social Sciences and Humanities Research Council of Canada (see <www.vserp.ca>).[9]

In 2003, VSERP published the results of a national survey of almost 2,000 voluntary organizations, selected to be broadly representative of charities and nonprofits in Canada, and over 300 funders,

---

[8] Gomery Inquiry Report, *Restoring Accountability — Phase 2*, available online: <www.gomery.ca/en/phase2report/index.asp>.

[9] The Co-Directors of VSERP were Susan Phillips from Carleton University and Michael Hall from Imagine Canada.

including federal, provincial and municipal governments, private foundations and United Ways (Hall *et al.* (2003)).[10] As the first survey of performance assessment practices in Canada's voluntary sector, the goals were to identify the nature and extent of the pressures and challenges in this area, obtain a snapshot of how voluntary organizations were doing and using evaluation, and get a sense of what might aid them in being more effective.

It came as no surprise to find that expectations and pressures on the part of funders for performance assessment have increased in recent years, both in terms of the amount and the type of information expected. Almost half of the voluntary organizations surveyed said that funder expectations had risen over the past three years. Almost as many (44 per cent) indicated that funders are requiring more information than they had three years previously and 49 per cent said they are requiring information about outcomes or impacts. And, funders agreed: they too said they are expecting more by way of evaluation. As part of their funding packages, almost half of funders indicated that they require evaluations and 40 reported that they "encourage" but do not require evaluations.

Although government funders reported greater increases in expectations than foundations, particularly in financial reporting and program evaluation, requirements for assessment have risen across the board. These were felt somewhat more acutely by larger voluntary organizations, probably because they have multiple funders so are facing not only more but potentially competing demands.

In spite of rising external demands, the vast majority of voluntary organizations reported that they conduct performance assessments because they are internally motivated to do so, not because they are required to by funders. Indeed, 73 per cent of the participants in the survey indicated that they do evaluation routinely, primarily motivated by decisions of their own staff or boards, whereas only 4 per cent said they conducted evaluations only when required by funders. It is also evident that voluntary organizations are assessing all aspects of their operations. Although the main focus is still on programs (66 per cent) and projects (56 per cent), more than half reported that they had

---

[10] The survey took a grounded approach to research in that a series of discussion groups were first held with staff and volunteers of voluntary organizations in 12 communities across Canada. The results of these discussions were used to construct the telephone interview questions. Upon completion and before the final report was produced, the feedback on the results of the survey was obtained by holding a second series of discussion groups.

assessed the overall performance of the organization in the past year; in addition, 45 per cent had evaluated fundraising activities, 40 per cent volunteer experiences, and a third the performance of the board.

The methods of evaluation used were far-ranging and most used more than one approach. There was widespread use of informal methods (*e.g.*, meetings of staff and volunteers), but these were normally supplemented by more formal approaches as needed. For the most part, performance assessments were conducted with in-house resources, with only 8 per cent of voluntary organizations using external evaluators.

Performance assessment is also finding its way into the governance of voluntary organizations. In most cases, the board of directors had at least reviewed the results of evaluations, and in more than one-third of cases had both requested and reviewed the information. In only 20 per cent did the board have no involvement at all in performance assessment.

In general, voluntary organizations were satisfied with the quality and accuracy of the evaluations they had produced and about three-quarters indicated they have made effective use of the results. If the board at least reviewed the evaluation information, the likelihood that it was used very effectively increased significantly (Hall *et al.* (2003, at p. 26)). The use made of evaluation was mainly to improve programs and services (68 per cent) and for purposes of strategic planning (55 per cent). Although used to report to funders, the tendency was that performance assessment results were not widely shared with others (only 15 per cent indicated they effectively shared such information).

Interestingly, funders felt they were less effective at using the evaluation information submitted to them than they could be (less than half said they made either effective or very effective use of such information).[11] They said that this depended in part on the quality of information they received, and over one-third felt that the information was often not what they had asked for. The lack of use of evaluation information also reflects a lack of capacity, both a lack of time and resources, on the part of funders: more than one-quarter said they lack the capacity to review evaluation information fully.

---

[11] Note that foundations indicated they were more likely make use of evaluation information for all purposes, and particularly to determine future funding of organizations, than did governments (Hall *et al.* (2003, at p. 28)).

Even if they used the information effectively, funders did not seem to be communicating very well how they use such information. Almost 20 per cent of voluntary organizations believed that funders used their evaluation reports for "administrative purposes" only — that is, to close the file. There was also a considerable discrepancy over perceptions of the extent to which evaluation was used by funders to help improve the performance of the organizations they fund. While 60 per cent of funders said they used evaluation information in this manner, only 20 per cent of voluntary organizations perceived this to be the case. The sense of evaluation as a paper exercise by a fairly large segment of voluntary organizations surveyed, combined with a reported fear that evaluations with unfavourable results would lead to a loss of funding, points to serious underlying challenges that are more political than technical in nature.

Both funders and voluntary organizations agreed on the main challenges of performance assessment — overwhelmingly, a lack of internal capacity and money. Although funder demands for evaluation have risen, there was no corresponding increase in resources to support such evaluation. The perceived ways in which performance assessment could be improved relate to filling these gaps in capacity through more financial resources, access to better technology and better staff training.

A lesser, but nevertheless significant, problem (cited by almost one-third of voluntary organizations) was unclear expectations on the part of funders, including problems with evaluation language and terminology. Both voluntary organizations and funders noted the value of encouraging greater consistency in terminology and greater co-ordination among funders so that they ask for similar information, particularly in cases where there are multiple funders (50 per cent of funders noted that this is a "big" need).

Confusion over language is particularly evident in the survey's findings related to outcome measurement. It is surprising that three-quarters of the voluntary organizations surveyed indicated that they collect information on outcomes and that it is relatively easy to do so, as well as fairly easy to analyze and interpret such information. This is wildly out of step with what was said in a pre-test with focus groups and what the literature indicates about the complexity of identifying the right outcomes and in collecting data on such indicators in a timely manner. What became evident in follow-up interviews is that the concept of "outcomes" has become enormously elastic and thus imprecise. In effect, "outcome measurement" had essentially come to be equated with any kind of performance assessment. Given the evolution and infusion of new terms in the lexicon of evaluation research, this is perhaps not so surprising after all. For this reason, we briefly define our own terms before proceeding.

Performance Assessment as a Management Tool

When VSERP began work on the national survey of voluntary organizations and funders in 2000, we talked about *evaluation*. As the research progressed and it came time to report results, we were using the language of *performance assessment*. The shift reflects not only what we learned from the survey, that voluntary organizations are routinely evaluating a wide range of their activities beyond their programs and projects, but also a changing focus in the literature. So, what is the difference?

From Evaluation to Performance Assessment

The distinction between evaluation and performance assessment is one of focus and timing. Whereas evaluation is normally episodic and issue-specific, focused on a program or other activity at a point in time, performance assessment is ongoing and more encompassing. The latter should encourage the development of routinized processes of assessment and monitoring that can be applied to all aspects of an organization, including assessment of the organization as a whole (McDavid & Hawthorn (2001)). "Performance measurement systems are designed and implemented with the intention of providing regular and continuing information for program and organizational purposes" (McDavid & Hawthorn (2001, at p. 9-6)). Evaluation and performance assessment are obviously interdependent as evaluation provides the framework for developing appropriate measures and indicators for ongoing monitoring and performance assessment, *and* ongoing assessment often generates data that can be used in evaluation (European Commission (1997); Davies (1999)).

The even broader process of identifying intended results, measuring, reporting and using the information from performance assessment as a basis for decision-making and strategic planning is often referred to as performance *management* (Davies (1999, at p. 151)). Performance management then is using performance information effectively and building the organizational systems for ongoing improvement (see English & Lindquist (1998)). The challenge in making evaluation and performance assessment a foundation for performance management, and thus for ongoing learning and self-improvement, is to use it as a management tool.

Using Performance Assessment as a Management Tool

Data from evaluations and performance assessment, if collected in a meaningful way, can produce knowledge allowing leaders to manage programs more effectively. For example, evaluation can help program managers to:

- ensure that the program is doing what one thinks it is doing;

- understand if the program is making a difference and what effect it has on users;

- improve program delivery mechanisms and refine eligibility criteria, program objectives and other program processes to ensure that the program is delivered in the most effective and efficient way;

- identify the lessons learned, and act upon the findings (McNamara (1998a)).

How does an organization move from doing occasional evaluations of programs or other activities to being capable of ongoing performance assessment and management and of learning from this process for self-improvement? The first step, we suggest, is becoming competent and confident in doing evaluations of a variety of activities, from assessing programs to the organization overall. This involves knowing when and how to evaluate what.

The second step is to build assessment into governance processes and the routine operations of an organization, and develop the capacity as the organization (and ultimately as a sector) to do this. In the rest of this chapter, we examine in a practical way the key issues involved first in evaluation and then in the institutionalization of performance management.

EVALUATION ISSUES: THE META-QUESTIONS

Evaluation design depends on what decisions need to be made with regard to the program, what information is needed to make these decisions and what kinds of resources are available to managers. Thus the key considerations in designing evaluation are:

- *Evaluation purpose and audience*: Why is the evaluation being done and what should be decided as a result? Who will be the main users of the evaluation results, *e.g.*, clients, funders, board, management, staff?

- *Program readiness*: Is the program ready to be evaluated?

- *Focus of evaluation*: What should be the focus of evaluation, *e.g.*, is it process or outcomes? What kind of information is needed to answer the evaluation questions (information on how the program was delivered or the effect of the program on clients and community at large)?

- *Choice of evaluator*: Who will conduct evaluation: external or internal evaluators? Who else needs to be involved?

- *Data collection methods and sources of information*: How can the requisite data be collected, *e.g.*, surveys, interviews, focus groups, *etc.*? What are the possible sources of information, *e.g.*, employees, users, existing program documentation?

Why: Evaluation Purpose and Audience

The first evaluation question that needs to be asked is *why* evaluation is being undertaken. Understanding the purpose of evaluation will help determine what should be evaluated, using what methodology, who should be engaged and when the best time is to evaluate. Typically evaluations are undertaken to serve one or more of three general purposes:

- *Accountability*: to demonstrate the results of programs and account for the use of resources;

- *Program planning or improvement*: to identify strengths and weaknesses of a program or process, as well as appropriate changes to make (*e.g.*, redefine eligibility criteria, add new categories of staff, improve guidelines, *etc.*);

- *Knowledge generation or enlightenment*: to create a new understanding about what works and what does not, understand the nature of specific social interventions and generate new knowledge (Patton (1997)).

Evaluation for accountability purposes is often externally driven and frequently referred to as *summative* evaluation. Summative evaluations are done at the end of a program or project and are designed for decision-making purposes about whether to continue or end a program, extend it to other sites, or cut it back (Perrin (2002)).

The limitations and pitfalls of evaluation done for accountability purposes can be significant. If an evaluation is conducted strictly to demonstrate accountability for the use of money to external funders and fails to address "how" and "why" information, it probably cannot provide the information needed to assist with decisions about future directions (Perrin (2002)). Furthermore, evaluations that are done strictly for accountability purposes may result in the diversion of resources from program improvement to documentation, record-keeping, report writing, auditing, and related activities. It may compel program managers to focus more on the justification of programs as opposed to what can be improved in the future. Finally, it may lead to distortion of program activities in its attempt to reduce them to a small number of quantitative indicators when the reality may have been much messier than this.

Evaluation for program improvement is often referred to as *formative* evaluation. This type of evaluation is consistent with a focus on learning. Formative evaluations are designed to assist in the early stages those who are developing programs and can be used as management tools for identifying what works and what does not, and how things can be improved. As the national survey (Hall *et al.* (2003)) indicates, the majority of voluntary organizations in Canada utilize some form of formative evaluation, even if very informal, for management and planning purposes.

Audiences for evaluation findings range from funders, policy-makers and the general public to program clients, association members, program staff and boards of directors. Accordingly, expectations for the evaluation vary with a stakeholder's position. For instance, funders tend to ask for information that helps them make decisions about their support of a program (*e.g.*, to continue or cut), while program managers require information to help them run the program. These distinctions matter as they affect the overall evaluation design and methodology as well as the eventual use of the evaluation results.

When: Program Readiness

The "when to evaluate" question can be systematically thought about through a procedure called *evaluability assessment*. Initially developed by Wholey (1979), evaluability assessment seeks to determine in a systematic way whether or not programs are ready for evaluation. Wholey (1979) recommended evaluability assessment as an initial step to evaluating programs in order to increase the likelihood that evaluations will provide timely, relevant, and responsive findings for decision-makers:

> The products of evaluability assessment are: (1) a set of agreed-on program objectives, side effects, and performance indicators on which the program can realistically be held accountable; and (2) a set of evaluation/management options which represent ways in which management can change program activities, objectives, or uses of information in ways likely to improve program performance.

(Trevisan and Huang (2003)).

Readiness for evaluation is assessed against three main criteria: (a) Does the program operate as intended? (b) Is it relatively stable? and (c) Does it seem to be achieving positive outcomes? (Weiss (1997, at p. 74)). Assessing a program against these criteria requires clarifying the goals, boundaries and theory of the program; interviewing stakeholders and identifying their needs, concerns and differences in perceptions; determining the plausibility of a program model (how it is believed to work); and making specific recommendations with regard to evaluability of the program (Smith (1989); Trevisan & Huang (2003)). The evaluator clarifies the series of assumptions that link program activities with program goals and examines the logical plausibility of the linkages. The main caution in this process is against oversimplification of program reality or using depictions of program theory as all-encompassing illustrations of the program. It needs to be kept in mind that programs can often be recursive rather than linear and represent a complex set of outcomes, both intended and unintended.

Evaluability assessment can be time-consuming for various reasons. It may be difficult to get commitments from key stakeholders. Program documentation may be unorganized. The process may require building a team that includes stakeholder groups and program implementers. The proper use of evaluability assessment, however, may increase the probability that actual evaluations will be timely, relevant and responsive (Trevisan & Huang (2003)).

What: Focus of Evaluation

On a fairly regular basis, voluntary organizations evaluate most aspects of their operations, including organizational performance, programs and services, fundraising activities, the experiences of their volunteers, the performance of their boards of directors, and their products (Hall *et al.* (2003)). Although the literature has been dominated by a focus on *program* evaluation, it is not particularly useful to carve up evaluation approaches according to which activity is being evaluated. A more helpful distinction is to think of evaluation by contexts, processes and impacts.

Needs Assessment or Context Evaluation

Needs assessment or context evaluation focuses on the characteristics of communities, stakeholders and broad social, economic and environmental factors. This type of evaluation aims to assess the needs, assets, and resources of a target community and identify its political environment and human services context. This allows voluntary organizations to plan relevant and effective interventions and increases the likelihood that they will be supported by community leaders and other organizations (Kellogg Foundation (1998)).

Typically, needs assessment is conducted prior to the beginning of a program. Contexts are not static, however. In some cases, context assessment may also have to be undertaken in later phases as a project or program matures, when contextual information is required to modify plans and explain deviations from planned process and outcomes. At this stage, it also helps to examine how broad changes in the society, including political, social, and environmental factors, may affect project implementation and effectiveness. Context may also figure in the interpretation of results: if "environmental barriers to project implementation are understood, seemingly troubled projects might be deemed successful based on the barriers they overcame" (Kellogg Foundation (1998, at p. 21)).

Process Evaluation

Process evaluation focuses on how the program actually works and can shed light on why certain results or outcomes are or are not achieved. Process evaluation is distinguished from formative evaluation by its focus (an analysis of how things work) rather than its timing. Evaluation of the process can take place while a program is still being implemented and thus enhance its likelihood of success by providing indications of what is happening and why. That is, it may be part of formative evaluation.

Process evaluation can also be a part of the summative evaluation, conducted once the program or project is completed: "Successful implementation of new project activities typically involves a process of adapting the ideal plan to local conditions, organizational dynamics, and programmatic uncertainties" (Kellogg Foundation (1998, at p. 24)). In broad terms then process evaluation can help to:

- identify and maximize strengths of the process and minimize barriers to implementing activities;

- determine the nature of interactions between staff and clients or users;

- measure the performance, perceptions and satisfaction of staff and volunteers, and the adequacy of organizational control and delivery systems;

- monitor users' and other stakeholders' experiences with the project, and their satisfaction with and utilization of project services; and

- assess whether available resources can sustain project activities (Kellogg Foundation (1998, at p. 25)).

Understanding of process, however, is among the most common difficulties associated with performance assessment because process is not only difficult to measure, but sometimes difficult to identify and articulate (Funnell (2000)). How things are actually working is seldom documented and perceptions of participants may differ considerably. In addition, varying dynamics in organizational culture and broader contexts may yield variations to planned program activities, thus requiring continuous review with periodic adjustments in program theory assumptions (Brinkerhoff (2002)).

Outcome Evaluation

Outcome evaluation assesses the short- and long-term program results or impacts (what actually changed) and seeks to understand what difference the program made. It helps to answer questions about what works, for whom, and in what circumstances. Three broad categories of outcomes are often distinguished in the evaluation literature:

- *Individual, User-Focused Outcomes* — These types of results show how clients' or users' lives improve as a result of the program. In other words, this level of outcome evaluation answers the question "What difference does this program/initiative make in the lives of those served?"

- *Program and System-Level Outcomes* — This level illustrates the the program is trying to achieve for the broader system (*e.g.*, expanded job placement alternatives, improved capacity of organizations to conduct evaluations).

- *Broader Family or Community Outcomes* — This type takes individual-level outcomes to the next level in measuring the impact on families, neighbourhoods, and in some cases, whole communities (Kellogg Foundation (1998)).

The Limits of Outcome Measurement

The recent interest in measuring outcomes is that such assessments enable a voluntary organization to demonstrate its value, not just its good intentions or amount of activity, and they provide guidance as to where to direct resources with the greatest effect. The challenges associated with outcome measurement are significant, however. One of the key issues is revealing the link between cause (activities) and effects (OECD (2004)). The complex, multi-layered nature of programs and the dynamic character of relationships among people, systems, and communities often make it very difficult to ascertain the exact cause of an outcome (Brinkerhoff (2002)). Attribution requires a detailed analysis of cause-and-effect relationships, and even after such analysis, attribution may be problematic. Outcome measures also encounter the problems of timing. Particularly in preventative programs, the actual outcomes may take years to be realized, long after the evaluation period has ended. Also, good outcome measures may be expensive and time-consuming to collect and analyze. As well, due to the complex nature of community change, programs often produce *unintended* outcomes which may take extensive research at multiple levels to identify let alone measure (Kellogg Foundation (1998)).

Finally, an exclusive focus on outcomes may lead to overlooking equally important aspects of evaluation, such as understanding how and why the program works or does not work, and what factors and circumstances shape the program (see Brinkerhoff (2002, at p. 216)). Indeed, outcomes may fail to provide information on how to improve service delivery and enhance efficiency, especially when results are disappointing. As Perrin (1998, at p. 374) notes:

> A program may fail to meet its performance targets because the program theory is wrong, in which case it should be replaced with something else. But it also may fail to do so for a variety of other reasons such as: inappropriate targets or measures which are not identifying other possible program outcomes; faulty management or implementation, under (or over) funding, unique circumstances (e.g. an employment training program during a recession or when the only employer in a single-industry town closes); the right program in the wrong situation (e.g. effective for some, but not all, of the types of clients it has been serving), measurement of outcomes attempted too soon or at the wrong time, faulty statistics, and so on.

Outcome measurement has become fashionable, even faddish in performance assessment in recent years, and is increasingly required by funders and espoused by governments as a means of accountability and managing public expectations. A challenge for voluntary organization is to avoid the bandwagon effect. In many cases, outcome measurement may simply be overkill. It may in fact not answer the desired questions or all, or do so at such expense that it is not the best investment of resources. If the question is to understand whether volunteers are satisfied and doing a good job, for example, one does not need to know how volunteering has changed their lives. In many cases, a good process evaluation or assessment of outputs may be fully adequate, indeed more appropriate, and the time and money saved better directed toward program improvement. When outcome evaluation *is* warranted, voluntary organizations are generally well advised to have some control or input into the nature of these measures, rather than having them imposed by third parties.

Logic Models as a Means of Linking Contexts, Processes and Outcomes

Logic models are perhaps the most feared or at least seemingly mysterious part of evaluation for many voluntary organizations. If one thinks of logic models as simply theories — or hypotheses or hunches — about change, they are not nearly so abstruse.

A logic model is a means of connecting context, process and outcomes, and attributing cause and effect. It is important, as Mayne (1999) notes, "not to definitively prove that the program has made a difference but to build over time a convincing case of plausible association between the results observed and the activities and outputs of the program, as more and more evidence is gathered". A logic model thus ties together:

- *Context*: the relevant physical, social, economic, cultural or political circumstances in which a program or other activity is set;

- *Inputs*: the resources (*e.g.*, human, financial) that are required to implement the program;

- *Activities*: the processes, tools, events, technology and actions that are an intentional part of the program implementation;

- *Outputs*: the immediate products or consequences of program activities (such as number of workshops offered, personnel trained, etc.);

- *Outcomes*: the actual changes that are realized when the outputs are used. Outcomes may unfold over time and are thus differentiated on several time scales from *initial* (outcomes that can be directly attributed to the program activities) to *intermediate* (changes in behaviour once the immediate outcomes have been achieved) to *final outcomes* (longer term and organizational or system level change as an overall result of the program).[12]

An effective logic model is developed early, and continuously re-fined and changed throughout the program assessment process in order to reflect the changing nature of the environment and knowledge about what works and what does not (Kellogg Foundation, 1998).[13] Logic models, which have become virtually ubiquitous in evaluation, have attracted both staunch defenders and critics. The critics argue that the logic of logic models often supplants reality and that we need to keep in mind that they are in fact *models*, that is representations of reality, not reality itself. The risk lies in being lulled into a false confidence that in simply depicting the model, the job is done. Thus evaluators often do not put its logic to the test by critically examining whether it is meaningful, plausible, doable and testable. In addition, by presenting programs as a coherent sequence from objectives to outcomes, logic

---

[12]   OECD, 2004; TBS, "Results-Based Management Lexicon": <http://www.tbs-sct.gc.ca/rma/lex-lex_e.asp>.

[13]   Building a logic model and identifying causal relationships may reduce but not eliminate problems associated with attributing outcomes to specific causes. Other techniques to assess program contribution to the results include using multiple lines of evidence, exploring and discussing plausible alternative explanations, and gathering additional relevant evidence (Mayne (1999)). On theories of change, see also Kubisch *et al.* (1998).

models imply linearity whereas the reality may be much more complex, dynamic and circular.

While supporters acknowledge many of its limitations, they argue that, as a heuristic for sorting out causes and effects, logic models are about the best that evaluation has to offer. The challenge comes in how the tool is used, not with the tool itself.

Who: Choice of Evaluator and Participant Involvement

Insiders or Outsiders?

Are evaluations better conducted by internal or external evaluators? The answer to this question largely depends on the purpose of evaluation, as well as available resources. If the primary aim of the assessment is to maximize learning and use of evaluation results in order to improve programs or operations, it is usually preferable to have the assessment done internally. In this case, performance assessment may be integrated into the program cycle in order to give feedback on actions taken. On the other hand, if the main goal is to demonstrate accountability to funders, stakeholders and society at large, an external, independent assessment might have more weight.

Both approaches offer a number of advantages and disadvantages and the choice needs to balance the purpose of evaluation with other considerations (see Table 1). Traditionally, evaluations are done by external experts in order to ensure the objectivity, impartiality and credibility of the findings. However, as performance assessment is increasingly seen as a management tool, internal evaluations are being used more widely. Internal evaluators, in most cases, have better "insider" knowledge of how the program works and can help increase the likelihood of utilization of evaluation results. External evaluations may or may not be more costly, but do require internal personnel to manage consultants. Combining both internal and external assessment is another option that might allow voluntary organizations to obtain an external quality check "without losing the benefit of the internal evaluator's firsthand knowledge of the project" (OECD (2004, at p. 18)).

Table 1: Advantages and Disadvantages of Internal and External Assessment

	Internal Assessment	External Assessment
Advantages	• Maximizes learning; benefits stay in the organization • Findings can be put to use immediately • Can be adjusted according to new needs and new findings • Increases organizational skills and capacities	• External consultants have assessment competence; can buy rather than grow such skills • May increase perceived legitimacy of results • Usually faster • Can be subject to competitive bidding (may be less costly) • Brings new perspectives
Disadvantages	• Can obscure negative findings • Skills may be limited • Takes staff time • Necessitates ongoing commitment	• Can be irrelevant • Mostly evaluator who learns • Can be expensive • Difficult to change the process • Less ownership by stakeholders • Gap with decision-makers; harder to use results

Source: Kim Forss, "Evaluation framework for information, consultation and participation in policy-making". A study commissioned by the OECD (January 2003).

Participatory Performance Assessment

The decision as to who should be involved does not stop with determining the evaluator. In order to maximize the usefulness of evaluation, program stakeholders need to buy into the evaluation process and its results. This requires collaboration of stakeholders in evaluation design, identification of indicators, data collection and interpretation, and use of results.

Stakeholder involvement in evaluation may prove to be a challenging task, however. First, such engagement increases the number of people involved in discussions and meetings which potentially complicates evaluation activities, increases timelines and reduces work quality. Second, key participants such as senior officials, managers, and staff members must reach a certain level of agreement about program and evaluation goals and ways to achieve them, while often having diverse needs with regard to the evaluation (Wholey (1979); DeLancer Julnes (2001)). For instance, managers and staff members are inclined to focus on inputs and outputs over which they have more control; decision-makers at the policy level tend to focus on inputs and outcomes; and advocates for particular interests tend to focus on intended and unintended outcomes (Wholey (1979); DeLancer Julnes (2001, at p. 404)). Third, collaboration also requires new roles for evaluators, such as an ability to work with diverse stakeholders, educate them about measurement, and facilitate their participation and input. Finally, stakeholder involvement blurs the line between professional evaluators and users with the risk of losing the objectivity that traditionally detaches evaluators from the environments they assess (Annie E. Casey Foundation (1997)).

At the same time, despite the difficulty of getting various stakeholders to agree on performance measures, it can prove to be highly beneficial to the process of performance management. For example, participatory assessment can enable evaluators to ask the right questions in the first place. Participation may raise stakeholders' expectations that the research results will be noticed, considered, valued, and acted on (Annie E. Casey Foundation (1997)). It may "result in positive staff development, a feeling of empowerment, and a sense of competence in evaluation issues and procedures" (Lafleur (1995, at p. 53)) and improve evaluation validity and credibility (Thayer, Fine, Cousins, & Whitmore (1998)). Finally, it also increases interaction and communication between funders and voluntary organizations that can lead to improved dialogue around the needs and complexities of performance assessment.

How: Data Collection Methods and Sources of Information

Once one gets to the *how* question, many of the tough issues have already been addressed. That said, decisions about which methods to use and their design probably consume more time than any other aspect of evaluation. There are a variety of evaluation methods available to voluntary organizations, ranging from informal staff and volunteer meetings to more formal methods such as focus groups, surveys, interviews and experimental design (Hall *et al.* (2003)). The guiding determinant in the selection of measurement tools is to obtain the most valuable and credible information in the most appropriate and realistic manner. Other factors that influence the choice of data collection methods, besides the intended use of the evaluation findings and nature of users, include:

- accuracy, credibility and sufficiency of data;

- political sensitivity of collecting data;

- complexity of collecting, interpreting and analyzing data; and

- costs of collecting data (*e.g.*, money, timeframe, *etc.*).[14]

Most organizations use more than one evaluation method. For example, the VSERP (Hall *et al.* 2003) study revealed that the vast majority of survey respondents (84 per cent) reported that they used informal methods (such as staff and volunteer meetings) as well as more formal methods. This reflects the fact that different techniques are better suited to different research questions and capabilities. Thus measurement generally should be approached from a variety of perspectives and we can expect to capture the full story by using a toolbox of methods and approaches, as appropriate to what we want to know and how much time and resources we have to find out. As Murray (2003) argues, the choice of how formal and elaborate a method to use should be made on the basis of how much time, money, and skill an organization has, but more importantly on how much it needs large amounts of high quality, detailed information for making internal policy decisions or influencing important external stake-holders. Table 2 provides an overview of the major methods used for collecting data during evaluations.

Table 2: A Sample of Data Collection Methods

Method	Overall Purpose	Advantages	Challenges
Questionnaires, surveys, checklists	Get a slice of information from many people in a non-threatening way	• Can get data from many people, representative of a population • Can be completed anonymously	• Might not get careful feedback • Low response rates • Wording can bias participant's responses

---

[14] See OECD, 2004; McNamara (1998b).

Method	Overall Purpose	Advantages	Challenges
		• Relatively inexpensive to administer • Easy to compare and analyze	• May need sampling expert • Doesn't get full story, gets a thin slice of information
Interviews	Fully understand interviewees' impressions or experiences, or learn more about their answers to questionnaires	• Get rich range and depth of information • Develops relationship with participants • Can be flexible, more opportunity to follow up questions not anticipated	• Can take considerable time • Can be hard to analyze and compare • Can be costly • Interviewer can bias participant's responses
Documentation review	Understand how program was designed and officially operates without interrupting the program; preliminary step for other measurement	• Get comprehensive and historical information • Doesn't interrupt program or participant's routine in program • Information already exists • Few biases about information	• Info may be incomplete; gives "official" story • Not flexible means to get data; restricted to what already exists
Observation	Understand first hand how a program actually operates, particularly about processes	• View operations of a program as they are actually occurring • Can adapt to events as they occur	• Can be difficult to interpret observed behaviours without interviews • Can influence behaviours of program participants • Can be expensive and time-consuming

Method	Overall Purpose	Advantages	Challenges
Focus groups	Explore a topic in depth through group discussion, *e.g.*, about reactions to an experience or suggestion, understanding common complaints, *etc*.	• Quickly get common impressions • Can be efficient way to get considerable range and depth of information in short time • Can convey key information about programs	• Can be hard to analyze responses; challenge of moving between group and individual level analyses • Need good facilitator for safety and closure • Difficult to schedule 6-8 people together
Case studies	Understand or depict in detail participant's experiences in a program, and conduct comprehensive examination through cross comparison of cases	• Fully depicts participant's experience in program input, process and results • Powerful means to portray program to outsiders	• Usually quite time-consuming to collect, organize and describe • Represents depth of information, rather than breadth • May be highly selective, not representative

Source: McNamara (1998c).

Data collection is as much about process as expertise. Often programs require measurement across multiple systems and at multiple levels, over long periods of time, and of outcomes that are hard to capture (Annie E. Casey Foundation (1997)). In order to meet these challenges, evaluators need to refine and adapt their tools and methods for measuring program process and success. In addition, the involvement of stakeholders in the choice and design of instruments both helps in identifying the right questions and indicators and in building confidence and credibility that meaningful information has been collected, and thus is more likely to be used (Annie E. Casey Foundation (1997)).

TOWARD PERFORMANCE ASSESSMENT AND MANAGEMENT

The difference between an organization that can do good evaluation when needed and one that actually uses evaluation as a means of learning and self-improvement hinges on making effective use of the results of evaluation, dealing with the political dimensions, and developing the capacity for performance assessment.

Using Assessment Results

Evaluation information can be a powerful tool for a variety of stakeholders, including program managers, funders, and clients/users. The information can be used to improve program effectiveness and service delivery, increase awareness of the organization and facilitate information sharing, inform strategic planning and guide fundraising, as well as to report to funders. For their part, funders can ensure that they are funding effective programs, help funded organizations improve their programs through identifying best practices and facilitate their own strategic planning (Hall *et al.* (2003)). The question of how the evaluation information will be used is best considered at the very beginning of a project, not only at the end as is often the case. Planning *different* ways of using evaluation findings helps ensure evaluation is conducted and the results reported in a way that actually meets people's needs.[15] By involving various stakeholders from the beginning, their commitment and ability to use the results is considerably enhanced (Fine & Thayer (2000)).

Several strategies can help promote the effective use of the evaluation data:

* *Ensuring high quality of evaluation information.* Evaluation information should be adequate and legitimate, and meet stakeholder needs and expectations. For example, the VSERP study suggests that a little over one-third of funders agreed (32 per cent) or strongly agreed (4 per cent) that the information they receive is often not what they had asked for. The low quality of information may be due to "voluntary organizations' confusion

---

[15] Public Health Agency of Canada, "Guide to Project Evaluation: A Participatory Approach", available online at: <http://www.phac-aspc.gc.ca/ph-sp/phdd/resources/guide/using.htm>.

about outcome evaluation and to their lack of clarity about funder expectations" (Hall *et al.* (2003)).

- *Presenting evaluation results as a systematic, cumulative study of links between activities and outcomes.* This may help demonstrate credibility of findings and provide information on both process and program effectiveness.

- *Keeping specific audiences in mind in reporting evaluation results.* Data should be presented in a way accessible and useful for the people who are going to use it. Data presentation may range from simple fact sheets to lengthy and complex research papers; it could involve limited circulation to key decision-makers to widespread communication on the web and through other technology to strategic face-to-face briefings with local decision-makers and news media.

- *Building stakeholder capacity to interpret, disseminate and maximize information.* There is a need to build capacity of stakeholders to use evaluation information which may entail several strategies. For example, data can be used to develop action plans to address some of the issues revealed in the evaluation with input from stakeholders. Community members can be engaged in continuous program planning and management. Once community members start to use data, they begin to see more types of information that would be useful and more ways they can use the data to make their own decisions (Annie E. Casey Foundation (1997)).

- *Using strategies that anticipate and reduce opposition.* In the case of sensitive or controversial findings, holding meetings with interested stakeholders and keeping the focus on issues rather than on people and personalities may help find ways for the negative findings to inspire improvements (Annie E. Casey Foundation (1997)).

- *Ensuring that data are used fairly.* Information sometimes can be used for harmful purposes, and it is the role of evaluators to protect the information so it cannot be misused. For example, when evaluation information is of a sensitive or controversial nature, one strategy would be to release it to all stakeholders simultaneously explaining what it means and what it can and cannot affirm (Annie E. Casey Foundation (1997)).

The Political Dimensions of Performance Assessment

Finding the appropriate evaluation techniques and measures can certainly be demanding and complex in its own right. It would be a mistake, however, to see the main challenges of performance assessment to be only or even primarily technical in nature. Evaluation is not an objective, value-free process, but one that is inherently political. It often necessitates serious debates and conflicts over values and strategies. "Why are we doing this?" How would we define success?" "So what?" These are political rather than technical questions that run through performance assessment from its inception to the use of results for program or organizational change.

The political dimensions of evaluation may be manifest in several ways, some quite overt and others almost inadvertent. The most obvious ones range from the mere fact that evaluations involve *people* (*e.g.*, decision-makers, funders, consultants, program staff) with specific and different values, perceptions, and interests who may interpret assessment measurement in different ways. Cutt & Murray (2000) suggest that the phenomenon of *subjective interpretation of reality* arises when evaluation data have to be interpreted, and again when decisions need to be made. "When it comes to analyzing almost any aspect of human behaviour, there are too many variables and there is too little control over those variables to permit solid conclusions about causal connections" (Cutt & Murray (2000, at p. 40)). In addition, there may be many different, perhaps competing theories of change and beliefs about what works or does not work. Yet, decisions need to be made and the results of performance measurement figure in such decisions. Thus boards and staff, particularly if they have been close to a program or project and are committed to it, may tend to revert to pre-existing attitudes about what they "know" works.

Sometimes the politics are more conscious and intentional. Murray (2003) suggests that political behaviour may arise at each stage of the evaluation process, particularly when evaluators, evaluatees, and other interested parties disagree on various aspects of evaluation. For example, during the design and implementation stage, the stakeholders may have quite different perceptions of the real purpose of evaluation — whether to identify strengths and weaknesses for better decision-making (the official reason) or to identify aspects to cut (the feared reason).

Particularly when funders are driving evaluation or in performance contracting (when payment is provided only after the achievement of some pre-specified outcomes), there may be a more structural dimension to politics. This is the reluctance to present "bad" results, or the *Look-Good-Avoid-Blame* factor, as Cutt & Murray (2000, at pp. 39-40) call it. If an evaluation reveals problems or if the results are not as expected, a natural concern is that funding may be terminated. So, the temptation is to make the results look as good as possible or explain failures as being beyond the organization's control. This politicization of evaluation is likely to occur when the environment has little tolerance for failure as is the case in many governments today. Not only is innovation likely to be stifled in the first place, because innovative programs are by definition riskier, but it becomes more difficult to learn from innovation when it does occur because successes and failures are not reported openly and fully. As Frumkin (2002, at pp. 86-88) argues, because the current environment far outstrips the sector's capacity to deliver meaningful and reliable information on what works and what does not, "the temptation to cut corners or to engage in strategic gaming around performance issues is only getting stronger".

A different kind of political problem arises internally, particularly in small, collegial organizations. Boards are often reluctant to push for evaluation as it might be seen as portending a lack of confidence in staff and the executive director in particular, whom they often know well, consider a friend or have a great deal of deference toward. As a result, suggests Murray (2003), boards often fail badly in their governance roles related to performance assessment and in their fiduciary duties to hold management accountable.

Although politics in evaluation is inevitable, the solution is not to abandon evaluation research. Rather, knowing that political dimensions exist is a precondition for useable evaluation research (Guba & Lincoln (1989)). Murray (2003) suggests that there are three routes for dealing with political behaviour. The first is to build trust among the interested parties. In most cases, trust is built over time. If a prior relationship does not exist, there is a need for an open and participatory approach to evaluation in order to minimize the likelihood of political games. Such participation may be a process of co-operation, but it may also be one of negotiation. Indeed, Guba & Lincoln (1989) maintain that in evaluation all parties should negotiate their rights. This implies that the role of the evaluator is to solicit the co-operation of each party in return for a particular *quid pro quo*. Such negotiation gives the evaluator insight into the "obstacles and opportunities that impinge upon the evaluative effort, and the limitations and possibilities for putting the results to work — only with sensitivity to the politics of evaluation research — can the evaluator be as creative and strategically useful"(Weiss (1993, at p. 94)).

A second means is to pay more attention to articulating a clear logic model, that is, a theory about change, and ensure that it is agreed to by most stakeholders. A third path is better training for boards of directors so that they can minimize the political games, but also fulfil their responsibilities. This does not mean reverting to a strong accountability by control role, but encouraging them to develop appropriate assessment systems or mechanisms and establishing clear expectations regarding their interest and role in assessment.

These factors, even though falling short of completely eliminating the political nature of evaluation, may help create a non-threatening, trusting environment in which to more fully realize the benefits of a good evaluation.

Building the Capacity for Performance Assessment

The biggest barrier to effective performance assessment in Canada is not political but a lack of capacity (Hall *et al.* (2003, at p. 32)). As the national survey indicated, capacity issues include financial constraints, lack of skills and knowledge in conducting evaluations, and inadequate staff and time. The magnitude and frequency with which capacity was mentioned as a problem in the VSERP survey points to an acute need to enhance the infrastructure of voluntary organizations to conduct evaluation. Capacity for evaluation can be built through training, knowledge and information sharing, financial support, and closer collaboration and advice from funders.

Besides building the organizational capacity to undertake evaluation, it is important to build the capacity to involve stakeholders, including program staff, community organizations, clients and funders, in evaluation. Inculcating a leadership role into the governance of a voluntary organization, through the way in which the board understands its role in performance assessment, is critical. Creating greater capacity for performance assessment extends beyond individual organizations, however, to fostering greater collective and shared capacity at the community level and across the voluntary sector as a whole.

Major issues involved in helping communities and the sector as a whole participate and develop the capacity for evaluation include:

- *Building credibility and acceptance of capacity-building efforts within communities.* Community stakeholders often perceive and mistrust evaluators as having limited ability to understand local issues. In order to overcome such resistance, evaluators need to invest time and effort in building personal relationships with voluntary organizations and the relevant communities *before* an evaluation begins as well as demonstrate long-term commitment to community collaboration.

- *Institutionalizing increased capacity.* A core group of community participants could be involved in evaluation and research this core continuously expanded to establish a broad base of knowledgeable participants.

- *Recognizing cultural competence and its impact on community engagement in research.* In conducting research, evaluators should attempt to understand not the only socio-demographic character of a community, but also its values, politics, and history by involving community leaders in the study.

- *Building local capacity for using and disseminating data.* Evaluation results, indicating community assets and strengths can help build capacity in communities to advocate for their own needs (Annie E. Casey Foundation (1997)).

CONCLUSION

In a political environment that has become extremely evidence-driven and in which accountability has become a major concern, the pressures for evaluation and reporting on all aspects of a nonprofit's operations have grown dramatically in recent years. In large part, this pressure is generated by external forces, but it is also being driven internally as boards and staff seek creative ways of demonstrating their value and of making strategic choices among competing claims on time and resources. Not only the pressures but the resources for evaluation have increased in recent years. A plethora of Web sites provide advice on evaluation methods and a substantial consulting industry has developed around performance assessment. As we argue, however, the main issues of assessment are not so much technical in nature as they are the meta questions involving tradeoffs of what an organization needs to know and how much time and resources it has to dedicate to finding out.

While there are clear benefits to performance management, there is also a dark side. The transaction costs mean that the resources spent on measurement are probably diverted from service and other activities, which may not necessarily bring a long-term reward in performance improvement. As we saw from the VSERP national survey, funders are increasingly expecting evaluation to be conducted, but without providing financial support to cover the costs of it. The expanded lexicon of evaluation terms, particularly if they are copyrighted and trademarked, has created considerable confusion rather than greater clarity. Depending on how results are used, the possibility of goal displacement has been well documented. If funding is tied to positive results and if indicators become the objectives, there may be a tendency to cherry-pick the easiest people to serve or stick to the tried and true, rather than innovating or adapting.

A key challenge for the voluntary sector is to bring performance assessment closer to governance so that boards of directors are more actively involved in making policy decisions about performance management. A related challenge is to build greater capacity for assessment, both at the organizational and the sectoral level. This involves a greater role for intermediary organizations in providing expertise, information sharing and convening various interested parties. It also entails greater dialogue among funders *and* between funders and the organizations they fund in order to establish shared expectations, greater consistency in evaluation requirements and common terminology.

The most ominous prospect is that the current political environment is so focused on accountability as control — and in particular on compliance, justification and financial reporting — that control is crowding out the potential for accountability as learning. There is little room to have something go wrong or not according to plan, particularly when dealing with government funders, and thus there is little scope for innovation, adaptation to changing conditions, or learning. The overwhelming challenge then is to engage a serious debate about this narrow form of accountability and to keep spaces open for innovation and risk taking, thereby fostering a climate more conducive to learning and self-improvement across all parts of the voluntary sectors.

REFERENCES

Annie E. Casey Foundation (1997), *Evaluating Comprehensive Community Change. Research and Evaluation Conference.* Available online at: <http://www.aecf.org/publications/evaluation/index.htm>.

Aucoin, P., & M. Jarvis (2005), *Modernizing Government Accountability: A Framework for Reform.* Canada School of Public Service. Available online at: <http://www.myschool-monecole.gc.ca/Research/publications/html/p131/1_e.html>.

Aucoin, P., & R. Heintzman (2000), "The Dialectics of Accountability for Performance", in (2000), 66:1 *Public Management Reform. International Review of Administrative Sciences* 45-56.

Brinkerhoff, J. (2002), "Assessing and Improving Partnership Relationships and Outcomes: A Proposed Framework (2002), 25 *Evaluation and Program Planning* 215-231.

City of Toronto (2004), *Cracks in the Foundation: Community Agency Survey 2003* (Toronto: City of Toronto Community and Neighbourhood Services, 2004).

Cutt, J., & V. Murray (2000), *Accountability and Effectiveness Evaluation in Nonprofit Organizations* (London: Routledge, 2000).

Davies, I.C. (1999), "Evaluation and Performance Management in Government" (1999), 5:2 *Evaluation* 150-159.

DeLancer Julnes, P. (2001), "Does Participation Increase Perceptions of Usefulness? An Evaluation of a Participatory Approach to the Development of Performance Measures" (2001), 24 *Public Performance & Management Review* 403-418.

English, J., & E. Lindquist (1998). Performance Management: Linking Results to Public Debate, *IPAC New Directions* Number 2.

European Commission (January 1997). *Evaluating EU Expenditure Programmes: A Guide to Ex Post and Intermediate Evaluation* (Luxembourg: European Commission, 1997).

Fine, A.H., & C.E. Thayer (2000). "Evaluation and Outcome Measurement in the Non-profit Sector: Stakeholder Participation" (2000), 24 *Evaluation and Program Planning* 103-108.

Frumkin, P. (2002), *On Being Nonprofit* (Cambridge, MA: Harvard University Press, 2002).

Funnell, S.C. (2000), "Developing and using a program theory matrix for program evaluation and performance monitoring" (2000), 87 *New Directions for Evaluation* 91–101.

Good, D.A. (2003), *The Politics of Public Management* (Toronto: IPAC, 2003).

Guba, E.G., & Y.S. Lincoln (1989), *Fourth Generation Evaluation* (London: Sage, 1989).

Hall, M., S.D. Phillips, C. Meillat, & D. Pickering (2003), *Assessing Performance: Evaluation Practices & Perspectives in Canada's Voluntary Sector* (Canadian Centre for Philanthropy and Centre for Voluntary Sector Research and Development, 2003). Available online at: <www.vserp.ca/pub/VserpReport.pdf>.

Hatry, H., T. van Houten, M.C. Plantz & M.T. Greenway (1996), *Measuring Program Outcomes: A Practical Approach* (Alexandria, VA: United Way of America, 1996).

Kettl, D.F. (2005, December). *The Next Government of the United States: Challenges for Performance in the 21st Century.* IBM Center for the Business of Government.

Kubisch, A.C., K. Fulbright-Anderson & J.P. Connell (1998), "Evaluating Community Initiatives: A Progress Report", in *New Approaches to Evaluating Community Initiatives, Vol. 2: Theory, Measurement, and Analysis*, K. Fulbright-Anderson, A.C. Kubisch, and J.P. Connell, eds. (Washington, DC: The Aspen Institute, 1998). Available online at: <www.aspeninstitute.org/Programt3.asp?bid=1264>.

Lafleur, C. (1995), "A Participatory Approach to District-level Program Evaluation: The Dynamics of Internal Evaluation", in J.B. Cousins and L.M. Earl, eds., *Participatory Evaluation in Education: Studies in Evaluation Use and Organizational Learning* (London: Falmer, 1995), pp. 33-54.

Mayne, J. (1999), "Addressing Attribution Through Contribution Analysis: Using Performance Measures Sensibly" (Office of the Auditor General of Canada, June 1999). Available online at: <www.oag-bvg.gc.ca/domino/other.nsf/html/9 9dp1_e.html/$file/9at9dp1_e.pdf>.

Mayne, J. (2003) "Reporting on Outcomes: Setting Performance Expectations and Telling Performance Stories", Office of the Auditor General of Canada. Available online at: <http://www.oag-bvg.gc.ca/domino/other.nsf/html/200305dp1_e.html>.

McDavid, J.C., & L. Hawthorn (2001), *Program Evaluation and Performance Measurement: An Introduction to Practice* (Thousand Oaks, CA: Sage Publications, 2001).

McNamara, Carter (1998a), "Where Program Evaluation is Helpful", in *Basic Guide to Program Evaluation*. Available online at: <http://www.managementhelp.org/evaluatn/fnl_eval.htm#anchor1577333>.

McNamara, C. (1998b), "Selecting Which Methods to Use", in *Basic Guide to Program Evaluation*. Available online at: <www.management help.org/evaluatn/fnl_eval.htm#anchor1665834>.

McNamara, C. (1998c), "Overview of Methods to Collect Information" in *Basic Guide to Program Evaluation*. Available online at: <http://www.managementhelp.org/evaluatn/fnl_eval.htm#anchor1585345>.

Murray, V. (2003), "Evaluation Games: The Political Dimension in Evaluation and Accountability Relationships." Available online at: <http://www.vserp.ca/pub/CarletonEVALUATIONGAMES.pdf>.

OECD (2004), *Measures for Promoting Integrity and Preventing Corruption: How to Assess?* Report prepared for the 30th Session of the Public Governance Committee, Paris.

Ogata, K., & R. Goodkey (1998), *Redefining Government Performance*, Cambridge Paper presented July 16, 1998. Available online at: <www.finance.gov.ab.ca/publications/measuring/cambridge_paper.html>.

Panel on Accountability and Governance for the Voluntary Sector (PAGVS) (1999) *Building on Strength: Improving Governance and Accountability in Canada's Voluntary Sector* (Ottawa: PAGVS, 1999).

Patton, M.Q. (1997), *Utilization-focused Evaluation: the New Century Text*, 3rd ed. (Thousand Oaks, CA: Sage Publications Inc., 1997).

Perrin, B. (2002), "Towards a New View of Accountability". Paper presented to the European Evaluation Society annual conference, Seville, Spain (October 2002), as part of a symposium on *Promoting Organizational Learning via Evaluation: The New Accountability?*

Perrin, B. (1998), "Effective Use and Misuse of Performance Measurement" (1998), *American Journal of Evaluation* 367-379.

Phillips, S.D., & K. Levasseur (2004), "The Snakes and Ladders of Accountability: Contradictions between Contracting and Collaboration for Canada's Voluntary Sector" (2004), 47 *Canadian Public Administration* 451-474.

Phillips, S.D. (2003), "SUFA and Citizen Engagement: Fake or Genuine Masterpiece?", in S. Fortin, A. Nöel, and F. St-Hilaire, eds., *Forging the Canadian Social Union: SUFA and Beyond* (Montreal: Institute for Research on Public Policy, 2003), pp. 93-124.

Power, M. (1994), *The Audit Explosion*, London: Demos.

Saint-Martin, D. (2004), *Coordinating Interdependence: Governance and Social Policy Redesign in Britain, the European Union and Canada* (Ottawa: Canadian Policy Research Networks, 2004).

Smith, M.F. (1989), *Evaluability Assessment: A Practical Approach* (Boston: Kluwer Academic, 1989).

Social Development Canada (2004), *The Voluntary Sector Initiative Process Evaluation, Final Evaluation Report*. Available online at: <www.vsi-isbc.ca/eng/relationship/process_evaluation/index.cfm>.

Taylor, M. (1996), "Between Public and Private: Accountability in Voluntary Organisations" (1996), 24 *Policy and Politics* 57-72.

Thayer, C.E., A.H. Fine, J.B. Cousins & E. Whitmore (1998), "Framing Participatory Evaluation" (1998), 80 *New Directions for Evaluation* 5-24.

Trevisan, M.S., & Yi Min Huang (2003), "Evaluability Assessment: a Primer" (2003), *Practical Assessment, Research & Evaluation* 8:20. Available online at: <http://PAREonline.net/getvn.asp?v=8&n=20>.

Voluntary Sector Initiative (*Accord*), *An Accord Between the Government of Canada and the Voluntary Sector* (Ottawa: Voluntary Sector Task Force, Privy Council Office, 2001).

Voluntary Sector Initiative (*Code on Policy*), *A Code of Good Practice on Policy Dialogue* (Canada: Joint Accord Table, 2002).

Voluntary Sector Initiative (*Code on Funding*), *A Code of Good Practice on Funding* (Canada: Joint Accord Table, 2002).

W.K. Kellogg Foundation (1998), *Evaluation Handbook: Philosophy and Expectations*. Available online at: <http://www.wkkf.org/Pubs/Tools/Evaluation/Pub770.pdf>.

Weiss, C.H. (1997), *Evaluation: Methods for Studying Programs and Policies*, 2nd ed. (Upper Saddle River, NJ: Prentice Hall, 1997).

Wholey, J.S. (1979), *Evaluation: Promise and Performance* (Washington, DC: The Urban Institute, 1979).

Chapter 10

FINANCIAL MANAGEMENT IN NONPROFIT ORGANIZATIONS

Carolyn Bodnar-Evans
Ryerson University

INTRODUCTION

Financial management in nonprofit organizations is becoming increasingly important and complex. There are numerous challenges in managing both revenues and expenditures due to changes nonprofits face in their external environment. For example, competition for funds and, in some areas, competition with for-profit organizations is creating pressure to paint a favourable financial picture. Donors and the public increasingly equate financial efficiency (or the percentage of expenses spent on programs and services) with organizational effectiveness. Scandals in both the nonprofit and for-profit worlds have created a demand for increased scrutiny and accountability.[1] Finally, information about nonprofits is more accessible to the public; for example, more people are accessing the annual information returns for registered charities that are readily available on Canada Revenue Agency's Web site.[2]

This chapter will look at the basic elements of sound financial management. It will answer such questions as: what is financial

---

[1] In The Muttart Foundation's report, *Talking about Charities 2004: Canadians' Opinions on Charities and Issues Affecting Charities* (available online at: <www.muttart.org/surveys.htm>), nearly all those surveyed agreed that charities should be required to disclose how donations are spent and almost half of those surveyed do research prior to donating, which includes reviewing financial statements.

[2] <www.cra-arc.gc.ca>.

management, who is responsible for it, and how can it help organizations achieve their missions in our increasingly accountable environment as well as help them to better respond to the challenges in their communities?

Financial management focuses on generating financial information that can be used to improve decision-making oriented towards achieving the goals of an organization as well as maintaining a healthy financial situation. It encompasses the broad areas of:

(1) Managerial accounting, which relates to the generation of any financial information that managers find useful for the internal management of the organization. It incorporates activities such as developing and implementing budgets as well as various analytic techniques;

(2) Financial accounting, which is concerned with providing retrospective financial information to users both internal and external to an organization. It produces regular reports from the accounting system regarding the financial status of the organization at any point in time; and

(30 Finance, which focuses on sources and uses of an organization's financial resources such as cash and investments.

A recent study argues that the future economic success of a nonprofit will depend not only on the quality of its social and economic activities but also its ability to improve its internal accounting decisions and communicate results from its financial reporting systems to its stakeholder community (see Keating & Frumkin (2003)). Inherent in this is the notion that financial management is not an end in itself but rather a tool in the overall pursuit of the mission, albeit an increasingly essential and powerful one. Financial management provides an understanding of the current financial status of an organization — how well it is doing financially and what it can or cannot afford to do. Suffice it to say, without adequate financial resources an organization cannot achieve its mission. Financial management is also concerned with effectiveness (whether an organization is accomplishing its mission), and efficiency (whether an organization uses the minimum resources required to accomplish its mission).

RESPONSIBILITY FOR FINANCIAL MANAGEMENT

Ultimately, the board of directors is responsible for the management of a nonprofit's funds and assets. It cannot delegate this responsibility to employees or financial consultants but it can rely on the advice and assistance of such people. While day-to-day financial management duties are usually delegated to staff, the board remains responsible and must maintain proper supervision and control of the work of the employees (see Ministry of the Attorney General (2004a)). The board's work in this area may be led by a finance committee, headed up by a treasurer. Depending upon the needs of the organization, the board may also create a separate audit committee. The responsibilities of these committees are discussed in more detail later in this chapter.

Except in all-volunteer organizations, the board usually delegates the responsibility for carrying out many of the financial management duties to the Executive Director, who in turn may delegate further to other professional staff. Often there is a Chief Financial Officer or book-keeper who undertakes many of these duties, such as the preparation of the financial information needed for board and management decision-making, progress tracking and reporting to the organization's stakeholders. However, it is not the role of financial managers to say what an organization should do with the information they provide.

In small nonprofit organizations without access to professional accounting staff, the board of directors usually must retain the responsibilities more commonly played by staff in larger organizations. To assist them it is worth focusing effort on attracting a treasurer to keep the financial records of the organization or perhaps to oversee a part-time book-keeper. More detail regarding roles and responsibilities for financial management is contained in each of the three main sections of this chapter, and further information on the responsibility for financial management may be found in the Muttart Foundation's publication *Financial Responsibilities of Not-for-Profit Boards: A Self-Guided Workbook* referenced at the end of the chapter.

HOW THIS CHAPTER IS ORGANIZED

The first section, "Budgeting — The Financial Component of the Planning Process", discusses the budgeting process, including pitfalls to avoid, types of budgets, who should be involved and steps in the process. The second section, "Internal Control", discusses the scope and importance of an internal control system, provides examples of controls, and describes the role of finance and audit committees. To illustrate its importance it also presents a case study concerning the discovery of fraud. The third and final section, "Financial Reporting", touches on basic financial statement concepts and those unique to nonprofit organizations, the roles of those responsible for it and some key reporting issues in the sector today.

BUDGETING — THE FINANCIAL COMPONENT OF THE PLANNING PROCESS

Budgeting is an important step in the overall planning process. It follows from an organization's strategy for accomplishing its mission and a plan setting out its non-financial and financial objectives. The budget is a specific and detailed plan for the fiscal year that defines the resources needed to accomplish its goals and objectives, where the resources will come from, and how they will be used.

At its simplest, the budget is a plan expressed in monetary terms but, much more than this, it is a useful management tool to motivate, monitor and measure financial performance, and to assist in managing operations and costs. Budgets can also act as an accountability tool for the organization's stakeholders, board of directors and managers.

However, used unwisely, a budget also has the ability to unnecessarily limit an organization. For example, budgets should not act as a constraint on what the organization can and cannot do, or prevent it from doing the right things. No budget is perfect as none of us can predict the future with any certainty. For this reason many accountants view budgets as being out of date soon after they are assembled and therefore urge that they be treated as guidelines rather than rigid rules. To get the most from the budgeting process, it is important to know what the ideal process should be and how to avoid some of the pitfalls that can arise in it. There are four elements to the ideal process.

First, appropriate *involvement of staff* is important. If senior management, starting with the CEO and senior financial manager (henceforth to be referred to as the CFO or chief financial officer) are not sufficiently engaged in the process then budgets may get short shrift from front-line managers and others involved in the process. The tone is set at the top. However, budgeting is not the sole domain of the CFO and therefore should not be viewed as simply an exercise in adjusting expense numbers to equal revenue numbers. Virtually all managers should become involved in creating and using budgets. If staff feel personally vested in how well the organization does, the chances of a good outcome are substantially improved.

Second, budgeting requires a significant amount of *time and energy*. It can typically take one to three months in small organizations and four to six months in a larger organization. Some have estimated that 20 to 30 per cent of the time of senior managers can be taken up by budgeting, therefore in order to be worthwhile, budgets have to be intimately connected to the plan and goals of the organization. Too often budgeting becomes an exercise in number crunching, separated from the planning process. A budget should reflect the way the organization's strategy will be implemented in terms of how funds will be spent to reach desired goals.

To prevent a budget from becoming too inwardly focused on negotiated targets, sufficient attention should be given to the client or donor served by the organization. It may also help for a budget not to focus just on inputs such as staff time or needed supplies, but to link the budgetary resources to the outputs and outcomes generated by such inputs (these are discussed in more detail in Chapter 9.

Third, the process of developing the budget should be *engaging*, especially for line managers such as program and department heads. These managers are often reluctant to get sufficiently involved in the budgeting process, seeing it as a low-value activity compared to their primary mission-related responsibilities. Yet their participation in devising, reviewing and analyzing the budget ensures the creation of something that is of value to them and the other users. Connecting the budget to the strategic priorities of the organization will help line managers see how the budget better serves the mission of the organization.

One way to involve managers in the budgeting process is by adopting a bottom-up approach which starts by having managers provide specific targets or outputs that their programs or departments can accomplish in line with the organization's strategic plan. They then prepare the corresponding budget allocation request required to meet these targets. This kind of approach can also be combined with a partial top-down approach whereby the CEO provides the overall budget number that each program or department must work within and based on this, the line managers then prepare targets and their detailed budget information. Aside from the process itself, managers may feel more engaged if they are evaluated in terms of their contribution towards budget objectives, again connected with the mission.

Finally, the budget process should be *flexible*. It should contain appropriate procedures for approving changes when required so that it enables rather than disables the organization's ability to adapt to changing conditions. Too often budgets are treated as rigid rules with many organizations being unwilling to change their budgets within the fiscal year in spite of changing conditions. Fear of being punished for missing budget targets can lower service quality and inhibit needed innovation. It may also reinforce a dependency culture that encourages people to meet the target rather than exceed the target so improvements are only incremental. Another typical budget behaviour associated with inflexibility is the "use it or lose it" or protectionist mindset which occurs when managers are penalized for not using their total budget allocation by having their next year's budget reduced. Managers with this mindset are therefore motivated to expend their total budget despite sometimes not really needing the funds. This kind of behaviour not only creates waste and inefficiency but results in missed opportunities to reallocate resources to take advantage of circumstances that unexpectedly arise to further the mission.

Trying to accurately predict what will happen in 12 months and budgeting accordingly is an exercise in futility. Thus it is important that the budget process strikes the right balance between flexibility and control. This can be done by ensuring that everyone understands what the purpose of the budget is and what the process is for creating and changing it.

In some cases the board may decide to be more "hands on" and thus exercise more control and less flexibility when an organization's financial situation is more precarious. In other circumstances, where the financial situation is good and management has a solid track record, the board may agree that more flexibility is required such that the CEO can operate within the total budget and only when there are changes to the overall bottom line surplus or deficit, would board approval be needed.[3] The CEO may apply a similar principle to managers with budget responsibility. Some organizations have adopted a rolling budget process such that the approved budget is reviewed regularly and revised budget goals are agreed upon during the year within parameters set by the board.

So how does an organization get the most from its budgeting process? First it is important to more fully appreciate what a budget

---

[3]   The various options for a board's involvement in budgeting are further explained later in this chapter. Also refer to Chapter 3 on the role of the board.

can do, then to understand the different types of budgets and finally to be clear about the role of the people involved and the process itself.

Characteristics of a Well-prepared Budget

A well-prepared budget allows an organization to adjust plans, activities and spending as needed; spend money cost-effectively; reach specific goals it has set; receive clean audits; and avoid incurring questioned or disallowed costs or cost overruns that it may have to pay for from other funds. It also lets everyone in the organization know the goals to be achieved, the work to be done to reach the goals, the resources (people and things) available, the timetable for getting specific work done, and the individuals responsible and accountable for doing it.

More specifically a well-prepared budget:

- provides the financial and operational guidance needed to implement policies and directives established by the board of directors;

- allows management to measure and guide immediate and long-term financial health and operational effectiveness;

- guides the acquisition and use of resources;

- anticipates operational expenses and identifies income to pay for such expenses;

- is a tool for controlling spending and avoiding unplanned deficits;

- helps to integrate administrative, staff and operating activities;

- allows monitoring of actual income and expenses against those that were budgeted so management can assess the overall financial situation and alter plans as needed; and

- serves as one of the bases for performance reviews and in some cases, compensation.

Types of Budgets

While budgets are most commonly thought of in terms of an operating budget which shows revenues and expenses, there are two other types of budgets which are related and should be prepared as part of the overall budgeting process. These are: (1) the capital budget — a plan for the acquisition of capital assets such as buildings and equipment that provide benefits for more than one year; and (2) the cash budget

— a plan for expected cash receipts and expenses that alerts management to those times when there will be excess cash to invest or a shortage of cash to make up.

Capital Budget

This budget shows what capital assets are required for an organization to operate and the effects of these acquisitions on the operating budget. Because the capital budget often details large costs for major pieces of equipment and buildings it is important that it discusses the implications of these expenses for current and future operating costs and for the organization's cash flow. Depending on the results of this analysis it may be necessary to make special arrangements to finance these acquisitions.

One of the most significant effects it has on the operating budget is through the inclusion of amortization or depreciation expenses. For example, while the full cost of a van or the major improvement of a building will be accounted for in the capital budget, only a one-year portion of the cost will be included as an expense in the operating budget for each year that the van or the major building improvement is expected to provide useful service to an organization's mission. This one-year portion is called amortization expense and it recognizes that the addition of a capital asset has a future benefit to the organization and therefore it is not reasonable to charge the full cost of the asset's purchase as an expense in the year purchased.

The capital budget of some organizations also identifies purchases of specific items for the coming year, while other organizations may approve an overall dollar value for capital spending and then evaluate and approve individual items for acquisition throughout the year as the need for those items arises. The capital budgeting process may require a thorough review of the proposed purchase and a search for alternative options. This usually involves a detailed financial analysis of the impact of the purchase on the organization's mission and financial situation over its lifetime.

Decisions regarding the purchase of an expensive piece of equipment used in a program and whether it should be purchased outright, leased or shared with another organization require this kind of analysis. As a practical matter, limits are set such that only items over a certain dollar limit would be capitalized and amortized. A cut-off of $500 or $1,000 is a reasonable level for many nonprofits. Those purchases falling below the cut-off would be accounted for as an expense which is deducted from revenues in the statement of revenues and expenditures at the time of purchase.

Cash Budget

Regardless of whether a cash budget is required by the board, it is a good idea to prepare one so as to reveal times when there may be a shortage of cash to pay regular operating costs such as salaries and rent. This allows for specific financing arrangements to be made well ahead of any potential cash shortages or, alternatively, management can try to speed up the timing of cash receipts and slow down disbursements so no shortage occurs. If a shortage necessitates borrowing from the organization's banker, sufficient lead time will be required to make these arrangements and for the board to provide formal approval if this is required by the organization's by-laws. On the flip side, the cash budget will also identify those times when excess cash may be on hand and available for investment. The cash budget takes the information in both the operating and capital budgets and translates revenues and expenditures, as well as capital asset acquisitions and disposals, into cash flow showing when cash outflows will exceed cash inflows and *vice versa*.[4]

Operating Budget

The operating budget is based on a set of detailed assumptions about what the organization wishes to accomplish in the next fiscal year modified by an analysis of likely external influences on the organization's income and expenses, such as the state of the economy, inflation, employment market and interest rates. It should be based on the "accrual" method of accounting, which means that the revenues and expenses arising from providing the services of the organization are both recorded in the same fiscal year even though the cash associated with these revenues and expenses may be received or paid in a different fiscal year. The accrual method must be used in order to conform to generally accepted accounting principles.

---

[4] For more information regarding cash budgets and cash flow management refer to the reference at the end of this chapter — *The Cash Flow Management Book for Nonprofits: A Step-by-Step Guide for Managers, Consultants, and Boards.*

An organization should not be indifferent to budgeting either a surplus or deficit. While some stakeholders may frown on the prospect of a surplus, the organization may be planning a new program in the following year and require additional resources from the current year to accomplish this. It may also be acceptable for organizations with accumulated surpluses from prior years to incur a deficit in order to apply those accumulated resources for special needs such as expanding a program.

The preparation of operating budgets is often an iterative process of top-down and bottom-up budgeting so in many cases it does not matter whether organizations budget for revenues or expenses first since revisions are likely to be needed to arrive at an acceptable final product. Operating budgets may be prepared for a fiscal period on many bases — monthly, quarterly or even annually (although if prepared annually the value of the budget as a management tool will be limited). This will be determined by the particular needs of the organization.

Board and Staff Roles and Responsibilities in Budgeting

The roles played by board and staff will vary depending on a non-profit's size, organizational structure and income structure. However, whatever the division of responsibility, it is important to follow a specified process that is tailored to the organization. Ideally, budgeting policies and procedures should be understood by all those involved. Also, as previously noted, budgets are best developed collaboratively using the skills and knowledge of those at a number of levels in the organization.

Board of Directors

Ultimately the board is legally responsible for ensuring that budgets meet applicable laws and regulations, are fiscally sound, and will further the organization's mission. The Canada Revenue Agency establishes and monitors many of the financial regulations that nonprofits must comply with such as the remittance of various withholding taxes and other amounts from employees as well as the disbursement quota,[5] and advocacy expenditure maximum. More information regarding these regulations can be found on Canada Revenue Agency's Web site.

As noted earlier, some boards restrict their role in budgeting to that of reviewing and approving, while others participate in budget preparation from the beginning. The extent of the board's role will depend on many factors. If management's financial expertise is limited (or there are no paid staff) or the organization finds itself in a financial crisis, then a board could decide to take on roles that might normally be considered those of management. In either case there is usually value in creating a finance or budget committee with the specific responsibility for reviewing budgets before subjecting them to a formal review by the full board.

One of the key responsibilities of all boards is to establish general budget policies. Such policies would, for example, state that budgets must be balanced (and note any exceptions to this rule) and specify the use or development of reserve funds. The board should also set the framework for budgeting by making general policy decisions about new programs, capital projects, major fundraising efforts, salary increases and changes to the overall staff complement.

Following the approval of the budget, the board should receive regular updates on its implementation from the CEO and, where appropriate, approve any significant changes to the budget that become necessary during the year.

CEO

The CEO's role is to facilitate and oversee the preparation and approval of the budget as well as its implementation once approved. This includes:

- arranging and staffing early strategic planning sessions with the board;

- preparing options and recommendations to guide budget development;

---

[5]   A detailed description of the disbursement quota is beyond the scope of this text but in general a charity meets the quota when it expends at least 80 per cent of the previous year's receipted donations on programs and services.

- ensuring the budget is accurate and adheres to board policies and that the budgeting schedule is met;

- reviewing draft budgets and making resource allocation decisions;

- presenting the recommended budget to the board, explaining its provisions and possible consequences and answering the board's questions.

Upon approval it is the responsibility of the CEO to work with the CFO or senior finance manager and others to implement the budget. This includes clearly communicating the approved budget to the management and front-line staff so they understand it and the part they play. Monitoring includes reviewing financial reports that compare actual with budgeted results so that variances can be determined and corrective action taken as appropriate. It is very important that the CEO communicate financial results and any corrective action he or she has taken to the board. Depending upon the situation, the CEO may seek the board's input and/or approval for needed fiscal or program changes.

CFO or Senior Financial Manager

The CFO plays a major and sustained role, often having day-to-day responsibility for co-ordinating budget development, implementation and monitoring. This would include:

- creating the budget development calendar and ensuring deadlines are met;

- communicating budgeting policies and procedures to managers and line staff;

- establishing the format for budget drafts;

- developing income and expense forecasts based on reviews of economic and competitive trends when applicable;

- collaborating in setting expense and income targets in line with strategic plan and programs;

- evaluating draft budgets from program or unit managers for accuracy, reasonableness, applicable guidelines and anticipated resources;

- discussing draft budgets with the CEO and other managers as needed;

- writing up recommendations for reducing, increasing or reallocating requested resources;

- preparing the budget document once the CEO's budget decisions are made and possibly helping to present it to the board; and

- once approved, overseeing its implementation and monitoring; this includes preparing and analyzing budgeted versus actual income and expense reports, and overseeing any corrective actions needed.

In organizations that do not have a dedicated financial person, this role may be fulfilled by a combination of people such as the CEO, part-time book-keeper, office or business manager, treasurer, or other qualified program staff.

Program, Unit, Activity or Department Managers

Usually it is program managers (including those involved in fundraising and administrative functions) who are best equipped to provide information on current program needs, revenues, costs and the effects of reducing or expanding individual programs. Thus their involvement is essential to developing budgets that accurately reflect reality. Ideally they are responsible for developing draft budgets for their areas, consulting with other staff to evaluate revenue potential, current or new programs, operating costs and staff and equipment needs. They should meet with the CFO or CEO to review draft budgets, explore options for change and, once the budget is approved, inform staff about program and operational requirements for meeting the budget. They must also be held accountable for the allocated resources by regularly reviewing financial reports prepared by the CFO and developing corrective action plans when problems arise.

Others

Depending on the nature of the organization, others may be involved in the budgeting process such as clerical staff, selected clients or volunteers, and consultants or other outside specialists. The role of these others is usually to provide information or advice but, in any case, should be clear to all those involved in the process.

Steps in the Budget Preparation Process

Although the budget preparation process can generally be described as bottom-up and iterative, this is not the only approach. The steps that follow are general and, while typical in a traditional budgeting process, can be altered. There are also other methods of budget preparation and these are summarized at the end of this section. Employing these other methods would require changes to the process as described in this section.

A set of assumptions and guidelines is prepared that create the context within which managers will develop detailed budgets for their areas. The CEO, working with the CFO, will generally provide policies, goals and performance expectations stemming from the policies and strategy established by the board.

In many cases there is a requirement that budgets be prepared using a predetermined format to make it easier to aggregate them across the organization. It is also desirable to require that the budget be accompanied by a proposed work plan that can be evaluated along with the budget request.

Sometimes those preparing budgets are told to focus only on the operating fund without including any restricted funds but, in order to make decisions regarding the best allocation of all the resources available to the organization, budgets should be prepared taking into consideration all the funds or resources of the organization.

The assumptions and guidelines that are provided at the beginning of the budget preparation process should reflect the organization's strategic plans and take into consideration its projected income and expenses for the coming year. For example, the organization could be having a bad year and need to make up for an unplanned deficit with a surplus the following year. Assumptions and guidelines may also include specific program objectives and priorities, reserve fund targets or limits, policies governing the creation of new programs or positions, and projections of personnel costs. An organization could also have a guideline requiring those doing the preparation to provide measures of what will be accomplished with the money they receive — indicators such as the number of counselling sessions to be conducted, the hours of service to be delivered or the participants to be served that link the budget outputs and outcomes to be achieved.

Sometimes organizations have budget formats that distinguish between those for internal reports (to staff, volunteers and the board) and those for external reports to stakeholders. For example, in the year-end audited financial statements to stakeholders, some administration expenses may be allocated to the cost of programs or fundraising, while, for the internal budget, administration may be categorized separately to facilitate its management by the person(s) responsible. In this case the board may want to see both versions of the budget, the internally used version which may be more helpful to the board's oversight role, and the externally used version so that it is aware of how the organization's stakeholders will view the financials. In addition, depending upon the funding structure, certain funders may require budget information in their own format to consider when making their decisions on funding.

The co-existence of budgets in different formats can get very confusing for managers and the board as well as adding to administrative complexity and cost. However, while settling on one format may seem ideal, if it does not provide value to the organization it could be worth producing more than one. If this is the case then, at minimum, the translation between internally and externally oriented budgets should be as simple as possible.

Budget Review and Adoption

Once the budgets for the responsibility areas are complete, they are aggregated. It is very common that the total of all spending requests exceeds projected revenues. Thus begins a process of negotiation to first eliminate any inefficiency in the budget, then to either find more revenue or reduce expenses. Choices must be made to focus on the highest priorities of the organization in order to minimize the impact on accomplishing the organization's goals and objectives. Through this negotiation process managers should be given the opportunity to provide a rationale for why their budget requests fit with the priorities and should not be among the first things cut. It may also be necessary to rethink certain aspects of the strategic plan because of information that comes to light during the budgeting process.

In the budget review process it is important that a good understanding of "hard and soft revenues and expenses" be developed so that there is some sense as to the degree of flexibility and risk inherent in the budget. "Hard" revenues are those that have a relatively high degree of certainty such as membership or tuition fees or fundraising revenue from a long-standing donor base. Hard expenses include salary and benefit expenses of permanent staff in core programs and rent payments. "Soft" revenues may include variable donation revenue from general sources, a challenge target or bequests. Soft expenses are those that, if the organization had to make mid-year budget cuts, could be reduced, eliminated or deferred until the next year without severe consequences such as temporary staff and non-essential program expenses. Ideally an organization would not plan to make long-term commitments with soft revenue.

Budget Implementation

An effective budget presentation in written form communicates to managers the amount that can be spent and what it can be spent on. It assists the board in keeping management accountable. Managers will need additional detail that breaks down the budget at the account level. As we will see, an effective system of internal control can help an organization achieve its plan, as can effective financial reporting.

Evaluation

A comparison of variances from budgeted to actual results should be done on a periodic basis, typically monthly or quarterly, so that problems can be identified and corrected midstream. Things do not always go as planned and it is important to understand why and whether it is simply something that should be recognized and corrected, or something that is beyond the control of the organization.

Other Budget-setting Methods

There are other methods for the setting of budgets, and while a detailed discussion of these is beyond the scope of this book, they are briefly described below. As noted earlier, employing any one of these techniques would require changes to the process described earlier.

Zero Based Budgeting

This budget-setting method asks the question: "If we were not doing this program or activity today, would we start it?" The focus is on a thorough re-evaluation of every facet of an organization's operation to determine whether it should be continued; thus it assumes that the organization is starting from zero. Employing this type of budget-setting method is very time-consuming, requires reliable and detailed cost information about the organization's activities, and can be very threatening to managers and staff involved in the process. While the approach has its merits, unless an organization has the resources to do it right, its application is most appropriate during periods of financial crisis when it is important to reduce costs with the least damage to vital services. In this situation the zero-sum method forces careful consideration of what is "vital" and what is not.

Rolling Budgets

This is a relatively new approach to budgeting being employed by some business organizations looking for improvements to the traditional budgeting process. Rather than creating an annual budget that remains static for the year, a budget is prepared and reviewed regularly (*e.g.*, monthly) and updated. Unlike the periodic reviews in the traditional process which may yield occasional changes here and there, in this case the entire budget is systematically recalculated at each review period. In some circumstances the rolling budget is prepared for an 18-month period rather than a 12-month period so that the budget always provides a view into the next fiscal year. While it may provide better information since the budget for the current and future periods are regularly reviewed, it is more time-consuming. It also requires constant and effective communication to ensure that the goals, which are updated as needed, are clear. It would be worth investigating for those nonprofit organizations existing in very dynamic environments in which costs and income can vacillate extensively over short periods of time.

Activity-based Budgets

The focus here is on developing budgets for clusters of activities such as a particular program or a specific fundraising campaign, rather than the traditional method of line item costs. This approach allows the organization to know how much it is spending on what, thus informing resource allocation decisions differently than a traditional budget process. It forces managers to consider what resources are actually needed for programs and functions since it is based on the activities carried out by the organization. For example, the process would start out with a determination of how many clients are to be served by a given program and proceed to a detailed analysis of *all* the direct and indirect expenses required to provide this level of service. For example, the complete cost of an activity includes the associated overhead costs such as a proportion of the rent, or a CEO's salary that is devoted to supporting the program. Thus, key decisions regarding cost allocations as well as reliable and detailed accounting information are critical. The chief benefit of this approach to budgeting is that it allows the organization to do a more thorough comparison of costs and benefits for its various programs and functions. This kind of information is also very valuable when it comes to making applications for grants. It also helps in negotiating contracts with governments or other funders who want only to fund direct costs but are unwilling to consider indirect costs necessary to support programs. The difficulty with this budgeting method is that there are no universally agreed-upon standards for calculating these indirect costs and deciding on the proportions that can be allocated to given programs.

INTERNAL CONTROL

Internal control used to be considered the sole domain of an organization's auditor or accountant. But this is no longer true and a much broader definition of internal control has emerged in the last decade. The following definition of "internal control" was developed by the U.S.-based Committee of Sponsoring Organizations[6] (COSO) in its publication *Internal Control — Integrated Framework*:

> Internal control is developed to allow an organization to achieve plans, protect resources, motivate employees, evaluate performance, alert management to variations from the plan, and take corrective action. It can be defined as a process, effected by an organization's board of directors, management and other personnel, designed to provide reasonable assurance regarding the achievement of objectives in three categories:
>
> 1. Effectiveness (moves the organization towards its goals or objectives) and efficiency of operations (accomplishes its goals at the lowest possible cost).
>
> 2. Reliability of financial reporting.

---

[6] The Committee of Sponsoring Organizations (COSO) Framework. COSO consists of the American Institute of Certified Public Accountants, The Institute of Management Accountants, the Institute of Internal Auditors, Financial Executives International and the American Accounting Association.

3. Compliance with applicable laws and regulations.

(Committee (1992), at p. 3.)

The COSO Framework consists of five components that form an integrated system that can react to changing conditions. The internal control system is intertwined with the organization's operating activities and is most effective when controls are built into the infrastructure of the organization.

1. *Control environment.* Sometimes referred to as the "tone at the top" of the organization, this refers to statements about the integrity, ethical values and competence of the organization's people including management's philosophy and operating style (*e.g.*, the way it assigns authority and responsibility); and the attention and direction provided by the board of directors. It is the foundation for all other components of internal control.

2. *Risk assessment.* The identification and analysis of risks, both inside and outside the organization that threaten the ability of the organization to achieve its objectives. This assessment forms the basis for developing a plan for minimizing the most serious of the risks identified.

3. *Control activities.* Policies and procedures that help ensure that management directives are carried out. Control activities occur throughout the organization at all levels in all functions. These include policies on what needs approval, verification or reconciliation, and what reviews should be made of operating performance, security of assets and segregation of duties.

4. *Information and communication.* Information systems within the organization are key to an effective system of internal control. Internal information, as well as information about external events, activities and conditions must be communicated in useful ways to enable management to make informed decisions. It is also vital for meeting the accountability requirements of external stakeholders. For example, the control system surrounding the activity of putting on a fundraising event would consist of the budget for the event, the planned amount to be raised, the record of the expenses incurred in putting it on and the record of ticket sales. These sources of information of information would likely be recorded in various places but are of little value unless they are brought together and communicated to the responsible mangers in a clear and useful fashion. Only is this way can the information help them monitor how successful the event was compared to the planned outcome and decide whether it should be dropped or changed in the future.

5.   *Evaluating*. The internal control system (all of the above four components) must be regularly monitored and evaluated by management and the board of directors to ensure that it is working as planned. The failure to carry out and act on this kind of evaluation of control systems is in large part responsible for many of the scandals that have plagued both the business and nonprofit world in recent years.

Elements of an Internal Control System

Specific examples of the elements of an internal control system are discussed below. It should be recognized that this list is far from exhaustive and is only provided to give a sense of the breadth of controls that may be considered.

A clear audit trail. It should be possible to trace any transaction in the accounting system back to its source, *e.g.*, if an expense is significantly more than budget, one should be able to look at a detailed listing of expenses from the accounting system to see how much was spent on what. The audit trail should be documented and, in order to be effective as a control, it should be regularly used to identify and examine discrepancies or unusual spending patterns.

Reliable personnel. The organization must have a group of employees that are capable, trustworthy and appropriately supervised.

Segregation of duties. This is one of the most common elements albeit difficult to accomplish in small organizations. The person who approves the bills should not be the same person that writes the cheques (this could be the board member who is Treasurer in smaller organizations). The benefit of segregation is that one person may catch a problem missed by another; however it cannot help in the instance where there is collusion among several persons and therefore it goes back to having reliable people in place.

Proper authorization. All spending must be supported by proper authorization. Authorization limits should be established so operations are not bogged down. Established authorization practices should extend to contracts that commit an organization's resources.

Proper procedures. To reduce errors, internal control systems rely heavily on standard operating procedures in the form of policy and procedure manuals. To do this effectively both the procedures and manuals should be kept current.

Physical safeguards. Cash should be kept in the bank. Deposits should be made regularly, daily if possible. Blank cheques should be locked up when not in use. Computer backups should be kept in a separate location. Inventory should be locked up with appropriate access controls.

Other elements of internal control systems may be suggested by the organization's auditors or found in resources such as the workbook published by The Muttart Foundation, *Board Development: Financial Responsibilities of Not-for-Profit Boards*, which includes a section called *"Making Sure the Accounts are in Order"*, of particular relevance to smaller organizations. Larger organizations may find the American Institute of Certified Public Accountant's *Audit Committee Toolkit for Nonprofit Organizations* a useful resource.

What an Internal Control System Cannot Do

The design of an internal control system is a function of the resources available, implying that its cost must be at least be equal to the benefits derived from it. Because of this, even the best internal control system can only provide *reasonable* assurance to management and the board about the organization's progress, or lack of progress in achieving its mission. Breakdowns in the internal control system can occur due to a simple error as well as faulty judgments that could be made at any level of the organization. There is also a possibility that internal controls will be circumvented by collusion or management override. Breaches of the internal control system that lead to fraud are discussed later on in this chapter.

Responsibility for Internal Control Systems

Everyone in the organization has a role to play in the organization's internal control system.

Board of Directors. The primary role of the board is one of oversight of the internal control system. This is best carried out by its *Audit Committee.* For specific examples on what a board can do to fulfil its role, see the section called *"Audit Committee"* further on in this chapter.

CEO. The CEO has the ultimate responsibility for the internal control system. The CEO sets the "tone at the top" thus affecting the integrity, ethics and other factors that create the positive control environment needed for the internal control system to thrive. However, much of the day-to-day operation of the system would normally be delegated to other senior managers in the organization if they are available.

CFO or Senior Financial Manager (if available). The chief responsibility of this person is to provide critical technical leadership in the development, implementation and maintenance of the internal control system since much of the internal control structure flows through the accounting and finance area of the organization.

All other personnel. All other staff should understand why control systems are necessary, how they work and their responsibility for supporting the system through their own actions.

The Role of Board Committees

Finance Committee

The board of a nonprofit organization often has a finance committee that can provide support to both the volunteer treasurer and staff. In smaller organizations unable to afford professional finance staff, this committee can play an important part in the internal control system. These responsibilities may include monitoring performance against budget, providing advice on investment policies, making investment decisions on behalf of the organization and reviewing or deciding insurance coverage plans, pension plans, unusual fundraising matters or expense reimbursements.

Since 2002 the spotlight as been on standards of governance relating to the oversight of financial transactions and auditing procedures because of a number of very public corporate accounting scandals. Certain legislated measures have been taken in both Canada[7] and the United States to rebuild public trust in the for-profit sector, one of which is improved standards for audit committees. While nonprofits are not directly affected by these, some have suggested that it may be worthwhile for them to examine their practices as a precaution.

---

[7]   In Canada these measures have been taken by the Ontario Securities Commission; the Canadian Securities Administrators, a group that works to better harmonize securities regulation across Canada; and the Canadian Public Accountability Board, a group that helps ensure public confidence in the integrity of the financial statements of publicly traded companies.

Certainly if an organization subjects itself to an annual audit, best practice dictates that the board create an audit committee. The existence of an audit committee may also provide greater assurance to an organization's stakeholders of the integrity of its financial statements and the internal processes that guide the expenditure of funds on the mission. In lieu of having a separate audit committee, the finance committee may be constituted twice a year or on an as-needed basis as an audit committee.

Audit Committee

In general an audit committee has two main responsibilities: first, to assist the board of directors in assuring itself that appropriate accounting policies and internal controls are established and followed, and that financial statements and reports are issued on time and in accordance with regulatory obligations; and second, to encourage and facilitate communication among the board, management and external auditors.

The audit committee should meet at least twice a year, before and after the audit, and then on an as-needed basis to fulfil its responsibilities. The basic functions of an audit committee are as follows:

1. Audit planning and preparation — The committee should plan with the auditors the scope of the upcoming audit, including areas of identified risk or potential error. It should also ensure that appropriate assistance is provided by the staff, review control weaknesses and determine whether if all practical steps have been taken to overcome them, and approve the auditor's engagement letter, including fees and expenses.

2. Ongoing reviews of information and control systems — This includes checking control system changes during the year, the condition of records, the adequacy of resources committed to accounting and control, and responding to any unanticipated financial risks that occur during the year.

3. Review of annual financial statements — This includes checking accounting policies (particularly those applicable to the nonprofit sector) and reviewing the methods used to account for unusual or significant transactions such as when pledges of funds may be accounted for as receivables, or how to handle a large grant made by a foundation to an affiliated organization.

4. Review of audit results — This includes looking over the auditor's proposed report and commenting on the appropriateness

of accounting policies such as when to account for pledges or bequests as revenue. It also checks on management's behaviour during the audit looking for significant adjustments, misstatements or irregularities, attempts to restrict the scope of the auditor's examination and evidence of illegal acts or fraud.

5.   Appointment of auditors — Enquire as to the experience, capabilities, objectivity and independence of individuals being proposed to conduct the audit, then recommend to the board the auditors to be appointed for the following year.

(See Deloitte & Touche LLP.)

Other functions may include: reviewing compliance with funders' regulations; ensuring that the required documentation has been sent to Canada Revenue Agency and other regulators to maintain the organization's nonprofit and/or charitable status; reviewing the organization's fundraising methods for their propriety and adherence to ethical codes. Sometimes the audit committee is the best one to review human resources policies with a special emphasis on assessing the extent to which they reduce the risks of lawsuits for harassment, wrongful dismissal or poorly written employment contracts.

In general, therefore, it has more and more become the case that the audit committee becomes the body that focuses on risk management for the board, since, even though risk management is a central challenge for both boards and CEOs, this committee is in the best position to assess the risks faced by the organization in many areas.

Membership in this committee should consist of three or more directors who are independent (who have no financial, family or other personal ties to management) and financially literate. This means having the ability to read and understand the organization's financial statements and understand the audit process, and being willing and able to ask searching questions about the matters before them. If possible, one member should be a financial expert (*e.g.*, employed in finance or accounting or possessing a professional certification in accounting).

Of course it is understood that it is sometimes difficult for the boards of small, grassroots organizations to find someone with this kind of financial expertise, in which case, what can they do? Difficult though it may be, the board members themselves must do their best to understand their financial role by consulting various information sources available such as this book and The Muttart Foundation's publication on financial responsibilities of boards cited earlier in the chapter. It might also be possible to enlist someone in the community who might not be willing to join the board but might provide some volunteer consulting on financial matters. Local branches of professional accounting associations and organizations like local Volunteer Centres and service clubs or business associations might be helpful in identifying these kinds of volunteer resources.

What to Expect from an External Audit

The role of an audit by external professionals is to obtain reasonable (not absolute) assurance that management's financial statements fairly present the financial position of the organization in accordance with generally accepted accounting principles (GAAP). It is important to note that it is not always possible for an auditor to verify the completeness of all of an organization's cash receipts due to their nature. For example, if a door-to-door campaign is conducted and cash is collected, there are no tests that an auditor can do to ensure that all the cash collected in the campaign was actually deposited into the organization's bank account.

An alternative to an audit is a "review engagement", the product of which is a statement that nothing has come to the attention of the public accountants performing the review that would cause them to believe that the financial statements are not in accordance with GAAP. It is primarily done using procedures that are less intensive than those used in an audit, and based on information supplied by the organization. Because of this, review engagements cost less than audits but they are mostly reserved for specific purposes such as complying with regulations attached to government funding contracts or foundation grants.

In general, it is not recommended that a review be used as a replacement for an annual audit. How a nonprofit is initially registered as a legal entity and the terms of its Letters Patent will determine whether an annual audit is required. It is also possible that certain funders may require an audit as a condition of receiving their funds.

Fraud

Fraud does not occur simply because of a poor internal control system, but ineffective controls can certainly make it easier for it to happen.

One theory (which is captured by the acronym "GONE") is that the probability of fraud increases when there is a combination of Greed, Opportunity (presented by poor internal controls), Need (fueled, for example, by a gambling problem or excessive debts), and Expectation (the perception that one will not be caught).

Fraud can have a significant impact on an organization's continued viability not only due to monetary losses but also due to the reduction in public support that generally results from publicized allegations of impropriety. Although there is no research to determine whether the incidence of fraud is higher or lower in nonprofits than for-profit enterprises, several factors make nonprofits especially vulnerable to fraud: an atmosphere of trust within the organization in which it is considered unnecessary to check on matters related to finance; the existence of donations which, because they do not involve an exchange for goods or services, cannot always be tracked; reliance on inexperienced volunteers to perform important tasks related to finance; unpaid boards of directors with little or no financial expertise; and lack of income to hire staff with appropriate experience and skills in the financial area.

It is important to understand that it is not the job of an external auditor to detect mismanagement or fraud. Rather, the board of directors is ultimately responsible and the audit committee is key in fulfilling this responsibility.

Several steps can be taken to help reduce the occurrence of fraud.

1. Ensure that the organization has implemented an effective ethics and compliance program such as a signed code of ethics at the time of employment.

2. Ensure that the audit committee and management are creating internal controls that address the appropriate risk areas and are functioning as designed.

3. Maintain oversight of significant funding arrangements.

4. Make a member of the audit or finance committee one of the signatories on all large cheque payments.

5. Ensure that there is continuous and open communication between management and the auditor such that all financial and internal control systems issues are addressed on a timely basis.

6. Maintain an open door policy towards fraud such that employees feel free to report suspected fraud to upper-level management or the board of directors.

7. Develop a clear understanding of what is in each revenue and expense account, then compare actual to budgeted expenses and, when there are differences, insist on plausible explanations and further investigation of things not satisfactorily explained.

8. Train and develop board members in their duties as financial overseers of the organization.

What Happens When Fraud Is Discovered?

It is not often that organizations want to disclose a case of fraudulent action, but much can be learned from an article that appeared in *The Nonprofit Quarterly* (see Erickson (2005)). By fluke it was discovered that the trusted book-keeper of a mid-sized nonprofit organization had embezzled a significant sum of money over the three years she was employed. The strategy adopted by the board was to:

*   immediately institute internal controls to minimize the chance of embezzlement ever happening again;

*   contract with a Certified Public Accounting (CPA) firm to conduct an audit;

*   assemble a team of volunteers to review and reconcile all bank statements during the period of the embezzlement;

*   implement a complete recovery plan which helped the organization to operate while dealing with the realities of the embezzlement, including seeking restitution through the bonding insurance policy, launching a civil suit against the embezzler, negotiating with the bank and developing a communications plan.

In this particular case the fraud occurred because of pressure to reduce administrative costs, insufficient independent verification of the general ledger and financial statements and the use of a "review engagement" by an accounting firm instead of a full audit, to save money.

The organization learned several lessons from their unfortunate experience:

*   When a crisis like this happens, tell the truth to your members.

- Be sure that independent bank reconciliations and other random verifications of invoices and receipts are done on a monthly basis.

- Conduct yearly audits.

- Reinforce to board members their fiduciary and legal responsibilities.

- Make sure your financial and administrative employees share the values of the organization.

- Be sure to train management staff as well as volunteer treasurers in financial procedures.

- Good administrative and financial controls are expensive but worth it; and

- Maintaining good relationships among the board, management, members, funders and donors is critical in building and funding an organization, especially in times of crisis.

FINANCIAL REPORTING

The financial reporting process may be thought of as the concluding phase of the cycle that begins with planning then moves to implementing and controlling. Reporting helps managers, the board and outsiders understand the current financial status of the organization. Managers want to know if they are on track and if the organization has sufficient financial resources to be viable. Donors want to know whether donated resources are put to good use. Creditors want to know whether the organization is a good credit risk. Foundations and corporations require support for funding requests. The Canada Revenue Agency wants to know that sufficient expenditures are being made on charitable programs and that the organization has not expended more than 10 per cent of its income on advocacy activities.

Many different reports may be created to satisfy the needs of these stakeholders for financial information. This section deals mostly with general purpose financial statements which are reported to the board, membership, donors, funders, government and the public. Quite often a nonprofit organization does not have the resources to produce several different reports on a regular basis, and therefore the general purpose financial statements produced either monthly or quarterly normally must meet several needs. Ideally they should be adapted for the required level of detail; managers needing more detail than the board of directors who, in turn need more information than the general public. Of course the accounting system should be able to produce supplementary information whenever needed for managers and directors alike.

Board members should expect that the information they require will be presented in an understandable way. Financial reports can make a board's financial responsibilities more difficult to carry out if they are in different formats, do not contain sufficient detail or contain too much detail. It is inadequate, for example, for a report to contain a statement of operations only, without the balance sheet and other corresponding statements.

Generally Accepted Accounting Principles

It is advisable that all financial reports be prepared using generally accepted accounting principles or GAAP so that they are readily understandable by their users and somewhat comparable from organization to organization. It is important to understand that GAAPs is not a set of prescriptive rules. GAAP does not specify how a particular expense must be accounted for or how expenses have to be shown within the financial statements. GAAP encompasses broad principles with some specific rules and procedures which are spelled out in the Canadian Institute of Chartered Accountant's (CICA) Handbook and in related documents issued by the CICA's Accounting Standards Board. The CICA Handbook applies both to for-profit and nonprofit organizations, and a great deal of professional judgment is required in applying the concepts and principles, particularly in cases where the Handbook does not deal specifically with accounting and reporting for some transactions or events.

Accounting policy choices are possible under GAAP and these can impact the financial position of an organization. For example, as we will see later, the choice an organization makes to account for contributions using the restricted fund method or the deferral method of accounting will impact its bottom line. This is because there is a timing difference related to when contributions are recorded in the statement of operations. Choices must also be made in choosing accounting policies and procedures, which affect the degree to which the financial statements are accurate. For example, accurately calculating the cost of photocopied documents made with a copier shared among many departments would necessitate procedures to keep track

374 THE MANAGEMENT OF NONPROFIT AND CHARITABLE ORGANIZATIONS

of the number of copies made for each department. However, this may not be worth the time staff must take to do it and some staff may fail to record all copies they make. Thus it may be determined that the cost of photocopying will be established with an approximation based on something like the relative proportion of staff in each department. The end result may be that the cost of is not totally accurate but is deemed to be good enough so as to not to represent a significant financial misstatement in the overall cost of programs.

Another element of choice in deciding how to present an organization's financial statements is the grouping of accounts. Certain financial information must be disclosed in a certain fashion but in general an organization has a significant amount of latitude, particularly in the disclosure of revenue and expense items. (See the discussion of financial statements below.)

These choices should be guided by what is most useful in making decisions as well as what the organization believes users would find most useful for their purposes. For example, an organization which places a high value on accountability may decide that the users of its financial statement should have more information than less and therefore choose to disclose expenses of various programs and services separately rather than lumping them into one expense line called "programs and services". This same organization's donors may want to know what the organization spends to fundraise, in which case it may choose to report these costs on a functional basis rather than a line-by-line basis (such as the costs of all printing, telephone and advertising expenses).

Financial Statements

Financial statements for a nonprofit organization normally include a set of four different types of statements.

Statement of Financial Position or Balance Sheet

This statement is a snapshot of the organization at a particular point in time, which could be either today or tomorrow, the end of the month or the last day of the fiscal year. It helps in assessing whether an organization has the financial resources to continue. It has three components representing the basic accounting equation (thus the term balance sheet):

$$Assets = Liabilities + Equity \text{ (or Net Assets)}$$

Assets are what the organization owns or what is owed to them. They are a result of past transactions or events and therefore represent the collective history of the organization from its beginning to the date of the balance sheet report. Common examples of assets are cash, investments, accounts receivable, prepaid amounts and capital assets such as computer equipment, furniture and buildings.

Liabilities are what the organization owes to someone else. Common examples of liabilities are accounts payable, payroll payable, loans payable and deferred grant revenue (advanced to the organization before a project's completion).

Equity (more commonly referred to as net assets or fund balances) is what is left over from the assets once all the liabilities have been paid. The net asset section shows unrestricted net assets as well as those whose use is restricted to a particular purpose, such as a scholarship fund, particular program or endowment.

Statement of Operations

Also known as the Statement of Revenues and Expenditures or Income Statement, this statement shows what the organization received as revenue (income) and what was spent (expenditures) over a particular period of time. It shows the cost of operating the organization and whether the organization raised sufficient funds to pay for its expenses, and acts as a bridge between the balance sheets at two different points in time. Common examples of revenue include contributions, fee-for-service revenue and investment income. Common examples of expenses include salaries, rent, insurance and printing. The difference between what was received as revenue and what was spent as expenses is either a surplus or a deficit.

The only disclosure requirement for revenue is that contributions should be disclosed by major source. There are no disclosure requirements for expenditures, but typically an organization will report expenditures by function, for example, the costs for research, education, fundraising or various programs. It may also choose to report by object or type of expense, for example, salaries, rent and utilities. Reporting by object is more common in organizations operating one or a few programs. Reporting by function, while requiring more judgment especially where costs are shared among several functions, may be more useful to financial statement users who want to know how much an organization spends in such areas as fundraising or costs of administration.

Statement of Changes in Net Assets or Fund Balances

This statement is sometimes combined with the statement of revenues and expenses, and provides details regarding the changes between the opening and closing fund balances, including any transfers of resources between funds. Since they do not result in changes in the organization's overall economic resources, transfers should not be recognized as revenues or expenses. In general, this statement will reveal the extent to which an organization's operations have added to or depleted its net assets. As a specific example, it will also reveal the result of board decisions regarding fund transfers; for example, it could show funds from the operating fund being "put aside" for a specific purpose in an internally restricted fund.

Statement of Changes in Cash Flow

The statement of changes in cash flow is a record of all funds coming into the organization and all funds flowing out of the organization during a particular period of time. Financial information is presented on a "cash" basis versus that of the statement of operations, which is presented on an "accrual" basis. This statement shows the organization's ability to raise cash from various sources such as from grants or donations or the sale of assets or investments, and how it is used to support programs and services.

Unique Aspects of Nonprofit Accounting and Financial Reporting

The unique aspects of accounting and financial reporting for nonprofit organizations centre upon accounting for revenues from contributions; capital assets and collections held; and income from controlled and related entities (such as foundations set up solely to benefit the organization).

Contributions

One of the key aspects of nonprofit accounting is that contributors to nonprofit organizations, be they governments, individuals, corporations or other nonprofits, can impose restrictions on how the resources they contribute can be used. This influences the bases of many nonprofit accounting and reporting practices. It is absolutely critical for organizations to honour these restrictions and distinguish them in their financial statements so that readers understand what resources an organization has to spend at its discretion and what resources are designated for specific purposes. This is the genesis of fund accounting.

Restrictions on contributions can only be imposed by a contributor from outside the organization. A restriction may be implicit in the fundraising appeal by the organization or contributors may have imposed restrictions of their own making. For example, if the organization raised funds that it said would be used for a specific purpose such as health research, these funds would then have an implied restriction. (It should be noted that a board of directors may impose internal restrictions on contributions but these are generally referred to as appropriations and are treated differently from externally restricted contributions.)

Fund accounting is the breaking up of an organization's financial statements on the basis of the purposes of various funds. Funds are usually based on the requirements of the financial statement users. For example, separate funds could be established for general operations, research, capital assets and endowments. Elements of a fund can include assets, liabilities, net assets, revenues and expenses.

A key decision for any nonprofit is determining its accounting policy for contribution revenue. This policy not only determines the format of the financial statements but it also determines the bottom line, *i.e.*, it is possible that the number representing revenues less expenses (the annual surplus or deficit) will be different depending upon the policy selected. Two methods are permitted — the deferral method and the restricted fund method.

The two methods treat unrestricted contributions in the same manner in that they should be accounted for as revenue in the year received. The difference between them stems from the treatment of income from restricted funds and endowments. Under the deferral method, restricted contributions that cannot be expended in the year in which they are received (because of the nature of the restriction) must be deferred and accounted for as revenue in the year in which the related expenses are incurred. The balance of deferred contributions represents the accumulation of restricted resources subject to restrictions that have yet to be complied with.

Contributions to an endowment are accounted for as direct increases in net assets, *i.e.*, not revenue since these contributions are considered to be permanent and thus will never be available to meet expenses associated with the organization's service delivery activities (though of course the income from endowment funds would be available for this purpose depending how the donor of the endowment specifies its use).

Under the restricted fund method, contributions are accounted for as revenue in the year received regardless of whether the related expenses were incurred. The balance of the restricted funds represents the accumulation of resources subject to restrictions that have yet to be complied with. In the same vein, endowment contributions are accounted for as revenue of the endowment fund in the year received. In cases where a restricted contribution is received but there is no corresponding restricted fund, these contributions should be accounted for in the general fund using the deferral method.

The differences in the methods can be illustrated as follows:

Operating Statement	Deferral Method	Restricted Fund Method
Unrestricted Contributions	$30,000	$30,000
Endowment Contributions	$0	$20,000
Restricted Contributions	$0	$10,000
Total Revenues	**$30,000**	**$60,000**
Expenses	$25,000	$25,000
Revenues less expenses	**$5,000**	**$35,000**
Balance Sheet		
Assets	**$35,000**	**$35,000**

Liabilities	**$10,000**	**$0**
Unrestricted Fund	$5,000	$5,000
Restricted Fund	$0	$10,000
Endowment Fund	$20,000	$20,000
Total Net Assets	**$25,000**	**$35,000**
Total Liabilities & Net Assets	**$35,000**	**$35,000**

The decision of which method to choose is entirely organization-dependent and there are pros and cons for both. An organization with limited accounting resources might find the restricted fund method easier since it does not entail keeping track of deferred contributions. On the other hand, some may consider financial statements prepared using the deferral method easier to understand since there is only one column of numbers for each fiscal year, and the revenue number is more representative of what was available to be spent in that year.

Another unique aspect of nonprofit accounting occurs when an organization receives a contribution of materials and/or services. Currently, a choice exists as to whether or not these will be accounted for but, if they are, a fair value must be estimated using market or appraisal values and the goods or services must be used in the normal course of the organization's operations. Except in the case of donations of capital assets, accounting for donated materials and services does not affect an organization's bottom line since their value counted as both a contribution and an expense. For example, a donation of legal fees might be accounted for as a corporate donation and correspondingly as an administrative expense. Some volunteer staffed organizations find it too cumbersome to track this information reliably. Others with a tracking system use the value of donation receipts to record a contribution as revenue and corresponding expense. However, the Canada Revenue Agency does not allow receipts to be issued for services and thus any tracking system must be for internal or public relations purposes only. For example, the value of volunteer services is normally not calculated due to the difficulty in determining what it should be. Nevertheless, some organizations like to make this estimation for certain special reports in which they seek to impress external stakeholders with the value of volunteer contributions. For more on how to calculate the approximate value of volunteer work, see Quarter, Mook & Richmond (2003).

Often organizations are conservative when it comes to accounting for contributions and in many instances account for them only on a cash basis, *i.e.*, when a cheque or cash is received. However, it *is* possible to recognize pledges as contribution revenue if: (1) the amount to be received can be reasonably estimated; and (2) the ultimate collection is reasonably assured. Bequest revenue most often cannot meet these two criteria since wills must be probated and can be subject to legal challenges.

Financial Statement Analysis

As previously noted, the readers of a nonprofit's financial statements are a diverse group, but all are interested in understanding the general financial health of the organization. The following elements of financial statement analysis are generally considered useful for both external stakeholders and the organization's board members and CEO. Although the elements discussed here are generic to most nonprofits, several other types of analysis are possible that are unique only to certain subsectors such as the performing arts, health or membership associations.

Comparative Financial Statements

Significant understandings can come from comparing two years of financial information with one another, on both the balance sheet and statement of operations. While general purpose financial statements generally only have the preceding year's information as a comparison, the interim financial statements circulated to management and the board should at least compare actual year-to-date results with the current budget as well as the actual for the previous year (covering the same time period). The board should expect reasonable explanations of any significant differences.

The Bottom Line

Interpreting the bottom line (annual surplus or deficit) from operations is tricky in a nonprofit. Nonprofits are not supposed to earn profits by their very nature so incurring more than an inconsequential surplus is generally frowned upon by contributors who want their contributions used, not sitting in a bank. On the other hand, deficits are also generally frowned upon as a sign of poor financial management. So what is the right bottom line? The answer is that it depends on the organization's situation, and financial statements do not usually provide the kind of information needed to properly assess this. There are valid reasons why an organization may be accumulating annual surpluses, for example, to establish a permanent financial reserve to assist with cash flow during the year or to "save up" for a major capital expenditure in the future. It may also be the case that a substantial unexpected unrestricted contribution was received during the year that could not be prudently expended in the same year. And, as we saw earlier in this chapter, the choice of accounting policies will also affect the bottom line.

Expense or Cost Ratios

These days more focus is being placed on administration and fundraising costs by donors and funders. It is suggested by some that donors ask several questions before giving (see Ministry of the Attorney General (2004b)). Two such questions are "How much of my donation goes directly to helping others?" and "How much goes for administration and fundraising costs?" There are several ways to calculate this though no universal agreement exists as to which is the best one. The following are four examples.

Ratio of Program Expenses to Total Expenses. Dividing the program expenses by total expenses results in a percentage that indicates how much of every dollar spent is spent on programs. If an organization has more than one program area, these obviously need to be accumulated for purposes of this calculation.

Ratio of Administration Expenses to Total Expenses. Dividing the total administrative expenses by total expenses results in a percentage that indicates how much of every dollar spent by an organization is spent on administrative activities.

Ratio of Fundraising Expenses to Total Expenses. Dividing fundraising expenses by total expenses results in a percentage that indicates how much of every dollar spent is spent to raise money.

Ratio of Contribution Revenues to Fundraising Expenses. Dividing the total fundraising expenses by the total of all contributions or donated revenue indicates how much it costs to raise a dollar. This same formula can be applied to each type of fundraising revenue. For example, if special event revenue and expenses are reported separately then you can calculate how much it costs to raise a dollar using special events.

A word of caution — while these cost ratios may be important to know, they each have their limitations and shortcomings. First, there are many factors that influence these ratios that do not necessarily reflect the organization's efficiency in using its resources, its size, its age, or the degree of involvement of volunteers in its operation. For example, a relatively new organization trying to get established may have higher fundraising and administration costs than a more established one due to the degree of investment required to set up its programs and establish its base of donors.

Second, financial measurement is imprecise. There are no standards for what constitutes a program versus an administration versus a fundraising cost. The categorization of these costs is particularly troublesome in the case where some costs are shared. For example, how should the cost of rent incurred to operate the programs and house the administrative and fundraising functions be accounted for? Should this cost be allocated among these functions? If so, how? By determining the relative square footage occupied by these functions? By the relative number of staff assigned to these functions? What if some of the staff work in several functions? How should their costs be allocated?[8]

Third, these measures may act as indicators of efficiency but this is not the same as effectiveness. An organization may have comparatively high costs of administration and higher-than-average fundraising expenses but be much more effective than others in actually achieving the results it was created to achieve.

Finally there is the question of how efficient is efficient? As we saw in the fraudulent action case cited in the "Internal Control" section, administration costs were in a sense too efficient in that they were too low, which led to poor control systems and thus made it easy for embezzlement to occur. The same might be said of fundraising

---

[8]   A recent U.S. study revealed that tracking personnel time was a low priority for most organizations due to the low perceived benefit of the practice. When done at all, most of the organizations surveyed had one or two staff members make a judgment once a year about how everyone spent their time. The study questioned the value of these inaccurate cost ratios.

costs. Allocating too few resources to fundraising may be detrimental to an organization in the long term.

How is all this attention on cost ratios affecting nonprofits? A study done by Peter Frumkin and Mark T. Kim at the Hauser Centre for Nonprofit Organizations at The Kennedy School of Government suggests that, while donors seem to be more interested in ratios, so far this bottom line management approach does not appear to be helping nonprofits attract more contributions (see Frumkin & Kim (2000)). The nature of the organization's mission and the personal commitment that donors have to it still matter more.

In conclusion, while these ratios and other financial measures provide useful tools for examining a nonprofit's operations, it is important to understand their weaknesses and use them only in combination with other non-financial measures that address an organization's effectiveness in achieving its mission, and general information about the organization's plans for the future.

REFERENCES

Committee of Sponsoring Organizations of the Treadway Commission (COSO) (1992), *Internal Control — Integrated Framework* (Jersey City: American Institute of Certified Public Accountants, 1992).

Deloitte & Touche LLP, "Not-for-profit Audit Committees". Available online at: <www.deloitte.com/dtt/article/0,1002,sid%253D3667%2526 cid%253D5975,00.html>.

Erickson, T. (2005), "How We Survived an Embezzlement" (2005), 12:2 *The Nonprofit Quarterly.*

Frumkin, P., & M.T. Kim (2000), "Strategic Positioning and the Financing of Nonprofit Organizations: Is Efficiency Rewarded in the Contributions Marketplace? Working Paper No. 2" (Cambridge, MA: Hauser Center for Nonprofit Organizations and John F. Kennedy School of Government, Harvard University, October 2000).

Keating, K., & P. Frumkin (2003), "Reengineering Nonprofit Financial Accountability: Toward a More Reliable Foundation for Regulation" (2003), 6:1 *Public Administration Review* 3-15.

Ministry of the Attorney General (2004a), "Duties, Responsibilities and Powers of Directors and Trustees of Charities", Charities Bulletin #3 (Toronto: Information from the Public Guardian and Trustee's

Charitable Property Program, 2004). Available online at: <www.attorney general.jus.gov.on.ca/english/family/pgt/charbullet/bullet3.asp>.

Ministry of the Attorney General (2004b), *Charitable Donations — Get the Facts Before You Give* (Toronto: Government of Ontario, 2004). Available online at: <www.attorneygeneral.jus.gov.on.ca/english/family/pgt/charitabledonations.asp>.

Quarter, J., L. Mook & B.J. Richmond (2003), *What Counts: Social Accounting for NonProfits and Cooperatives* (Toronto: Ontario Institute for Studies in Education, University of Toronto, Prentice Hall, 2003).

ADDITIONAL RESOURCES

This chapter has served as an introduction to the budgeting, controlling and reporting aspects of financial management. Additional resources are available for those who wish to pursue more in-depth studies. Among those the interested reader might consult are the following:

American Institute of Certified Public Accountants, *The AICPA Audit Committee Toolkit: Not-for-Profit Organizations* (New York: AICPA, 2005).

Anthony, R.N., & D.W. Young, *Management Control in Nonprofit Organizations*, 7th ed. (Boston: McGraw-Hill/Irwin, 2003).

Board Development Program of Alberta Community Development, *Financial Responsibilities of Not-for-Profit Boards: A Self-Guided Workbook*, The Muttart Foundation; available from the Resource Centre for Voluntary Organizations, Grant MacEwan College, Edmonton 2000, homepage at: <http://www.rcvo.org/index.html>.

Danyluk, D., *Not-for-profit Financial Reporting Guide* (Toronto: The Canadian Institute of Chartered Accountants, 1998).

Dropkin, M., & B. LaTouche, *The Budget Building Book for Nonprofits: A Step by Step Guide for Managers and Boards.* (San Francisco: Jossey-Bass, 1998).

Dropkin, M., & A. Hayden, *The Cash Flow Management Book for Nonprofits: A Step-by-Step Guide for Managers, Consultants, and Boards* (San Francisco: Jossey-Bass, 2001).

Finkler, S.A., *Financial Management for Public, Health, and Not-for-Profit Organizations*, 2nd ed. (Upper Saddle River, NJ: Pearson Education Inc., 2005).

Persaud, S., & A. Mason, *Finance and Audit Committees Can Play a Key Role Both in Detecting Fraud and in Preventing It*, Canadian Fundraiser, October 2003.

Ruppel, W., *Not-for-Profit Accounting Made Easy* (New York: John Wiley & Sons, 2002).

The Canadian Institute of Chartered Accountants, *CICA Handbook* (Toronto: CICA).

Voluntary Sector Initiative, *Resources for Accountability and Financial Management in the Voluntary Sector*, A Project of the Capacity Joint Table funded by the Government of Canada. Available online at: <www.vsi-isbc.ca>.

Chapter 11

MANAGING THE HUMAN DIMENSION IN NONPROFIT ORGANIZATIONS: PAID STAFF AND VOLUNTEERS

Agnes Meinhard
Ryerson University

INTRODUCTION

An organization is a complex social system comprising various groups of individuals working together towards a common purpose. A fundamental challenge for management is to co-ordinate the actions of these individuals in order to ensure the achievement of the organization's goals. At a minimum, this requires knowledge of the organization's technologies and specific task requisites in order to match the people best suited for the jobs. At a higher level, this entails understanding the diversity of individuals in the organization with respect to their personalities, cultural backgrounds, values, attitudes, emotions, abilities, motivations and ambitions; and being able to leverage this knowledge to ensure the smooth functioning of the organization. Whether or not an organization has a formal Human Resource (HR) department or manager, a foundation of good human resource practices is essential to the long-term success of an organization.

Although there is a common basis for good human resource practices that pertains to all organizations, nonprofit organizations differ with respect to several characteristics: governance structure, incentive structure and reliance on volunteers. These unique features warrant special consideration. Therefore, this chapter focuses on both identifying the basic concepts and discussing the unique aspects of managing the human dimension in nonprofit organizations. The chapter begins with a snapshot of volunteer and paid participation in the nonprofit sector in Canada. This is followed by a discussion of key concepts related to managing people in organizations, and the particular challenges faced by nonprofit organizations. Since volunteers are an integral part of most nonprofit organizations, the chapter's third section focuses on the special case of recruiting and managing volunteers. The chapter ends with some concluding observations on how nonprofit organizations can apply the insights raised in the chapter to benefit their operations, even in low-budget conditions.

LABOUR AND VOLUNTEER PARTICIPATION IN THE NONPROFIT SECTOR

The importance of the nonprofit and charitable sector in providing social, cultural, and recreational benefits to Canadians has long been valued, however the size of its contribution to Canada's economy and job market is only now being recognized. Nine per cent of Canada's employers are nonprofit organizations, employing 20 per cent of the nation's labour force (McMullen & Schellenberg (2002, at p. 20-21)). This translates into more than two million jobs (NSNVO (2005)). Mostly on the strength of the wages, salaries and supplementary income paid out by nonprofit organizations, the sector accounts for 6.8 per cent of the nation's GDP. This compares favourably to the contributions to GDP by the agriculture (1.5 per cent), mining, oil and gas (4.0 per cent), retail (5.0 per cent) or food and accommodation (2.3 per cent) sectors. Even without considering the contribution of hospitals and post-secondary institutions, which are the major employers of the nonprofit sector, the rest of the nonprofit sector still accounts for 3.9 per cent of the GDP (Statistics Canada (2004, Figure 2, at p. 6)).

Almost three-quarters of the jobs in the sector are concentrated in the largest 2 per cent of organizations; half of them are to be found in hospitals and universities (NSNVO, 2005). The majority of nonprofit organizations (63 per cent) are small and operate with an annual budget of less than $100,000. Only 30 per cent of these small organizations have paid staff and they generally number fewer than two full-time employees. More than two-thirds of the employees in the nonprofit sector are women, compared with less than half in the for-profit sector. The majority of managers in the sector are women as well, ranging from 50 per cent in hospitals and universities to 66 per cent in other nonprofits. This compares favourably with the for-profit sector, where only 36 per cent of managers are women (McMullen & Schellenberg (2002, at p. 40)). There are no statistics available with respect to the ethnic composition of the nonprofit workplace.

Most nonprofit organizations (54 per cent) rely exclusively on volunteers to carry out their missions (NSNVO (2005)). Six and one half million Canadians volunteer in nonprofit organizations (Hall *et al.* (2001)), but because many volunteer at several organizations, "nonprofit and voluntary organizations report a combined volunteer complement of over 19 million" (NSNVO (2005, at p. 32)). This translates into somewhere between 1.1 and two billion hours[1] of volunteer labour representing about 7.5 full-time jobs per voluntary organization.

HUMAN RESOURCE MANAGEMENT IN CANADIAN NONPROFIT ORGANIZATIONS

In the broadest sense of the term, human resource management (HRM) refers to all management and leadership practices involving the co-ordination of paid and/or unpaid members of a social, political, cultural or economic enterprise, to work towards achieving organizational goals. In the narrowest sense of the term, it refers to a specialized field of organizational management dealing with the administrative functions associated with staffing an organization: hiring, training, compensation and firing. However, even in its narrowest sense it is far more complex, involving the creation of an organizational infrastructure that enables employees and volunteers to accomplish their tasks and reach their goals. This entails clearly defining the jobs, resources and skills needed to fulfil the organization's mission, ensuring a safe and positive work environment where people are treated fairly, providing mechanisms for managing conflict, maintaining open lines of communication, giving timely feedback and rewarding good work. It also involves finding people with the appropriate knowledge and abilities to accomplish required tasks, helping them navigate organizational change through training and development, and engaging in strategic human resource planning.

---

[1] The estimates differ in the NSGVP and the NSNVO.

The vast majority of nonprofit organizations do not have specialized HR units, nor even designated HR officers. It is not surprising then, that human resource management was earmarked by the Voluntary Sector Initiative (VSI) as an area that needs to be developed. With VSI funding, a thorough and informative Web site was created providing detailed descriptions of the various HR functions. The site, called *Human Resources in the Voluntary Sector*, also has explicit "how to" instructions for organizations that are interested in developing and/or improving HR practices: <http://www.hrvs-rhsbc.ca/>.

A Brief History of Human Resource Management

Torrington and Hall (1987) describe six distinct stages in the evolution of human resource management as a field of practice. Although these stages unfolded in a chronological sequence, the practices described in each of the stages build on, rather than replace, one another.

Stage 1 can be traced back to the abuses of the Industrial Revolution in Britain. With the passing of workers' rights legislation in the mid-nineteenth century, social-minded factory owners hired "welfare officers" not only to help their organizations comply with the new legislation, but also to attend to the social needs of their employees. Later, under enlightened owners, the functions of these welfare officers were expanded to include managing unemployment benefits and sick leave, and sometimes even providing subsidized housing (Stage 2). Further expansion of human resource functions occurred in the early twentieth century as two competing schools of thought influenced the direction of human resource management. On the one hand there were the rationalist economic efficiency models best exemplified by Frederick Taylor's (1911) *Principles of Scientific Management*, which espoused the division of labour and basically viewed workers as extensions of machines. On the other hand, the Human Relations School (Mayo (1945)) emphasized the importance of extending responsibility and trust to the workers through job enrichment and improved relations both among the workers, and between workers and management. In Stage 3 of the development of HR, welfare officers or personnel managers were concerned with improving conditions in the workplace by boosting workers' morale and providing them with a social network. This stage also marked the earliest use of staffing, placement and training strategies.

In these three early stages, even though they were paid agents of the factory owners, welfare officers saw their role as representing the interests of the workers in their quest for benefits and advocating for ever more enlightened management practices. Stage 4 represented a change in orientation as unionization became more prevalent after the First World War and the HR officer became management's representative in contract negotiations. Stage 5 saw a further integration of HR into the realm of management as staffing and training were seen by management to afford the organization with a competitive advantage. Finally, in Stage 6, employees are seen as an important resource, and the HR function has been elevated to a senior management position, where strategic human resource planning forecasts the long-term staffing, skills and training needs of organizations in a rapidly changing environment. The evolution of human resource management to a strategic function was necessitated by the volatility of the business environment, the complexity and size of modern organizations, and the demand for interesting and challenging work and life-work balance by more highly educated employees (Beer, *et al.* (1984)).

Human Resource Management as Practised in Canadian Nonprofit Organizations

As already stated, few Canadian nonprofit organizations have formal HR departments or specially designated HR managers. However, despite the lack of formal HRM mechanisms, for the most part, nonprofit employers furnish their workers with good working conditions and opportunities for full participation. As a series of reports published by the Canadian Policy Research Network (CPRN) on nonprofit employers indicates, the smaller and less hierarchical workplaces in the nonprofit sector are more likely to create an atmosphere of mutual trust and respect through shared responsibility and decision-making practices. They are also more likely to provide personal and family support systems (McMullen & Brisbois (2003)), as well as offer their employees training opportunities, most of which occur outside the organization (McMullen & Schellenberg (2003, Table 11, at p. 28)). These positive working conditions are important because nonprofit organizations are often at a disadvantage in terms of their ability to offer salaries that are competitive with the for-profit and public sectors. In fact, employee satisfaction in the nonprofit sector is similar to that in the for-profit sector, despite significant wage differentials (McMullen & Schellenberg (2003)).

A study comparing human resource management as practised in Canadian and British nonprofit organizations in the late 1980s revealed that Canadian organizations tended to be at Stages 2 and 3 of Torrington and Hall's classification, whereas British organizations tended to be at the more advanced Stages 5 and 6 (Haiven (1998)). Canadian nonprofit organizations tend not to align their human resource management practices with their organizational strategy (Akingbola (2005)). This difference in HR practice may reflect the general lack of strategic planning in Canadian nonprofit organizations (Meinhard & Foster (2003)). It may also reflect a reluctance to become too business-like in their operations (Meinhard & Foster (2003)). Human resource practices in Canadian nonprofit organizations appear to focus on mediating solutions to problems in the workplace and ensuring that workers' needs are met, rather than on forecasting and long-term planning (Haiven (1998)). This may well be regrettable because whether or not a nonprofit organization has a formal human resource management position, planning its human resource needs has distinct benefits.

The Benefits of Human Resource Planning

Nonprofit organizations in Canada, as elsewhere, are working in an environment characterized by continuous change, uncertain and scarce financial resources, and increasing demands for services as the government continues to withdraw from directly providing a social safety net. In order to survive and fulfil their missions in such an environment, nonprofits cannot afford to waste any of their resources, especially human resources. They therefore have to anticipate organizational needs, avoiding both shortages and surpluses of human resources. They can control labour costs by determining the optimal complement of volunteers and staff. By planning ahead, they can co-ordinate recruitment campaigns to achieve cost efficiencies when hiring new workers or bringing in new volunteers. Well-developed HR planning helps to improve performance, increase productivity and reduce employee and volunteer dissatisfaction and turnover (Macaleer & Jones (2003)).

On the other hand, inadequate human resource planning can be both financially and organizationally costly. Without proper planning, organizations may be unable to fill their specific human resource needs, thus weakening their performance capabilities. For example, unfilled positions can be costly both from a productivity perspective

— work not done, and from a human perspective — needed services are not provided. In such cases, additional stress is placed on remaining staff as they work extra hours to compensate for vacant positions. In large organizations, poor planning and/or lack of communication between departments about their anticipated needs can result in one department laying off individuals while another department in the same organization is acquiring individuals with the same or similar competencies. The impact on morale is unmeasurable, but its disruptive effect on the social fabric of the organization is palpable. Given the benefits of forecasting human resources needs, and the potential costs to the organization of inadequate planning, it would seem negligent not to engage in strategic human resource management. Yet, for a variety reasons, most nonprofit organizations do not plan ahead.

The Challenge of Human Resource Management for Nonprofit Organizations

Nonprofit managers face several challenges in creating an infrastructure that provides optimal conditions for maximizing their human resource potential: (1) a dearth of relevant guidelines for managing human resources; (2) a lack of HR management training; (3) insufficient financial resources; (4) employment uncertainty under project funding; and (5) tension between volunteers and paid staff.

Dearth of Relevant Guidelines

Although much has been written about volunteer recruitment and retention, human resource management in the nonprofit sector has not been a focus of study among scholars researching the nonprofit sector. Thus there are few, if any, guidelines written specifically for nonprofit organizations. This is not surprising as more than half of all nonprofit organizations rely exclusively on volunteer labour. Only 20 per cent of the total number of organizations in the sector hire more than four paid employees (NSNVO (2005)). Research and textbooks on human resource management and practices focus on the for-profit sector and usually on large, corporate and bureaucratic organizations. This does not reflect the reality of the smaller nonprofits with limited funds and very few employees. Nevertheless, HR management is relevant to all organizations, irrespective of organizational size and whether organizational goals are pursued by paid employees or volunteers.

Lack of HR Management Training

Only large nonprofit organizations can afford to hire a manager of human resources and only the largest have human resources departments. In the remainder of the organizations, HR functions are left to the executive director and/or a committee of the organization's Board of Directors. In either case, the day-to-day HR issues that arise are the concern of the executive director, who is rarely trained in HR management (Brudney (1999)). Generally, the executive director in a nonprofit organization is promoted or hired to the top position because of her knowledge and skills in the particular service provided by her organization. Lacking HR training, many of the necessary mechanisms for such matters as harassment control and conflict management, as well as all the other needs mentioned above, are not in place, so these issues often remain unrecognized and neglected. This in turn, can lead to strained relations in the workplace. Most executive directors (EDs) are already over-extended in their workload, trying to guide their organizations through changing conditions and dealing with higher priority problems; understandably they are loath to add the tasks of HR management to their already heavy loads.

Insufficient Financial Resources

Most nonprofit organizations operate with very tight budgets, influencing not only their employee component, but also their financial incentive structures. Salaries in the nonprofit sector are generally lower than in the for-profit sector. With the exception of hospitals and universities, managers in the nonprofit sector earn approximately 18 per cent less than those in the for-profit sector and professionals earn 14 per cent less, despite the fact that 28 per cent of nonprofit employees have university degrees as opposed to 15 per cent in the for-profit sector. Wages are equivalent at the clerical level (McMullen & Schellenberg (2003)). For-profit organizations can offer their employees monetary incentives and other tangible rewards to motivate their employees to reach their production, market and profit goals. In nonprofit organizations, there is little room for significant financial rewards; they therefore rely on the goodwill and dedication to the cause of both their paid workers and volunteers. As one staff member in an organization dedicated to helping women said, "I was hired to work half-time, but there is no way the work can get done on a half-time position, so I basically volunteer the rest of the hours I need to complete the work" (Meinhard *et al.* (2004)). In nonprofit organizations the problem is not only how to motivate employees and volunteers, but also how to prevent burn-out.

Employment Uncertainty under Project Funding

By and large, governments are increasingly funding individual projects rather than providing stable, long-term operational grants (Pal (1997)). Because nonprofit organizations are so heavily reliant on government funding, the uncertainty inherent in these new funding practices makes it more difficult for them to plan their human resource needs, and attract skilled people (Akingbola (2005)). This is as true for the larger organizations with a formal HR department as it is for the small organizations. In the smaller organizations, the situation is exacerbated as the juggling of hiring and firing decisions is placed on the shoulders of an already over-extended executive director. In a climate of increasing accountability concerns, governments and other funders are demanding more frequent and more detailed reports. This is also placing a strain on nonprofit organizations, as employee time spent on preparing reports is at the expense of time spent on mission activities. This leads to frustration, dissatisfaction and a drop in productivity.

Tension between Volunteers and Paid Staff

Tensions between volunteers and paid staff can occur at two levels. First, there may be tension among employees and volunteers at the front lines. Because of insufficient financial resources, nonprofit organizations are often forced to supplement their paid staff with volunteer labour. In long-term situations, this may lead to resentment, especially when volunteers are doing work similar or identical to that done by paid staff. On the other hand, inappropriate expectations of volunteers by paid employees may cause frustration and lead to conflict. A second source of tension and conflict lies in the governance structure of nonprofit organizations, which is characterized by a shared, but legally unequal, leadership between the chairperson of the volunteer board and the paid professional executive director. As O'Connell (1985, at p. 52) points out, "The greatest source of friction and breakdown in voluntary organizations of all types, sizes, ages and relative degrees of sophistication and excellence relates to misunderstandings and differing perceptions between the voluntary board president and staff directors." This creates role ambiguity and role conflict. Role ambiguity occurs when boundaries between board and staff are blurred and people are uncertain about their job duties, performance expectations, level of authority and other job conditions. Often volunteer board members misinterpret their responsibilities and try to micro-manage the organization's paid employees. This frequently occurs when an organization grows and begins to hire staff. In small volunteer-run organizations there is often little difference between those who carry on the work of the organization, and those who also sit on the board. The tasks of governance, management and operations are undifferentiated as everyone chips in to fulfil the organization's mission and goals. As an organization grows and recruits professional staff, management is delegated to the executive director, who is directly accountable to the board. However, it is often hard for board members to stand back, and thus they continue to "work in the trenches", functioning as volunteers doing staff work or providing expertise to staff as they do their work. This mixing of roles can often lead to conflict. On the other hand, lack of involvement in the organization by board members may cause paid employees to feel directionless.

Many of these challenges are being addressed. The dearth of human resource guidelines specifically tailored for the nonprofit sector is being rectified through easily accessible HR information repositories such as the HRSV. In addition, during the past decade several Canadian universities and colleges have begun to offer programs in nonprofit management studies to address the lack of management skills among leaders in the nonprofit sector. With respect to insufficient financial resources and reliance on government funding, recent statistics and surveys indicate that nonprofit organizations are increasingly seeking partnerships with corporations (Meinhard & Foster (2003)) and diversifying resources in order to decrease their dependence on government (Foster & Meinhard (2005)). The most recently available statistics indicate that between 1996 and 2003, the corporate sector's share of support for the voluntary sector has increased from 1 per cent to 3 per cent of the total nonprofit revenue. The nonprofit sector's earned income, from dues, sales, rentals and other commercial activities now accounts for 35 per cent of the proportion of income to the sector, up from 30 per cent, while the government's share is down to 49 per cent from 56 per cent (Standing Committee on Finance (1996); NSNVO (2005)). This trend in revenue diversification has implications for greater independence for at least some nonprofits and their ability to plan for their human resource needs. Finally, as suggested in the following section, there are ways to mitigate the tensions created by the leadership duality that is characteristic of nonprofit organizations.

The Role of the Board in Human Resource Management

Canadian law stipulates that nonprofit Boards are fully responsible for the affairs of the organization and the conduct of all its members. They have ultimate jurisdiction over staff. Normally the board delegates this responsibility to a chief executive officer if there is one, however, if the organization is too small to have a staff, the board can fulfil the HR functions itself usually through an HR committee with, if possible, an HR expert to sit on it.

In any case, well-functioning nonprofit Boards set the tone for their entire organization. First, they must ensure that the organization is in compliance with the various provincial and federal laws governing employment relationships such as employment standards, collective agreements and labour standards, occupational health and safety, pension benefits, pay equity, employment equity, and human rights. Second, the board is responsible for ensuring that the quality of work life for those in the organization is high. This means fair compensation and benefits, good working hours, and policies that ensure equitable treatment of staff and volunteers. These are the cornerstones of a good workplace. Furthermore, the board should ensure that the organization has in place systems that lead to performance evaluation of staff and volunteers and enable them to receive feedback about organizational effectiveness and staff morale. It is also the board's job to ensure that the organization's work values and ethics are conveyed to all their members, both paid staff and volunteers. This is critical in the case of organizations that serve vulnerable clients such as people with disabilities, at-risk children and youth, and abused women and children, to name but a few.

Much of the role ambiguity found in nonprofit organizations stems from the lack of clearly defined role descriptions for members of the board and staff. When the roles of board members and staff are clearly delineated, and feedback mechanisms are in place, there is less room for role ambiguity. And when the relationship between the board and the executive director is more realistically defined as a partnership, rather than a hierarchy of power, role conflict may be averted. A partnership model of governance recognizes that EDs are the *de facto* leaders, given that they have information and expertise about how their organizations operate on a day-to-day basis. The organization is more central their lives than it is in the lives of the board members they serve, many of whom hold other jobs and may not have been members for a long time (Herman & Heimovics (1991)). Therefore, realistically, it is EDs who assure that the governance function is properly organized and maintained (Herman & Heimovics (1991); Drucker (1990)). Executive directors are expected not to usurp the board's role, but to work with it, not only on decision-making and policy formulation, but also in providing criteria for the evaluation of programs and individual performance. The challenge is to find the middle ground between a rubber-stamp board that abdicates its responsibilities to the ED, and an overbearing, micro-managing board that creates tension among the staff. Regular board development sessions, and board orientation programs for new board members can go a long way to enhance board and staff members' understanding of their roles in the organization. (See Chapter 3 for more on boards.)

THE SPECIAL CASE OF VOLUNTEERS

As the statistics at the beginning of this chapter indicate, volunteers are the backbone of the nonprofit sector. No estimates of their financial worth can truly gauge the value of their contribution to Canadian society. They invigorate our communities, preserve our parks and waterways, champion our arts and cultural institutions and support recreational facilities and amateur sports. They also help immigrants settle in their new communities and enrich the lives of our less fortunate citizens, thus strengthening Canada's social capital.

The noun "volunteer" is commonly understood to refer to someone who engages in an activity of his/her own free will for the benefit of others, without receiving monetary remuneration. There is some controversy in the literature with respect to the parameters of the term (Wilson (2000)), as the word is often used in ways that extend beyond this basic meaning. A prime example of this would be high school students who "volunteer" in order to fulfil curriculum requirements, or experts who "volunteer" their time to give free advice but accept symbolic monetary honoraria. Cnaan and associates (1996) identified four dimensions that underlie the concept of volunteering: (a) free choice (is there any coercion?); (b) remuneration (is any reward of monetary value received in exchange for an activity?); (c) context (does the activity take place in a formal or informal setting?); and (d) beneficiaries (who benefits from the activity?).

In this chapter, the term "volunteer" is used in a broad sense to include all those who freely engage in an activity within a nonprofit organizational context to benefit others in some way, without receiving monetary compensation. Volunteers serve their chosen organizations in many ways: providing direct service to clients, helping with administrative activities, contributing expertise, and serving as a director on an organization's board.

Formal volunteering most likely originated in religious institutions. It was an active expression of the religious obligation of performing charitable deeds — a cornerstone of all religions (de Schweinitz (1943)). As institutions run by religious orders were set up to help care for the physical needs of the sick, the orphaned and the handicapped, lay people began to contribute time as well as alms to the poor (de Schweinitz (1943); Feingold (1987); Martin (1985)). Because of the nature of the work, most of these early volunteers were women. Voluntary association was one of the few socially sanctioned extra-domestic activities available to women. Thus, for many, volunteerism played a liberating role in their lives, giving them their only experience in the public realm (McCarthy (1990)). Eventually, women began forming their own associations and by the mid-1800s, they were administering organizations in the fields of philanthropy, arts and sciences, and social reform (Kaminer (1984)), that were both efficient and effective in carrying out their missions (Scott (1990)). These organizations laid the foundations of the modern voluntary sector (Lewis (1994); Odendahl (1994)) and strongly influenced the creation of the social welfare state (O'Neill (1994)). By the beginning of the twentieth century, helping the poor and the handicapped became more secularized and professionalized as social workers and other professionally trained workers gradually replaced volunteers. Congregational voluntary action declined as the state formed a partnership with nonprofit organizations to provide essential social and cultural services (Cnaan *et al.* (1993)). With generous funding, some nonprofit organizations were able to hire professionals; in these organizations, volunteers became adjuncts. However, the bulk of organizations now, as then, still rely on volunteers.

There are concerns, however, about the sustainability of this valuable resource. After a steady increase in volunteering rates, from 15.2 per cent of the population in 1980 to 26.8 per cent in 1987

(Dreesen (2000)), and peaking at 31.4 per cent in 1997, in 2000 the rate slipped back down to 27 per cent (Hall *et al.* (2001)). This represents a decline of about one million volunteers in three years and comes at a time when nonprofit organizations are looking towards volunteers to help them maintain service levels in the face of government cutbacks and downloading (Foster & Meinhard (1996); Meinhard & Foster (1997)). Even more disturbing than the decrease in participation rates is the drop in average hours volunteered annually. In 1987 the yearly average was 193 hours, dropping to 170 hours in 2000. These hours are not distributed equally among the volunteers. One-quarter of volunteers contribute almost three-quarters of volunteer hours. This means that voluntary organizations in Canada rely on 7 per cent of the population to do the bulk of volunteering.

It is not surprising then, that many organizations claim they are facing "a crisis in volunteering". The earliest signs of this crisis coincided with the entry of women into the workforce in large numbers in the late 1970s and 1980s. At that time, both the number of women volunteers, and total volunteer hours, dropped substantially (Kaminer (1984); Masi (1981)). And although the number of volunteers has increased significantly since the 1980s, its growth has not been commensurate with the demand (Beerli, Diaz & Martin (2004)). Fears of a deepening crisis are mitigated in part by hopeful projections that the downward trend in volunteering will be reversed when the baby boomers start retiring *en masse* (Independent Sector (2003)). This hope may be based on a common misconception that there are legions of retirees volunteering. In truth, in 2000 the 65+ cohort accounts for the lowest volunteering rate: 18 per cent compared to 30 per cent among the 35-44 and 45-55 age cohorts. However, their low participation rate is tempered by the fact that they contribute the largest amount of time, averaging more than 269 hours per year (Hall *et al.* (2001)). According to the 1980 and 1987 statistics (Duchesne (1989)), this same cohort volunteered in greater numbers when they were younger, so their volunteering rates have decreased as they aged. It is therefore not a foregone conclusion that baby boomers will volunteer in greater numbers when they retire, than current retirees. As a matter of fact, baby boomers are not volunteering at the rates at which current retirees volunteered when they were younger. Ambitious campaigns are being planned in the U.S. to attract this cohort (Mareck (2004)).

Who Volunteers and Why?

Two questions have long intrigued researchers: who volunteers, and why do they volunteer? There is a broad consensus in research findings from many countries that the most important predictors of adult volunteering are related to three factors: whether their parents volunteered, whether they volunteered as children or young adults, and whether they are affiliated with a religious institution (Reed & Selbee (1999); Hodgkinson & Weitzman (1997)). Additionally, being a woman, having a university education and holding a job also increase the likelihood of volunteering. Age plays a role as well: adults between the ages of 35 and 44 make up the highest proportion of volunteers.[2] This may partly be a reflection of their participation in child-related activities in sports, education, music and arts.

So, why do people volunteer? There are many theories that attempt to answer this question. (For a thorough review of theories, see Wilson (2000)). An idea central to volunteering is altruism — giving without expectation of reward and indeed "helping others" is the most frequently cited reason given for voluntary affiliation (Duchesne (1989); Carter (1975); Beerli (2004)). This notwithstanding, more probing investigations suggest that altruism is only a minor motivator (Smith (1982); Gluck (1975); Clary *et al.* (1996)). Social catharsis (Langton (1982)), such as fulfilling a religious or social obligation, and collective identification with a "good cause" (Kramer (1981); Duchesne (1989)) are other reasons for volunteering. Some researchers suggest that volunteering, like other human behaviour, is best be explained as the pursuit of personal benefits and rewards. These may be either instrumental, such as acquiring skills and job experience, building one's resume or gaining social recognition (Olson (1965); Clark & Wilson (1961); Flynn & Webb (1975); Masi (1981); Taylor (1989)); or affective, such as gaining new friendships and establishing social networks (Knoke (1986); Flynn & Webb (1975); Gluck (1975); Beerli (2004)).

No doubt, all of these incentives play a role in determining volunteering behaviour, but at certain times, different factors will predominate. For example, when embarking on a new career, volunteering may help round out resumes or provide skills needed to gain a competitive edge in the job market. Volunteering also opens possibili-

---

[2] Calculated from aggregated statistics from 1980, 1987, 1997, 2000.

ties for new friendships after moving to a new city or neighbourhood. Parents volunteer to organize or help in their children's recreational and educational groups. Often people join groups when invited to by a friend. Finally, there are times, such as in disaster situations, when people are moved by altruism and join in an effort to help irrespective of personal benefit.

The latest theories and research have identified two separate clusters of reasons for volunteering. The first may be labelled as "traditional" and involves collectivist values, with a focus on institutional loyalty and the collective common good. This is closely related to affective incentives. The second may be labelled "modern" and is characterized by individualistic values expressed in self-organized and/or program-based volunteering, with a focus on instrumental incentives and personal gains (Hustinx & Lammertyn (2003)).

Figure 1: Traditional and Modern Volunteer Clusters

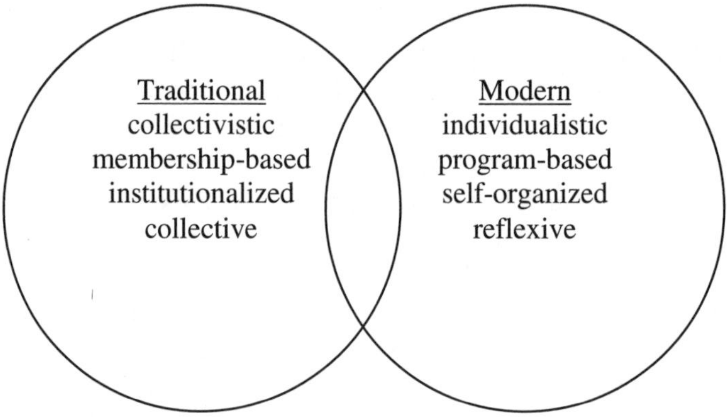

Traditional
collectivistic
membership-based
institutionalized
collective

Modern
individualistic
program-based
self-organized
reflexive

These clusters are not mutually exclusive, and an individual may hold both traditional and modern values, but research indicates that younger volunteers fall more clearly into the "modern" cluster. There has been a shift from group/community induced volunteering, characteristic of older volunteers, to more individual self-serving volunteering defining the younger generation. Whereas in the past, people volunteered because they were, or aspired to be, members of a group that served a cause that they believed in (for example, being a life member of Rotary Club or the National Council of Women), today's young volunteers seek to benefit both the organization and themselves. They fulfil that purpose by working on a specific project without a long-term commitment to the group. Or alternatively, because they tend to mistrust institutions, they may self-organize for a specific project and then disband. Whether this is a distinguishing characteristic of the current cohort of young volunteers that will define them even as they age, or whether this is a phenomenon related to life cycles, is yet to be seen.

Attracting Volunteers

Attracting volunteers has been a major challenge for the nonprofit sector. Volunteer recruitment manuals and Internet Web sites abound with commonsense advice aimed at appealing to both the affective and the instrumental needs of potential volunteers. For example, they urge recruiters to be personable, friendly and enthusiastic (Schindler-Rainman & Lippitt (1977); Routh (1972)), while suggesting that organizations set up peer programs and encourage members to bring along their friends (The Economist (2005)). On the instrumental side, these manuals recommend that organizations create interesting programs (Jackson (2005)), define tasks and jobs carefully, and offer training opportunities (Jackson (2005)). Finally they advise organizations to know their target population (Beerli, Diaz & Martin (2004)), advertise (Izon (2005)), and market themselves much like they would a product (Beerli *et al.* (2004)). This last strategy is now a recurring theme in the literature; there are even journals dedicated to the subject of the marketing for nonprofit organizations.[3]

Essentially, there are two different ways in which nonprofit organizations appeal to prospective volunteers. One is through focusing on membership orientation, where the emphasis is on satisfying the affective needs of the volunteer (*i.e.*, needs that relate to emotions and feelings); the other is through a task/program orientation, where the focus is on instrumental gains — for example, the practical benefits of volunteering for making contacts or learning skills (Meijs & Hoogstad (2001)).

---

[3]   *E.g.*, International Journal of Nonprofit and Voluntary Sector Marketing, Journal of Nonprofit & Public Sector Marketing.

Membership Orientation

In organizations characterized by membership orientation, the primary focus is on the needs and goals of the members. Initially this is what defines the organization's mission. New members join because they either identify with the organization's mission or have an affinity with the other members. Loyalty is cultivated through informal socialization rather than formal training. Membership organizations seek equilibrium between individual and organizational goals by emphasizing the pleasure of social activity while doing good. There is a progression of involvement from passive membership to active volunteering. Over time, membership in the organization becomes a part of the individual's identity. Service clubs (*e.g.*, Kiwanis, Rotary, Lions) and churches are examples of membership-oriented organizations (Meijs & Hoogstad (2001)).

Task/program Orientation

In these organizations the focus is on tasks and programs. Volunteers are sought, not to become members of the organization, but to complete specific tasks. Emphasis is on training to provide the volunteer with new skill sets. Task accomplishment takes priority over social activities. In the absence of demands for organizational loyalty, organizations find it easier to attract people to do specific, but time-limited jobs. The task/program management orientation seeks equilibrium between individual and organizational goals by encouraging individual gain, with an emphasis on training, work experience and merit reward, all for a good cause. Volunteers tend not to identify with the organization as much. Examples of these kinds of organizations would be food banks, hospitals or social service agencies (Meijs & Hoogstad (2001)).

Recruitment strategies for organizations with a membership orientation target people who share the organization's values, and emphasize the social and friendship benefits the organization can offer. Organizations with a program orientation are more likely to seek individuals with skills needed by their organization. They offer instrumental incentives such as learning new skills and the opportunity to enhance personal benefits (Meijs & Hoogstad (2001)).

In the past it was generally believed that "the cause" was the main source of attracting volunteers, and that those who identified with it would join the organization, form friendships, become loyal members and do whatever task was necessary to help the organization achieve its mission. The emphasis was on the shared effort towards furthering the mission. Indeed, this was a strategy that seemed to work quite well until recently. Most organizations are still geared to that kind of recruitment despite the fact that research shows a growing trend toward episodic volunteering for instrumental gains.

New Trends

As funding for social and cultural services continues to decrease (Hall & Banting (2000)), provincial and federal governments have encouraged increased volunteerism by supporting initiatives such as the 1998 Ontario Voluntary Forum and the 2001 International Year of the Volunteer. In some sectors however, there is strong opposition to any suggestions of replacing professional services with volunteer labour. High volunteer turnover rates, high costs of training, threat of job losses for paid employees, and the risks involved in replacing university-trained professionals by volunteers, are all potent arguments that have been put forward against the replacement of paid staff by volunteers (*e.g.*, Lefebvre (1996)). And, in fact, there is little evidence that any large-scale replacement of paid staff has taken place (NSNVO (2004)).

Nevertheless, given severe funding cuts, organizations may benefit from a larger and better educated pool of volunteers. Indeed, in a recent study of the value added contribution of hospital volunteers, Handy and Srinivasan (2004) calculated that for every dollar spent on the volunteer program, the hospital derived an average of $6.84 in value. Volunteers provided invaluable non-medical support to patients while freeing professionals to spend more time on medical care. Several new volunteer initiatives are occurring in Canada. The largest and most ambitious of these are government-mandated programs in the secondary schools of several provinces. Other initiatives include employee volunteer programs sponsored by corporations, and social-entrepreneurial ventures aimed at enticing young people to volunteer.

Education

Although during the past decade the voluntary sector has become more visible thanks to increased media attention, greater research interest and the establishment of various graduate and undergraduate nonprofit management programs, many members of the general public are still not aware of the size and importance of the voluntary sector. Education is essential not only to increase awareness of the critical role of the voluntary sector for societal well-being, but also to help develop an ethos of giving and participating (Salamon & Anheier (1996)). This has traditionally been a role played by religious institutions, however in an increasingly secularized society it is unrealistic to rely solely on religious institutions to encourage community involvement and social action (Cnaan *et al.* (1993); Wuthnow (1991)). Evidence from school-based "service learning" programs in the United States indicates that schools can play a significant role in encouraging civic responsibility. The concept of service learning dates back to the turn of the last century when John Dewey wrote about the "importance of social and not just intellectual development; and the value of actions directed towards the welfare of others" (Kraft (1996, at p. 133)). "Service learning" links community service directly to the school curriculum. It has enjoyed renewed interest in the latter decades of the twentieth century as a potential brake to the worrisome decline in civic participation (Barber (1992); Bellah *et al.* (1985); Putnam (2000)).

In many Canadian provinces, community service programs have long existed as part of co-op placements, extracurricular activities, and specific courses. Nonetheless, Ontario and British Columbia are the only provinces with mandated community service requirements for high school graduation. Technically, high school students who volunteer in nonprofit organizations in order to fulfil credit requirements would not fall into the category of volunteer as defined above. However, a recent study of the Ontario program indicates that many of the students were already volunteers before the program, and many actually continued freely volunteering more than their required hours (Meinhard *et al.* (2006)).

These relatively new programs highlight government interest in playing a more active role in socializing youth to the importance of community involvement and charitable giving. For example, the stated intention of the service component in Ontario is to "encourage students to develop awareness and understanding of civic responsibility and of the role they can play in supporting and strengthening their communities" (Ontario Ministry of Education (1999)). In fact, a lack of awareness — "not knowing" where to volunteer — is the most common reason given by young people for not volunteering (Hall *et al.* (2001)). This barrier has been effectively eliminated by the new program, as schools and parents help students organize their volunteering activities to fulfil their requirements.

Although the long-term success of this program is not yet known, other studies show that the greatest benefits occur when community service is linked to a structured school activity, and when placements are arranged in active partnership with nonprofit agencies. (Meinhard & Foster (1999); Foster & Meinhard (2000); Raskoff & Sundeen (1998)). Simply requiring 40 hours of service over four years of high school in the absence of a structured program is not likely to achieve the intended long-term results of increased civic-mindedness and community participation.

Employer-supported Volunteering

While the government has been cutting funding to the nonprofit sector, the corporate sector has increased its involvement. The most recently available statistics indicate that the corporate sector has more than doubled its support of the voluntary sector from $1.2 billion in 1996 (Standing Committee on Finance (1996)) to $2.8 billion in 2003 (Statistics Canada (2003, at p. 23)). This relatively newfound sense of corporate social responsibility is, in part, in response to shareholder concerns for community involvement and social responsibility (Austen (2000); Schmid & Meinhard (2000)), and in part a result of an in-creased realization of the marketing potential of such involvement (Berger *et al.* (2005a)). To this end, organizations try to offer support in different, and at times innovative, ways, both through direct giving and by facilitating employee volunteer programs. These volunteer programs include: volunteer recognition events, making donations to the volunteers' charities in recognition of their work, sponsoring events that employees organize, providing time off, arranging flexible scheduling, and "lending" employees to nonprofit organizations for periods of time.

One of Canada's major banks has just launched an innovative paid leave of absence program where employees can request a sec-ondment to a nonprofit organization for a period of from 3 to 12 months. The bank will not only pay the employees' salaries and guarantee equivalent movement in the ranks when they return, it will also give a $5,000 grant to the nonprofit organization to cover space and equipment costs. Other programs capitalize on the widespread use of the Internet by providing a service to match volunteers from the corporation with nonprofit boards in need of their skills.

Employer-supported volunteering is a three-way partnership that benefits all involved as summarized in Table 1.

Table 1: Mutual Benefits from Employer-supported Volunteering

Nonprofits gain from:	Businesses	New partnerships and sponsorships, support and better understanding
	Employees	A supply of volunteers with needed skills, exposure to their cause
Businesses gain from:	Nonprofits	Improved image, which leads to increased sales and greater customer loyalty
	Employees	More loyal workforce, better morale and pride in organization
Employees gain from:	Nonprofits	New skills, sense of giving back, social network
	Business	Recognition, support for community work, time off to volunteer

Entrepreneurial Initiatives

There are many individual efforts by young people to get their peers involved in volunteering and community activity. One example is the creation of the Framework Foundation, conceived and executed by a young man who was worried about the lack of community participation among his peers. He engaged several of his friends and with them organized a unique art auction to attract 22- to 35-year-olds to volunteer. Called a *Timeraiser*, people pledge volunteering hours, instead of bidding money, to purchase paintings by young Canadian artists. The art is purchased by Framework Foundation with money raised through corporate sponsorships and fundraising. Everyone gains, the artists get important exposure and sell their paintings, the corporate donors and partners get exposure and recognition, voluntary agencies get skilled and educated volunteers, and volunteers not only get to purchase art but also contribute to their community and learn about its needs. In the words of the Framework Foundation:

> The Framework Foundation empowers Canadians between the ages of 22 and 35 to "get in the picture" and help build stronger communities through volunteer involvement. Our Framework Foundation "picture" celebrates the power of collective dedication, recognizing its importance in addressing community needs.

(<http://www.frameworkfoundation.ca/about/index.php>.)

The first *Timeraiser* was launched in 2004 in Toronto and was a great success with almost 10,000 hours of volunteering completed at over 40 agencies. Volunteers and agencies track their hours by a computerized tracking system that was specially devised for this project. In 2006 *Timeraisers* are planned for other Canadian cities.

Volunteer Diversity

As noted above, volunteer participation rates in Canada are decreasing just as voluntary organizations are becoming more reliant on volunteers. In order to expand the pool of volunteers and supporters, leaders of nonprofit organizations are increasingly recognizing the need to engage Canada's growing ethnic communities. Currently, the participation rate among Canada's newer ethnic communities is lower than that of older, more established communities. The challenge for nonprofit organizations is to find a way to reach out to these groups. This means recognizing that volunteering is a function of many interrelated factors: prevailing cultural norms and values, available opportunities, individual and societal barriers, and past experience, all of which influence personal attitudes. These factors may differ among the various ethnic communities. Thus, for example, in a culture where volunteering has a connotation of "forced labour" as in Communist China, where individuals were forced to "volunteer" to engage in an activity deemed necessary by the authorities, volunteering outside the home or family may have little appeal.

When members of various ethnic groups were asked why they do not volunteer, the two main reasons given were lack of time and not being asked (Hall *et al.*, 2001). Lack of time, although not unique to newer Canadians, is all the more pertinent to immigrants who are struggling to make ends meet. "Not being asked" may be an indication of subtle social barriers that may exist in the recruitment of volunteers. Thus, while members of some social groups may be actively courted by voluntary organizations, thereby increasing their knowledge of where and how to volunteer, members of other groups may receive no attention or may be approached in culturally inappropriate ways, thereby impeding intentions to volunteer. Recruiters must recognize these subtle barriers and mitigate them by learning more about the myriad ethnic communities in Canada today.

Diversity is also an issue when it comes to the composition of nonprofit boards. Although there is no definitive Canadian count, American studies estimate the extent of minority representation on boards to be between 12 per cent to 16 per cent (Constance-Huggins & Bangs (2003)). This trend continues, despite clauses in the by-laws of many nonprofit organizations calling for a board composition representative of the community's population. In Canada, ethnic diversity in the nonprofit sector is reflected by the diversity of ethno-cultural organizations across the sector rather than diversity within individual organizations, which means that the problem here is probably as great as in the United States.

Volunteering in nonprofit organizations can play a bridging role in helping new Canadians integrate into society. Thus, a concerted effort by voluntary organizations to attract new immigrants serves not only the organization but also society as a whole, not to mention the newcomer (Onyx & Maclean (1996)). However, new immigrants are more likely to volunteer and join organizations within their ethnic community. This may provide them with important bonding experiences, especially in a new and strange country, but it can also delay their integration into Canadian society (Berger *et al.* (2005b)). Low volunteering rates among certain ethnic minorities continue even into the second generation, indicating that cultural and normative influences, as well as discriminatory barriers, have deep roots in a country that encourages the celebration of multiculturalism (Berger *et al.* (2005b)).

It is perhaps in the area of gender diversity that the voluntary sector has made the greatest strides. Although women were always active in voluntary organizations, access to leadership was denied them. In their frustration, they founded and led their own organizations. Today, many nonprofit organizations, including large national ones, have women at their helm. For example, data from a large Canadian study (Meinhard & Foster (2003)) involving more than 300 organizations that were not specifically serving women or advocating their causes, indicate that 53 per cent of them were led by women in either paid or unpaid positions. This figure dropped to 48 per cent when considering only those organizations with revenues exceeding one million dollars.

On the other hand, women's representation on boards of directors is considerably lower, averaging around 36 per cent in American studies (Mayorova (1995)) and 43 per cent in the Canadian one, including the large organizations (Meinhard & Foster (2003)). However, compared to the corporate sector, these figures are encouraging.

The concept of diversity on boards is not limited to gender and ethno-racial background. Diversity in terms of age, education, economic status and type of work will give boards access to a variety of different perspectives that will help them function better in Canada's diverse environment. Achieving diversity is not an easy task and can only be accomplished if the board deliberately sets policy to attract people of various backgrounds.

Managing Volunteers

The ultimate challenge in employee management is how to improve worker productivity. Organizational behaviour literature identifies two separate but related avenues for achieving high performance from workers. One is devising an appropriate and fair incentive structure. This must be coupled with creating a favourable workplace climate and attractive job design. These two pillars of management are pertinent for volunteers as well, but the emphasis and balance between them is different.

Incentive Structure

Organizational management practices are predicated on the principle of exchanging rewards for services rendered to the organization in pursuit of its goals. The rewards are primarily monetary in nature, although they may also include promotion through the ranks and non-tangible reinforcements such as recognition and praise. In addition, there may be intrinsic rewards associated with an activity, such as feeling good about an outcome or enjoying the activity itself. Various theories of motivation describe the relationship of human performance to the satisfaction of basic needs and the achievement of desired rewards (Hertzberg *et al.* (1959)). These theories posit that as basic needs for food and security are fulfilled through the performance of certain activities, humans strive to satisfy more complex ones such as needs for affiliation, esteem, achievement power and self-actualization (Alderfer (1972); Maslow (1943); McClelland (1961)). Whether or not they continue to pursue certain activities depends on the value of the extrinsic and/or intrinsic rewards associated with the activity (Lawler (1973)). In a paid workplace, mundane, uninteresting work may be well tolerated in exchange for sufficient monetary compensation, which acts as an incentive to perform the task. However, even in the workplace, increasing monetary rewards has diminishing returns after a certain level of reward satisfaction has been reached (McShane (2005)). Therefore, in order to improve performance it is often the case that the answer lies in improving the structure and characteristics of the job and/or the workplace.

Workplace Climate and Job Design

Often called simply job design, this refers to a combination of factors that together affect the performance of an individual. The key components are: clarity of the task (*i.e.*, what exactly needs to be done); level and variety of skills needed (*i.e.*, mundane and boring versus challenging and varied work); perceived significance of the work (*i.e.*, the importance to key stakeholders); level of autonomy (*i.e.*, is the job highly standardized or does one have discretion to make decisions?); identification with the completed task (*i.e.*, participation in the entire process versus performing a specific part exclusively); and finally, level and quality of feedback (Hackman & Oldham (1980)). In theory, the better the job design, and the more socially fulfilling the workplace, the more satisfied the worker will be, which in turn increases motivation and ultimately leads to better performance.

In the case of volunteers, monetary reward is not a motivator, nor is the activity undertaken by the volunteer to satisfy basic existence needs. Therefore, the challenge for management is to find the right combination of incentives and job characteristics that will induce the volunteer to stay interested in helping the organization. In terms of incentives, both the academic and practitioner literature has identified the following "best practices":

- Understand the volunteers' needs and match them with the appropriate job (Wilson & Pimm (1996)).

- Emphasize and communicate the social meaningfulness of the activity (Onyx & Maclean (1996)).

- Link the activity to generalizable skills (Janey *et al.* (1991)).

- Value their time, give them feedback, and publicly and privately recognize their contributions, and reimburse their expenses (Brudney (1999))

Furthermore, job and workplace characteristics take on added importance in managing volunteers. Although there are many non-monetary incentives related to volunteering, such as those discussed above, they may not be enough to mitigate the deleterious effects of poor workplace/job characteristics. The academic and practitioner literature identifies the following work and job factors as important and beneficial for a volunteer program:

- Provide a budget for a dedicated volunteer manager (Brudney (1999)).

- Train paid staff members in how to work with volunteers (Brudney (1999)).

- Train volunteers to lead other volunteers (Brudney (1999)).

- Clearly communicate roles and define jobs (Ross (1992)).

- Provide orientation and job training (Wilson & Pimm (1996)).

- Ensure work variety and delegate responsibility (Netting *et al.* (2005); Wilson & Pimm (1996)).

- Create a positive ambiance in the workplace (Puffer & Meindl (1995)).

Effective volunteer management is highly correlated with a volunteer's commitment to continue volunteering with the organization (Farmer & Fedor (1999)). On the organizational side, time devoted to managing volunteers is strongly related to organizational benefits accruing from the use of volunteers (Brudney (1999)). This notwithstanding, evidence from a study of 1,800 nonprofit organizations suggests that 80 per cent of organizations using volunteers lack the capacity to manage them effectively (GUI Program News (2005)). Budgetary constraint is the foremost reason put forward as preventing organizations from instituting structured volunteer programs with trained managers whose primary focus is the volunteer contingent (Hager & Brudney (2004)).

Besides the size of the budget, there are three other determinants of whether or not an organization adopts formal volunteer management practices: task variety, size of volunteer contingent and type of organization. The greater the variety of tasks performed by volunteers and the greater the number of volunteers, the more likely that the organization will adopt formal volunteer management practices. Additionally, the type of organization will also be a determinant; for example, health and human service organizations were found to be more likely to adopt a formally structured volunteer program than educational and arts institutions (Brudney & Nezhina (2005)).

Challenges for managing volunteers differ depending on whether the organization's activities are performed for the most part by volunteers, or whether they are carried out by paid employees, with some additional help from volunteers (Adams & Shepherd (1996)). In the former, it is usually volunteer leaders who organize other volunteers. The foremost problems incurred in these situations are related to lack of leadership training in managing others and lack of job descriptions and role clarity (Adams & Shepherd (1996)).

In organizations where volunteers and paid staff members work together, the success of the volunteer program depends on the relationship between volunteers and paid staff (Adams & Shepherd (1996); Colomy *et al.* (1987); Mausner (1988)). Tension between the two tends to be higher in organizations without trained volunteer managers, where volunteers are often supervised by staff managers who, on average, devote less than one-third of their time to volunteer coordination (Brudney (1999), and who are often unfamiliar with the characteristics of volunteers (Wilson (1981)). Wilson and Pimm (1996) identify three main areas of misunderstanding. The first relates to mutual misperceptions. Employees often fear that they may be replaced by volunteers and resent the favoured treatment that they believe is afforded to volunteers. On the other hand, volunteers often feel exploited, believing they are given the least important, least interesting jobs and experience higher role uncertainty (Farmer & Fedor (1999)). The second involves managerial discomfort as supervisors recognize the limits of their authority with respect to volunteers. This leads to attitudes among staff that "volunteers are a nuisance, work has to be found to occupy them and then resources diverted to supervise them" (Wilson & Pimm (1996, at p. 27)). The third misunderstanding stems from a clash of values with respect to paid and volunteer labour, the latter generally considered of higher moral value.

Each of these areas of misunderstanding can be overcome with good volunteer management practices that involve open communications clearly identifying the roles of volunteers and staff members as mutually supportive (Adams & Shepherd (1996)), building a relationship of trust between supervisors and their volunteers (Farmer & Fedor

(1999)), and reiterating the importance of both volunteers and employees in furthering the mission of their organizations.

BOARD, STAFF AND VOLUNTEERS WORKING TOGETHER FOR ORGANIZATIONAL SUCCESS

In many nonprofit organizations, the sandwiching of paid professional staff between a voluntary board of directors and volunteer workers presents a situation prone to role ambiguity and role conflict. On the one hand there may be tensions between staff and board members over the direction of the organization in light of an imbalance between knowledge and information on the part of the part-time board volunteers and the full-time paid organizational leadership. Conflict may also occur over issues of supervision, as boards may be prone to micro-managing their staff. On the other hand, tensions may arise between paid employees and volunteer workers over misperceptions about their respective roles and miscommunication in the work they do together. Solutions are not simple, but problems can be minimized and their impact mitigated through the application of sound human resource practices. Interestingly, with the exception of a few articles, most treatises on how to best recruit and manage volunteers do not mention the importance of having basic human resource management structures in place.

Basic Human Resource Functions

"Board, staff and volunteers working together for organizational success" is not a just cliché when an organization has guidelines to address human resource challenges and opportunities. Using Wilson's & Pimm's (1996) framework, the seven basic HR functions will be reviewed and their applicability to all levels of the organization — board, staff and volunteers — will be demonstrated.

Recruitment

Finding the right people for the right job is basic to all organizations, however in nonprofit organizations finding a fit with the organization, its cause and its people often has more weight than job skills. Recruitment entails preparation and planning in terms of predicting organizational needs, identifying target markets, clearly defining the purpose and content of the job or jobs, devising a profile of the ideal person, marketing the organization through informative advertisements that appeal both to the instrumental benefits of participating and to the affective benefits of belonging to the organization, and finding the right channels through which to communicate. Even in membership organizations, where recruitment for a specific job will target the organization's own membership, such planning and segmentation of potential recruits is recommended (Wilson & Pimm (1996)). A common problem in nonprofit organizations is that without an HR structure, response to applications is slow and people go elsewhere. Proper recruitment helps to forestall later problems associated with lack of fit. These principles apply not only to the recruitment of volunteer workers, but also to board volunteers and staff members.

Selection

Although the nonprofit literature is replete with recruitment sugges-tions, selection processes are barely mentioned. Yet this is a key element of HRM, as not all potential recruits are suited for the job. In the for-profit world there are many tools for selection, depending on the job. In nonprofit organizations the most viable tool is the structured job interview. The interview should not only be a means for the interviewer to gauge the suitability of the prospective volunteer or employee, it should also include an opportunity for the organization to clearly define the parameters (task, skills needed, time required, flexibility *etc.*) of the activities the volunteer will be engaged in. This will give potential recruits a chance to (re)consider their application if the parameters do not fit with their needs and abilities. It also gives both parties the opportunity to explore shared values. The selection process should be completed for board members as well as staff and volunteers. As with recruitment, proper selection processes mitigate the chance of a poor fit. This is important because frequent turnover is disruptive, but also can lead to disaffection among the existing employees and volunteers.

Orientation

Once the selection process is complete, the most important, and often most neglected part of the HRM process, especially where there is no one designated to oversee these functions, is orientation (Wilson & Pimm (1996)). Formal orientation serves many purposes, but basically it is a process of organizational socialization (McShane (2005)), in which new members learn about the organization, its values, and how things are done. They meet key people and see how their activities fit in with the rest of the organization. During the orientation, new members should be informed about the organization's policies with respect to their rights and obligations, and be informed about the organization's liability insurance. Most importantly, a formal orientation is an opportunity to revisit the job description, and to clearly understand the reporting relationships and performance expectations. Without a formal orientation, the learning process is extended and it takes longer for the new member to play an active and beneficial role in the organization. Formal orientation can also be an opportunity for self-selection, without incurring large costs to either the leaving member or the organization. Orientation of new board members is a crucial board activity as well, as so many people who join nonprofit boards have little experience and knowledge of boards in general, and certainly not of the specific board.

Supervision

This not only involves providing direction and oversight for the work to be done, it also includes training in both technical skills pertaining to the job and leadership skills for filling leadership positions and supervising volunteers in the future. In the absence of direct control mechanisms through managerial authority, supervision of volunteers requires more negotiation and persuasion than direction. Thus, training supervisory staff is important. They need to learn that volunteers have different needs and values associated with their voluntary work, and that therefore, they have to be approached in different ways. In addition, they need to respect constraints facing volunteers, and not overburden them during busy times. On the other hand, in times of low activity, they must keep their volunteers involved in the affairs of the organization, to prevent them from leaving. Training staff members in how to supervise and work with volunteers paves the way for smoother staff-volunteer relations. Boards should be training their members as well, outlining the limits of their authority vis-à-vis staff.

Performance Appraisals

This is perhaps the most neglected HR function in nonprofit organizations. There is often a reluctance to give negative feedback to a volunteer in fear of losing their support. But poor performance has ripple effects that can lead to covert and even overt conflict, a lowering of work norms among other volunteers and staff, and a decrease in morale. Formal performance evaluations for the purposes of wage or career advancement should be instituted for every staff member. However, formal appraisals may be counter-productive with respect to volunteers (Wilson & Pimm (1996)). In their case, it may be more beneficial to provide feedback through informal chats. Asking them how things are going, whether they are happy in their work and how the organization is treating them, can lead to openings where the supervisor can suggest how things can be improved and express their concerns without discrediting volunteers' work. Supervisors need training in this as well.

Performance evaluation of the ED by the board of directors is another oft-neglected task. Here the opposite is true. The board should engage in regularly scheduled formal evaluations. For more on this see Chapter 3.

Termination

Informing an organizational member that his or her services are no longer needed is always a difficult task, except when circumstances involve illegal or immoral activities. It is even more difficult with respect to volunteers. Paid supervisors may find the task less daunting, but voluntary staff members or board members find it almost impossible as there may be social and personal repercussions. However, keeping a poorly functioning volunteer is detrimental to the organization. It takes skill to terminate a voluntary relationship in a way that will hurt neither the volunteer nor the organization. These skills have to be learned and practised. Fortunately it is more often the case that volunteers initiate the termination. An exit interview to determine the reasons for withdrawal is an important tool to improving recruitment and selection practices.

CONCLUSION

Knowledge and application of basic human resource practices is beneficial to nonprofit organizations not only with respect to paid staff members, but also with respect to volunteers and volunteer board members. That these practices are not widespread, especially in smaller, volunteer-driven organizations, is often a function of budgetary constraints. However, there is a distinct lack of awareness on the part of many voluntary organizations of the importance and benefits of exercising human resource practices. There is sometimes a mistaken belief that the attraction of a voluntary organization is its informality and lack of professionalism, and that adding formal HR practices may detract from the organization's appeal. It is not essential for a small organization to have a paid, trained person designated for HR issues. However, since the board has ultimate legal responsibility for what happens in the organization, it is in its interests to pay more attention to HR issues. Therefore, as part of their resource planning, they should consider sending their volunteer leaders or staff supervisors to attend seminars and workshops that teach basic HR practices. Sometimes simply by raising awareness of HR issues, relations among board, volunteers and paid staff can be improved for future organizational success.

This chapter has highlighted some of the basic issues around managing human resources in voluntary and nonprofit organizations. The overarching goal of HRM is to bring together the various groups of players in ways that enhance an organization's capacity to pursue its mission efficiently and effectively. Although many of the practices are similar to those in the private sector, the dimensions of the challenge are magnified because of the dual nature of nonprofit governance, the budgetary constraints so many of them face, the reliance on voluntary commitment to carry out goals, and the relatively undeveloped state of human resource practices in nonprofit organizations.

REFERENCES

Adams, C.H. & G. J. Shepherd (1996), "Managing Volunteer Performance: Face Support and Situational Features as Predictors of Volunteers' Evaluations of Regulative Messages" (1996), 9:4 *Management Communication Quarterly* 363-389.

Akingbola, O. (2005), *Strategy, Human Resource Management and Government Funding in Nonprofit Organizations*, Unpublished Doctoral Dissertation, University of Toronto.

Alderfer, C.P. (1972), *Existence, Relatedness and Growth* (New York: The Free Press, 1972).

Austin, J.E. (2000), "Strategic Collaboration Between Nonprofits and Businesses" (2000), 29:1 *Nonprofit and Voluntary Sector Quarterly* 69-97.

Barber, B. (1992), *An Aristocracy of Everyone* (New York: Ballantine, 1992).

Beer, M., P.R. Lawrence, D.Q. Mills & R.E. Walton (1984), *Managing Human Assets* (New York: Free Press, 1984).

Beerli, A., G. Diaz & J.D. Martin (2004), "The Behavioral Consequences of Self-Congruency in Volunteers" (2004), 9:1 *International Journal of Nonprofit and Voluntary Sector Marketing* 28-48.

Bellah R., R. Madsen, W. Sullivan, A. Swidler & S. Tipton (1985), *Habits of the Heart* (Berkeley: University of California Press, 1985).

Berger, I.E., P.H. Cunningham & M.E. Drumwright (2005a), "Social Alliances: Company/Nonprofit Collaboration" (2005), 47:1 *California Management Review*, 58-90.

Berger, I., M. Dinca, M. Foster & A. Meinhard (2005b), *Ethnicity, Voluntary Behaviour and Social Integration.* Proceedings of the Annual Conference of the Administrative Sciences Association of Canada, Toronto, ON.

Brudney, J.L. (1999), "The Effective Use of Volunteers: Best Practices for the Public Sector" (1999), 62:4 *Law and Contemporary Problems* 219-255.

Brudney, J.L., & T.G. Nezhina (2005), "What is Old is New Again: Achieving Effectiveness with Volunteer Programs in Kazakhstan" (2005), 16:3 *Voluntas* 293-308.

Carter, N. (1975), *Trends in Voluntary Support for Non-Governmental Social Service Agencies* (Ottawa: Canadian Council on Social Development, 1975).

Clark, P.B., & J.Q. Wilson (1961), "Incentive Systems: A Theory of Organizations" (1961), 6 *Administrative Sciences Quarterly* 129-166.

Clary, E.G., M. Snyder & A.A. Stukas (1996), "Volunteers' Motivations: Findings from a National Survey" (1996), 25:4 *Nonprofit and Voluntary Sector Quarterly* 485-505.

Cnaan, R., A. Kasternakis & R.J. Wineburg (1993), "Religious People, Religious Congregations, and Volunteerism in Human Services: Is

There a Link?" (1993), 22:1 *Nonprofit and Voluntary Sector Quarterly* 33-51.

Cnaan, R., F. Handy & M. Wadsworth (1996), "Defining Who is a Volunteer: Conceptual and Empirical Considerations" (1996), 25:3 *Nonprofit and Voluntary Sector Quarterly* 364-383.

Colomy P., H. Chen & G.L. Andrews (1987), "Situational Facilities and Volunteer Work" (1987), 6:2 *Journal of Volunteer Administration* 20-25.

Constance-Huggins, M., & R.L. Bangs (2003), *Diversity Within and Among Nonprofit Boards in Allegheny County* (Pittsburgh: University Center for Social and Urban Research, University of Pittsburgh, 2003).

de Schweinitz, K. (1943), *England's Road to Social Security* (New York: Barnes, 1943).

Dreesen, E. (2000), *What Do We Know About the Voluntary Sector? An Overview.* Statistics Canada, Cat. No. 75F0048MIE-No. 06. Available online at: <http://www.statcan.ca/english/research/75F0048MIE/75F0048MIE2002006.pdf>.

Drucker, P.F. (1990), "Lessons for Successful Nonprofit Governance" (1990), 1:1 *Nonprofit Management and Leadership* 7-14.

Duchesne, D. (1989), *Giving Freely: Volunteers in Canada.* Statistics Canada, Labour Analytic Report, Cat. No.: 71-535 No. 4 (Ottawa: Minister of Supply and Services, 1989).

Economist, The (March 12, 2005), "Britain: Subsidizing Virtue; Volunteering" (2005), 374:8417 *The Economist* 57.

Farmer, S.M., & D.B. Fedor (1999), "Volunteer Participation and Withdrawal" (1999), 9:4 *Nonprofit Management and Leadership* 349-368.

Feingold, M. (1987), "Philanthropy, Pomp and Patronage: Historical Reflections upon the Endowment of Culture" (1987), 116:1 *Daedalus* 155-178.

Flynn, J.P., & G.E. Web (1975), "Women's Incentives for Community Participation in Policy Issues" (1975), 4:3-4 *Journal of Voluntary Action Research* 137-145.

Foster, M.K., & A.G. Meinhard (2005), "Diversifying Revenue Sources in Canada: Are Women's Voluntary Organizations Different?" (2005), 16:1 *Nonprofit Management & Leadership* 43-60.

Foster, M.K., & A.G. Meinhard (2000), *Structuring Student Volunteering Programs to the Benefit of Students and the Community.* Presented at the Fourth International Conference of the International Society for Third Sector Research, Dublin, Ireland.

Foster, M.K., & A.G. Meinhard (1996), *Toward Transforming Social Service Organizations in Ontario.* Presented at the Babson Conference on Entrepreneurship, Seattle, WA.

Gluck, R. (1975), "An Exchange Theory of Incentives of Urban Political Party Organization" (1975), 4:1-2 *Journal of Voluntary Action Research* 104-115.

GUI Program News (April 1, 2005). "New Fundraiser Volunteer Module Eases Management Tasks", 16(4) *GUI Program News.*

Hackman, J.R., & G.R. Oldham (1980), *Work Redesign* (Reading, MA: Addison-Wesley, 1980).

Hager, M., & J.L. Brudney (2004), *Volunteer Management Practices and Retention of Volunteers* (Washington, DC: The Urban Institute, 2004).

Haiven, J. (1998), *The Right People for the Job: The Not-For-Profit Sector and its Human Element.* Presented at the Association for Research on Nonprofit Organizations and Voluntary Action Conference, Seattle, Washington.

Hall, M., & K.G. Banting (2000), "The Nonprofit Sector in Canada: An Introduction", in K.G. Banting, ed., *The Nonprofit Sector in Canada: Roles and Relationships* (Montreal and Kingston: School of Policy Studies, Queen's University, 2000).

Hall, M.H., L. McKeown & K. Roberts (2001), *Caring Canadians, Involved Canadians: Highlights from the 2000 National Survey of Giving, Volunteering and Participating.* Catalogue No. 71-542-XIE (Ottawa: Statistics Canada, 2001). Available online at: <http://www.givingandvolunteering.ca/pdf/n-2000-hr-ca.pdf>.

Handy, F., & N. Srinivasan (2004), Valuing Volunteers: An Economic Evaluation of the Net Benefits of Hospital Volunteers" (2004), 33:1 *Nonprofit and Voluntary Sector Quarterly* 28-54.

Herman, R.D., & D.R. Heimovics (1991), *Executive Leadership in Non-Profit Organizations* (Oxford: Jossey-Bass Publishers, 1991).

Hertzberg, F., B. Mausner & B.B. Snyderman (1959), *The Motivation to Work* (New York: Wiley, 1959).

Hodgkinson, V.A., & M.S. Weitzman (1997), *Volunteering and Giving Among American Teenagers 14 to 17 Years of Age: 1996 edition* (Washington, DC: Independent Sector, 1997).

Human Resources Council for the Voluntary/Non-profit Sector (2005), *The Canadian Centre for Philanthropy and the Canadian Policy Research Networks*. Available online at: <http://www.hrvs-rhsbc.ca/hr_overview/pg001_e.cfm>.

Hustinx, L., & Frans Lammertyn (2003), "Collective and Reflexive Styles of Volunteering: A Sociological Modernization Perspective", 14(2) *Voluntas* 168-187.

Independent Sector (2003), "Independent Sector Report Illustrates Philanthropic Potential of the American Baby Boom Generation". Press Release. San Francisco, CA, November 4, 2003. Available online at: <http://www.independentsector.org/media/experiencePR.html>.

Izon, L. (January 15, 2005), "Volunteer Vacations Target the Tsunami Zone" *Globe & Mail,* p. T2.

Jackson, J. (2005), "Volunteers: Not Free Labour" (2005), 115:4 *Municipal World* 39-40.

Janey, J.P., J.E. Tuckwiller & L.E. Lonnquist (1991), "Skill Transferal Benefits from Volunteer Experiences" (1991), 20 *Nonprofit and Voluntary Sector Quarterly* 71-79.

Kaminer, W. (1984), *Women volunteering* (Garden City: Anchor Press, 1984).

Knoke, D. (1986), "Associations and Interest Groups" (1986), 12 *Annual Review of Sociology* 1-20.

Kraft, R. (1996), "Service Learning: An Introduction to Its Theory, Practice and Effects" (1996), 28:2 *Education and Urban Society* 131-159.

Kramer, R. (1981), *Voluntary Agencies in the Welfare State* (Berkeley: University of California Press, 1981).

Langton, S. (1982), "The New Voluntarism", in J.D. Harman, ed., *Volunteerism in the Eighties: Fundamental Issues in Voluntary Action* (Washington, DC: University Press of America, 1982) (pp. 3-22).

Lawler, E.E. (1973), *Motivation in Work Organizations* (Monterey, CA: Brooks/Cole, 1973).

Lefebvre, B. (1996). From Minutes of the Standing Committee on General Government, Government of Ontario. Timmins, ON.: June 16, 1996.

Lewis, J. (1994), "Gender, the Family and Women's Agency in the Building of the 'Welfare States': The British Case" (1994), 19:1 *Social History* 37-55.

Macaleer, B., & S. Jones (2003), *"Does HR Planning Improve Business Performance?"* (2003), 45:1 *Industrial Management* 14-21.

Marek, A.C. (2004), "Volunteer" (2004), 137:23 *U.S. News & World Report* 84.

Martin, S. (1985), *An Essential Grace: Funding Canada's Health Care, Education, Welfare, Religion and Culture* (Toronto: McClelland and Stewart, 1985).

Masi, D.A. (1981), *Organizing for Women: Issues, Strategies, and Services* (Lexington, MA: Lexington Books, 1981).

Maslow, A. (1943), "A Theory of Human Motivation" (1943), 50 *Psychological Review* 370-396.

Mausner, C. (1988), "The Underlying Dynamics of Staff Volunteer Relationships" (1988), 5:3 *The Journal of Volunteer Administration* 5-9.

Mayo, E. (1945), *The Social Problems of an Industrial Civilization* (Boston: Harvard University, 1945).

Mayorova, O.V. (1995), *Corporate and Nonprofit Boards: Have Women Gained Power?* MA Thesis submitted to the Graduate School of the University of Louisville.

McCarthy, K.D., ed. (1990), *Lady Bountiful Revisited: Women, Philanthropy, and Power* (New Brunswick, NJ: Rutgers University Press, 1990).

McClelland, D. (1961), *The Achieving Society* (New York: Van Nostrand, 1961).

McMullen, K., & R. Brisbois (2003), *Coping With Change: Human Resource Management in Canada's Non-Profit Sector*, CPRN Research Series on Human Resources in the Non-profit Sector, No. 4 (Ottawa: Canadian Policy Research Networks, 2003).

McMullen, K., & G. Schellenberg (2003), *Job Quality in the Non-Profit Sector*, CPRN Research Series on Human Resources in the Nonprofit Sector, No.2. Ottawa: Canadian Policy Research Networks, 2003).

McMullen, K., & G. Schellenberg (2002), *Mapping the Non-Profit Sector*. CPRN Research Series on Human Resources in the Non-profit Sector, No. 1 (Ottawa: Canadian Policy Research Networks, 2002).

McShane, S.L. (2004), *Canadian Organizational Behaviour*, 5th ed. (Toronto: McGraw-Hill Ryerson, 2004).

Meijs, L., & E. Hoogstad (2001), "New Ways of Managing Volunteers: Combining Membership Management and Programme Management" (2001), 3:3 *Voluntary Action* 41-61.

Meinhard, A.G., M.K. Foster & P. Wright, "Rethinking School-Based Community Service: The Importance of a Structured Program" (2006), 20:1 *The Philanthropist* 5-22.

Meinhard, A., M. Foster & I. Berger (2004), *The Process of Institutional Isomorphism in Ontario's Voluntary Sector*. Presented at the annual conference of the Administrative Sciences Association of Canada, Quebec City, Quebec.

Meinhard, A.G., & M.K. Foster (2003), "Differences in the Responses of Women's Voluntary Organizations to Shifts in Canadian Public Policy" (2003), 32:3 *Nonprofit and Voluntary Sector Quarterly* 366-396.

Meinhard, A.G., & M.K. Foster (1999), *The Impact of Community Service Programs on Students in Toronto's Secondary Schools*. Presented at the annual conference of the Association for Research on Nonprofit Organizations and Voluntary Action, Washington, DC.

Meinhard, A.G., & M.K. Foster (1997), *Women's Voluntary Organizations and the Restructuring of Canada's Voluntary Sector: A Theoretical Perspective*. Proceedings of the Annual Conference of the Administrative Sciences Association of Canada, St. John's, NF.

Netting, F.E., M.K. O'Connor, M.L. Thomas & G. Yancey (2005), "Mixing and Phasing of Roles Among Volunteers, Staff, and Participants in Faith-Based Programs" (2005), 34:2 *Nonprofit and Voluntary Sector Quarterly* 179-205.

NSNVO (2005), *Cornerstones of community: Highlights of the National Survey of Nonprofit and Voluntary Organizations*, Catalogue No. 61-

533-XIE (Ottawa: Statistics Canada, Minister of Industry, 2005). Available online at: <http://www.statcan.ca/bsolc/english/bsolc?catno= 61-533-X>.

O'Connell, B. (1985), *The Board Member's Book: Making a Difference in Voluntary Organizations* (New York: Foundation Center, 1985).

Odendahl, T. (1994), "Women's Power, Nonprofits and the Future", in T. Odendahl and M. O'Neill, eds., *Women and Power in the Nonprofit Sector* (San Francisco: Jossey-Bass, 1994) (pp. 183-222).

Olson, M. (1965), *The Logic of Collective Action: Public Goods and the Theory of Groups* (Cambridge, MA: Harvard University Press, 1965).

O'Neill, M. (1994), "The Paradox of Women and Power in the Nonprofit Sector", in T. Odendahl and M. O'Neill, eds., *Women and Power in the Nonprofit Sector* (San Francisco: Jossey-Bass, 1994) (pp. 1-16).

Ontario Ministry of Education, *Ontario Secondary Schools, Grades 9 to 12: Program and Diploma Requirements* (Toronto: Queen's Printer, 1999). Available online at: <http://www.edu.gov.on.ca/eng/document/ curricul/secondary/oss/oss.pdf>.

Onyx, J., & M. Maclean (1996), "Careers in the Third Sector" (1996), 6:4 *Nonprofit Management and Leadership* 331-345.

Pal, L.A. (1997), "Civic Re-alignment: NGOs and the Contemporary Welfare State", in R.B. Blake, P.E. Bryden, & J.F. Strain, eds., *The Welfare State in Canada: Past, Present and Future* (Concord, ON: Irwin Publishing, 1997) (pp. 88-104).

Puffer, S., & J. Meindl (1995), "Volunteers from Corporations: Work Cultures Reflect Values Similar to the Voluntary Organizations" (1995), 5:4 *Nonprofit Management and Leadership* 359-376.

Putnam, R.D. (2000), *Bowling Alone: The Collapse and Revival of American Community* (Toronto: Simon & Schuster, 2000).

Reed, P., & K. Selbee (1999), *Distinguishing Characteristics of Active Volunteers in Canada: Nonprofit Sector Knowledge Base Project* (Ottawa: Statistics Canada, 1999).

Ross, D. (1992), "Managing Volunteers: When the Carrot is not a Paycheque" 66:9 *CMA Magazine* 30.

Routh, T. (1972), *The Volunteer and Community Agencies* (Springfield, IL: Thomas Books, 1972).

Raskoff, S., & R. Sundeen (1998), "Youth socialization and civic participation: The role of secondary schools in promoting community service in southern California" (1998), 27:1 *Nonprofit and Voluntary Sector Quarterly* 66-87.

Salamon, L.M., & H.K. Anheier (1996), *The Emerging Nonprofit Sector: An Overview* (Manchester: Manchester University Press, 1996).

Schmid, H., & A.G. Meinhard (2000), *A Comparative Analysis of Emerging Partnerships Between Corporations and Nonprofit Social Service Organizations in Canada and Israel.* Presented at the annual conference of the Association for Research on Nonprofit Organizations and Voluntary Action, New Orleans, LA.

Scott, A.F. (1990), "Women's Voluntary Associations: From Charity to Reform", in K. McCarthy, ed., *Lady Bountiful Revisited: Women, Philanthropy, and Power* (New Brunswick, NJ: Rutgers University Press, 1990) (pp. 35-54).

Schindler-Rainman, E., & R. Lippitt (1977), *The Volunteer Community: Creative Use of Human Resources*, 2nd ed. (La Jolla, CA: University Associates, 1977).

Smith, D.H. (1982), "Altruism, Volunteers, and Volunteerism", in J.D. Harman, ed., *Volunteerism in the Eighties: Fundamental Issues in Voluntary Action* (Washington DC: University Press of America, 1982) (pp. 23-44).

Standing Committee on Finance (1996), *The 1997 Budget and Beyond: Finish the Job*. Fifth report of the Standing Committee on Finance, December 1996. Available online at: <http://www.parl.gc.ca/35/Archives/committees352/fine/reports/05_1996-12/fine-05-cov-e.html>.

Statistics Canada (2005), *Business Dynamics in Canada, 2001*, Catalogue No. 61-534-XIE, Ottawa: Minister of Industry.

Statistics Canada (2004), *Satellite Account of Nonprofit Institutions and Volunteering*, Catalogue No. 13-015-XIE. (Ottawa: Minister of Industry, 2004). Available online at: <http://www.statcan.ca/english/freepub/13-015-XIE/13-015-XIE2004000.pdf>.

Taylor, F.W. (1911), *The Principles of Scientific Management* (New York: Harper Brothers, 1911).

Taylor, H.L. (1989), "Volunteer Work Develops Many Skills: Keys to Effective Management" (1989), 14:2 *Canadian Manager* 27.

Torrington, D., & L. Hall (1987), *Personnel Management: A new Approach* (London: Prentice-Hall, 1987).

Wilson, J. (2000), "Volunteering" (2000), 26 *Annual Review of Sociology* 215-240.

Wilson, M. (1981), "Reversing the Resistance of Staff to Volunteers" (1981), 21 *Voluntary Action Leadership* 21-24.

Wilson, A., & G. Pimm (1996), "The Tyranny of the Volunteer: The Care and Feeding of Voluntary Workforces", 34:4 *Management Decision* 24-39.

Wuthnow, R. (1991), *Acts of Compassion: Caring for Others and Helping Ourselves* (Princeton, NJ: Princeton University Press, 1991).

Chapter 12

OPTIMIZING THE POTENTIAL OF INFORMATION AND COMMUNICATIONS TECHNOLOGY IN NONPROFIT ORGANIZATIONS

Yvonne Harrison
Seattle University

INTRODUCTION

In his book, *Making Nonprofits Work*, new governance scholar Paul Light (2000) concludes that nonprofit work is more difficult now than ever before. He points to "funders, be they governments, charitable foundations, or individual givers ... [being] so insistent about economy and results" and "clients, be they communities or individuals ... [being] more demanding about efficiency and responsiveness" (p. v). These pressures have placed a new emphasis on the need for nonprofit organizations to perform efficiently and effectively. One of the major new tools with the potential for providing help in doing this is information and communications technology (ICT).

Generally, the normative literature on ICT use in nonprofit work is enthusiastic and supportive. Several studies point to the benefits of ICT use in the nonprofit sector on a number of levels, including increases in organizational efficiency and effectiveness and enhanced relationships with constituents (*e.g.*, Blau (2001); Burt & Taylor (2000); Saxton & Game (2001); Te'eni & Young (2003)). In the U.K.,

Burt & Taylor (2000) report that the benefits "extend beyond conventional enhancements of administration and operational efficiency and effectiveness ... Embedded within electronic networks is the potential to reshape organizations internally, reconfigure relationships across networks of organizations, and redefine relationships with individual citizens" (p. 131).

A review of the ICT adoption literature suggests that Canada is a world leader in the adoption of the Internet (OECD (2004)) and in the adoption of it by the voluntary sector (Pargmegiani & Sachdeva (2000)). The rate of Internet adoption in Canada is not surprising given commitments made by the Government of Canada to be the world leader in connectivity (see Canada (1999) for Speech from the Throne; Industry Canada (2002) for voluntary sector adoption; available online at: <http://www.voluntarygateway.ca/en/main> for Canadian voluntary sector Internet portal).[1]

Though Canada may be a leader in the adoption of new ICT tools, there is mounting evidence that not all nonprofits are making full use of these resources, nor are they benefiting from them to the same degree (*e.g.*, Blau (2002); Hall Aitken (2001); Ipsos Reid (2001); Kirschenbaum & Kunamneni (2001); Ludgate & Surman (2004); Nonprofits' Policy and Technology Project (1998); Murray & Harrison (2002a); (2002b); Harrison & Murray (2006); Pitkin & Manzo (2002); Ticher, Maison & Jones (2002)). Of course this problem is not confined to the nonprofit sector. It has been a concern to all those who study the "new economy" for some time (*e.g.*, Cooper (2004); McLoughlin & Harris (1997); OECD (2004); Te'eni & Young (2003); Zuboff (1988)).

Te'eni & Young (2003) describe how the new economy[2] challenges and changes the role of nonprofits by "making disclosed information more readily available and also raising the expectations of consumers ..." (p. 403). They caution that those who do not adopt the

---

[1]   As an example, an area of nonprofit activity where the Internet is being heavily promoted in Canada is in sports. For a national example of an online "community of practice" that facilitates sport policy development see <www.sportmatters.ca>. For a range of ICT tools to meet sport practice needs from the grassroots to governance level see <www.sportweb.ca>. For an example of a sporting event volunteer management system, see <www.volweb.ca> and for a virtual sport club see <www.clubvpa.com>.

[2]   Te'eni & Young (2003) define the new economy as the "general trend toward global organizations and marketplaces, a move from mainly tangible to combinations of tangible and intangible goods, and a leap into an intensely interlinked network of goods and agents" (p. 397).

new technology that lies behind this new economy will suffer serious consequences including a loss of "relative advantages ... compared to business and government, in providing services ..."(p. 397). However, failure to make use of ICT effectively results in a waste of the money and time invested (Quinn (2005); Van Grembergen (2000)).

While ICT can act as a "double-edged sword" depending on how well it is used, the question nonprofits must be concerned with in the new economy is not "should we or shouldn't we adopt ICT?", but rather, "*why* should we adopt it and how do we get the most out of what it has to offer?" Typical is this comment from an anonymous Executive Director:

> The simple truth is that the use of technology is one of the more challenging aspects facing those who manage nonprofit organizations. First, it is complicated ... Second, it is hard to have a clear idea of how to think about technology in the unique context of running a nonprofit organization. Third, it is hard to determine the best way to implement technological solutions when there are so many being thrown at us. Lastly, how can we be sure we're following best practices?

Acknowledging that there is limited literature on the nature of the nonprofit ICT effectiveness challenge, this chapter draws from the huge volume of industry reports and guidelines on ICT use as well as results from survey research conducted on the topic in the Canadian nonprofit sector. It will address a range of questions nonprofits face with regard to new ICT tools:

1. What is information and communications technology (ICT)?

2. What are the common types of ICT applications used by nonprofits?

3. How much success have nonprofits had with the use of ICT tools?

4. What factors influence the adoption and effective use of ICT?

5. How should the management of ICT be approached by nonprofits?

WHAT IS INFORMATION AND COMMUNICATIONS TECHNOLOGY (ICT)?

While there is no generally accepted definition of ICT, one way to understand it is to look at the makeup of the ICT sector, delineated by the Organisation for Economic Cooperation and Development (OECD) (1997) as "limited to industries which facilitate, by electronic means, the processing, transmission and display of information" (p. 1). It follows then that information and communications technology (ICT) is any technology that facilitates the passage of information, whether through conversion, storing, processing, and/or transmission. ICT includes such things as computer hardware (*e.g.*, cellular phones, handheld computers, desktop computers (PCs), and fax machines), software (*e.g.*, the operating systems like Windows, Mac OS, GNU/Linux), and the applications (off-the-shelf computer-based programs, Web-based software that is accessed from remote servers over the Internet, and "open source",[3] the code and licence that allows an organization to make use of and further develop software applications for free)[4][5] that "run the computer" (<http://www.gnu.org/philosophy/ICT-for-prosperity.html>), and the network infrastructure, such as an Intranet or the Internet, that make information sharing between computers possible. While each component has a separate function, they work in concert to form what is known in the literature as an information system (IS) (Clarke (2001)).

The OECD (2000) reported that ICT is an example of a new general-purpose technology that has had pervasive effects on practically all sectors of the economy. Furthermore, a larger proportion of investment is now spent on ICT than all other general-purpose technologies making the case for the emergence of a new economy. A review of the literature shows that ICT has evolved over a 30-year period. Initially it emerged in the area of manufacturing to give organizations more information than employees could provide them about production efficiency. Soon it evolved to enable these same organizations to gather other types of information about what, where, and how something should be done (Warren & Weschler (1999)).

Most recently, advancements in the Internet and the World Wide Web (WWW) have enabled organizations of all types and sizes to make more use of ICT. Tim Berners-Lee revolutionized communications when he created the WWW, a "single global space" for people to gather and share information (Carvin (2005)). While he did not create the networks that make up the Internet, he did develop two important technologies that made global information sharing possible:

---

[3]   For information on "open source" see <http://directory.fsf.org/>.

[4]   "Free" is defined by GNU as providing users with "the freedom to run, copy, distribute, study, change, and improve the software" <http://www.gnu.org/philosophy/free-sw.html>.

[5]   For categories of free software, see <http://www.gnu.org/philosophy/categories.html>; for a "free" software directory; see <http://news.zdnet.com/2100-3513_22-5934144.html>.

1. HyperText Transfer Protocol (HTTP), the technological infrastructure that makes information accessible from a server to a computer through a software application known as a Web browser.

2. HyperText Modern Language (HTML), the technical language used to make information on a Web page viewable on a computer.

With the introduction of these and other new communications technologies, electronic commerce and business applications have emerged that have have redefined the nature of work and organization. Casey (1998, at p. 7) elaborates:

> Electronic commerce is the buying and selling of goods and services using a variety of technologies singly or in combination. These tools include the Web, electronic data interchange (EDI), e-mail, electronic funds transfer (EFT), electronic catalogs and credit and smart cards. In contrast, electronic business is the leveraging of these same technology tools to redefine core business processes and thereby improve the performance of the enterprise and to reduce operating costs.

Arnant (2002) has pointed out that this "'redefining' process can be applied to just about any area of a business or organization: sales and marketing, accounting and finance, training and education, customer service, manufacturing or new business development" (p. 7).

With the current wave of e-commerce and business applications well advanced, ICT has evolved into Web-based applications (not just Web sites) that are hosted externally to the organization by way of an "application service provider" (ASP). McDonald (2003, at p. 2) defines these Web Services, as a movement "away from transactional-based business processes to a service oriented approach, often involving collaboration of multiple organisations to provide an integrated service to customers". The rationale behind Web Service Technology (WST) has less to do with the inadequacy and performance of older technologies and more do with the cost and performance challenges of developing technologies that can be accessed and shared within a network environment. For more details on the use of WST and other online tools in nonprofits see: <www.compasspoint.org/enonprofit/>.

Though there is limited information on the uptake of partnerships between nonprofits and private sector WST firms, a review of the literature suggests that there is a history of "partnering" between nonprofits and software developers. As a result, many nonprofits are moving to adopt computer operating systems (*e.g.*, Linux) and "open source" software applications that allow them to use their own resources (*e.g.*, virtual software development volunteers) to further develop and make use of WSTs for free.[6] For information on the history of this movement see: <http://www.gnu.org/gnu/thegnuproject. html>. For information on the nature of "partnering" to produce electronic systems and services see Langford & Harrison (2001).

With ICT now well advanced, and a new generation of the Internet fast approaching, organizations are rethinking their institutional arrangements in order to "combine the advantages of small scale with the economies of scale provided by 'clusters' and networks" (OECD, 2000, p. 9). In this new context "collective innovation is fed by the interaction among a variety of learning players within multidisciplinary technological networks" (Antonelli, Guena & Steinmueller (2000, at p. 90)). It is this combination that "has emerged as the dominant mode of organization and the production of new knowledge" in the new economy (Antonelli *et al.*, at p. 90).

WHAT ARE THE COMMON TYPES OF ICT APPLICATIONS?

With the number and range of ICT tools now well advanced, the concern of many nonprofit managers is in knowing what types of ICT applications to use and how to make effective use of them. In considering the different kinds of ICT applications available, it might prove helpful to review some of them within the four broad components of nonprofit management — people; operations; financial resources; and performance.

People

There are a number of ICT applications on the market designed for the purpose of engaging and managing people. Email, instant messaging, Web-conferencing, and online learning are examples of direct communications applications that have transformed the way people share information and interact. Indirect applications, on the other hand, are those that facilitate engagement by way of a third party. For example, information is shared with a large number of people by way of a Web Blog, or Real Simple Service (RSS) feed (*i.e.*, digital text is translated

---

[6] For information on the motivations of "free and open source" software developers, see: <http://freesoftware.mit.edu/papers/lakhaniwolf.pdf>.

to digital audio to be placed on a digital audio device like an iPod). In the former case, ICT applications mimic or extend traditional forms of engagement. In the latter, they involve new forms of engagement.

Direct ICT Applications

Email

Defined by Wikipedia (2005) as "a method of composing, sending, storing and receiving messages over electronic communication systems" (*i.e.*, through a computer, email software application and Internet network), email brings people who are physically or geographically separated, together. Email is thought to provide nonprofit organizations with many benefits. At the individual level, email provides a new means of communicating internally with staff, board members, and volunteers and externally with colleagues in other organizations, community groups, funding and regulatory bodies, as well as actual and prospective donors (see Gilbert (2003); Murray & Harrison (2002a)).

In Canada, email is generally widely adopted. Murray and Harrison (2002a) showed that 86 per cent of a national sample of voluntary organizations they surveyed made use of email to meet organizational purposes such as sharing information externally with colleagues in other organizations and internally with paid staff. On the other hand, at that time, email was much less used in the management of volunteers. For example, 74 per cent of respondents used it for communicating with volunteers about meetings or events, 64 per cent used it to communicate about specific jobs or work schedules, and 53 per cent used it to send recognition messages for good work. The use of email applications to share information with members or other interested stakeholders in the organizations through such tools as listserves was even less (27 per cent), and more advanced applications such as obtaining feedback from them through electronic surveys was very rare (6 per cent). No doubt these figures will have increased since this survey was conducted in 2002 but they reveal the tendency of nonprofits to neglect the application of ICT to volunteers, members and external stakeholders relative to staff.

In his 2003 book, *The Basics of Nonprofit Email*, leading nonprofit ICT consultant Michael Gilbert questions whether email is having as positive an impact on nonprofits as it could. Though he refers to email as the "killer application" of the Internet, he is quick to point out that, as the Canadian research showed, nonprofits "have only scratched the surface" of email use and usefulness. He points to survey data he collected from 900 U.S. nonprofit organizations that showed (at p. 17):

- 44% of organizations had email addresses for fewer than 20% of their supporters;

- 64% did not collect email addresses on their Web site;

- 75% could not survey their stakeholders online;

- 78% did not have an email strategy.

He suggests that nonprofits should use email to build relationships, share (*e.g.*, electronic newsletters) and collect information (*e.g.*, electronic questionnaires), connect with prospective and traditional donors, and promote the sale of goods and services ("e-commerce"). As an example of the benefits of doing this, he reports that nonprofits that used email to survey their stakeholders were five times more likely to be able to do email fundraising (p. 22). Gilbert (2003) uses the following keywords as the basis for his advice to nonprofits wanting to increase their effectiveness through the use of email:

Collect

Never pass up an opportunity to collect an email address. Gilbert (2003) describes access to email addresses as the "most important level of engagement" (p. 32). He suggests nonprofit Web sites be set up to collect email addresses on each Web page. As well, nonprofits should ensure that in every form of communication, the opportunity to collect email addresses is presented. For information on the use of email marketing see: <http://www.charityvillage.com/cv/research/rmed 36.html>.

Respond

Treat email as you would the telephone. In the private sector, many managers believe that not answering a telephone call from a customer translates into loss of the customer. Not answering email is similar. Gilbert suggests that "people expect email to be returned on much the same schedule as they expect phone messages to be returned, but many organizations fail to meet that expectation" (p. 34). In the context of online recruitment system use, Harrison & Murray (2006) report findings that suggest nonprofit managers who fail to use ICT effectively will not only lose contact with the prospective volunteer but may suffer the social consequences of having the prospective volunteer say negative things about their experience.

Humanize

Communicate in the online world the same way you would in the offline world. Gilbert argues for a "human" response to email communications. He cites Locke, Levine, Searls & Weinberger's (2001) *The Cluetrain Manifesto* as the impetus for "genuineness in communication between people" even when some of those communications take place in the online world (p. 34). They describe 95 theses about online markets. The first is in knowing that "markets are conversations" (p. 1). Gilbert describes how communications in the online world can be thought of "as the very lifeblood of an organization … an invitation to deeper engagement" (p. 34).

Responsible

Take responsibility for email by safeguarding your contacts and accessing new ones responsibly. Gilbert suggests using email to "convert existing stakeholders to the new channel of communication" (p. 33). He cautions against purchasing email lists as they "create the slippery slope toward becoming a spammer" (p. 33). To establish new email relationships, Gilbert suggests asking stakeholders to introduce you to their contacts. New relationships are more likely to develop if an existing relationship is in place.

Trusting

Manage email relationships in a way that builds trust. Gilbert suggests giving stakeholders control over how they wish to be involved. According to Friedman, Kahn & Howe (2000), giving stakeholders control over how they wish to be involved in the online environment helps to build a trusting relationship by "easing cooperation among people and fostering reciprocal care-taking" (p. 34). Another way to build trust electronically is to let stakeholders know that your organization has adopted a code of ethics for online conduct. There are several useful codes of conduct available to assist nonprofits in this regard. One code that relates to email comes from TRUSTe, a nonprofit email accrediting organization. TRUSTe offers a privacy seal based on an assessment of email practices (see <http://www.truste.org/businesses/email_privacy_seal.php> for more information). E-philanthropy.org has developed a code of conduct that describes expectations for nonprofit online behaviour. The code was initially developed for the purpose of "fostering the effective and safe use of the Internet for philanthropic purposes" but can be used for any application (see <http://www.ephilanthropy.org/site/DocServer/ePhilan thropy_Code_of_Ethics.doc?docID=101>).

Relationship

Use email to build relationships first, content second. Gilbert describes an overabundance of "issueheads" in nonprofits. He says that "issue-heads" are those "deeply engaged with the subject matter of their work" (p. 37). He claims that being "issue" oriented "can lead non-profits to have a deeper relationship with the content that they send to their supporters, rather than with the supporters themselves" (p. 37). He argues that the direction of email communications should flow from relationship to content, not the other way around. To build effective email relationships, Gilbert suggests nonprofits adopt electronic newsletters because the cost is lower than print and the opportunity for stakeholder engagement is high, particularly when the newsletter contains electronic links to the sending agency.

For information on open source software to strategically manage and keep track of nonprofit constituent communications see: <http:// www.openngo.org/aboutcivicrm>. For information on low-cost databases see: <http://www.idealware.org/articles/fgt_low_cost_dbs.php>.

Instant Messaging (IM)

Defined by Wikipedia (2005) as "the act of instantly communicating between two or more people over a network such as the Internet" (see <http://en.wikipedia.org/wiki/Instant_messaging>), IM puts millions of users in direct person-to-person communication with one another. It is mostly useful in the work world when one needs to have direct and immediate contact with others at a distance and a telephone is not available or desirable. Wikipedia (2005) reports that of all IM applications, America Online's AOLs Instant Messenger has the most active users at 53 million, followed by Microsoft's MSN Messenger at 29 million and Yahoo! Messenger at 21 million.

One potential application of this could be in the area of volunteer management as a way of contacting volunteers or putting volunteers in touch with one another, especially at certain times, such as while a special event or campaign is underway. Former United Nations

Volunteers co-ordinator Jayne Cravens recently wrote that she prefers IM to email because it is much easier "to build a relationship with a volunteer and get much more of an idea of his or her personality via IM than email". What Cravens is referring to is the capability of IM to provide users with "presence". (See (<http://www.techsoup.org/fb/index.cfm?fuseaction=forums.showSingleTopic&forum=2019&id=48669&cid=117&cg=searchterms&sg=IM>.)

While IM has a number of functions, Richards (2001) does caution against using IM applications for file sharing because of copyright violation. He recommends that managers become aware of the legal implications of file sharing and adopt ethical file sharing practices to ensure compliance with copyright law (Richards (2001)). For open-source IM software see: <http://directory.fsf.org/livecomm/chat/IM/>.

Web Conferencing

Web-conferencing applications combine a number of ICT components to provide audio, video, instant messaging and file sharing capability within an online "community of practice". While providing partici-pants with as much information as a traditional on-site meeting would provide, most Web-conferencing software applications can be downloaded and accessed over the Internet. There is one application on the market that incorporates free Internet telephone (*e.g.*, <www.skype.com>) to provide nonprofits with a low-cost Web-conferencing solution (see <www.nortia.com> for NetPresenter). For open-source Web-conference software see <http://directory.fsf.org/livecomm/conference/>). For information on the use of Web-conferencing applications see: <http://www.charityvillage.com/cv/research/rtech3.html>.

Online Learning

In the "knowledge economy", a number of applications exist to inform and educate managers about nonprofits and nonprofit work. One application that has been informing managers in Canada about non-profit management issues since 2002 is the Voluntary Sector Knowl-edge Network (VSKN) (<www.vskn.ca>). Run out of the Centre for Nonprofit Management in Victoria, British Columbia, VSKN is an interactive online learning site which offers knowledge and manage-ment support in the following two ways:

- The *Read About It* component offers a vast array of information and materials about a topic gleaned from scouring the Web for the "best sites".

- The *Ask a Mentor* component offers one on one online mentoring sessions, for a limited time, with experts in the various areas of non-profit management (<http://www.vskn.ca/vskn.htm>).

There are a number of other similar sources of online nonprofit management education in Canada though most do not have an interactive component. Among them are the library of Imagine Canada (<http://www.nonprofitscan.ca/>), and the "Resources and Library" area of Charity Village (<http://www.charityvillage.com/CV/charity village/ires.asp>). Each of these in turn will direct the reader to many other more specific Canadian websites with educational content such as those of the United Way/Centraide, Volunteer Canada, Community Foundations Canada, *etc*.

With respect to the effectiveness of online learning tools, Dziuban, Moskal & Dziuban (2000) claim that they have created a new context for learning. Within this context, user and content deliverer roles have shifted. For users, the role is that of responsible "life-long learners" who are in charge of what they learn and how they interact with the new media. For the content deliverer, the role is of "facilitator of incremental and interactive cyber pedagogy" (p. 174). While the learning context has changed, they present research that shows most learners prefer a "mixed" learning environment that combines online and traditional pedagogy. For information on online learning in Canada see: <http://www.charityvillage.com/cv/research/rdl.html>. For open source education software see: <http://directory.fsf.org/education/>.

Indirect ICT Applications

Blogs

This relatively recent phenomenon has been defined by Smith, Kearns & Fine (2005) as "web-based applications used to post journal-like commentaries" (p. 36) hence the name "blogs" for "Web logs". According to Sifry (2005), there are currently about 18.9 million blogs, a number that he says "has doubled every five months for the past three years" (p. 2). "Bloggers" are individuals who informally publish their opinions in the online environment using text, images, media objects and data.

Rudolf (2005) describes two types of blogs: "aggregation" and "open-ended". Aggregation blogs are issue-specific whereas open-ended blogs place no restriction on blogger content. Open-ended blogs allow for free access (*i.e.*, any blogger can participate) while issue-specific blogs may place restrictions on participation (*e.g.*, must be a registered or be approved blogger to join). Nonprofits can make use of blogs to become informed about issues or to engage "issueheads". For more information on nonprofit use of blogs and blogging applications see: <http://www.charityvillage.com/cv/research/rtech32.html>. For an example of a free blogging application see: <http://www.blogger.com>; for a listing of open-source blogging applications see: <http://directory.fsf.org/search/fsd-search.py?q=blogging>.

Podcasting

"Podcasting's essence is about creating content (audio or video) for an audience that wants to listen or watch when they want, where they want, and how they want" (<http://en.wikipedia.org/wiki/Podcasting>). Using Really simple Syndication (RSS) feed, podcasts allow written material to be transformed into audio or video formats and vice versa.

While no data exists on the use of podcasts by nonprofits, the rate of adoption of RSS feeds is staggering. Hart, Pierson & Hull (2005) cite statistics that showed over 1,700 RSS feeds were available for podcasting within the six months of being made available: see <http://www.burningdoor.com/feedburner/archives/001029.html>. Podcasting is potentially a useful tool in nonprofits for a number of reasons:

1. It provides busy managers with an opportunity to listen to information that they have little time to read (*e.g.*, in the car radio by way of an FM transmitter).

2. It reduces the amount of work by providing a means of translating audio into digital text (*e.g.*, minutes of board meetings).

3. It can increase knowledge and transparency (*e.g.*, by sharing RSS feeds with others on specific topics or posting them on the organization's Web site).

For information on Podcasting see: <http://en.wikipedia.org/wiki/Pod casting#Regular_radio-based_podcasts>.

Operations

Web Sites

The use of the Internet and its billions of Web sites has become more and more diverse and sophisticated in recent years. This makes the value of Web sites for managing many aspects of the nonprofit organization more important than ever. A Web site consists of a series of HTML Web pages. The pages of a Web site will be accessed from a common root Universal Resource Locator (URL) called the homepage, and usually reside on the same physical server. The URLs of the pages organize them into a hierarchy, although the hyperlinks between them control how the reader perceives the overall structure and how the traffic flows between the different parts of the sites.

Having private (internal) and public (external) sides or interfaces, Web sites can be customized or created using a standard template. For many small nonprofits and voluntary associations, a template that provides public and private member access is all that is needed. In Canada, nonprofits can create a free Web site for themselves at <http://www.envision.ca/tools/memberwebs.asp>. For an example of a source of low-cost Web sites, see <www.clubvpa.com>. For medium to large nonprofits, a custom-designed site is usually more appropriate. For information on access to open source Web site tools see: <http://directory.fsf.org/webauth/content/>. For general use of nonprofit Web sites see: <http://www.charityvillage.com/cv/research/rtech47.html>.

Cukier & Middleton (2003) report that nonprofits in Canada use Web sites to share information, fundraise, conduct advocacy, provide member support, develop community and recruit volunteers. However, 80 per cent of these sites are used for "information provision and organizational promotion" only (p. 109). Harrison, Murray & Mac-Gregor (2004) assessed how NPOs in Canada were making use of Web sites specifically for the purpose of managing their volunteer program according to the following four levels of "e-connectivity":

- Level 1: Web sites used for "hosting information" about the volunteer program.

- Level 2: Web sites used for hosting information as well as interactive features such as online volunteer applications, listservs, or online survey capabilities.

- Level 3: Level 2 features as well as the capability of accessing other databases remotely by those within the organization.

- Level 4: Level 3 features as well as access to internal databases by "outsiders" across organizations.

While overall access to Web sites in the volunteer programs they surveyed (total n=494) was high (90 per cent in a national e-enabled sample (n=365); 78 per cent in a regional traditional sample (n=129)), the overall level of e-connectivity was low at 1.5. This finding indicates that most volunteer programs were making use of their Web sites solely to host information about their volunteer programs. Fewer were using their sites to interact with their members and volunteers (level 2, interactivity, was 20 per cent) and a very small percentage were using them at the remaining levels of interactivity.

According to private sector financial systems expert Juliana Cafik, the key to getting the most value out of an organizational Web site is to think of it in terms of how it can help meet business objectives. Once overall objectives have been established and agreed upon, a technological strategy should be identified to achieve them. With respect to what kinds of strategies should be incorporated into Web sites, Michael Gilbert (2003) suggests that nonprofits incorporate "email strategies" into them (*e.g.*, include interactive forms that allow nonprofits to collect email addresses and sort information within a database). Grobman (2001) provides more guidance by classifying Web site strategies into "push" and "pull" categories. Push strategies are those that "enable content providers to automatically 'push' information to users of their service" (*e.g.*, through an electronic mailing list) (p. 95). "Pull" strategies on the other hand, require that the user take the initiative to "acquire the information" (p. 95) (*e.g.*, looking up a topic in the virtual library or completing an online registration form).

Along with push and pull strategies, Grobman encourages nonprofits to pay attention to the *design* of their Web site as well as its content. For example, they should consider the speed at which the Web site loads, its ease of use, the accuracy and timeliness of information posted, its scalability (how easily it can grow with increased traffic) and its capability for facilitating nonprofit work (*e.g.*, interaction, collaboration and service delivery). For a directory of open-source Web site systems see: <http://directory.fsf.org/webauth/content/>.

Schultz & Fristedt (2005) also suggest that nonprofits monitor the popularity of their Web sites and determine whether it is "optimized — that is easily found among the multitude of other sites a seeker may happen upon" (p. 8). Nonprofits can check on the optimization level of their Web sites through a process Schultz and Fristedt refer to as "search engine optimization (SEO)". This type of information provides the nonprofit with information about the likelihood that their Web site will be found if actively searched (Schultz & Fristedt (2005)). To check Web site optimization levels see: <http://www.linkpopularitycheck.com/>.

Virtual Volunteering

ICT can be a useful means to facilitate different activities associated with the volunteering process. Whereas in traditional volunteering, each step of the process is carried out through face-to-face interaction with those in the voluntary organization, now the individual volunteer can use ICT to search for volunteer opportunities, select an organization to volunteer for, and perform specific forms of work at a physical distance from the organization. For the manager of volunteer resources, the process is similar. The virtual volunteer manager may use ICT to perform any or all necessary functions at a physical distance from the volunteer, from identifying the need for volunteers and the nature of the work required to searching for and locating a potential pool of volunteers (recruitment), making selections, putting them to work, and overseeing their performance. The hope is that this use of ICT will increase volunteering by providing volunteer program managers with new tools for performing volunteer work and reaching and recruiting more volunteers from traditional sources and from new sources such as the ICT community, youth, those who are housebound or those who face time and travel restrictions.

The extent to which ICT is used to find and perform volunteer work at a physical distance is very low in Canada as it is in the U.S. (Brudney (1999); Murray and Harrison (2002b; 2005)). Murray & Harrison (2002b; 2005) report that while "pure" virtual volunteering is rare, the majority of prospective volunteers who use ICT do so to look for volunteer work but perform it on-site. The same holds true for managers of volunteer programs in that they use ICT to recruit volunteers to do work on site. This finding suggests that, whereas ICT appears to be accepted as a means for finding volunteers, its value as a means for performing work is less established.

When ICT is used for work, the typical tasks virtual volunteers perform are those that involve the use of ICT such as desktop publishing, research, Web site development and fundraising (see Cravens (2000); Murray & Harrison (2002b; 2005); Tyler (2002); <www.unv. org>). However, it has been shown that virtual volunteers can also perform direct service delivery work such as mentoring agency clients by email and telephone (Cravens (2000)). This suggests that, in addition to those tasks that require ICT use, it is possible to re-engineer volunteer work to include tasks that have typically been thought of as requiring face-to-face interaction. This will require that managers identify volunteer position requirements first, ensure the technological infrastructure is in place to meet them, then actively recruit virtual volunteers and manage them as they would any other volunteer — albeit through technological means (*i.e.*, use ICT to communicate about a position or schedule, gather information, provide support, track and monitor work, and provide recognition).

With regard to the demographic profile of the virtual volunteer, online recruitment users in Canada are more likely than volunteers who find work in traditional ways to be young, new to volunteering, female, educated and motivated to volunteer in order to learn new skills or find paid employment (Murray & Harrison (2002b; 2005)).

Though virtual volunteers can be found in existing volunteer programs, the best source of them is online. Murray & Harrison (2002b) found that users of online recruitment systems were significantly more likely than traditional volunteers to have virtual volunteer experience. The key to "landing" a virtual volunteer is to make early contact with them. About half of the prospective volunteers that had been in email contact with a volunteer agency about a volunteer position were recruited. For more information on how to build and manage a virtual volunteer program see: <www.serviceleader.org>.

Financial Resources

Online Fundraising

Of all the nonprofit ICT applications on the market, online giving or e-Philanthropy applications appear to have generated the most interest.

While no estimates are available for Canada, ePhilanthropy (2005) reports that giving in the United States in 2004 reached over five billion dollars worldwide with online giving representing approximately half of this amount (2.62 billion USD). The increase in online giving is thought to be "driven by significant increases in online giving for both small and large organizations and the unprecedented use of the Internet for tsunami and hurricane relief efforts ..." (<http://www.imakenews.com/ephilanthropy/e_article000413576.cfm?x=b5wpwKf,b3D0cyPh,w>). Shaver (2006) offers the following statistics as a way of predicting the acceptance of online giving in Canadian nonprofits:

> The estimated 45% of donations to Hurricane Katrina made online was higher than the 22% for the tsunami, which in turn was higher than the percentage for any previous disaster — including 9/11. Nonprofits are taking note, and fewer will be on the digital sidelines in 2006.

See <http://www.canadianfundraiser.com/newsletter/article.asp?ArticleID=1859>.

While the potential for online giving is great, Grobman (2001) cautions that nonprofits consider the following factors[7] prior to adopting an online giving/fundraising strategy:

1. *Legal*. New Antiterrorism legislation adopted in Canada after the September 11, 2001 attacks on the United States includes money-laundering legislation. The federal government of Canada has set up a Financial Action Task Force (FATF) to sort through the policy implications of the legislation. According to its Web site: "the FATF is an intergovernmental body whose purpose is the development and promotion of national and international policies to combat money laundering and terrorist financing" (see <www.fatf-gafi.org/pages/0,2987,en_32250379_32235720_1_1_1_1_1,00.html>). As part of a "due diligence", nonprofits will need to review and consider the implications of this legislation on online fundraising before engaging in e-commerce activities.

2. *Ethical*. Nonprofits should also be aware of the threat that online fundraising may be used fraudulently. It is up to nonprofit managers and boards of directors to protect individual donors. One way to ensure authenticity is to include online giving/fundraising in a code of ethics. The Salvation Army, for example, has adopted a Code of Fundraising Ethics, which lays out SA's

---

[7]   Grobman's considerations are expanded to reflect the Canadian nonprofit context.

fundraising "obligations" for individual donors (see <http://www.salvationarmy.ca/fundraisingethics>).

3. *Tax.* As of 2005, the Canada Revenue Agency (CRA) requires that registered charities include the CRA's Web site on all charitable donation receipts. The CRA also requires that all online receipts be delivered in an unalterable format (*e.g.*, PDF document).

4. *Service Provider.* Nonprofits must consider the costs associated with developing e-commerce capability. E-commerce involves technical providers using software to facilitate the transaction between the giver and bank. Many e-commerce providers are private technology companies that take a percentage of the donation to make a profit (*e.g.*, to facilitate the transaction between the donor and the bank). The banks also take a percentage of the transaction to cover processing costs. It is important to know that while e-commerce is a standard and "seamless" practice, it involves a host of relationships.

5. *Marketing.* Once the e-commerce service is operational, nonprofits must be sure to market it vigorously. Promoting online sites through direct email marketing is important as is ensuring Web site search engines are updated with the appropriate key words or "meta tags".

For an example of open source fundraising and contact management system see <http://directory.fsf.org/calendula.html>; for an example of an open source nonprofit funding application see <http://directory.fsf.org/productivity/special/affero.html>; for tips on selecting an online fundraising database see <http://www.idealware.org/articles/ten_common_mistakes_in_selecting_donor_databases.php>; for an online giving software report see <http://www.idealware.org/donations/idealware_online_donations.pdf>.

Performance

Performance management is an aspect of nonprofit reform that places emphasis on accountability and value for money (Light (2000); Cutt & Murray (2000)). Light notes that the call for greater accountability and levels of performance comes from a number of sources, including current reforms in the government and business sectors, government legislation, and funders and clients wanting to determine the appropriateness and responsiveness of services. ICT provides nonprofits with new means to collect performance measures such as "the number of clients served, client demographics, satisfaction of clients, and initial and immediate outcomes" (Collins (2003, at p. 3)). While manual methods can be used to collect and keep track of information, Collins states that the use of ICT allows nonprofits to "streamline" what is often perceived as a difficult and time-consuming process. He provides four reasons why ICT applications should be adopted by nonprofit organizations:

1. Digital information can be indexed, sorted, and cross-tabulated in more complex ways than are feasible in a manual system.

2. Computerized systems can store far more data much faster and, given an appropriate back-up system, more securely.

3. Computerized systems can standardize data collection, much like using forms does, but also offers opportunities to integrate data systems from other areas in the agency, such as billing to create an enterprise wide-database that reduces redundant work efforts.

4. ICT allows for the collection and analysis of different kinds of data such as qualitative or "soft" data (*e.g.*, Collins describes that qualitative data can be collected systematically as a result of data "coding", while analysis can produce outcomes by way of "results mapping".

While Collins (2003) recommends that nonprofits adopt ICT methods in this regard, he also asks that they do not adopt them blindly. He advocates due diligence in determining the suitability of performance measurement ICT applications by:

(a) reviewing the capability of existing ICT applications;

(b) reviewing other ICT applications in relation to existing applications;

(c) involving staff and stakeholders in the purchase and/or design, training and evaluation of new ICT applications, and the development of performance measures.

While all too often the responsibility for ICT rests in the hands of technical experts (*e.g.*, developers and vendors), Collins claims that "careful planning, implementation flexibility, and a clear strategy will guide the process towards creating maximum value" (p. 7). For a comprehensive list of performance measurement software applications see: <http://www.gse.harvard.edu/hfrp/content/eval/issue27/harris_table.pdf>. For open source examples see: <http://directory.fsf.org/search/fsd-search.py?q=performance+assessment>.

One way to ensure that the use of ICT applications adds business value to the nonprofit organization is to adopt an IT performance management framework. A good example is Van Grembergen (2000) IT balanced score card (IT BSC). The IT BSC is a take-off of Kaplan & Norton's (1992), balanced score card approach (BSC), a framework to organize and monitor an organization's performance in relation to its strategic plan. The BSC originally emerged in the private sector as a way to identify performance measures beyond the financial level (*e.g.*, financial, customer, innovation and learning, and internal business perspectives). While originating in the for-profit world, the BSC has also been used to assess performance in the public and nonprofit context (see Cutt & Murray (2000); Kaplan (2001)).

Van Grembergen (2000) borrows the BSC logic to create an IT-enabled BSC framework to ensure IT "returns business value" to the organization. Like the BSC, the IT BSC approach includes a variety of performance measures at different levels of analysis, including the level of the user, operations, business contribution and future orientation. Van Grembergen elaborates further on the use of this framework (p. 1124):

> Each of these perspectives has to be translated into corresponding metrics and measures that assess the current situation. These assessments have to be repeated periodically and have to be confronted with goals that have to be set beforehand and with benchmarking figures. Very essential is that within an IT BSC the cause-and-effect relationships are established and the connections between the two types of measures, outcome measures and performance drivers, are clarified.

He argues for the inclusion of independent and dependent variable relationships within the framework to illustrate the inter-connectedness of perspectives. Figure 1 provides an illustration of the causal logic Van Grembergen describes in his article.

Figure 1: Illustration of Van Grembergen's IT BSC from an Individual Level Perspective

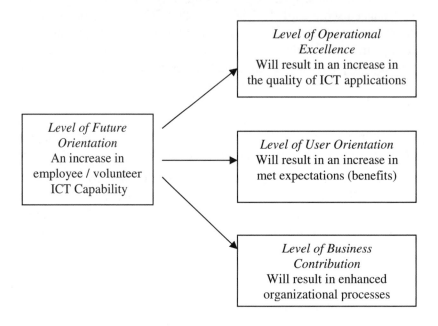

Adopting ICT performance measurement tools and an IT BSC approach to monitoring the use of them can assist nonprofits in determining the effectiveness of ICT from different perspectives and at different levels of analysis (*e.g.*, individual, organizational, work, program, client, formal and informal stakeholders, community, society).

HOW MUCH SUCCESS HAVE NONPROFITS HAD WITH THE USE OF ICT TOOLS?

Even though survey research has indicated that Canada is a leader in terms of funding and voluntary sector access to ICT (Pargmegiani & Sachdeva (2000)), the leadership, according to several evaluations, stops there (Phillips (2000); Schneider (2003)). One report based on the VolNet program experience (through which 10,000 voluntary organizations in Canada were provided with computers, software, and the Internet) revealed that the program had failed to achieve its original objective. The numerous problems found with the program included "ill-defined mandate, poor communication … overly ambitious targets … and an inability to develop online resources and further partnerships

... stressed in its original plan" (Phillips (2000, p. 2)). Brock (2002, at p. 7) also cited problems with this strategy:

> The strategy is incomplete because it lacks a small picture view. More specifically, it must evolve beyond "network" or infrastructure goals and should include a focus on the finer details of knowledge and skills development as well as expanded "opportunities and resources" and "knowledge about implementation".

A 2001 research study conducted by *Volunteersonline* and sponsored by the Province of Ontario on Internet usage echoed concerns similar to those voiced by Phillips and Brock. This study, *Making IT Work for Volunteers*, examined how connected voluntary organizations were and how much ICT they had access to. The study report concluded that there was significant progress in the area of connectivity and basic access to the Internet but, at the same time, much of the voluntary sector lacks the tools, training and financial resources necessary to use the Internet strategically and effectively (Volunteers online (2001)).

A similar theme was noted in research findings from the U.S. and U.K. (Hall Aitken (2001); Pitkin & Manzo (2002); Princeton Survey Research Associates (2001); Ticher, Maison & Jones (2002)). For example, in the U.S., Pitkin & Manzo's (2002) study of ICT use by nonprofit organizations in the Los Angeles region showed that, while these organizations were well equipped with the basic tools, they were not making effective use of them. Schneider (2003) suggested that in the U.S. ICT use in the nonprofit sector has "raised the bar for many kinds of agency administrative activities, making it difficult for agencies lacking resources to compete" (p. 391). As a result, new expectations and structural issues are emerging within the sector, and, in the small minority-based nonprofit organizations she studied, Schneider found that "IT is becoming an additional problem rather than a way to make these NPOs work easier" (p. 395). Similarly, in the U.K., Hall & Aitken (2001) reported that while the Internet had improved the delivery of services to clients, and provided organizational benefits in terms of increases in efficiency, there were also barriers to ICT use including managerial attitudes ("ICT is not recognized by senior management and/or management committees") and a lack of ongoing support and training. Another U.K. study by Ticher, Maison & Jones (2002) revealed that the biggest barriers to effective ICT use are internal and included a lack of managerial "vision" about how best to use it and "confidence and determination to take ideas forward" as well as a lack of capacity to develop, implement and manage complex ICT projects (p. 2).

WHAT FACTORS INFLUENCE THE ADOPTION AND USE OF ICT APPLICATIONS?

One recent approach to understanding the factors that influence the adoption and use of ICT can be found in the research of Harrison and Murray (see Murray & Harrison (2002a); Harrison, Murray & Mac-Gregor (2004); Harrison & Murray (2006)). This work found that barriers to adoption and use of ICT in the volunteer management context exist along several dimensions. For example, there is evidence of barriers at the level of the *individual* (*e.g.*, work experience), the *organization* (*e.g.*, size of budget, job stress), the *social group* (*e.g.*, amount of involvement of staff in new applications and decisions), and the *technical systems* (*e.g.*, prior experience with ICT, ease of use of systems) levels. Moreover, different barriers influence different types of ICTs resulting in different patterns of effectiveness suggesting that ICT effectiveness is not a singular but rather, a multidimensional construct (see Harrison, Murray & MacGregor (2004)).

This work also found that levels of adoption and effective use of ICT applications in volunteer management varied according to type of user and ICT application being used. This was consistent with the innovation diffusion literature, which contends that the factors associated with the adoption of innovations change over time as they become more accepted and used (Rogers (2003); van Dijk & Hacker (2003)). This finding is also consistent with the information system success literature which supports the notion that different usage contexts will have different measures of effectiveness (Seddon, Staples, Patnayakuni & Bowtell (1999)).

Factors Associated with ICT Availability for Volunteer Programs

The amount of information and communications technology adopted by managers of volunteer programs was associated with demographic characteristics and their prior experience with ICT. At the level of demographics, gender was a factor, with male managers more likely to have adopted more ICT than female managers. Other factors were related to prior experience. Specifically, the more years of experience in using ICT, the more ICT was adopted. It is also positively related to

ICT confidence, with managers who were the most positive in their feelings of capability having adopting the most. Not surprisingly, the more experience female managers had with ICT, the more positive their feelings of capability and the more they adopted. This observation suggests that even though volunteer programs having male managers tend to be predisposed to more physical access to ICT, the gender divide in volunteer programs exists only until such time as female managers gain experience with ICT.

At the organizational level, the findings showed a "size divide", with large volunteer organizations with budgets greater than $250,000 having adopted the most ICT. The findings further suggest that organizational slack (surplus resources), rather than volunteer program innovation, may account for the digital divide between large and small sized volunteer programs.

The most influential factor related to ICT adoption by volunteer programs was demand for volunteers. As demand increased, so did the amount of ICT adopted. This finding suggests that availability of ICT in volunteer programs is associated with need, with larger volunteer programs in excess of 75 volunteers demonstrating the most need.

Participation in training and involvement in decisions related to ICT were also positively associated with the amount of ICT adopted by volunteer programs. This finding is consistent with the innovation diffusion literature, which has described innovative organizations as more participative and therefore more prone to ICT adoption (Rogers (2003)).

Finally, the more positive the perception that ICT resulted in net benefits in the volunteer program, the more ICT the managers reported adopting in their volunteer programs.

Factors Associated with How Much ICT Is Actually Used

It is one thing to acquire the computers and software that make up ICT but this does not always mean it will be fully or effectively used. The Harrison and Murray research attempted to look separately at availability and actual use. For example, even though gender was related to the amount of ICT available, it was not significantly related to its use. Conversely, the volunteer programs that were predisposed to using ICT to fill volunteer opportunities and have work performed virtually were those in which their managers were *newer* to the job. This finding suggests that differences in the use of ICT may be attributed to an "experience divide" between those who are newer to the position and those who have spent more time performing "old ways" of volunteer management.

At another level, participation by the manager in ICT and other policy decisions in the organization combined with feelings of ownership of them were positively associated with the use of ICT to fill volunteer opportunities and have work performed virtually. Similarly, participation in deciding on a new ICT application such as online recruitment was positively associated with its adoption and use. Clearly the more involved and integrated the volunteer program manager is with organizational decision-making the more ICT will be used.

The more demanding the manager perceived the job to be, the more ICT was used. Similar findings were found at the work level, lending further support for the positive association between demand and use of ICT in volunteerism. For example, the more virtual volunteers the manager had placed in the volunteer program, the more likely the manager had used an online recruitment system to contact them about a position. Similarly, the more that managers used the Internet as a means of communication, the more likely they used ICT to fill volunteer opportunities and have volunteer work performed. These findings lend support to the earlier claim that the more use or experience managers have with ICT in a particular context, the more uses will be found for it in that same context.

It was also found that the easier ICT applications were to learn and the higher the perceived quality and capacity of them in the volunteer program, the more ICT was used by the managers to share tasks at a distance. However, the quality of available ICT systems in the volunteer program was not significantly related to the adoption of an external Web-service application such as online recruitment. Likewise, the quality of online recruitment applications that were adopted was not significantly related to their use. These findings suggest that differences in the adoption of online recruitment may not be solely attributable to differences in the quality of the application.

Managerial perceptions that ICT is useful (or important, beneficial, and so forth) were associated with general use of ICT by managers to fill volunteer opportunities and have volunteer work performed at a distance. Similarly, perceptions that the online recruitment application was a useful tool were associated with its adoption.

All of these findings lend support for the conclusion that high expectations of benefits from ICT are a positive influence on ICT adoption. For information on how these factors integrate into a theory of ICT adoption, see Harrison & Murray (2006).

HOW SHOULD THE MANAGEMENT OF ICT CHANGE BE APPROACHED BY NONPROFITS?

While new ICT applications have provided nonprofits with improved tools for conducting their work, not all make the most effective use of them. To do this requires a new approach to the management of technological change. Remenyi, White & Sherwood-Smith (1999, p. 18) characterize ICT effectiveness in the following ways:

1. Whether or not an information system succeeds is a function of management orientation and management processes rather than the simple application of the technology itself; mechanistic solutions or processes such as the software development cycle are increasingly unlikely to deliver satisfactory results.

2. Information systems are not the property of the information systems department. Every system requires a user owner. Information systems themselves do not deliver benefits but rather facilitate improvements to business performance. This being the case, information systems benefit delivery is the responsibility of the management who requested and commissioned the system. Successful systems development needs the commitment of multiple stakeholders — both multiple primary and multiple secondary stakeholders.

3. Information system requirements evolve over time starting from the statement of the information system concept and will continue to evolve until the system is discontinued; these changes in an information system's requirements may reflect changes in information technology, business requirements or environmental conditions or business growth.

4. Information system's actualization is frequently a compromise of the requirements of the various stakeholders. When stakeholders have starter values and are prepared to ensure that the interests of their own personal domain are aligned with the interests of the organization as a whole, satisfactory results will be achieved. Thus, the information leadership role needs to be defined in terms of the ability to capture attention, create meaning, and thus shared values, and build trust.

5. A process of continuous and dynamic evaluation and debate between knowledgeable stakeholders recognizing the need for shared values,

individual autonomy and ambiguity, provides the best chance for information systems optimization.

In keeping with this approach, several practical suggestions come to mind to assist the leaders of nonprofit organizations with the management of ICT change:

1. ICT changes should be introduced in manageable pieces so that they take place over time within an evolving rather than a static process. One purpose of managing change in this way is to create opportunities for success, so that ICT does not seem overwhelming and the new demands created by ICT are not overly stressful to managers, especially those who have been in the job longer or have only been performing their work in traditional ways. Success becomes incremental and cumulative, with one successful change setting the stage for another as managers and users develop positive attitudes and experience with new applications. This represents a more flexible, longer term approach to ICT change and organizational development, a contrast to some of the more rigid approaches used to facilitate ICT reform in the past (Brock (2002); Phillips (2000)).

2. In addition, participation strategies should target individuals who are not predisposed to adopting new ICT applications in their work. Among managers, this group would include those who have been in the job for more than five years and/or who lack experience using ICT applications in a management context. It would also include individuals who are older and lack ICT literacy. The critical success factor is that users actively engage and gain experience with ICT both formally — in such activities as the design, training, and evaluation stages of new ICT applications — and informally; for example, in conversations with colleagues. Involvement in ICT can come from many sources (*e.g.*, from programs offered by vendors, local volunteer centres and professional associations) but the best source is training provided by the organization itself. Making experienced users into champions of ICT change and recognizing them for their efforts in the organization as well as more broadly within the community at large should set the stage for future success (see Murray & Harrison (2002a); Harrison & Murray (2006)).

3. The role of the ICT support specialist needs to be redefined so that it emphasizes the importance of that person as a "facilitator of change" rather than a lone problem solver who hands out solutions for others' difficulties. By playing this new role, the ICT specialist becomes an advisor/coach for the end users, thus

encouraging them to develop their own ICT capabilities and become more confident in their use.

4. Special attention should be paid to making sure that ICT applications are relevant, easy to learn, user friendly and rewarding, so users perceive them as adding positive value to their work.

5. The ICT budget should contain sufficient resources to cover the costs of ICT planning and proper introduction processes.

6. It is always necessary to monitor, measure and celebrate progress.

Failure to manage ICT change in the ways suggested may result in a digitally deficient nonprofit organization — one that lacks the capacity to meet the demands of the new economy.

CONCLUSION

Increasing the capacity of nonprofit organizations to meet the demands of the new economy requires that they understand ICT, the range of nonprofit management applications, and the factors that challenge their adoption. To be effective users of ICT, it is important that nonprofit leaders recognize that there is no "one size fits all" strategy for ICT change and that there will be competing interests and needs surrounding ICT issues. Managing ICT is thus as much about managing change as it is about mastering technology. While this task may seem daunting, the research suggests that it is worth undertaking because of the many benefits that well-planned and implemented ICT use can provide for clients in need of more efficient and responsive services, stakeholders in need of involvement and accountability, and citizens seeking to satisfy their needs for engagement in the community.

REFERENCES

Antonelli, C., A. Geuna & W. E. Steinmueller (2000), "Information and Communication Technologies and the Production, Distribution and Use of Knowledge (2000), 20:1-2 *International Journal of Technology Management* 72-94.

Arnant, G. (2002), "At the dawn of the e-evolution", *Globe and Mail*, Report on Business, November 21, pp. 6 and 11.

Blau, A. (2001), More than Bit Players: How Information Technology Will Change the Ways Nonprofits and Foundations Work and Thrive in the Information Age (New York: Surdna Foundation, 2001). Available online at: <www.surdna.org>.

Brock, K.L. (2002), "Antagonists and Allies: Voluntary Organizations, Business and the Policy Process". Paper presented at the Institute of Public Administration of Canada Meetings, Halifax (August 27, 2002).

Brudney, J. (1999), "Effective Use of Volunteers: Best Practices in the Public Sector" (1999), 62:4 *Law and Contemporary Problems* 219-255.

Burt, E., & J. A. Taylor (2000), "Information and Communication Technologies: Reshaping Voluntary Organizations" (2000), 11:2 *Nonprofit Management and Leadership* 131-143.

Cafik, J. Principal, Stonebridge Solutions, Telephone Interview, January 10, 2006.

Carvin, A. (2005), "Tim Berners Lee: Weaving a Semantic Web" (Newton, MA: EDC Center for Media & Community, 2005). Available online at: <http://www.digitaldivide.net/articles/view.php?Article ID=20>.

Casey, J. (1998), "Card-Based Purchasing and Effective Government" (1998), 1:4 *The Business of Government* 7.

Clarke, S. (2001), *Information Systems Strategic Management* (London: Routledge, 2001).

Collins, M. (2003). "Wanted: Information Technology Solutions for Problems of Measuring Outcomes." Unpublished Paper.

Compeau, D.R., C.A. Higgins & S. Huff (1999), "Social Cognitive Theory and Individual Reactions to Computing Technology: A Longitudinal Study" (1999), 23:2 *MIS Quarterly* 145-158.

Compeau, D.R., & C.A. Higgins (1995), "Computer self-efficacy: Development of a measure and initial test" (1995), 19:2 *MIS Quarterly* 189-211.

Cooper, J.C. (2004, March 22), "The Price of Efficiency". *Business Week*, pp. 38–46.

Cooper, J., & K. D. Weaver (2003), *Gender and Computers: Understanding the Digital Divide* (Manwah, NJ: Lawrence Erlbaum Associates, 2003).

Cravens, J. (2000), "Virtual Volunteering: Online Volunteers Providing Assistance to Human Services" (2000), 17:1 *Journal of Computers in Human Services* 119-136.

Cukier, W., & C. Middleton (2003), "Evaluating the Web Presence of Voluntary Sector Organizations: An Assessment of Canadian Web Sites" (2003), 1:3 *IT & Society* 102-130.

Cutt, J., & V. Murray (2000). *Accountability and Effectiveness Evaluations in Nonprofit Organizations* (London: Routledge, 2000).

De', R., & B. Mathew (1999), "Issues in the Management of Web Technologies: a Conceptual Framework" (1999), 19:6 *International Journal of Technology Management* 427-447.

Dziuban, C., P. Moskal & E. Dziuban (2000), "Reactive Behavior Patterns Go Online" (2000), 17:3 *Journal of Staff, Program, & Organizational Development* 171-182.

Ferndig, R.E., & K. D. Trammell (2004). "Content Delivery in the 'Blogosphere'" (2004), *T.H.E. Journal* 12-20.

Fountain, J. (2001), *Building the Virtual State: Information Technology and Institutional Change* (Washington, DC: Brookings Institution Press, 2001).

Friedman, B., P.H. Kahn & D.C. Howe (2000), "Trust Online" (2000), 43:12 *Communications of the ACM* 34-40.

Gilbert, M. (2003), *The Basics of Nonprofit Email* (Seattle: Gilbert Center, 2003).

Government of Canada, Parliament, House of Commons, Speech from the Throne (Adrienne Clarkson), Debates and Proceedings (Hansard). 37th Parliament, 1st Session, October 12, 1999 (Ottawa: Public Works and Government Services, 1999). Available online at: <http://www.pco-bcp.gc.ca/default.asp?Language=E&Page=InformationResources&sub=sftddt&doc=sftddt1999_e.htm>.

Grobman, G. (2001), *The Nonprofit Organization's Guide to E-commerce* (Harrisburg, PA: White Hat Communications, 2001).

Hall Aitken (2001), *E-enabling the Voluntary and Community Sectors: Final Report*. Glasgow: U.K. Government Online, Office of the E-envoy. Available online at: <www.e-envoy.gov.uk/reports-e-enabling-top/$file/index.htm>.

Hampton, K., & B. Wellman (2003), "Neighboring in Netville: How the Internet Supports Community and Social Capital in a Wired Suburb" (2003), 2:4 *City and Community* 277-311.

Harrison, Y., V. Murray & J. MacGregor (2004), *The Impact of ICT on the Management of Canadian Volunteer Programs, Information and Communications Technology: Beyond Anecdotes* (Toronto: Canadian Centre for Philanthropy, 2004).

Harrison, Y., & V. Murray (2006 forthcoming), "Bridging the Effectiveness Divide in ICT Use: The Case of Volunteer Recruitment in Canada".

Hart, P.E., K. Pierson & J.J. Hull (2005), "Refocusing Multimedia Research on Short Clips" (2005), 12:3 *IEEE Multimedia* 8-13.

Industry Canada (2002), *VolNet Final Report* (Ottawa: Government of Canada, 2002).

Ipsos Reid (2001), *Volunteer Opportunities Exchange (VOE): Summary of Findings* (Ottawa: Ipsos Reid, 2001).

Kaplan, R.S. (2001), "Strategic Performance Measurement and Management in Nonprofit Organizations" (2001), 11:3 *Nonprofit Management & Leadership* 353-370.

Kaplan, R.S., & D.P. Norton (1992), "The Balanced Scorecard-Measures that Drive Performance" (1992), 70:1 *Harvard Business Review* 71-79.

Kirschenbaum, J., & R. Kunamneni (2001), *Bridging the Organizational Divide: Toward a Comprehensive Approach to the Digital Divide* (Oakland, CA: Policy Link, 2001).

Langford J., & Y. Harrison (2000), "Partnering to Produce Electronic Government" (2000), 44:4 *Canadian Public Administration* 393-416.

Locke, C., R. Levine, D. Searls & D. Weinberger (2001), *The Cluetrain Manifesto* (New York: Perseus Publishing, 2001).

Light, P.C. (2000), *Making Nonprofits Work. A Report on the Tides of Nonprofit Management Reform* (Washington, DC: The Brookings Institution, 2000).

Ludgate, C., & M. Surman (2004), *Beyond the Box*: *Thinking Strategically about Technology Grantmaking in Canada's Voluntary Sector* (Ottawa: Government of Canada through the Voluntary Sector Initiative, 2004).

McDonald, D. (2003), *Web Services Technologies Report*. For the JISC Technology Watch Service. Available online at: <www.jisc.ac.uk/uploaded_documents/tsw_03-04.pdf>.

McLoughlin, I., & M. Harris (1997), *Innovation, Organizational Change and Technology* (London: International Thomson Business Press, 1997).

Meyer, C.A. (1997), "The Political Economy of NGOs and Information Sharing" (1997), 25:7 *World Development* 1127-1140.

Murray, J. (2003), *The Connector*. Retrieved on May 8, 2005 from http://firstsearch.oclc.org.ezproxy.library.uvic.ca/WebZ/FSPage?paget ype=return_frameset:sessionid=sp02sw11-34270-e8hq42ws-29z6z5: entitypagenum=29:0:entityframedurl=http%3A%2F%2Fgateway.uvic. ca:entityframedtitle=:linktype=librarylink:entityframedtimeout=15: entityopenTitle=:entityopenAuthor=:entityopenNumber=:

Murray, V., & Y. Harrison (2002a), "The Impact of Information and Communications Technology (ICT) on Volunteer Management" (Toronto: Canadian Centre for Philanthropy, 2002).

Murray, V., & Y. Harrison (2002b), "Virtual Volunteering: Current Status and Future Prospects" (Toronto: Canadian Centre for Philanthropy, 2002).

Nonprofits Policy and Technology Project (1998), *Speaking up in the Internet Age: Use and Value of Constituent E-mail and Congressional Web Sites* (Washington DC: OMB Watch, 1998).

Organisation for Economic Co-operation and Development (1997), "Use of information and communications technologies at work" DSTI/ICCP/IE ((1997)8/FINAL) (Paris: OECD, 1997).

Organisation for Economic Co-operation and Development (2000), "Science, Technology and Innovation in the New Economy" (Policy brief) (Paris: OECD, September 2000).

Organisation for Economic Co-operation and Development (2004), *OECD Information Technology Outlook* (Report), Available online at: <http://www1.oecd.org/publications/e-book/9304021E.PDF>.

Pargmegiani, M., & T. Sachdeva (2000), *Information and Public Policy Concerning Voluntary Sector Use of Information Technologies, the Internet and the World Wide Web: An International Report* (Toronto: Canadian Centre for Philanthropy, 2000).

Phillips, S. (2000), *Renewing Governance: Voluntary Sector Network Support Program (VolNet): Citizen Engagement Through Information and Communication Technology* (Ottawa: Industry Canada 2000). Available online at: <http://www.volnet.org/english/Sue_Phillips_ report:_Renewing_Governance.html> (retrieved July 23, 2001).

Pierce, J.C., & N.P. Lovrich (2003). "Internet Technology Transfer and Social Capital, Aggregate and Individual Relationships in American Cities" (2003), 1:1 *Comparative Technology Transfer and Society* 49-71.

Pitkin, B., & P. Manzo (2002), *The IT Revolution and Nonprofit Organizations in Los Angeles* (Los Angeles: Center for Nonprofit Management in partnership with the School of Social Policy and Research, UCLA Advanced Policy Institute, 2002).

Princeton Survey Research Associates (2001), *Wired, Willing and Ready: Nonprofit Human Service Organizations' Adoption of Information Technology* (Princeton, NJ: Independent Sector and Cisco Systems, 2001).

Quinn, L.S. (2005, September), *"Software Costs and Usage: Findings of a Nonprofit Sector Survey"*. Idealware. Available online at: <www. idealware.org/IW_software_survey_report.pdf>.

Remenyi, M., T. White & M. Sherwood-Smith (1999), "Language and a Post-modern Management Approach to Information Systems" 17:6 *International Journal of Information Management* 17-32.

Richards, Jr., H. (2001), "Is the Whole Greater than the Sum of Its Parts? The Applicability of the Fair Use Doctrine to the New Breed of Instant Messaging Software" (2001), 8:2 *The Richmond Journal of Law and Technology* 15. Available online at: <http://www.law. richmond.edu/jolt/v8i2/article3.html>.

Rocheleau, B. (1999), "The Political Dimensions of Information Systems in Public Administration", in D.G. Garson, ed., *Information Technology and Computer Applications in Public Administration* (Hershey, PA: Idea Group Publishing, 1999) (pp. 23-40).

Rogers, E.M. (2003), *Diffusion of Innovations*, 5th ed. (New York: Free Press, 2003).

Rudolph, W. (2005 November 19). "Engaging Citizens in On-Line Politics: Technology Tools in On-Line Community". Paper presented to the ARNOVA conference, Washington, DC.

Saxton, J., & S. Game (2001). *Virtual Promise: Are Charities Making the Most of the Internet Revolution?* (London: Third Sector, 2001). Available online at: <www.virtualpromise.net/vp_docs/Complete.pdf>.

Schneider, J. (2003), "Small, Minority-Based Nonprofits in the Information Age" (2003), 13:4 *NonProfit Management and Leadership* 383-399.

Schultz, J. & J. Fristedt (2005), "Calling All Search Engines" (June 2005) *Association Management, Supplement* 8-13.

Seddon, P.B., D.S. Staples, R. Patnayakuni and M. Bowtell (1999), "Dimensions of IS Success", Communications of the AIS, 20, 165-176.

Segil, L. (2001), *FastAlliances: Power your e-business* (New York: Wiley & Sons, 2001).

Shah, Z.S. (2003), "What's a Blog, and Why Should Nonprofits Care?" (2003), 10:4 *Nonprofit Quarterly* 1-5.

Shaw, D.V., N. Kwak & R.L. Holbert (2001), "Connecting and 'Disconnecting' with Civic Life: Patterns of Internet Use and the Production of Social Capital (2001), 18:2 *Political Communication* 141-162.

Sifry, D.L. (October 2005). "The State of the Blogosphere." (Powerpoint presentation.) (Technorati, Inc.).

Smith, J., M. Kearns & A. Fine (2005), *Power to the Edges: Trends and Opportunities in the Online Civic Engagement*, e-Volve Foundation. Available online at: <www.justvote.org/press/Pushing_Power_to_the_Edges.pdf >.

Te'eni, D., & D. R. Young (2003), "The Changing Role of Nonprofits in the Network Economy" (2003), 32:3 *Nonprofit and Voluntary Sector Quarterly* 397-414.

Ticher, P., A. Maison & M. Jones (2002), *Leading the Way to ... ICT Success* (London: The Baring Foundation, 2002).

TimeBank.org (2005, January 12). "About Giving Time: Virtual Volunteering". Retrieved from <http://www.timebank.org.uk/aboutgiv ing/virtual.htm>.

Tyler, R. (November 15, 2002), "Online volunteering", *Digital Journal.* Retrieved from: <www.digitaljournal.com>.

UN Volunteers. (2005). "Online Volunteering: What Is It?" Available online at: <http://www.unvolunteers.org/volunteers/options/online/ whatisov.htm>.

Van Dijk, J., & K. Hacker (2003), "The Digital Divide as a Complex and Dynamic Phenomenon (2003), 19:4 *The Information Society* 315-326.

Van Grembergen, W. (2000), "The balanced scorecard and IT governance" (2000), 2 *Information Systems Control Journal* 40-43. Available online at: <www.isaca.org/Content/ContentGroups/Journal1/20002/The_ Balanced_Scorecard_and_IT_Governance.htm>.

Vogiazou, Y. (2002), *Wireless Presence and Instant Messaging* (United Kingdom: Knowledge Media Institute, Open University, 2002). Available online at: <http://www.jisc.ac.uk/uploaded_documents/tsw_02-07.pdf>.

Volunteers on line (2001), "Making it Work for Volunteers", retrieved October 15, 2002 from <www.volunteersonline.ca/news/environmentals can.htm>.

Warren, M.A., & L.F. Weschler (1999), "Electronic Governance on the Internet", in D.G. Garson, ed., *Information Technology and Computer Applications in Public Administration: Issues and Trends* (Hershey, PA: Idea Group Publishing, 1999) (pp. 118-136).

Wellman, B., A. Quan-Haase, J. Witte & K. Hampton (2001), "Does the Internet Increase, Decrease or Supplement Social Capital"? (2001), 45:3 *American Behavioural Scientist*, 436-455.

Wikipedia: <http://en.wikipedia.org/wiki>.

Zuboff, S. (1988), *In the Age of the Smart Machine: The Future of Work and Power* (New York: Basic Books, 1988).

INDEX

A

Accountability, *see also* **Evaluation practices**; **Evaluation issues**; **Performance assessment**
- control issue, 307
- demands for, sources of, 307
- evaluation vs. performance assessment, 309
- generally, 307-09
- learning issue, 308

Accounting. *See* **Financial reporting**

Advocacy, 11, 30, 183

Alliances. *See* **Corporate sector partnering**; **Government relations**

Audits, 367-69

B

Board of directors
- advisor role, 59
- advisory board, 85
- appointment/reappointment, terms of, 79-80
- assessment procedures, 84
- attendance at meetings, 80
- board culture, 89-92
- • changing. *See* leadership
- • commitment to action, 91
- • defined, 89
- • diversity and equity, acceptance of, 91
- • how-to-run-a-meeting culture, 90
- • openness to change, 90
- • roles and responsibilities, convictions re, 91
- board manual, 83
- board self-management, 58
- boundary spanning, 57
- CEO selection and evaluation, 57, 67-68
- cliques, 79
- committees, 76-79
- • executive committee, 78
- • finance committee, 78
- • "governance" committee, 79
- • nominating committee, 78
- • policy committees, 76
- • standing committees, 77-78
- • working committees, 77
- community relations, 57, 68-70
- • "bringing the outside in" issues, 69
- • "taking the inside out" issues, 70
- composition, 84-89
- • balance, importance of, 89
- • business skills, importance of, 87
- • commitment, 84
- • diversity, 85
- • experts vs. laypeople, 86
- • low-profile organizations, 88
- • non-popular organizations, 88
- • personality characteristics, 87-88
- • prestigious people, 85
- • stakeholders vs. community representatives, 86
- • time and energy, 84
- decision-maker/evaluator role, 58
- diversity on, 411
- executive director's relationship with, 111-14
- fiduciary role of, 53-54
- financial management, responsibility for, 346-47, 354-55, 366-69
- fiscal/legal oversight function, 57, 67
- formal offices, 75-76
- fundraising role, 70
- governance-only board, 61
- governing function, 53-55
- human resources, role re, 397-98
- implementer role, 59
- improving performance of, 95-96
- informal groups, 79
- leadership, 92-95
- • chair, 92-94
- • executive director, 94-95
- • leadership roles, 92

Board of directors — *cont'd*
- • meetings, skills re, 93
- • leadership positions on, 75-76
- • management systems, development and assessment of, 58, 71-73
- • • balanced scorecard management system, 72
- • • CCAF-FCVI framework for performance reporting, 72-73
- • meetings
- • • agenda formats, 82
- • • attendance at, 80
- • • frequency of, 80-81
- • • length of, 81-82
- • • rules, 83
- • • time of, 81
- • "mixed model boards", 61-63
- • organizational design and, 299
- • orientation program, 83
- • procedural issues, 74
- • purpose and priorities assessment, 57
- • resource development, 58, 265-66
- • roles and responsibilities, 56-59
- • rubber-stamp boards, 54
- • size of board, 74-75, 168
- • strategic direction issues, 63-67
- • • information sources/overload, 66-67
- • • mission and values, 64
- • • program and operating policies, 65
- • • rules and procedures, 65
- • • strategic priorities, 64
- • structural issues, 73-74
- • working board, 60
- • types of boards, 60-63

Budgets. *See* **Financial management**

C

Canada Corporations Act, 132

Canada Not-for-Profit Corporation Act, 131

CEO, 57, 67-68, 265, 355-56

Charitable foundation, 146, 251, 257

Charities
- • heads of, 128
- • *Income Tax Act* definition, 128
- • nonprofit organization, distinguished from, 129
- • registered. *See* **Registered charities under ITA**

Committees. *See* **Board of directors**

Community relations
- • board and. *See* **Board of directors**
- • changing nature of, 206
- • executive director and, 119-20

Competition, 13, 180, 183, 197, 276

Computers, use of. *See* **Information and communications technology**

Corporate sector partnering
- • alliances between nonprofits, 201-04
- • • effectiveness of, 202
- • • features of, 202
- • • forced arrangements, 203
- • • funder-imposed partnerships, 203
- • • VSI, effect of, 203
- • cheque book philanthropy, 198
- • community investment, 198
- • competitor relationships, 197
- • corporate citizenship, 198
- • corporate social responsibility, 198
- • examples of, 195, 196
- • generally, 195
- • nonprofit partnering continuum, 198
- • partnership/alliance relationships, 197-98
- • • globalization, effect of, 200-01
- • • guidelines for finding, 199
- • • mutual self-interest analysis, 200
- • publicity motivation, 196
- • shift to partnerships, 195-96
- • strategic philanthropy, 198

D

Demographics, 19-20

Donors. *See* **Resource development**

E

E-commerce, 433

Email. *See* **Information and communications technology**

E-philanthropy, 238, 270

Evaluation information, use strategies, 334-35

Evaluation issues, *see also* **Accountability**; **Evaluation practices**; **Performance assessment**
- audiences for evaluation findings, 321
- context evaluation, 323
- data collection methods, 330-33
- design considerations, 320
- evaluation focus, 323-26
- evaluation purposes, 320-21
- • accountability, 321
- • knowledge generation, 320
- • program improvement, 321
- evaluator, 328-29
- • insiders vs. outsiders, 328-29
- information sources, 330-33
- logic models, 326-28
- • critiques of, 327
- • described, 326-27
- • value of, 328
- needs assessment, 323
- outcome evaluation, 324-25
- outcome measurement, limits of, 325-56
- participatory performance assessment, 329-30
- process evaluation, 323-24
- readiness for evaluation, 322
- stakeholders, involvement of, 329-30

Evaluation practices, *see also* **Accountability**; **Evaluation issues**; **Performance assessment**
- changing environment factors, 310-14
- control-based accountability regime, 314

- federal *Results for Canadians* framework, 311
- generally, 309-10
- New Public Management, introduction of, 310
- Panel on Accountability and Governance in the Voluntary Sector, 312-13
- results focus, 312
- Social Union Framework Agreement, 311
- Voluntary Sector Evaluation Research Project (VSERP), 314-18
- • evaluation methods, 316
- • funder expectations re performance assessment, 315
- • outcome measurement, 317
- • problems identified, 317
- • survey, 314
- Voluntary Sector Initiative, 312-13

E-volunteers, 206

Executive director
- challenges facing, 120-22
- • compensation, 121
- • interpersonal issues, 121
- • isolation, 120
- • powerlessness, 121
- • role, confusion re, 121
- • tunnel vision, 121
- • unreasonable expectations, 122
- competencies, 104-09
- • case studies re, 107-08
- • complexity, 106
- • levels of demonstration, 109
- • relationships, 105
- • strategies and resource management, 105
- • vision and alignment, 105
- defined, 100
- "director", defined, 101
- effectiveness assessment, 110-20
- • boards, ED relationship with, 111-14
- • • board-centred perspective, 112
- • • strategic planning, 112
- • • team analysis, 113
- • community, ED relationship with, 119-20
- • decision process model and, 111

Executive director — *cont'd*
- • financial oversight, ED and, 117-19
- • • accounting function vs., 118
- • • reasonable expectations re, 118, 119
- • • responsibilities, 117, 118
- • goal model analysis and, 111
- • organizational effectiveness and, 111
- • staff, ED relationship with, 114-17
- • • ED views re, 116-17
- • • HR management activities, 114-15, 116
- • • HR management information, 114
- • • planning framework, 115
- • "executive", defined, 101
- • leadership and, 103-09
- • • competencies. *See* competencies
- • • management vs. leadership, 103-04
- • personal beliefs and values of, 109
- • role of, 101
- • stakeholder groups, relationship with, 102-03

Executive management
- • described, generally, 99-100, 122-23
- • executive director. *See* **Executive director**

F

Fiduciary duties, 53-54, 164

Financial management
- • board responsibility for, 346-47
- • budgets, 348-62
- • • activity-based budgets, 361-62
- • • adoption of, 359
- • • characteristics of good budget, 351
- • • described, 348
- • • evaluation, 360
- • • flexibility requirement, 349-50
- • • implementation of, 360
- • • managers, involvement in, 349
- • • preparation process, 358-59
- • • • assumptions and guidelines, 358

- • • • format varieties, 359
- • • review, 359
- • • roles and responsibilities re, 354-57
- • • • board, 354-55
- • • • CEO, 355-56
- • • • CFO/senior financial manager, 356
- • • • managers, 357
- • • • staff, generally, 357
- • • rolling budgets, 361
- • • staff involvement in, 348
- • • time and energy requirements, 349
- • • types of, 351-54
- • • • capital budget, 352
- • • • cash budget, 353
- • • • operating budget, 353-54
- • • zero-based budgeting, 360-61
- • external audit, 369
- • fraud, 369
- • • discovery of, actions on, 371-72
- • • effect of, 370
- • • prevention strategies, 370-71
- • • probability of, circumstances, 370
- • generally, 345-46
- • internal control, 362-72
- • • audit committee, 367-69
- • • COSO Framework, components of, 363-64
- • • defined, 362
- • • finance committee, 366
- • • limits on, 365
- • • responsibility for, 365-66
- • • role of board committees, 366-69
- • • system, elements of, 364
- • responsibility for, 346-47
- • review engagement, 369

Financial oversight, 57, 67, 117-19

Financial reporting
- • accounting policy choices, 373
- • accounts grouping, choice re, 374
- • financial statements, 374-76
- • • balance sheet, 374-75
- • • fund balances, 376
- • • nonprofits, peculiarities re. *See* nonprofits
- • • statement of changes in cash flow, 376
- • • statement of changes in net assets, 376

Financial reporting — *cont'd*
- • statement of operations, 375
- GAAP, application of, 373
- generally, 372-73
- nonprofits and, 376-83
- • contributions, 377-80
- • • deferral method, 377-79
- • • materials and/or services, 379
- • • restricted fund method, 377-79
- • financial statement analysis, 380-83
- • • bottom line, 380
- • • comparative financial statements, 380
- • • expense/cost ratios, 381-83
- use analysis, 374

Financial resources. *See* **Nonprofit organizations**

Foundation. *See* **Charitable foundation**

Fraud. *See* **Financial management**

Funding. *See* **Nonprofit organizations**; **Resource development**

Fundraising. *See* **Nonprofit organizations**; **Resource development**

G

Giving. *See* **Nonprofit organizations**; **Resource development**

Government relations
- accountability, 177
- accountability in government, 178-80
- • acceptance of, 179
- • bureaucratization problem, 179
- • described, 178
- • governance model and, 178
- • independence issue, 179
- • professionalism issue, 180
- advocacy role of organization, 183
- collaborative model, 182-83
- competitive nature of, 180, 183
- complexity of, 181
- corporate sector allies, 174
- development and maintenance, 187-91
- • access to relevant government actors, 187
- • control analysis, 188
- • funding. *See* funding, amount and type of
- • policy access, 187
- • resource adequacy analysis, 188
- dual model, 182
- federal regulatory scheme, 184-86
- • access to policy formulation, 184
- • accountability, 184
- • corporate status of organization, 184
- • electoral regulations, 186
- • ITA status of organization, 185
- • lobbying regulation, 185
- • tax expenditure funding, 185
- functional analysis, 183
- funding issues
- • amount and type of, 188-90
- • • contribution agreements vs. sustaining grants, 189
- • • innovation, need for, 190
- • • unpredictable environment, dealing with, 189-90
- • relationships, 183, 186
- generally, 173-76
- "governance" vs. "command and control" models, 174
- government levels, differences between, 181
- government scrutiny, 175
- "market failure" theory, 174
- monitoring role, 177
- "new public management", meaning of, 180
- partnerships between organizations, 175
- public funding, 176
- sector analysis, 182
- Voluntary Sector Initiative (VSI). *See* **Voluntary Sector Initiative**

H

Human resource functions
- orientation, 416
- performance appraisals, 417-18

Human resource functions — *cont'd*
- recruitment, 415-16
- selection, 416
- supervision, 417
- termination, 418

Human resources management, *see also* **Human resource functions**; **Volunteers**
- board, role of, 397-98
- Canadian practices re, 391-92
- challenges re, 44, 393-97
- • amelioration of, 396
- • financial resources, insufficient, 394
- • guidelines, lack of, 393
- • HR management training, lack of, 394
- • paid staff vs. volunteers, tensions between, 395-96
- • project funding insecurities, 395
- generally, 40-43, 387-90
- history of, 390-91
- HR departments, 391
- paid staff, statistics re, 388
- planning, benefits of, 392-93
- volunteers, statistics re, 389

I

Income. *See* **Nonprofit organizations**; **Resource development**

Income Tax Act
- application of, 132
- "charities" defined, 128
- exemptions under, 139-40

Information
- HR management information, 114
- overload, 66-67
- sources, 21, 330-33
- systems, 302

Information and communications technology, *see also* **Media relations**; **Organizational design**
- adoption of, 430,
- • actual use, 453-55
- • availability for voluntary programs, 452-53
- • factors affecting, 452-55
- applications, 434-42
- benefits of, 429
- blogs, 440-41
- communication technologies, 434
- components of, 432
- described, 431-34
- e-commerce, 433
- email, 435-38
- • collection of e-dresses, 436
- • humanizing, 437
- • relationship building through, 438
- • responses to, 436
- • responsibility for, 437
- • trust relationships through, 437
- • use of, 435
- generally, 429-31
- instant messaging, 438-39
- Internet, 432-33
- investment in, 432
- literature re, review of, 429-31
- management of technological change, 455-57
- online fundraising, 445-47
- online learning, 439
- performance management, 447-49
- • framework re, 449
- podcasting, 441
- success through use of, 450-52
- virtual volunteering, 444-45
- Web conferencing, 439
- Web Service Technology firms, 433
- Web sites, 442-44

Internet. *See* **Information and communications technology**

J

Johns Hopkins Comparative Nonprofit Sector Project, 26

L

Leadership. *See* **Board of directors**; **Executive director**

Legal structures
- co-operative without share capital, 139
- corporation without share capital, 138
- income tax exemptions, 139-40
- legal capacity, 140-41
- liability, 141
- national nonprofit corporate structures, 142-44
- • association agreements, 144
- • centralized chapter model, 143
- • national association model, 142-43
- overview, 134-35
- perpetual existence, 142
- registered charities. *See* **Registered charities under ITA**
- set-up costs, 140
- trusts, 135-36
- • certainties requirement, 135
- • trustees, 136
- unincorporated association, 136
- • legal personality, absence of, 138
- • memorandum of association, 137

Legislation
- federal, 132
- provincial, 133-34
- regulations. *See* **Government relations**

Liability, *see also* **Risk management**
- charitable immunity doctrine, 160
- directors and officers
- • due diligence in operations, 167-68
- • duties of, 163-64
- • independent legal advice, seeking, 168
- • liability of, 164-65
- • rights and powers of, 165
- • statutory protection of, 166
- • transfer of personal assets by, 169
- vicarious liability of organization, 159-62

M

Management, *see also* **Evaluation practices**

- financial. *See* **Financial management**
- generally. *See* **Board of directors**; **Executive management**
- human resources. *See* **Human resources management**
- model, 16-22
- external concerns, 17-20
- • demographics, 19-20
- • economics, 18
- • politics, 18
- • social values, 19
- • technology, 19
- internal concerns, 20-22
- • information, 21
- • money, 21
- • organization and planning, 21-22
- • people, 21
- project. *See* **Project management**
- risk. *See* **Risk management**
- strategic. *See* **Strategic management**
- technology. *See* **Information and communications technology**

Media relations
- benefits of sustained media relations, 205
- "e-volunteers", 206
- fair coverage, issue re, 204
- generally, 204
- VSI sector-wide public awareness campaign, 204-05
- Web site development, 205

Mission, 3-4, 64, 276, 282-83

N

National Survey of Nonprofit and Voluntary Organizations (NSNVO), 26

Nonprofit organizations
- activity types, 28-30, 31
- • arts and culture, 29
- • business and professional associations, 30
- • charity promotion, 30
- • development and housing, 30
- • education and research, 29

Nonprofit organizations — *cont'd*
- • environment, 30
- • health, 29
- • hospitals, 29
- • international understanding, 30
- • law, advocacy and housing, 30
- • religion, 30
- • social services, 29
- • sports and recreation, 29
- • universities and colleges, 29
- board of directors, 7
- business organizations vs., 3
- Canadian perspective, 25-26
- • economic contributions, 32-35
- • • GDP statistics, 33-34
- • • volunteers vs. paid staff, 34-35
- • • workforce employed, 34
- • geographic area of focus, 32
- • public vs. mutual benefit, 32
- • size and scope of nonprofit sector, 30-31
- challenges of, 43-48
- • demand for services/products, 44
- • external funding issues, 46-48
- • finances, 44
- • human resources, 44
- • infrastructure and processes, 44
- • planning and development, 44
- • relationships with networks, 44
- charitable status, CRA registration re, 28
- charity, distinguished from, 129
- definitions, 26-28, 129
- development stage, 14-16
- distinctive features, 3
- expressive functions, 29
- financial resources, 37-40
- • competition for, 13
- • concentration of revenues, 39
- • distribution of revenues, 40
- • government funding, reliance on, 37-38
- • income sources, 12, 37
- • scarcity, 13
- • types of organizations, relative revenues, 39
- generally, 48-49
- goals, 5
- government organizations vs., 3
- human resources, 40-43
- • paid staff, statistics re, 42-43
- • staff activities statistics, 42

- • staff size statistics, 41
- • volunteers, functions of, 41
- • volunteers vs. paid staff, 41
- *Income Tax Act* definition, 129
- international comparisons, 35-37
- legal structures. *See* **Legal structures**
- management. *See* **Management**
- mission, 3-4
- priorities, 5
- service functions, 29
- types of, 8-11
- • advocacy-oriented organizations, 11
- • membership benefit nonprofits, 8-9
- • public benefit organizations, 9-11
- • self-help groups, 8
- • service-providing organizations, 10
- • work-related organizations, 9
- values, 3-4
- voluntarism, degree of, 11
- volunteers, use of, 6

O

Organizational design
- committees, 303
- conflicts between functions, 297
- defined, 296
- formalization, degree of, 301
- functional grouping, 296
- horizontal structure, 301-02
- information systems, 302
- line functions, 296
- mechanistic design structures, 297-99
- organic design structures, 297-99
- program, by, 296
- program databases, 302
- staff functions, 296
- task forces, 303
- vertical structures, 299-301
- • board of directors, 299
- • centralized vs. decentralized, 300
- • non-hierarchical structures, 300
- • spans of control, 299
- • tall vs. flat hierarchy, 300
- work teams, 303

Organizational form
- design vs., 294
- non-traditional, 295
- varieties of, 294

P

Partnerships. *See* **Alliances**

Performance assessment, *see also* **Accountability**; **Evaluation issues**; **Evaluation practices**
- building capacity for, 338-39
- evaluation vs., 318
- management tool, as, 318-19
- ongoing performance assessment, creation of, 319
- performance management, as, 318
- political dimensions of, 336-38
- • dealing with, 337-38
- • design stage, 336
- • funders, where evaluation by, 337
- • small organizations, in, 337
- • subjective interpretation, 336

Philanthropy
- cheque book, 198, 247
- e-philanthropy, 238, 270
- meaning of, 230
- philanthropic culture, 261
- strategic, 198, 247

Planning. *See* **Strategic management**; **Strategic planning**

Politics
- generally, 18, 279
- performance assessment and. *See* **Performance assessment**

Project management
- examples, 291
- project life cycle, 292-94
- • business case, 292
- • communication plan, 293
- • feasibility study, 292
- • impact analysis, 293
- • post-project review, 293
- • risk management, 292
- • scope, 292
- • sponsor, 293
- • terms of reference, 292
- • project phases, 293-94
- • types of projects, 291

Public relations. *See* **Media relations**

R

Registered charities under ITA
- borrowing, 152
- charitable activities, 151
- charitable foundation, 146
- • public vs. private foundation, 146
- charitable organization, 145-46
- "contribution" vs. "control" test, 147-49
- control of other corporations, 152
- directors/trustees and control, relationship between, 146
- disbursement quota rules, 149-51
- new regulatory regime re, 155-57
- • appeals process, 157
- • interim sanctions, 155-57
- related business, carrying on, 151
- rules affecting, chart re, 154-55
- types of charities, 145-46

Regulations. *See* **Government relations**

Relationships. *See* **Corporate sector partnering**; **Government relations**; **Media relations**

Resource development, *see also* **Nonprofit organizations**
- accountability, 267
- defined, 215-16
- development program, 230-43
- • annual giving, 232-38
- • • described, 232-33
- • • direct mail, 233-35
- • • door-to-door campaigns, 238
- • • e-philanthropy, 238
- • • special events, 235-36
- • • telemarketing/phone solicitation, 236-37
- • donor pyramid, 231-32
- • generally, 230-31
- • major and special giving, 239-43

Resource development — *cont'd*
• • • capital campaign, 240
• • • endowment giving, 240-41
• • • major gift campaign, 240
• • • major gift program, 240
• • • planned giving, 242-43
• • resources. *See* resources analysis
• donor pyramid, 231-32
• donors, identifying, 243-52
• • corporate donors, 246-51
• • • cause marketing, 249-51
• • • cheque book philanthropy, 247
• • • corporate social responsibility,
    247, 248
• • • in-kind donations, 249
• • • matching gifts, 249
• • • opportunities analysis, 248
• • • sponsorships, 249
• • • strategic community investment,
    247
• • • strategic philanthropy, 247
• • foundations, 251
• • groups and associations, 252
• • individual donors, typography,
    245-46
• • stakeholder groups, concentric
    circles re, 244
• • table re, 243-44
• ethical fundraising, 268
• fund development, *see also*
    development program
• • defined, 216
• • fundraising activities, profession-
    alism of, 226, 270
• • fundraising profession, growth in,
    225, 270
• • giving, increase in Canada, 224
• • individual donors, 225
• • leadership focus, 227
• fundraising, *see also* donors,
    identifying; fund development; roles
    and responsibilities
• • core operating needs, for, 252
• • defined, 217
• • ethical, 268
• • evaluation and measurement, 263
• • percentage-based, 269
• • philanthropic culture, knowledge
    of, 261
• • planning and implementation,
    261-62
• • principles, 227-30

• • strategic and annual planning, 262
• • types of, table re suitability,
    253-56
• income sources
• • auxiliaries/guilds, 221
• • business activity (profit-based),
    222
• • earned income, 219
• • entrepreneurial ventures, 221
• • fees for services, 220
• • gaming, 220
• • gifts and donations, 219
• • government, 219
• • hybrid activity (profit and social
    benefit-based), 222
• • membership fees and dues, 221
• • related businesses, ITA reform re,
    224
• • social enterprises, 222-23
• • social service (needs-based), 222
• • statistics, 219
• "institutional advancement",
    defined, 216
• nonprofits vs. registered charities,
    217-18
• philanthropy. *See* **Philanthropy**
• privacy legislation, 269
• sources analysis, 257-61
• • fundraising costs, 259-61
• • • solicitation activities, costs of,
    260-61
• • non-staff resources, 258-59
• • parallel foundation, establishment
    of, 257
• • software programs, use of, 259
• • staffing, 258
• roles and responsibilities, 263-67
• • board, of, 265
• • board members, of individual,
    265-66
• • CEO, of, 265
• • development committees, 266
• • development professional, of, 264
• • generally, 263
• • volunteers vs. staff, 264
• stewardship, good, 267

Risk management, *see also* **Liability**
• anti-terrorism legislation, compli-
    ance with, 162-63
• checklists, use of, 169

Risk management — *cont'd*
- choice of nonprofit or charitable structure, 158
- definitions re, 157-58
- directors and officers, role and duties of, 163
- • fiduciary duties, 164
- indemnification, 166-67
- insurance, 167
- legal risk management committees, 168
- size of board, 168
- standard of care, 159

S

Staff. *See* **Human resources management**; **Volunteers**

Stakeholders
- community representatives vs., 86
- concentric circles re, 244
- executive director relationship with, 102-03
- involvement of, 329-30
- strategic planning re, 281-82

Strategic management, *see also* **Board of directors**
- competitive business strategies, 276
- components of, 277
- history of, 278
- mission statements, 276
- process diagram, 277
- strategic thinking, 277-78
- "visioning", 278

Strategic planning
- activating, 279
- agreement re, securing, 281
- circular/circuitous nature of, 280
- consultants, roles of, 279
- environmental scan, 284-85
- • emerging issues, 284
- • forecasting trends, 285
- • monitoring, 285
- history of, 278
- internal scan, 285
- mandate, confirming, 281
- mission statement, 282-83
- opportunities, 286
- political dimensions of, 279
- process diagram, 280
- project management. *See* **Project management**
- stages of, 280-81
- stakeholder analysis, conducting, 281-82
- strategic issues, definition of, 287
- • "scenario building/planning", 288-89
- • vision statement, connection to, 288
- • volunteering analysis, 287
- strategic plan
- • formulation of, 289
- • implementation of, 290-91
- strengths, 286
- SWOT analysis, 286
- threats, 286
- values, 284
- vision, 283, 288
- weaknesses, 286

T

Technology. *See* **Information and communications technology**

Trustees. *See* **Board of directors**

U

Uniform Charitable Fundraising Act, 131

V

Values, 3-4, 19, 64, 109, 284

Vicarious liability. *See* **Liability**

Voluntary Sector Initiative, 181, 191-94
- *Accord*, described, 192
- *Code on Funding*, 193, 313
- *Code on Policy Dialogue*, 192, 313
- *Codes of Good Practice*, 192, 313
- data collection systems, 193

Voluntary Sector Initiative —
cont'd
- described, 191
- performance improvement objective, 193
- purposes of, 191-93
- regulatory reform objectives, 194
- Sectoral Involvement in Departmental Policy Development, 193
- volunteers, awareness and capacity of objectives, 193

Voluntary Sector Evaluation Research Project (VSERP). *See* **Evaluation practices**

Voluntary Sector Task Force, 191

Volunteering, 284, 401-02

Volunteers, *see also* **Human resources management**
- age statistics, 400
- attracting, 403-05
- • membership orientation, 404
- • strategies, 403
- • task/program orientation, 404-05
- benefits of volunteering, 401-02
- community service programs, 406
- contributions of, 398
- crisis re, 400
- diversity, 409-11
- • boards, on, 411
- • ethnic, 409-10

- • gender, 410
- education, 405-06
- employer-sponsored volunteering, 407-08
- entrepreneurial initiatives, 408
- e-volunteers, 206
- Framework Foundation, 408-09
- managing, 411-15
- • formal practices, use of, 413-14
- • incentive structure, 411-12
- • job design, 412
- • paid staff and volunteer mix, 414
- • productivity, 411
- • workplace climate, 412
- motivations of, 401-02
- • traditional collectivistic vs. modern individualistic, 402
- origins of volunteering, 399
- paid staff vs., 34-35, 41, 264
- recruitment. *See* attracting
- self-serving, 402
- statistics, 400
- sustainability of, 399-400
- *Timeraiser*, 408-09
- trends, 405-09
- virtual volunteering, 444-45
- "volunteer", meaning of, 398-99

W

Web sites. *See* **Information and communications technology**